Sartre and the International Impact of Existentialism

Alfred Betschart • Juliane Werner
Editors

Sartre and the International Impact of Existentialism

palgrave
macmillan

Editors
Alfred Betschart
Sartre Society, Chur, Switzerland

Juliane Werner
University of Vienna
Vienna, Austria

ISBN 978-3-030-38481-4   ISBN 978-3-030-38482-1   (eBook)
https://doi.org/10.1007/978-3-030-38482-1

This Palgrave Macmillan imprint is published by the registered company Springer Nature Switzerland AG.
The registered company address is: Gewerbestrasse 11, 6330 Cham, Switzerland

Preface

Forty years have passed since the death of the French philosopher, dramatist, and novelist Jean-Paul Sartre. Yet, there are few thinkers who to this day excite so many emotions. Condemned by those who perceive him as a Marxist and a communist, and hold him responsible for the miseries of failed identity politics, he is, on the other hand, praised for his philosophy of authenticity and his political commitment, earning him the reputation of being the "world's conscience": his tireless fight against war, (neo-)colonialism, and all kinds of oppression, including that of women, Jews, blacks, and homosexuals.

Sartre was a dominating figure in the intellectual discourse in the time between 1945 and 1968, and his work continued to influence writers and thinkers worldwide. Our collection aims at bringing together multidisciplinary research on Sartre's reception outside of France, with many countries still waiting to be explored. The contributions of this volume reflect on existentialism's presence in various areas (e.g. literature, philosophy, and psychology) and, through an analysis of different forms of cultural transfer (e.g. translation, censorship) in multiple mediums (e.g. literary periodicals, plays) and institutions (e.g. universities, libraries), seek to re-examine the impact of the first global intellectual movement of modern time.

The editors thank everyone who supported this project, especially the Department of Comparative Literature at the University of Vienna,

Austria, and the Sartre Society in Germany for organizing the conference "The International Reception of Existentialism" in Vienna in September 2018. We extend our gratitude to the North American Sartre Society for their yearly conferences; it was at one of their worthwhile events that the editors met for the first time and where the idea that led to this book was born. Finally, we thank our partners with Palgrave Macmillan for their support and *Yale French Studies* for their permission to reprint two essays.

Chur, Switzerland   Alfred Betschart
Vienna, Austria   Juliane Werner

Contents

Notes on Contributors

Hamid Andishan works part-time as professor in the Department of Philosophy at the University of Ottawa. His areas of work include phenomenology, existentialism, political philosophy, human rights, and Middle Eastern philosophies.

Jamie Andrews leads Cultural and Learning Programming at the British Library, and previously led the development of the library's literature collections. He is a Fellow of the Clore Leadership Programme, a Trustee of Oxford House and the Forward Arts Foundation, and has previous non-executive experience in the cultural and higher education sectors.

Ronald Aronson is Distinguished Professor Emeritus of the History of Ideas at Wayne State University in Detroit. His writings include *Jean-Paul Sartre—Philosophy in the World, After Marxism, Living Without God, We: Reviving Social Hope*, and recent essays on contemporary themes in *Boston Review*.

Norbert Bachleitner is Professor of Comparative Literature at the University of Vienna. His fields of interest include literary translation and transfer studies, social history of literature, censorship, literature in periodicals, intertextuality, and digital literature. His most recent book publications are *Die literarische Zensur in Österreich von 1751 bis 1848* (2017) and *Brüchige Texte, brüchige Identitäten* (2018).

Cameron Bassiri is professorial lecturer in the Department of Philosophy and Religion at American University, Washington, D.C. His research interests include phenomenology, existentialism, the history of philosophy, and the philosophy of education. His book on Edmund Husserl and the phenomenology of time was published in 2018.

Robert Bernasconi is Edwin Erle Sparks Professor of Philosophy and African American Studies at Penn State University, Pennsylvania. He is the author of two books on Heidegger, of *How to Read Sartre*, and of numerous articles. He is the editor of *Critical Philosophy of Race*, *Levinas Studies*, and *Eco-Ethica*.

Alfred Betschart is a board member of the Sartre Society in Germany. His areas of work include the history of existentialism, existentialist ethics, and existentialism and politics, on which he has published and edited several contributions and books. He is the responsible editor of the website www.sartre.ch.

Damon Boria is Associate Professor of Philosophy at Franciscan Missionaries of Our Lady University in Baton Rouge, Louisiana. His publications include articles on existential and environmental ethics, social philosophy, and philosophy of literature. He is also serving as president of the North American Sartre Society.

Francesco Caddeo received his PhD in philosophy from Université Jean Moulin Lyon 3 in 2016, as well as in literature studies from Università degli Studi dell'Aquila. His dissertation is entitled *Sartre chez les philosophes structuralistes et poststructuralistes*. His research focuses on political thought in Jean-Paul Sartre, contemporary French philosophy, and postcolonial studies.

Ayşenaz Cengiz is an assistant professor and teaches undergraduate and graduate courses in the Department of Translation and Interpreting Studies at Boğaziçi University, İstanbul. Her main research interests are feminist approaches to translation, traveling theories, and paratexts and translation. Her master's thesis was published in 2010 under the title *Migration of Theories: The Journey of Sartrean Existentialism into Turkey Through Translation*.

Yoav Di-Capua is Professor of History at the University of Texas in Austin, where he teaches modern Arab intellectual history. He received his PhD from Princeton University in 2004. He is the author of *Gatekeepers of the Arab Past: Historians and History Writing in Twentieth-Century Egypt* (2009) and *No Exit: Arab Existentialism, Jean Paul Sartre and Decolonization* (2018).

Julia Elsky is Assistant Professor of French at Loyola University Chicago. Her research on the theater of the absurd has appeared in *PMLA*, and she is writing a book on the topic. She co-edited the seventieth-anniversary issue of *Yale French Studies* that revisits the journal's first issue on existentialism. She has also completed a book manuscript on Jewish émigré writers under Vichy.

Adrian van den Hoven is professor emeritus at the University of Windsor in Windsor, Ontario. He is the translator (with B. Kingstone) of Jean-Paul Sartre, Philippe Gavi, and Pierre Victor: *It Is Right to Rebel* (2018); the editor (with R. Aronson) of Jean-Paul Sartre: *We Have Only This Life to Live: The Selected Essays of Jean-Paul Sartre, 1939–1975* (2013); and an author of papers and articles on Sartre and Camus.

Raoul Kirchmayr is Adjunct Professor in Aesthetics at the University of Trieste and member of the editorial board of the journal *Aut Aut*. He is the author of *Il circolo interrotto. Figure del dono in Mauss, Sartre e Lacan* (2001), *Merleau-Ponty* (2008), and *Passioni del visibile* (2018). He has translated and edited various works by Sartre in Italian, such as *Qu'est-ce que la subjectivité?* (2013, with M. Kail).

Rony Klein teaches literature at Tel Aviv University, Israel. His fields of research are contemporary philosophy, especially French and Jewish-French, contemporary French literature, and Jewish thought. He is the author of *Letter, Body, Community—Between Jewish Thought and French Contemporary Philosophy* (2014).

Nariaki Kobayashi is a PhD student in the Department of Language and Society at Hitotsubashi University, Japan. His main research interests are French literature, French philosophy (in the twentieth century), and Japanese philosophy. For the Japanese Association of Sartre Studies he organized a symposium on Yoshirô Takeuchi in 2017.

Maria Russo is a lecturer in moral philosophy at the Faculty of Philosophy at Vita-Salute San Raffaele University, Milan, and a member of the International Research Centre for European Culture and Politics (IRCECP). Among her publications are *Freedom in Situation: The Human Finitude in Kant and Sartre* (2015) and *For a Critical Existentialism. The Relationship Between Ethics and History in Jean-Paul Sartre's Moral of Authenticity* (2018).

Alan Patricio Savignano is co-founder and director of the Círculo Sartre. He is a PhD student in philosophy at the National Academic of Sciences of Buenos Aires and at the University of Buenos Aires. His doctoral thesis deals with the theory of intersubjectivity in different periods of Jean-Paul Sartre's philosophy and its effects on phenomenology.

Hiroaki Seki is a PhD student at the University of Tokyo and is writing a thesis on the theme of salvation through art in Sartre's works at Sorbonne University, Paris. His research interests include twentieth-century French literature, with a special focus on Sartre. His principal publication is "Sartre et la figure de Cassandre" in *International Sartre Studies* (2017).

Matthew Senie is an independent scholar who completed his MA in philosophy at American University, Washington, D.C. His research interests include existentialist literature, particularly the fiction of Jean-Paul Sartre and Albert Camus, and the relations of philosophy to psychoanalysis and psychiatry. He has presented on topics ranging from Sartre's philosophy of education to literature and existential psychoanalysis.

Juliane Werner is a postdoctoral researcher and lecturer in the Department of Comparative Literature at the University of Vienna, Austria. Her principal research is concerned with transcultural exchanges between Austria, France, and the United States, literature and psychiatry, and philosophical fiction. She is the author of *Thomas Bernhard and Jean-Paul Sartre* (2016) and of the forthcoming monograph *Existentialism in Austria. Cultural Transfer and Literary Resonance (2020)*.

Vincent von Wroblewsky has been the president of the Sartre Society in Germany since its foundation in 1993, and is a philosopher and translator. Born in France, he grew up in East Berlin, the capital of the former

GDR, where he finished his studies at the Humboldt University in 1967. From 1967 to 1991 he worked at the Central Institute of Philosophy with the Academy of Sciences in East Berlin. He translated many texts by Sartre and other philosophers and writers. For his own writings, see http://franc-all.de/.

1

An Overview of the International Reception of Existentialism: The Existentialist Tsunami

Alfred Betschart

The frequently mentioned 'existentialist wave' in the years following the end of World War II was not a wave, but rather a tsunami. It was a tsunami that went around the world. It started in December 1944 with the publication of Jean-Paul Sartre's *The Republic of Silence* (*La république du silence*) in the U.S. Thereafter it reached countries like Italy, the U.K., Sweden, and Germany, as well as East Asia and Latin America, particularly Japan and Argentina. In the 1950s even communist countries like the Soviet Union (Betschart 2018a) and the People's Republic of China (Zhang 2008) could not elude the tsunami. In this decade, existentialism became one of the dominant intellectual currents in the Middle East, too. Turkey, Brazil, and South Vietnam were hit by it in the early 1960s. There had been other waves before, such as Marxism and Freudian psychoanalysis; however, none had spread as quickly around the globe as the existentialist tsunami and none was as broadly positioned as the existentialist movement. Existentialism was not only a philosophical, but also a

A. Betschart (✉)
Sartre Society, Chur, Switzerland
e-mail: infos@sartre.ch

© The Author(s) 2020
A. Betschart, J. Werner (eds.), *Sartre and the International Impact of Existentialism*,
https://doi.org/10.1007/978-3-030-38482-1_1

1

literary movement. Particularly in the Third World, it had a significant political impact through its concept of engagement. And the existentialist tsunami reached out to the arts, too, and, with its black turtlenecks, even to fashion. William McBride's declaration that "few if any other modern Western philosophical movements have had as strong an impact on the general culture as has existentialism" (McBride 2012, p. 50) is an understatement.

The existentialist tsunami was caused by Sartre and his friends, Simone de Beauvoir and Albert Camus. Although philosophers such as Gabriel Marcel, Martin Heidegger, and Karl Jaspers partly figure among the existentialists—an error caused by Sartre in his most widely read philosophical essay *Existentialism Is a Humanism* (*L'existentialisme est un humanisme*)[1]—they never took part in the existentialist tsunami. The rehabilitation of the Nazi Heidegger started to gain a real foothold only in the 1950s, and Jaspers was rather a phenomenon of the German-speaking countries. Since the literary opus, via novels and plays, was more important than the philosophical oeuvre in the spread of the existentialist tsunami, Heidegger and Jaspers, who were only philosophers, had a significant disadvantage in comparison to Sartre and his friends. Only Marcel published a literary work, too. However, it never reached as large an audience as his French fellow citizens' works. Marcel, the Catholic, neo-Socratic philosopher, was rather used by critics as an argument against Sartre.

The focus in this book lies—in Sartre's terminology—on the French atheist existentialists, although there are certain references to philosophers and writers who did not strictly adhere to this current. Søren Kierkegaard's reception partly preceded, partly ran parallel to Sartre's and played an important role in preparing the field for French existentialism. At the same time, Kierkegaard was an important Christian alternative to French existentialism for those who opposed the atheism of Sartre and his friends (BORIA[2]). Among artists and writers, but also among psychologists, there were important currents that ran parallel to French atheist

---

[1] All three rejected the designation 'existentialist'. Not to confound them with Sartre and his friends, their philosophy should rather be called the 'philosophy of existence'.

[2] Names in small caps refer to the essays by the respective authors in this book.

existentialism, partly influenced by Sartre's version, partly as developments in their own right. What according to Sartre is valid for Gustave Flaubert (Sartre 2006, p. 25) is valid for the existentialists too: they not only influenced their time in many ways, but they were also an expression of their time. Many important examples of parallel developments can be found in literature. Richard Wright, Allan Ginsberg and other beatniks, Iris Murdoch, Hanoch Levin (KLEIN), and many Italian and German authors could be mentioned. One of the most intriguing examples is Max Frisch's play *Andorra*, which seems to be a theatrical version of Sartre's *Anti-Semite and Jew* (*Réflexions sur la question juive*). However, although this play was published only in 1961, its sketch dates from 1945, when Sartre was writing his *Anti-Semite and Jew*. Similar correspondences can be found in the relationship between Sartre's existential psychoanalysis and the psychotherapies of Carl Rogers, Abraham Maslow, Rollo May, Erich Fromm, and Viktor Frankl. When investigating the reception of existentialism in Latin America, many parallel developments can be detected, partly due to the influence of the Spanish philosopher Miguel de Unamuno, partly due to local circumstances such as the question of commitment in the fight against the indigenous élite and the dictators, and the question of *mestizaje* and the relationship of the Latinos to the Other.

With regard to time, our focus is on the period between 1944 and 1968. Of course, the first existentialist texts were translated before 1944: Sartre's *The Wall* (*Le mur*) was published in English and German in 1938, in Japanese in 1940, his short story *The Room* (*La chambre*) in Spanish in Argentina in 1939. As a global cultural event, however, the existentialist tsunami started only with the end of World War II approaching, and in the 1960s, the tide was already falling. The support Sartre lent to Israel after the Six-Day War led to the complete breakdown of Arab existentialism and impaired existentialism in other countries of the Third World too. Frantz Fanon's wife no longer allowed Sartre's introduction to be published together in new editions of *The Wretched of the Earth* (*Les damnés de la terre*). In the years before 1968, there was discussion between Sartre and the structuralists (Claude Lévi-Strauss, Michel Foucault) about the importance of man in history.[3] The events in Paris in May 1968 proved that Sartre was right against the structuralists that (wo-)men can make history; even Michel Foucault became a political activist thereafter and collaborated with Sartre on several occasions. Nevertheless, structuralism and postmodernism quickly supplanted existentialism as the leading non-Marxist philosophies in the 1970s. Already during the 1960s, existentialism had lost ground to Marxism, which became for about ten years the philosophy *à battre*. Even the Sartreans lost interest in Sartre. Sartre's move away from Marxist to anarchist political philosophy in the 1970s went almost unnoticed. *It Is Right to Rebel* (*On a raison de se révolter*), an important work for Sartre's political philosophy in the last ten years of his life, was translated into English forty-three years after its French publication in 1974.

Evidently, 1968 was not the end of existentialism as a philosophy. In some countries like the People's Republic of China and Russia, where existentialism had for a long time been banished to the poison cabinet, existentialism saw a wider reception only in the 1980s and 1990s. Several Americans—Mark Poster, John Lawler, Thomas Flynn—tried to find a synthesis of Marxism and existentialism after 1975. Beauvoir's *The Second Sex* (*Le deuxième sexe*), the historically most important work ever published by an existentialist, became the theoretical base of feminism, although Beauvoir's existentialist feminism was soon superseded by an essentialist version (Moi 2008, pp. 200–202). Questions of identity (gender, ethnicity, sexuality), which have been dominating politics more and more since the 1970s, have their theoretical foundations with Sartre and Beauvoir. However, even Judith Butler—she wrote her doctoral thesis about desire with Alexandre Kojève, Jean Hyppolite, and Sartre—prefers to keep her existentialist heritage at a distance.

Our focus on this quarter of a century between 1944 and 1968 has its implications with regard to the subjects treated in this book. Maurice Merleau-Ponty, Sartre's close political collaborator between 1945 and 1950, was virtually nonexistent on the international scene during the time of the existentialist tsunami. His reception as a philosopher—he did

---

[3] See Sartre's interview *Replies to Structuralism* (*Jean-Paul Sartre répond*) with Bernard Pingaud in the journal *L'Arc* in 1966.

not write any literary works—began only slowly with the first transla-tions in the 1960s.[4] The reception of Beauvoir and Camus, too, was sig-nificantly behind Sartre. Beauvoir suffered for a long time, until the 1970s, from the neglect *The Second Sex* experienced. Betty Friedan, with her *The Feminine Mystique* (1963), always kept herself at a distance from Beauvoir, although acknowledging that it was *The Second Sex* that intro-duced her to what later was called feminism (Friedan 1985, p. 304). Only after Kate Millet's *Sexual Politics* and Shulamith Firestone's *The Dialectic of Sex* (both 1970) did Beauvoir stand more in the limelight. In the time before, Beauvoir was rather perceived as '*la Grande Sartreuse*', whose major works were of a biographical character.

Not very different was the situation with Camus. As a proclaimed author of the Résistance, he received a lot of attention in the years imme-diately after the war. Thereafter, the interest in his work lowered signifi-cantly. *The Rebel* (*L'homme révolté*) was translated into English only five years after its publication in French, *The Just Assassins* (*Les justes*) seeing a delay of nine years. His less pronounced political attitudes and less overt atheism in comparison to Sartre made him the preferred existentialist author with the Christian middle-of-the-road readership; however, this segment was not very large, with the exception particularly of the U.S. When seven years ahead of Sartre, Camus was awarded the Nobel Prize for Literature in 1957, this was a compromise between the need to reward existentialist literature and not giving the prize to Sartre. Camus experienced a revival only after the collapse of communism in Eastern Europe in 1989/1991, mainly in his role as a representative of an ethics of conviction in opposition to Sartre as an ambassador of an ethics of responsibility. The fact that this book about the international reception of existentialism mainly focuses on Sartre very much reflects the situation at the time of the existentialist tsunami: it was mostly Sartre who was the driving force.

---

[4] One of the rare exceptions was Mexico, where Merleau-Ponty, together with Sartre, was intro-duced into philosophical discussions by Emilio Uranga, a member of the Grupo Hiperión, at a series of lectures at the French Institute of Latin America in 1948 (Alberto Sánchez 2016, pp. 20–26). The interest of Latin America in Merleau-Ponty is confirmed by the fact that his *Phenomenology of Perception* (*Phénoménologie de la perception*) was translated into Spanish in 1957, five years ahead of the English translation (Domingo Toledo 2011, p. 215).

A Question of Methodology—Communication Theory

The reception of existentialism in France is very well explored. Anna Boschetti did groundbreaking work with her book *Sartre et "Les Temps Modernes"*, which was based on Pierre Bourdieu's sociology (Boschetti 1985). There was the late German professor Ingrid Galster, who followed a more classical way of analysis focusing on Sartre's life and oeuvre. Further important contributions came from Randall Collins with his network approach (Collins 1998), and from Patrick Baert, who published his book *The Existentialist Moment* based on his new approach of positioning in 2015.

When it comes to the reception of existentialism outside France, the situation looks quite different. So far, a good number of books and articles about the reception in various countries outside France has been published. However, it is a jigsaw puzzle with many missing pieces. To achieve a better understanding of existentialism, with regard to both its achievements and its failures, these lacunae have to be closed. In this essay, I shall give an overview of what we already know about the international reception of existentialism. The model used is adopted from communication theory, which is better suited to reflect the complexity of the reception process than other models focusing on the author, his social situation, and his oeuvre. In this model based on communication theory, *senders* are transferring *messages* to *receivers*. Transferring messages on different *channels* allows to enlarge the number of receivers considerably. On the way from the sender to the receiver, the messages are forwarded by *repeaters* and partly jammed by *noise*. In comparison to the national reception, repeaters and noise play a much more decisive role on the international level. In accordance with Hans Robert Jauss and his reception esthetics, based on Hans-Georg Gadamer's *Truth and Method*, the fate of a work is finally decided by the readers. This thesis is in line with Sartre's own conception of literature where the reader is a second creator in literature on a par with the writer. However, in contrast to Jauss, the focus in this overview is not on the existentialists' works, but on their messages. It is important to differentiate between work and message, since a work can contain several messages and the same message can appear in different works. Not all the messages sent are received and some are only received in a distorted form, since sending and receiving of messages is a process of encoding and decoding. In accordance with Sartre's epistemological perspectivism, there can be significant differences in content between the messages encoded by the senders and the messages decoded by the receivers.

The Senders—Sartre, Beauvoir, Camus, Merleau-Ponty

As to the senders, of the four authors generally considered French atheist existentialists, Sartre, Beauvoir, Camus, and Merleau-Ponty, we can ignore Merleau-Ponty. The international reception of his work was very low. As to Sartre, Beauvoir, and Camus, although their major focus was on France, they were very much interested in the international reception of their work, as their journeys abroad prove. However, Camus, who was afraid of flying, traveled significantly less than Sartre and Beauvoir. His major trips were those to the U.S. in 1946, to Latin America in 1949, and to Sweden in 1957, which resulted in a significant increase in translations, in the U.S., Argentina, and, after he had received the Nobel Prize in Sweden, all over the world.

Camus's traveling schedule is in stark contrast to the many journeys Sartre and Beauvoir made. In the years between 1945 and 1951, Sartre and Beauvoir traveled to the U.S. six times. On his second trip in 1945/1946, Sartre gave lectures at the universities of Yale, Harvard, Princeton, and Columbia, as well as at Carnegie Hall. The first trip in Europe outside France led him to Brussels in October 1945, where Iris Murdoch, the British writer and philosopher, happened to hear him. Further important trips were those to the USSR in 1954 and to China in 1955, which led to the publication of *The Respectful Prostitute* (*La putain respectueuse*) in both countries. In contrast to his many trips to communist Eastern Europe—nine trips to the USSR between 1954 and 1955 and between 1962 and 1966, six visits to Yugoslavia from 1953 to 1969,[5] additional journeys to the German Democratic Republic (GDR), Poland, and Czechoslovakia—Sartre's visits to Brazil in 1960 and to Japan in 1966 had significant impacts. With his lectures in Japan, Sartre caused another wave of discussion about the role of the intellectual (Müller 2016, pp. 194–195; Suzuki and Sawada 2011), and his visit to Brazil left a long-lasting imprint with Caetano Veloso's and Gilberto Gil's *tropicalismo* (Ibiapina Ferreira n.d.). Sartre and Beauvoir made many more journeys to other countries. Some, like the trips to Germany in 1948 and to Egypt in 1967 could have had a great impact but failed due to political events shortly after the visit (Cold War, Six-Day War). How prominent Sartre and Beauvoir were at that time is best shown by the number of prominent political leaders they met: Palmiro Togliatti (Italy), Mao Zedong and Chen Yi (China), Fidel Castro and Che Guevara (Cuba), Josip Broz Tito (Yugoslavia), Juscelino Kubitschek (Brazil), Nikita Khrushchev (USSR), Gamal Abdel Nasser (Egypt), and Levi Eshkol (Israel). No other philosopher has ever matched this record.

The country with which Sartre and Beauvoir had the closest connection was Italy. As Rossana Rossanda described it, this was not only a political/intellectual relationship, but a love affair (Rossanda 1987, p. 262). In 1946—after a trip to Switzerland including its German-speaking part which was their first trip to a non–French speaking area in Europe—they met important intellectuals of the Italian left such as Elio Vittorini, Carlo Levi, Ignazio Silone, and Alberto Moravia. From 1952 to 1979, Sartre and Beauvoir normally spent a part of their summer holidays in Italy, where they had frequent discussions with their Italian friends. Time and again, Sartre gave lectures and interviews and wrote

---

[5] In his introduction to Louis Dalmas's book *Le communisme yougoslave depuis la rupture avec Moscou* (*Yugoslavian Communism Since the Break with Moscow*) in 1950, Sartre supported Yugoslavia's independence from the USSR. Thereafter, several of his works were translated and he became a topic of philosophical discussion—the prominent Marxist Boris Ziherl was involved in one of them in 1953; in 1965, Danilo Pejović penned a sympathetic portrait of Sartre in the journal *Praxis* (Pejović 1965). Sartre influenced writers such as Radomir Konstantinović in Serbia and Edvard Kocbek in Slovenia. He met Mihailo Marković, a major proponent of the Praxis School, as a co-speaker at a conference in Rome in 1964. And he was befriended by Vladimir Dedijer, with whom he had worked at the Russell Tribunal. In 1983, Sartre was honored with a Serbo-Croatian translation of selected works in twelve volumes.

articles that were printed in Italian publications. Among them were the lectures at the Gramsci Institute in Rome in 1961 and 1964 on subjectivity and ethics (CADDEO; KIRCHMAYR).

The Repeaters—Translators, Publishers, Emigrants, Journalists

Repeaters play a very significant role in international reception. Of utmost importance are translators and publishing houses. Without Hazel Barnes, the American translator of *Being and Nothingness* (*L'être et le néant*), the reception of existentialist philosophy would have been much less pronounced in the U.S.; a similarly important role was assumed by Traugott König for German-speaking countries. Partly the translations were accompanied by cuts and errors. There were frequent inaccuracies which served to adjust the text to local customs and to render it less offensive with regard to local moral standards, particularly in the field of sexual behavior (BACHLEITNER). However, there were also significant errors and cuts. The case of Howard M. Parshley's first English translation of Beauvoir's *The Second Sex* in 1952 is well known. Not only were technical terms translated incorrectly, but more important were the cuts he made. According to Margaret A. Simons, Parshley deleted half of one chapter, cut a quarter of another, and eliminated the names of seventy-eight women (Simons 1999, p. 62). Not surprisingly, Parshley had a bigger problem with Beauvoir's chapter 'The Lesbian'. Sartre's preface to the first American translation of *The Wretched of the Earth* also showed a significant distortion which made the English version appear more aggressive than it was originally conceived.[6] Without the publishing houses Alfred A. Knopf in the U.S. and Rowohlt in Germany (both published many works by Sartre, Camus, and Beauvoir), their reception in these countries would have been significantly weaker. Rowohlt was the

---

[6] Sartre's original text calls the colonialist an oppressor and an oppressed one at the same time, a point which was very important to Sartre. This idea of double oppression was however lost in the first translation into English and was corrected only in the second translation by Richard Philcox, published in 2004 (Sartre 2004, p. lv).

publishing house that fostered the French existentialists' work on a par with, if even not better than, Gallimard in France. The lack of success of existentialist philosophy in Germany, a country steeped in academic philosophy, is certainly not due to Rowohlt, but rather due to the strong local competition by Heidegger and Jaspers.

A second important category of repeaters is constituted by professors who had emigrated from continental Europe and students who had returned to their countries from France where they had come into contact with existentialism. In the U.S., for example, where philosophical academia was in the hands of analytical philosophy, immigrants such as Jean Wahl, Herbert Marcuse, Hannah Arendt, and Hans Jonas, and other today less well-known persons like Henry Peyre (ELSKY) and Walter Kaufmann played a significant role in the American reception of existentialism. Kaufmann's book *Existentialism from Dostoevsky to Sartre* became one of the most widely read philosophy books among American college students (Fulton 1999, p. 85). For Kaufmann, Wahl, and others, it was a chance to excel in a field of philosophy they knew much better than the indigenous philosophers: continental philosophy. In Asia, former students in France were of similar importance, for example, Suhayl Idris and Ali Shariati in Lebanon and Iran, Suzuki Michihiko (KOBAYASHI/SEKI) and Sawada Nao in Japan, Luo Dagang in China, and Nguyen Van Trung in South Vietnam. They had experienced existentialism in Paris not only as a philosophy, but also as a lifestyle and a political force, and in contrast to the emigrant philosophers, they kept this understanding of existentialism alive in their respective countries.

Other important categories of repeaters were foreign journalists in France and generally French critics publishing abroad. American journalists like John Lackey Brown for the *New York Times* and Janet Flanner for the *New Yorker* and the *Partisan Review* took on roles as important in the years after the end of World War II as did Lutfi al-Khuli for Egypt and Simha Flapan for Israel in the 1960s. French critics of existentialism like Emmanuel Mounier and Jacques Maritain and the communist Roger Garaudy and the Belgian Jesuit Roger Troisfontaines were of equal importance in a negative way. A very special and very influential case was that of György Lukács, a Hungarian communist philosopher, with whom Sartre led an indirect debate in *Combat* in 1949. With his books

Existentialism or Marxism and *The Destruction of Reason*, Lukács's criticism of existentialism as an irrationalist philosophy in the tradition of Arthur Schopenhauer, Friedrich Nietzsche, and Heidegger, and therefore as being close to fascism, became highly influential throughout the whole communist world.

Another special role was assumed by the various military governments in occupied Germany and Austria, particularly the French administration. They acted simultaneously as repeaters and as noise. The performance of Sartre's *The Flies* (*Les mouches*) was prohibited in Germany until the spring of 1947 because it was considered too subversive (Rahner 1993, p. 133). Although existentialism was the major export item during these years, the attitude of the French military administration in Germany was ambiguous, and it even suppressed it in Austria (WERNER; for the French military administration in Germany see Högerle 2013).

Noise—Censorship, Social Taboos

While repeaters reinforce a message, noise jams it. Talking about noise, we first think of censorship. The communist régimes in the Soviet Union and China[7] allowed at first only the translation of *The Respectful Prostitute*, and even this only in a version with an optimistic end (VAN DEN HOVEN; Betschart 2018b). They principally maintained their ban on existentialist works until the 1960s and 1980s respectively. In line with the policy of Andrei Zhdanov, the Stalinist secretary of the Communist Party of the Soviet Union in charge of propaganda and agitation, Alexander Fadeyev, the general secretary of the Union of Soviet Writers, condemned Sartre together with other writers such as Eugene O'Neill, John Dos Passos, Henry Miller, and André Malraux as reactionary writers praising the abnormal and the immoral at the World Congress of Intellectuals in Defense of Peace in Wrocław, Poland, in 1948.

A sad case of censorship was that of Trân Duc Thao in North Vietnam. Trân tried to combine phenomenology and Marxism and met Sartre for

---

[7] One of Sartre's texts, *The Room*, had been translated into Chinese in 1943 before the Communist revolution.

discussions in 1950, when Trân lived in Paris. Upon his return to North Vietnam in 1951/1952, he was forbidden to continue his work. As to the GDR, its situation was quite peculiar. On the one hand, communist ideologists heavily criticized the existentialists, first as nihilistic and then as decadent petit bourgeois. In 1948, the philosophy of existence was even criticized by the East German Prime Minister Otto Grotewohl. The philosopher Ernst Bloch, not generally a communist propagandist, condemned Sartre in a Stalinist style in 1956 even after Khrushchev had dismantled Stalinism at the 20th Party Congress. On the other hand, until the construction of the Berlin Wall, the border to the Federal German Republic was open, which would have made it a futile exercise not to publish at least the less 'dangerous' literary works (VON WROBLEWSKY).

It was not only the communists that jammed the existentialist messages. Sartre and Beauvoir were observed by both the KGB and the CIA/FBI. A second important player in the field of jamming was the Catholic Church. Sartre's complete work was put on the *Index librorum prohibitorum* in 1948. The same happened to Beauvoir's *The Second Sex* and *The Mandarins* in 1956. In 1950, the pope had condemned existentialism *in toto* in his encyclical *Humani generis*. These condemnations significantly impaired the reception of existentialism in Catholic countries, and generally in Catholic schools everywhere in the world, for example, in Austria, Bavaria, and most of Catholic Italy. The Catholic Church's ban was one of the major reasons why the center of reception of existentialism in the Hispanic world was not in Spain but in Argentina (SAVIGNANO), although the régime under Juan Perón was only slightly milder than Francisco Franco's in Spain.[8] The vehement opposition to existentialism by the two most powerful ideological centers in the world, communism and the Roman Catholic Church, may surprise the reader. It is hard to find another philosophical and literary movement that experienced a similar rejection, but it is understandable when considering that at that time

---

[8] At the philosophy congress in Mendoza/Argentina in 1949, Perón called Sartre's *Nausea* (*La nausée*) "trash", while Camus's play *The Misunderstanding* (*Le malentendu*) was even banned.

Franco's Spain prohibited the sale of Camus's work for political reasons until 1955/1958. The Catholic Church had not put him on the index.

there existed only three important ideological camps: Karl Marx, Jean-Paul Sartre, and Jesus Christ[9] (Rahner 1993, p. 209).

Another important kind of noise was social taboos. Sartre's and Beauvoir's criticism of the bourgeois patriarchal morality with regard to sexuality and particularly the position of women in our society was severely subjected to social taboos. Nothing proves this better than the virtually nonexistent reception of Beauvoir's *The Second Sex* in Europe, until Beauvoir's theses were reimported to Europe from the U.S. in the early 1970s (Galster 2015, pp. 211–212). For a large part of the general public, and in particular the academia, Sartre's and Beauvoir's work showed a pornographic character to be rejected *in toto*.

Channels—Visits, Books, Theater, Articles, Film

Regardless of the many acts of jamming, the existentialist tsunami quickly spread around the world between 1945 and 1950. This had a lot to do with the fact that the messages of Sartre, Beauvoir, and Camus were sent through most of the channels available at the time: personal visits, books, theater performances, articles in journals, magazines, and newspapers, even films. Existentialism was a media event, too. The personal visits by Sartre, Beauvoir, and Camus have already been mentioned. Analysis of their books shows that their reception spread mainly via literature and not philosophy (see also Kaufmann 1975, p. 40). Their literary works were remarkably quickly translated into the three major languages English, Italian, and German. After 1945, translation of Sartre's major literary works into English took on average 1.3 years, with Beauvoir 3.6 years, with Camus 5.3 years. Into Italian, the translation of Sartre's literary works took on average about 3.2 years and into German only 2.3 years, although the book market there only revived in 1948. These figures also show us the relative relevance of the markets and authors. The first

---

[9] In the years after World War II, the Christian Democrats were the leading parties in the major countries on the European continent (MRP/France, CDU/Germany, DC/Italy). They became the godparents of the European Community. On the intellectual level, Sartre's Christian opponents were philosophers like Gabriel Marcel and the representatives of the *Renouveau Catholique*, authors such as Georges Bernanos, Paul Claudel, and François Mauriac (WERNER).

and major market in terms of the reception of existentialism was the Anglo-Saxon, and in particular the American market, followed by the German and Italian markets. The figures also confirm the clear dominance of Sartre over Beauvoir and particularly Camus when it comes to the reception of their work outside France.

As to the major philosophical works, they were translated slowly. It is obvious that the reception of Sartre's philosophy took place rather through his plays and secondary philosophical writings such as *Existentialism Is a Humanism* and *What Is Literature?* (*Qu'est-ce que la littérature?*). *Being and Nothingness* was first translated into German in 1952, followed by English in 1956 and Italian in 1964. The slower translation into Italian can be explained, however, by the good knowledge of French in Italian philosophical circles. Of particular note is the fact that in the early Sixties the first translations of the *Critique of Dialectical Reason* (*Critique de la raison dialectique*) and the preface to *The Wretched of the Earth* into one of the three major languages appeared in Italian in 1963 and 1962 respectively. This proves the interest in Italy in a Marxian version of existentialism that was largely lacking in the U.S. and Germany.[10] The only country that could compete with Italy in this regard was Japan, where the *Critique* was translated in 1962.

There were also translations into many other languages. Among the forerunners with regard to translations was Sweden where many texts were published between 1946 and 1949; *Existentialism Is a Humanism* was translated into Swedish in 1946, the same year that the French edition appeared and before the German and the English translations. Another hotspot for translations was Argentina. There, the reception of the Spanish thinkers José Ortega y Gasset and Unamuno and the Germans Max Scheler and Heidegger had prepared the field for the first translation ever of *Being and Nothingness* into a foreign language in 1949. And finally, in the Sixties, there was a boom of translations of Sartre's work into Turkish (Cengiz; Koş 2004, pp. 37–38) and Arabic, but with a clear focus on literary and political texts, while the philosophical texts, apart from *Existentialism Is a Humanism*, were mostly neglected.

---

[10] However, even in Italy, the interest in Sartre's philosophy waned quickly in the 1960s. Already in 1967, Antonio Santucci called the *Critique* outdated (Invitto 1987, p. 182).

With the translation of the plays, performances in theaters started. This significantly broadened the audience exposed to existentialist messages. This was of particular importance in Germany and Italy, where, after years of deprivation by the fascist régimes the élite eagerly visited the theaters. Several of Sartre's plays were staged by the most prominent theater directors in Europe. Luchino Visconti directed *No Exit* (*Huis clos*) in the Teatro Eliseo in Rome in 1945. Giorgio Strehler followed with *In the Mesh* (*L'engrenage*) at the Piccolo Teatro in Milano in 1953 (Tessari 1987, pp. 158, 164). The performances of *The Flies* by Gustav Gründgens in Düsseldorf and by Jürgen Fehling in Berlin in 1947/1948 were major cultural events and a highlight of the debate about the Germans' collective guilt that had started in 1945.[11] Peter Brook staged *No Exit* (at a theater club in London), *The Victors* (*Men Without Shadows*; *Morts sans sépulture*) and *The Respectful Prostitute* in the U.K. in 1946/1947.

And to the theater performances we have to add the films. What today has been widely forgotten, even by Sartreans, is the fact that there was an astonishing number of films based on plays or scripts by Sartre—works like *The Chips Are Down* (*Les jeux sont faits*), *Typhus* (as a film, *The Proud and the Beautiful*), *False Noses* (*Les faux nez*), *Kean*, and *The Trojan Women* (*Les Troyennes*). The most interesting film from the perspective of the international reception of existentialism was *The Witches of Salem* (*Les sorcières de Salem*), a film Arthur Miller later prohibited to be shown. This film adaptation of Arthur Miller's play *The Crucible* was a French-GDR cooperation.

Last but not least we have to take into consideration the role of articles in journals, magazines, and newspapers. These were journals like *Partisan Review* and *Politics* in the U.S., *Politecnico* in Italy, *al-Adab* in the Arab world, and *Sur* in Argentina, partly built after the model of Sartre's and Beauvoir's *Les Temps modernes*. The situation in Germany, where the Allied Forces maintained a strict control over the media, was exceptional.

---

[11] In this debate in which Jaspers also participated, Sartre took the 'scandalous' position that the Germans should not fall into self-denial, as the past cannot be undone; they should rather honestly commit themselves to a future in freedom.

In a survey in Germany in 1948, Sartre's *The Flies* and Carl Zuckmayer's *The Devil's General* were mentioned as two most important cultural events in the time after the end of World War II (Rahner 1993, p. 305).

As a kind of compensation, many small journals came into existence and some of them, such as *Der Ruf*,[12] *Die Quelle, Dokumente, Umschau*, and *Frankfurter Hefte*, became platforms for the discussion of existentialist thoughts (Rahner 1993; Koberstein 1996).

Another special case was the importance of articles in newspapers and popular journals such as *Life, New York Times Magazine, Time*, and *Newsweek* in the U.S. Sartre and Beauvoir even wrote essays for the fashion magazines *Vogue* and *Harper's Bazaar*. This allowed them to reach out to a public they could have never met by using the more traditional channels—however, at the price that their personal lifestyle gained in importance in comparison to their philosophy (Cotkin 2003, p. 92). As Alfred Andersch remarked in 1951, the fact that the existentialists published novels and plays, too, very much hampered the reception of existentialism as a serious philosophical and literary movement (Andersch 2004, p. 281). Even more detrimental were the publications in newspapers and popular journals. The criticism by Brown, the *New York Times* correspondent in Paris, that the Sartreans led a lifestyle of drinking, partying, and sexual adventures (Fulton 1999, p. 32) determined the long-term perception of existentialism in the U.S. more than the articles in *Partisan Review*.

First Message—An Absurd, Contingent World Worth Rebelling Against

There are four different existentialist messages that have proved to be highly influential. The first and most basic existentialist message is based on the thesis that the world is absurd (Camus) and contingent (Sartre) with *The Myth of Sisyphus* (*Le mythe de Sisyphe*) and *Nausea* as the most important texts. Man is conceived as an individual subject who is confronted with an adverse environment. Human existence is always

---

[12] *Der Ruf* with Andersch, a Sartrean, as editor was the mouthpiece of the young generation of writers of *Group 47*. The journal was influenced by American writers such as Ernest Hemingway and William Faulkner and advocated a socialist humanism similar to Sartre's ideas.

being-in-situation. The conflict between man and his environment—in Sartre's later terminology, specifically the practico-inert—is the reason behind alienation. In the *Critique*, Sartre specifically mentions in this regard scarcity, counter-finality, and exigences/constraints as important factors contributing to alienation. With their idea of an absurd world, the existentialists laid the ground for the Theater of the Absurd with Samuel Beckett, Eugène Ionesco (ELKSY), Jean Genet, Harold Pinter, Tom Stoppard, and Friedrich Dürrenmatt among its most prominent authors. According to Dürrenmatt, Sartre had invented absurd theater with *No Exit*.

With the existentialists, this message of an absurd, contingent world goes together with the idea that man's destiny is failure: "man is a useless passion", as Sartre wrote in *Being and Nothingness* (Sartre 2012, p. 662). This pessimistic worldview allowed existentialism to continue a line of thinking for which the field had already been tilled before World War II by philosophers such as Kierkegaard, Jaspers, and Heidegger, and writers like Franz Kafka. Outside their own existentialist community, Camus and Sartre found support for this message particularly from the Christian Left—the American-German Paul Tillich was one its most prominent promoters—who conceived the individual as a subject suffering in Jesus Christ's succession. For the Swiss-American photographer Robert Frank, Sartre's phenomenological view on the contingent world became an important source of inspiration to shoot pictures of poor people and miserable conditions all over the U.S. This pessimistic existentialist message however experienced rejection by the communists and the vast majority of Americans for whom it stood in conflict with their general optimistic attitude (Fulton 1999, pp. 28–29).

This pessimism however was just one part of the first existentialist message. In contrast to earlier 'existentialists', the French existentialists gave this pessimistic worldview an optimistic turn by stating that man can rebel against the situation he is thrown into. This is a very important difference between Sartre, Beauvoir, and Camus on the one side, supported by Nietzsche, and Kierkegaard, Jaspers, and Heidegger on the other. Sartre's and Camus's positive figure is a man who rebels, not unlike the heroes in the novels by Hemingway and Malraux. This rebellious optimism was the basic message in *Existentialism Is a Humanism* and *The Rebel*. As Camus wrote in *The Myth of Sisyphus*, one must imagine Sisyphus happy.

This combination of a general pessimism with a possible positive turn by an individual rebellion was particularly well received in countries that were going through or had just been through difficult circumstances. This explains the positive reception in Italy, Germany, and Japan (KOBAYASHI/SEKI) after the war, but also in the Arab countries in the 1950s after the breakdown of the old traditional systems (ANDISHAN; DI-CAPUA), in Turkey in the 1960s after the fall of the nationalist regime of Adnan Menderes (Koş 2004, p. 93), and in South Vietnam during and after the Ngo Dinh Diem regime (Gadkar-Wilcox 2014). Among the young writers and intellectuals, many supporters of Castro's revolution in Cuba had read Sartre's works before (Rowlandson 2018, pp. 59–60). The birth of Brazilian *tropicalismo* in 1967/1968, which owes so much to existentialism, can only be understood in the context of artists' opposition to the military dictatorship (Ibiapina Ferreira n.d., p. 7). In the 1980s, existentialism was revived in the People's Republic of China after many years under Mao Zedong (Song and Xu 2007).

But there was also significant opposition to this message of the individual's rebellion. Traditional Christians like all other conservative forces opposed the idea that people could rebel against their fate. The existentialist message that one can rebel—Sartre wrote in both *Being and Nothingness* and the *Critique* that even the slave in chains is ultimately free to rebel (Sartre 2012, p. 594; Sartre 1985, p. 666)—was always rejected by the traditional right, but also by the communists, when it was about rebelling against their own real socialist system.

In the context of this first message of a contingent world, Shūzō Kuki should be mentioned, a Japanese student the young Sartre tutored in 1928. Since Shūzō handed in a doctoral thesis about contingency at the University of Kyoto five years later, Japan can be considered the first country ever where an existentialist message was published.

Second Message—You Are Free, Therefore Choose

The second important existentialist message was the one about the individual's absolute ontological freedom: since, in Sartre's words, existence precedes essence, man has to choose his self and his values. The promoters of this message were Sartre and Beauvoir. Since Camus—particularly the later one[13]—did not support it, his refusal to be called an existentialist is correct in this regard. For Sartre and Beauvoir, all values are created by (wo)man, and therefore, whatever (wo)man chooses is of equal right. There is no God, no religion, no tradition, no ideology that can prescribe to (wo)man how to act: as Fyodor Dostoevsky said: if God doesn't exist, everything is permissible (Sartre 2007, pp. 28–29). Among the supporters of this second message, younger people and people from arts and literature can particularly be found. Many of them were introduced to this message by Sartre's play *The Flies*, which as a free adaptation of a Greek drama found access to school curricula more easily than most other existentialist works.

A very important part of this message was that the subject should live authentically. Both Sartre and Beauvoir criticized living in bad faith with regard to facticity and to transcendence. The subject has to accept the situation she/he is in and assume responsibility for her/his choice. These existentialist postulates concurred with those of other existential philosophers and humanist psychologists—from Jaspers and Heidegger to Rollo May and Erich Fromm. Especially positive in this regard was the reception in the U.S., where the call for living authentically had become very loud after World War II.

The call for embracing one's individual freedom sparked great interest with writers and artists. During the dark years of the economic crisis of the 1930s and World War II that followed it, the pressure on literature, music, and the arts had risen. The existentialists were the loudest voice for their liberation after World War II. This call was particularly eagerly

---

[13] Whereas Meursault killed an Arab without regret in *The Stranger* (*L'étranger*), the later Camus rejected nihilism in *The Rebel* and advocated an ethics of measure.

trust

listened to in the former fascist world. Sartre and Beauvoir met many prominent Italian writers personally, including Carlo Levi, Silone, and Alberto Moravia. In Germany, Andersch, one of the founders of *Group 47*—with Heinrich Böll and Günter Grass as its two most prominent members—was a strong supporter of existentialist ideas (see also Littler 1991). The Swiss author Max Frisch started his literary career after he had assisted in a rehearsal of *The Flies* at the Zurich Playhouse in 1944 and published several works, among them *I'm Not Stiller*, close to existentialist ideas. Norman Mailer, who described himself as an American existentialist, the Swedish-German writer Peter Weiss, and the Englishman Colin Wilson are other authors to be mentioned here. The art critic Harold Rosenberg and his concept of action painting along with the Italian film directors Michelangelo Antonioni and Federico Fellini (Pamerleau 2009, pp. 85–112, 165–192) (Russo) were very much influenced by existentialist ideas. Sartrean views can even be found in artists outside the traditional European-American world, such as the Japanese filmmakers Ōshima Nagisa and Yoshida Yoshishige. The French-Polish composer René Leibowitz, a friend of Sartre, Beauvoir, and Camus, led an international debate in defense of the artistic freedom of the twelve-tone technique against the communist Prague Manifesto of 1948 supported by Igor Stravinsky and Nicolas Nabokov.

Sartre's and Beauvoir's call for assuming one's ontological freedom was based on a relativist view of morality. With their criticism of traditional conservative morality, whether in its bourgeois or its communist form, Sartre and Beauvoir met a lot of opposition. The communists criticized them as nihilistic and decadent and so did the conservative bourgeois critics, among them also Jaspers and Hans Jonas. Nihilism was still the major target in the Zurich literary dispute of 1967. Only very few, like the German writer Andersch, defended Sartre's nihilism *expressis verbis*. Most of the critics, whether bourgeois or communist, opposed a literature in Genet's style with representatives of the lumpenproletariat, criminals, and homosexuals. Sartre, Genet's most prominent supporter, and Beauvoir had severely criticized bourgeois patriarchal morality in their books[14]

---

[14] *Nausea, The Childhood of a Leader* (*L'enfance d'un chef*), *Being and Nothingness, She Came to Stay* (*L'invitée*), *No Exit, The Age of Reason* (*L'âge de raison*), *The Reprieve* (*Le sursis*), *The Respectful Prostitute, Dirty Hands* (*Les mains sales*), *Troubled Sleep* (*La mort dans l'âme*), *The Second Sex, Must*

where they describe many examples of unmarried couples, *ménages à trois*, homosexuals, prostitutes, abortion, and other kinds of acts and behaviors 'normal' people considered unnatural or perverted at that time.

Most of the criticism directed toward Sartre and Beauvoir was carried out in a disguised form. Open statements like the ones by Brown and Jaspers, who blamed the existentialist followers for their erotic licentiousness (Fulton 1999, p. 32; Jaspers 1968, pp. 497, 500), were rare. However, Sartre and Beauvoir also had their followers with respect to their criticism of bourgeois patriarchal morality. In this regard, Murdoch's novels and the work by the beatniks stand in the tradition of Sartre and Beauvoir. Allen Ginsberg dedicated his masterly poem *Howl* to Carl Solomon who had followed the existentialist scene in Paris. Whereas in our Christian culture explicit discourses about sexuality were mostly shunned, this topic was more freely discussed in other cultures. In Japan, Sartre's early writing was considered part of what was called "the literature of the flesh" (Slaymaker 2002, p. 78; Suzuki and Sawada 2011, p. 183). In South Vietnam, too, existentialism was openly associated with sex (Hiên 2009, pp. 15–16), and when Sartre traveled to Egypt in 1967, he was shown a copy of a translation of *Existentialism Is a Humanism* with a naked woman on the front cover (Di-Capua 2018, p. 208). Arab existentialism had already developed a scene in Baghdad/Iraq where drinking alcohol and 'fornication' were a central part of the lifestyle (Di-Capua 2018, p. 132).

This message of ontological freedom even reached the general society. The Parisian existentialist scene with Juliette Gréco[15] and Boris Vian extended to many cities around the globe. Listening to jazz (bebop, cool jazz), wearing black turtlenecks and black trousers, girls with short hairstyles and ballerinas—this was fashionable among young people from the second half of the 1940s into the 1950s. Young people formed a very important segment of Sartre's following (Fulton 1999,

---

We Burn de Sade? (Faut-il brûler Sade?), Saint Genet, The Mandarins (Les mandarins), The Condemned of Altona (Les séquestrés d'Altona), The Prime of Life (La force de l'âge), Force of Circumstance (La force des choses).

[15] Gréco and Georges Brassens stood at the origin of a tradition of chansons with an existentialist tinge, which was picked up by Luigi Tenco and Fabrizio De André in Italy and by Franz Josef Degenhardt in Germany.

pp. 130–131; Cotkin 2003, p. 1): Sartre was the Socrates of the twentieth century, a corrupter of the youth who wanted to express their desire for freedom. In Germany, there existed an existentialist movement among students of high schools and universities called the 'exi movement' (Krüger 1986). These were young people wearing black, listening to cool jazz, reading Sartre—young people who rejected the old role models of men and women and who advocated sexual freedom. When the Beatle Paul McCartney was asked who their audience in Hamburg was, he referred to the members of this movement (Perone 2009, p. 78). Two members of the 'exi movement' in Hamburg were the originators of the Beatles' mop-top haircut, a milestone in the development of the most prominent symbol of the hippie generation, the long hair. Not surprisingly, several figures of the German 68 generation from Rudi Dutschke and Benno Ohnesorg to Alice Schwarzer, Udo Lindenberg, and Rüdiger Safranski were influenced by existentialist oeuvres they had read in their college years. When we ask the question today who the spiritual parents of the sexual liberation of the generation of 1968 were, there is no easy answer. Ginsberg and Jack Kerouac had a certain influence, particularly in the U.S.; Marcuse and Wilhelm Reich were important with regard to Freudo-Marxism, but both were reluctant to accept sexuality in its broad form, as their attitude toward homosexuality proves. The sexual liberation that took place in the 1960s and 1970s most probably owes more to Sartre and Beauvoir, since no other intellectuals stood for free sexuality in any form as much as Sartre and Beauvoir (Betschart 2019).[16]

---

[16] For decades, existentialism was perceived as a philosophical and literary movement with a strong political tinge rather than as one with a strong concept of lifestyle. This has changed in the last few years with contributions by Sarah Bakewell (*At the Existentialist Café*, 2016; *Think big, be free, have sex … 10 reasons to be an existentialist*, https://www.theguardian.com/books/2016/mar/04/ten-reasons-to-be-an-existentialist, 2016), Agnès Poirier (*Left Bank. Art, Passion, and the Rebirth of Paris 1940–1950*, 2018), and most recently Skye C. Cleary (*Being and drunkenness: how to party like an existentialist*, https://aeon.co/ideas/being-and-drunkenness-how-to-party-like-an-existentialist, 2019).

Third Message—No to Discrimination Against Women, Jews, Blacks, Homosexuals

Individual freedom presupposes equality and particularly nondiscrimination, the third important existentialist message. Whereas ontological freedom is absolute, practical freedom is always limited: as Sartre wrote in *Being and Nothingness*, (wo-)man is always in a situation. What Sartre and Beauvoir opposed all their life was discrimination. Beauvoir wrote *The Second Sex* in opposition to discrimination against women. Although it was quickly translated—into German two years after its French publication, one year later into English—opposition from a male-dominated patriarchal society prevented any adequate reception of the book. Even in France and even among her friends—with the exception, of course, of Sartre, who always supported her work—Beauvoir experienced rejection. Camus, who was never a supporter of this third important existentialist message with regard to women or to discrimination for race or sexual orientation, accused Beauvoir of ridiculing the French man. The world had to wait fourteen years until Betty Friedan's *The Feminine Mystique* (1963), the first important book published that picked up Beauvoir's ideas.

Nevertheless, Beauvoir was an important role model for young female intellectuals: the British philosopher and author Iris Murdoch and the Austrian poet Ingeborg Bachmann, but also the Lebanese writer Layla Ba'albakki led independent lives similar to Beauvoir's. Sartre's and Beauvoir's partnership served as a role model for many young intellectual couples who were convinced that a partnership of equal rights between a woman and man was possible on an intellectual level, too. How innovative this was at the time is shown by Beauvoir when she recounts her visit to Berlin in 1948. She was always addressed as Mrs. Sartre and not as Mlle or even Mme Beauvoir, because at that time it was unthinkable that a woman could be intellectually independent of a man. Beauvoir's novels *She Came to Stay* and *The Mandarins* and the (auto-)biographies *The Prime of Life* and *Force of Circumstance*—describing the partnership between Beauvoir and Sartre and their lovers—were highly influential in this regard. Suhayl Idris and Aida Matraji led a life in Beirut/Lebanon that was a copy of Sartre's and Beauvoir's. Among the early Sartreans, the prominence of women is remarkable (Fulton 1999, p. 79). With Murdoch, Marjorie Grene, Hazel Barnes, and Mary Warnock, four important existentialist scholars were women—although we have to concede that this was partly due to the fact that existentialism was not considered a philosophy on a proper academic level in the world of Anglo-Saxon universities.

Before Beauvoir's publication of *The Second Sex*, Sartre had published works opposing antisemitism and racism. No other theoretical work of Sartre's was as quickly translated into the major foreign languages as *Anti-Semite and Jew*, the first book about antisemitism published by a major European intellectual since World War II. Although existentialism in the early years of the existence of the state of Israel was not an issue for the Jews there (KLEIN), Sartre's literature and philosophy found quite some echo among Jewish writers and intellectuals, not only in France, but also in other countries: Jean Améry (Austria; KZ prisoner), Paul Celan (Romania), Peter Weiss (Sweden/Germany), Fritz Heinemann (U.K.), Allen Ginsberg, Norman Mailer, Arthur Miller, and Susan Sontag (all U.S.).

In 1947/1948, Sartre supported black African authors such as Léopold Sédar Senghor and Aimé Césaire in their fight for recognition. In *Black Presence* (*Présence noire*) and *Black Orpheus* (*Orphée noir*), he recognized the importance of the black skin which stigmatizes the Black in the sense that, unlike the Jew, a black person cannot choose to become another white European. Sartre's work particularly influenced Frantz Fanon in his *Black Skin, White Masks* (*Peau noire, masques blancs*, 1952), which then led to *The Wretched of the Earth* (BERNASCONI). Directly and indirectly via Fanon, Sartre's theoretical views on racism influenced Edward Said and his concept of orientalism, and Stuart Hall, a founding father of cultural studies. Black existentialism started in the 1960s—for example, with Steve Biko in South Africa. Stokely Carmichael cited Camus, Sartre, and Fanon in his famous 1966 speech at UC Berkeley. Carmichael and Sartre cooperated shortly thereafter in the Russell Tribunal about the Vietnam War. Angela Davis had intensively studied Sartre as an undergraduate. The attraction existentialism exerted on black intellectuals is also shown in the case of African American writers such as Richard Wright and Ralph Ellison. Sartre's engagement on behalf of ethnical minorities even reached

Japan where Suzuki Michihiko, a specialist in French literature, became famous for his involvement in favor of the Zainichi, ethnic Koreans living in Japan as a scorned minority (KOBAYASHI/SEKI).

Sartre was also one of the first prominent heterosexual intellectuals to defend the equal rights of homosexuals. Although his biography *Saint Genet* was only translated later, his defense of the explicitly homosexual writer Jean Genet was well noted. Beauvoir wrote with *Must We Burn de Sade?* an essay about an equally disputed writer. The International Committee for Sexual Equality, an international organization for the defense of the rights of homosexuals, almost invited Sartre as main speaker for their conference in 1953. That Oreste Pucciani, one of the more important representatives of existentialism in the U.S., was a homosexual and partner of Rudi Gernreich, a co-founder of the Mattachine society, an early gay rights society in the U.S., was hardly a coincidence. Another prominent member of the Mattachine society, Wallace de Ortega Maxey (see de Ortega Maxey 1958), was an existentialist, too. In Germany with Fritz J. Raddatz and Hubert Fichte, there were prominent homosexual and bisexual intellectuals who stood in the tradition of Sartrean existentialism.

As attractive as the message of nondiscrimination was for women, Jews, Blacks, and homosexuals, the amount of resistance to this message was considerable—not in terms of outright opposition, but rather, as *The Second Sex* shows, by maintaining silence. This was as true for the conservative religious majorities in the West as for the communists all over the world. *No Exit*, Sartre's most performed piece today, was not allowed by the Lord Chamberlain to be shown at larger British theaters until 1959 because one of the three major characters was a lesbian (ANDREWS). Since Lucien, the main figure in *The Childhood of a Leader*, temporarily chose to become a homosexual, this book, originally printed in the GDR in 1957, was banished to the poison cabinet after an intervention by Alfred Kurella, a writer and candidate to the Politburo of reigning communist Socialist Unity Party (SED) (VON WROBLEWSKY).

Fourth Message—Engage Yourself

The fourth important existentialist message was the one of engagement. This was certainly the most widely spread message the existentialists sent out to the world. Although Merleau-Ponty's *Humanism and Terror* (*Humanisme et terreur*) was translated only late (into German in 1966, into English in 1969), all four French existentialists—Sartre, Beauvoir, Camus, and Merleau-Ponty—were involved in this message so closely associated today with Sartre's name. Camus can even be called a forerunner to Sartre in this regard. With his early political engagement in Algeria before World War II—for a short time, he was even a member of the Communist Party—and his position as political commentator and editorialist of the newspaper *Combat* 1944–1947,[17] Camus was involved in politics much earlier than Sartre.

Sartre published his programmatic essay *What Is Literature?* about the committed writer in 1947. Translations into English and German followed soon, and later into Italian, Japanese, Spanish, even Turkish and Farsi. Already in October 1945, Sartre had published a text known among Sartre scholars as *Présentation* [*des Temps Modernes*] explaining the idea behind *Les Temps modernes*. This eminent text was an enlarged version of what the journal *Horizon* in the U.K. and shortly thereafter *Partisan Review* had previously published as *The Case for Responsible Literature*. The unique blend of philosophy, literature, and politics that is so characteristic of existentialists had already attracted attention at the end of 1944 when the American press presented existentialism as an intellectual movement of Résistance fighters.

Sartre's political position before 1952 was ambiguous. He was for a unified, liberal, left-wing Europe and against the threats of the Cold War. However, his relationship with the Communists was tense. Apart from his engagement in the Rassemblement Démocratique Révolutionnaire (RDR) 1948–1949, which the Communist Party strictly opposed, his

---

[17] As Raymond Aron correctly remarked, Camus was not the editor in chief of *Combat*; this was Pascal Pia (Aron 1983, p. 208).

political activities were mostly limited to purely intellectual forms.[18]
Sartre became the *animal politique* he is remembered for today only after
1950, after Merleau-Ponty had stopped working as a political director of
Les Temps modernes. However, Sartre was regarded as a politically committed figure outside France even in the years before, as the break between
Sartre and the *Partisan Review* and *Politics* proves. The understanding
abroad of what engagement meant definitely exceeded Sartre's own
actions at the beginning. Only in the 1950s, when Sartre for a short time
became involved with the French and Soviet Communists (1952–1956
and 1954–1956 respectively) and when he fought against keeping Algeria
as a French colony (1955–1962), did Sartre become the politically committed writer the world had seen in him before.

Wherever there were politically committed writers outside the
Communist parties, they were regularly associated with Sartre's concept
of engagement. In Italy, from Alberto Moravia and Silone to Pier Paolo
Pasolini, the line of committed writers was long. Most members of *Group
47* that dominated German literature in the 1960s and 1970s adhered to
a slightly mitigated version of Sartre's concept. In their discussions with
the representatives of the *nouveau roman*—Alain Robbe-Grillet, Nathalie
Sarraute—the members of *Group 47* defended Sartre's concept of the
committed writer, at the COMES meeting in Leningrad in 1963 and
thereafter in the discussions in Germany (Ächtler 2016, pp. 115–117).
In the Arab world, *iltizam*, the Arabic word for commitment, was one of
the key words in literary criticism in the 1950s—commitment in its
Sartrean as well as its communist meaning (Di-Capua 2018, p. 78).
Engagement became a central topic, too, for many writers in Latin
America, from the group around the journals *Sur* and *Contorno* in Buenos
Aires (Savignano 2016) to Mario Vargas Llosa in Peru (Vargas Llosa
1996, pp. 131–143) and other writers in Colombia, Mexico, and Cuba.
The impact of Sartre's visit to Japan in 1966 that caused another wave of
discussions about the role of the intellectual has already been mentioned.
Several of the writers and intellectuals most engaged in politics in Japan—

---

[18] At this time, Sartrean engagement was not much more than a modern version of *qui tacet consen-
tire videtur*. In his *Introduction to Les Temps Modernes* of 1945 he blamed the brothers Goncourt and
Gustave Flaubert for not having written a single line against injustices and oppression and not for
not having taken arms against the repression after the defeat of the Paris Commune.

among others, Oda Makoto, Kaikō Takeshi, Ōe Kenzaburō, and Yoshimoto Takaaki (Müller 2014, p. 250)—were influenced by Sartre.

Sartre's request for the writer's political engagement was particularly popular because, unlike the communists who also called for it, Sartre additionally advocated the writer's right to choose his own political values and ideas freely. This was the reason why the communists rejected the Sartrean version of commitment. That the right-wing bourgeoisie opposed the politically committed writer and intellectual and preferred a concept of *l'art pour l'art* with the writer kept in his ivory tower does not really surprise. Strangely, the Frankfurt School, too, and particularly Theodor Adorno, opposed Sartre. Adorno mistrusted any kind of active social involvement so much that he rejected Sartre's concept of commitment (Adorno 1981, pp. 409–430).

Distorted Messages—Limits of Freedom, Politics

The transfer of messages is frequently accompanied by more or less serious distortions. Communication is a process of encoding and decoding in which errors may occur. Once the sender has encoded his message, he has mostly lost his influence over the process of decoding. The second message of the individual's absolute freedom was very powerful and became, together with the concept of engagement, Sartre's most important trademark, but at the price of a significant distortion. Sartre's idea of ontological freedom never implied practical freedom. The human being is always situated. The slave's absolute freedom never implied that the slave is free from any shackles, but only referred to the fact that slaves are able to decide to rebel, as they did in history on several occasions. Sartre's intention was to exhort us that, however difficult the circumstances, we still can and have to try to change them.

Other prominent examples of distorted messages concern Sartre's political engagement. In 1945, the American press already blamed Sartre for being anti-American. *Partisan Review* and *Politics*—both led by anti-Stalinist (ex-)Trotskyites—and other former communists such as Sydney

Hook accused Sartre of being too Soviet-friendly at a time when the French Communists and Sartre were still quarreling with each other. Today Sartre is still associated with labels such as communist, Marxist, and even Maoist. His association with the respective political movements seems to justify this message; however, these allegations are based on the failure to differentiate between ideological alliances and considerations of usefulness. His alliances with the French (1952–1956) and Soviet communists (1954–1956, 1962–1964/1968), the Algerian rebels (1955–1962), Castro's Cuba (1960–1961/1971), and several 'Maoist' New Left groups in France (Gauche Prolétarienne, Vive La Révolution etc., none of them recognized by Beijing, 1970–1971/1973) were not ideological partnerships, but rather cases of tactical cooperation. Finally, Sartre was faithful only to his own values, to his four big noes to militarism, colonialism, racism, and bourgeois morality. As the short periods of cooperation indicate, Sartre broke with his partners easily when they violated his core values.

The failure to understand the true nature of Sartre's political tactics had serious repercussions. His theory of commitment derived from his almost behaviorist view that only observable acts count and not thoughts—with speaking considered as an act—and, from his ethical standpoint, that being responsible for one's acts means that we have to justify them vis-à-vis the Other. However, most receivers understood this message not as a general ethical statement—man is free to choose, as shown in *The Flies*, but has to justify his actions to the Other, as shown in *No Exit*—but rather as a political one closely associated with Sartre's own political standpoint—with the effect, that many politically engaged writers disapproved of Sartre's position on committed literature because they did not distinguish between Sartre's general theory and his own political stance.

Many progressive writers all over the developed world, from the U.S. with, for example, Arthur Miller to the German Group 47, refused to follow Sartre's collaboration with the Communists as short-lived as it may have been. Together with his less pronounced atheism,[19] Camus's

---

[19] On the occasion of the premiere of Camus's *The Misunderstanding*, André Rousseaux, critic for *Le Figaro*, wrote that with Sartre God is dead, with Camus only hard of hearing.

refusal to any cooperation with the Communists was a major reason that Camus, too, became a source for political inspiration, particularly in the U.S. Bob Moses, a leader of the Student Nonviolent Coordinating Committee, was very much inspired by him. This was also the case with Tom Hayden, one of the initiators of *Students for a Democratic Society* (SDS) and a leading figure in the movement against the war in Vietnam. There was just a short period of a few years around 1968 and 1970 when Hayden—like other radical students such as Jerry Rubin—followed Sartre rather than Camus because of the latter's more pacifist attitude (Cotkin 2003, pp. 225–230).

Sartre's manifold criticisms of the Communist, and in particular the Soviet, world were forgotten. With his defense of Kafka at the World Peace Congress in Moscow 1962, Sartre had sent an important signal that contributed to the Kafka Congress in Liblice in Czechoslovakia the following year which in turn was a place of inspiration for the Prague Spring.[20] Sartre was one of the very early supporters of Soviet dissidents, too. Already in 1963, Sartre's *Les Temps modernes* had published two of Alexander Solzhenitsyn's novels. However, Sartre never lost the label of being a communist or at least of being their fellow traveler.

Sartre's political engagement also found its supporters. His commitment to the Algerian cause gave him a lot of credentials in the Arab world, which, however, resulted in a fatal misunderstanding. Most of the Arabs erroneously believed Sartre to be on their side in their conflict with Israel. When Sartre supported Israel's claim to existence after the Six-Day War, Arab existentialism collapsed completely (Di-Capua 2018, pp. 229–249). The engagement for Algeria was followed by other commitments in favor of the Third World. Sartre supported Castro's Cuba and fought against the War in Vietnam, particularly as the executive president of the Russell Tribunal 1966/1967. These actions gained him a lot of support among progressive students in the U.S. (ARONSON) and in other parts of the world. When Sartre visited Japan in 1966, Vietnam was at the top of the agenda. *The Wretched of the Earth* by Fanon with Sartre's

---

[20] Sartre had a good relationship to the movement that led to the Prague Spring. Already in 1965, *Les Temps modernes* published an article written by Ota Šik, the father of the economic reforms during the Prague Spring. Two years later, *Men Without Shadows*, *Dirty Hands*, and *The Trojan Women* were published in Czech with a postscript by Milan Kundera.

preface became the Bible for many activists fighting for the Third World and the independence of its countries. Sartre was definitely one the spiritual fathers of the Third World movement that became so popular in the First World in the 1960s and 1970s.

Distortion however affected not only Sartre's political views, but also Camus's. Particularly because of his praise of Scandinavian social democracies in *The Rebel*, Camus was and is still mainly perceived as a middle-of-the-road social democrat. His anarchist leanings as expressed in his collaboration with the Italian Nicola Chiaromonte and the American Dwight Macdonald were overlooked (Marin 2013). In this regard, Camus shared the fate of Sartre whose return in the 1970s to his early anarchism of the time before World War II was never properly perceived by either his followers or his foes (Betschart 2016).

Failed Messages—Marxism, Ethics, Philosophy, Psychology

There were not only distorted messages, but also messages that were not received at all. A major one was Sartre's criticism of Marxism as expressed in *Search for a Method* (*Questions de méthode*) and the *Critique*.[21] The only exception in the developed world was Italy where Sartre was invited twice to the Gramsci Institute in the 1960s and where he later engaged in a dialogue with the group *Il Manifesto*. Neither heterodox Eastern European Marxists such as Adam Schaff and Danilo Pejović (Schaff 1965; Pejović 1965) nor the Marxist left in Europe and North America ever adopted Sartre's ideas on how to 'improve' Marxism—most probably because they intuitively felt that Sartre's talk in *Search for a Method* about Marxism as the philosophy of our time was just kind words which would have finally led to the replacement of Marxism by existentialism. The Marxist students around 1970 rather preferred Marxism in the version of Marcuse,

---

[21] Sartre's major criticism concerned the reductionist approach of Marxism to the individual. Marxists reduce Paul Valéry to a petit bourgeois; however, not every petit bourgeois is Valéry. Individuals are what they make out of what is made of them. Sartre's critique has its foundation in his differentiation between 'explaining' and 'understanding'—nature is characterized by causality, human mind by teleology—which finds its root with Wilhelm Dilthey and Jaspers.

Adorno, and Louis Althusser or even Mao's crude theories. It was rather at a later time, in the mid-1970s and early 1980s, that some American philosophers came up with the idea of existential Marxism: Mark Poster with *Existential Marxism in Postwar France* in 1975, John Lawler with *The Existentialist Marxism* in 1976, and Thomas Flynn with *Sartre and Marxist Existentialism* in 1984. Additionally, intellectuals from the Third World have to be mentioned: they tried to combine existentialism with Marxism to find their own national way for a new political ideology, partly including their major national religion. The Japanese Tanabe Hajima and the South Vietnamese Ngyuen Van Trung combined existentialism and Marxism with Buddhism (Müller 2014, p. 254; Hiên 2009, p. 11), the Iranian Ali Shariati with Shia and Sufism (Rahnema 2000, pp. 294, 360).

Another important message not received at all concerned the ethical problem of the relationship between ends and means. In the years between 1943 and 1952, Camus, Sartre, and Beauvoir led an intensive but indirect discussion about this issue in several plays and essays. On the one hand, Sartre and Beauvoir defended an ethics where ends and means form a unity—in Max Weber's terms, an ethics of responsibility—in *Moral Idealism and Political Realism* (*Idéalisme moral et réalisme politique*) and *The Useless Mouths* (*Les bouches inutiles*) in 1945, *The Responsibility of the Writer* (*La responsabilité de l'écrivain*) and *What Is Literature?* in 1947, *In the Mesh* and *Dirty Hands* in 1948, and *The Devil and the Good Lord* (*Le diable et le bon dieu*) in 1951; Camus, on the other hand, advocated an ethics of conviction in *Letters to a German Friend* (*Lettres à un ami allemand*) in 1943–1945, *Neither Victims nor Executioners* (*Ni victimes ni bourreaux*) in 1946, *The Just Assassins* in 1949, and *The Rebel* in 1951. This indirect discussion finally ended in the break between Camus and Sartre in 1952. As much as this break was noted, little attention was given to the underlying difference in ethics that caused it. A big chance to discuss one of the most important ethical questions was missed. That Camus has today to a large extent closed the gap with Sartre in terms of popularity finds its reason very much in the fact that we live in a world of an ethics of conviction today and no longer in a world of an ethics of responsibility, as was the case until the 1970s.

The most important failure in the transmission of messages, however, concerned Sartre's philosophy in its proper sense. In comparison to his other messages, his philosophical ones were of secondary importance. Sartre had few discussions with other philosophers of the quality of those he had with Enzo Paci in Italy (KIRCHMAYR, CADDEO; Rovatti 1987). In the Anglo-Saxon countries particularly, the discussion about existentialist philosophy was largely limited to the undergraduate level where it mainly served as a bait to lure young students to study philosophy.[22] Sartre's ontology and epistemology hardly got any proper attention from philosophical academia. What Mary Warnock said about the Cambridge and Oxford of the 1950s—"There was a deep hostility to the very idea of 'continental philosophy'" (Woessner 2012, p. 159), with the possible exception of the young A. J. Ayer—was valid for most of the North American universities, too, where only a few philosophers such as John Wild and William Barrett showed a serious interest in existentialist philosophy. This is surprising for several reasons. Sartre's existentialism was one of the last, if not the last systemic philosophy, before Jean-François Lyotard discredited universalizing theories in his 1979 text *The Postmodern Condition*. Existentialism is a philosophy that comprises almost all philosophical disciplines. It starts with ontology, epistemology, and philosophy of science, goes on to psychology, along with social and political philosophy and ends with normative ethics and meta-ethics.

Even in relation to particular questions such as the mind-body problem, the existentialists' inventive solutions were overlooked for a long time. Sartre's proposal to understand consciousness as empty and as pure intentionality and the lived body (*Leib*) as the mode by which consciousness is in the world—herewith he rejected the Cartesian and later Kantian separation between consciousness and outer world and offered a way to overcome the subject/object separation—has never found its proper reception. If any of the existentialist philosophers is cited today by philosophers with regard to the mind-body problem, it is Merleau-Ponty

---

[22] The major exceptions were the translations of *Esquisse d'une théorie des émotions* (as *The Emotions* in 1948, and later as *Sketch for a Theory of the Emotions*) and *L'imaginaire* (as *Psychology of the Imagination* in 1949, and later as *The Imaginary*) into English. These very early translations—which were, however, widely neglected—can be best explained by the fact that Sartre stood in the tradition not only of Henri Bergson's, but also of William James's criticism of association psychology.

rather than Sartre. Another important differentiation Sartre introduced into philosophy was the distinction between pre-reflective and reflective consciousness, by which he made the ego an object of consciousness. This concept, too, was met mostly with disregard by philosophical academia. Even in the field of ethics, Beauvoir's and Sartre's theses found little resonance. Warnock's *Existentialist Ethics* 1967 and Barnes's *An Existentialist Ethics* 1978 remained exceptions.

The situation in psychology is not very different. One would expect that Sartre's existential psychology, with fundamental choice as its key concept, would have found an appropriate reception in psychology, since with Alfred Adler and Ludwig Binswanger there were two important representatives of a humanistic psychotherapy with similar concepts. Frankl's logotherapy is maybe even influenced by Sartre. With Rogers, Maslow, May, and Fromm there were humanistic psychologists with ideas quite close to those of Sartre (Bassiri/Senie). However, here again, existentialism's reception in the world of psychotherapists and psychologists was virtually nil. Even Heidegger, who had written against Sartre's blend of philosophy and psychology in his famous *Letter on Humanism*, had a better entry into the world of psychotherapy through Medard Boss's *Daseinsanalysis* than did Sartre. The only traces Sartre left in this field were via his influence on anti-psychiatry with David Cooper and Ronald D. Laing (U.K.), and partly Franco Basaglia (Italy).

Sartre's alleged pessimism, atheism, and anti-Americanism are mentioned as reasons for the neglect in philosophy. However, the cases of Kierkegaard, Heidegger, and Camus speak against this interpretation: Kierkegaard definitely lacks Sartre's optimistic view of a human being that can rebel; Heidegger was a Nazi, and both, Camus and Heidegger were atheists, too. It seems rather that Sartre's and Beauvoir's second message, the one about individual freedom with its strong criticism of bourgeois patriarchal morality was the reason why the scientific community did not allow them to enter the premises of academia. Existentialist philosophy was considered café philosophy (Fulton 1999, p. 22). The early presentations of existentialism in the U.S. as well as in Europe and on other continents focused on existentialism as a lifestyle movement. The existentialists' refusal—with the exception of Merleau-Ponty—to follow an academic career and their readiness to promote their philosophical ideas by such unacademic means as literature, film, and even interviews in 'vulgar' journals, were met with significant opposition from academia in its ivory tower. Their rejection of the existing morality experienced even greater objection: Sartre's and Beauvoir's nihilistic and relativistic view of morality was understood by the vast majority of professors as an offense.

This was particularly true in the field of sexuality. The role of sex in Sartre's and Beauvoir's work leaves "*Lady Chatterley's Lover* sleeping at the door-post", as Walter Kaufmann wrote (Kaufmann 1975, p. 45). The American-Austrian philosopher Alfred Stern stated that a part of Sartre's work was "pornographic" (Stern 1967, p. 250). The first German translation of *Being and Nothingness* cut Sartre's explanation of the hole—the publishers most probably assumed that more than one opening in the human body could be meant. The British-German philosopher Fritz Heinemann who otherwise was rather a promoter of existential philosophy wrote that *Being and Nothingness* contained *scènes amoureuses* (amorous scenes) that are a scandal in the history of metaphysics (Heinemann 1971, p. 189). Similar reasons for the very weak reception must be assumed in the fields of psychology and psychotherapy, whose representatives had quite bourgeois conceptions of morality. The lifelong one-to-one heterosexual relationship was their moral standard. In his *Saint Genet*, however, Sartre had idealized a writer who was a homosexual and a thief. This was completely unacceptable in a world where the American Psychiatric Association and the American Psychoanalytic Association maintained until 1973 and 1991 respectively that homosexuality was a mental illness to be cured.

With his analysis of the relationship of the individual to the Other in *Being and Nothingness* and *Anti-Semite and Jew*, Sartre had ventured into the field of sociology, too. Although Sartre showed a vivid interest in American sociology—he read David Riesman's *The Lonely Crowd* (1950) and William Whyte's *The Organization Man* (1956) with great interest, and Sartre and Beauvoir were befriended by C. Wright Mills when he lived in Paris—his impact on sociology exceeded that on psychology only minimally. With Alfred Schütz and Erving Goffman, Sartre exerted at least some influence. Said with his concept of orientalism and Hall with his cultural studies are other well-known representatives of sociology where traces of Sartre's earlier work can be found. However, when it comes to Sartre's later work, his *Critique*, an appropriate reception is still completely missing, although the *Critique* with its analysis of the various kinds of groups—from the series, the milieu, the group-in-fusion to the simple group, the pledged group, the organized group, and finally the institutionalized group—was mainly a work about social philosophy. Sartre's social philosophy could have provided ample material to discuss sociological questions such as alienation, identity, and recognition.

Feed-back

Finally, since reception is communication and communication is always reciprocal, an overview of the international reception of existentialism would not be complete without dealing briefly with how the international reception fed back to the existentialists. The distorted performance of *Dirty Hands* (as *Red Gloves*) in New York in fall 1948 and the discussions about the same play in Vienna in 1952 (Werner 2017) led Sartre to the decision to prohibit any performance of *Dirty Hands* without the approval of the local Communist party—a ban lifted only in 1964 on the occasion of a performance in Turin (Italy). Sartre wanted to prevent the representation of *Dirty Hands* as an anticommunist play, whereas it was rather one about the conflict between a younger idealist communist as the representative of an ethics of conviction and a more experienced *Realpolitiker* as the representative of an ethics of responsibility. Another kind of reaction to experiences abroad was Sartre's permission to change the ending of his piece *The Respectful Prostitute* from a pessimistic to an optimistic one in the Soviet Union and China in accordance with the more optimistic communist view (VAN DEN HOVEN; Betschart 2018b).

A less known event with an even more influential impact concerns the reception of existentialism in the U.S. The first existentialist text published in the U.S. was *The Republic of Silence* in December 1944. This was Sartre's text written for the first issue of *Les Lettres françaises* after the liberation of Paris in August 1944. This text, written in a very triumphalist style, was appropriate for the immediate days after the liberation and for *Les Lettres françaises* as the leading intellectual Résistance publication.

However, it was no longer suitable several months later when it was published in New York. It gave the wrong picture that the existentialists were intellectuals and writers representative of the Résistance. Although Sartre and Beauvoir in particular never claimed to have been very active in the Résistance and indeed they—including Camus—never were very active members, they praised each other in this regard to enhance their reputation with the Americans (ARONSON).

The Existentialist Tsunami

Existentialism spread around the globe in the years after World War II like a tsunami. The existentialists, particularly Sartre and Beauvoir, were the first modern, truly global intellectuals using any kind of means to spread their messages and commenting on very different subjects. Much-traveled artists and musicians, among them Peter Paul Rubens and Wolfgang Amadeus Mozart, had previously promoted their work in much of the world accessible to them at the time. Sigmund Freud and Alfred Adler traveled not only in Europe, but also to North America. William James, Henri Bergson, John Dewey, and Bertrand Russell were philosophers who made journeys to many parts of the world, and found a certain audience outside the ivory tower of philosophy. However, none of them was as successful as the existentialists.

This overview shows that there were several factors that contributed to the existentialist tsunami. As already Boschetti noticed for the case of France, the fact that Sartre, Beauvoir, and Camus communicated through different channels was very important. The wide network of repeaters proved to be more effective than the noise with which existentialism was confronted unlike any other modern intellectual movement. The decisive factor was that the needs of that time were met by the four major existentialist messages of 'an absurd, contingent world worth rebelling against', 'you are free, therefore choose', 'no to discrimination against women, Jews, blacks, and homosexuals', and 'engage yourself!'. However, this overwhelming success came at a price: some of the messages were distorted, some others were never received at all, particularly by philosophers.

The existentialist tsunami was an event in history not yet surpassed. And it was not just a fad, but it left permanent traces in history. With their ideas of individual freedom and authenticity, the existentialists anticipated and exerted a considerable influence on our way of life today. No feature has characterized the politics of the last fifty years as much as the battle against discrimination in terms of gender, ethnicity, and sexual orientation—although we have forgotten today that the intellectual godparents of this political movement were Sartre and Beauvoir.

References

Ächtler, Norman. 2016. Zwischen Existentialismus und Strukturalismus, Engagement und Degagement—Alfred Anderschs Poetik des Beschreibens. In *Alfred Andersch. Engagierte Autorschaft im Literatursystem der Bundesrepublik*, ed. Norman Ächtler, 111–131. Stuttgart: J.B. Metzler.

Adorno, Theodor W. 1981. Engagement. In *Noten zur Literatur*, ed. Rolf Tiedemann, 409–430. Frankfurt a. M.: Suhrkamp.

Alberto Sánchez, Carlos. 2016. *Contingency and Commitment. Mexican Existentialism and the Place of Philosophy*. Albany: SUNY Press.

Andersch, Alfred. 2004. Jugend am Schmelzpott einer Kultur. In *Gesammelte Werke*, Bd. 8: Essayistische Schriften 1, 279–292. Zürich: Diogenes.

Aron, Raymond. 1983. *Mémoires. 50 ans de réflexion politique*. Paris: Julliard.

Baert, Patrick. 2015. *The Existentialist Moment. The Rise of Sartre as a Public Intellectual*. Cambridge: Polity.

Betschart, Alfred. 2016. Sartre's Anarchist Political Philosophy—A Draft for a Diverse Society? Accessed June 26, 2019. http://sartre.ch/Sartre-anarchy-NASS-16.pdf.

———. 2018a. Sartre und die Sowjetunion. Die Geschichte eines komplizierten Verhältnisses. Accessed June 26, 2019. http://www.sartre.ch/Sartre-SSSR.pdf.

———. 2018b. Die ehrbare Dirne. Drei Versionen der 5. Szene im Zweiten Bild. Accessed June 26, 2019. http://www.sartre.ch/Die%20ehrbare%20Dirne.pdf.

———. 2019. Von Freud zu Sartre—Die Vordenker der sexuellen Revolution. In *1968—soziale Bewegungen, geistige WegbereiterInnen*, ed. Jens Bonnemann et al., 149–165. Springe: zu Klampen.

Boschetti, Anna. 1985. *Sartre et "Les Temps Modernes"*. Paris: Éditions de Minuit.

Collins, Randall. 1998. *The Sociology of Philosophies. A Global Theory of Intellectual Change*. Cambridge, MA: Harvard University Press.

Cotkin, George. 2003. *Existential America*. Baltimore: John Hopkins University Press.

Di-Capua, Yoav. 2018. *No Exit. Arab Existentialism, Jean-Paul Sartre, and Decolonization*. Chicago: University of Chicago Press.

Domingo Toledo, Roberto. 2011. Existentialism and Latin America. In *The Continuum Companion of Existentialism*, ed. Felicity Joseph et al., 215–237. London: Continuum.

Friedan, Betty. 1985. *"It Challenged My Life". Writings on the Women's Movement*. New York: W. W. Norton.

Fulton, Ann. 1999. *The Apostles of Sartre. Existentialism in America 1945–1963*. Evanston: Northwestern University Press.

Gadkar-Wilcox, Wynn. 2014. Existentialism and Intellectual Culture in South Vietnam. *The Journal of Asian Studies* 73 (2): 377–395.

Galster, Ingrid. 2015. *Simone de Beauvoir und der Feminismus*. Hamburg: Argument.

Heinemann, Fritz. 1971. *Existenzphilosophie lebendig oder tot?* Stuttgart: Kohlhammer.

Hiên, Thu Lương. 2009. *Vietnamese Existential Philosophy: A Critical Reappraisal*. Diss., Temple University.

Högerle, Daniela. 2013. *Propaganda oder Verständigung? Instrumente französischer Kulturpolitik in Südbaden 1945–1949*. Frankfurt a. M.: Peter Lang.

Ibiapina Ferreira, Adriano. n.d. Influências do existencialismo sartreano na música brasileira: o caso tropicalista. Accessed June 26, 2019. https://www.academia.edu/33310391/influ%c3%8ancias_do_existecialismo_sartreano_na_m%c3%9asica_brasileira_o_caso_tropicalista.

Invitto, Giovanni. 1987. Sartre e filosofi Italiani. In *Sartre e l'Italia*, ed. Ornella Pompeo Faracovi and Sandra Teroni, 181–199. Livorno: Belforte.

Jaspers, Karl. 1968. Was ist Existentialismus? In *Aneignung und Polemik, Gesammelte Reden und Aufsätze zur Geschichte der Philosophie*, ed. Hans Saner, 497–501. München: Piper.

Kaufmann, Walter. 1975. *Existentialism from Dostoevsky to Sartre*. Rev. and exp. ed. New York: New American Library.

Koberstein, Anja. 1996. *"Gott oder das Nichts". Sartre-Rezeption im frühen Nachkriegswerk von Alfred Andersch im Kontext der zeitgenössischen Existentialismusdiskussion*. Frankfurt a. M.: Peter Lang.

Koş, Ayşenaz. 2004. *An Analytical Study on the Migration of Sartrean Existentialism into Turkey through Translation*. Istanbul: Master Thesis Boğaziçi University.

Krüger, Heinz-Hermann. 1986. Viel Lärm um Nichts? Jugendliche 'Existentialisten' in den 50er Jahren. In *Schock und Schöpfung. Jugendästhetik im 20. Jahrhundert*, ed. Willi Bucher and Klaus Pohl, 263–268. Darmstadt: Luchterhand.

Littler, Margaret. 1991. *Alfred Andersch (1914–1980) and the Reception of French Thought in the Federal Republic of Germany*. Lewiston: Edwin Mellen.

Marin, Lou. 2013. *Albert Camus: écrits libertaires (1948–1960)*. N.p.: Égrégores.

McBride, William. 2012. Existentialism as a Cultural Movement. In *The Cambridge Companion to Existentialism*, ed. Steven Crowell, 50–69. Cambridge: Cambridge University Press.

Moi, Toril. 2008. *Simone de Beauvoir. The Making of an Intellectual Woman*. 2nd ed. Oxford: Oxford University Press.

Müller, Simone. 2014. Begriffsverständnis und Rezeption der Existenzphilosophie in Japan unter besonderer Berücksichtigung des Sartreschen Existentialismus. In *Begriff und Bild der modernen japanischen Philosophie*, ed. Raji C. Steineck et al., 233–268. Stuttgart: Frommann-Holzboog.

———. 2016. Von Arishima Takeo zu Jean-Paul Sartre. Rezeption und Assimilation des Intellektuellenbegriffs im modernen Japan. In *Wort—Bild—Assimilationen. Japan und die Moderne—Japan and Modernity*, ed. Simone Müller et al., 190–223. Berlin: Gebr. Mann.

de Ortega Maxey, Wallace. 1958. *Man is a Sexual Being, An Existential Approach To the Subject*. Fresno: Fabian Books.

Pamerleau, William C. 2009. *Existentialist Cinema*. Houndmills: Palgrave Macmillan.

Pejović, Danilo. 1965. Jean-Paul Sartre. *Praxis. Revue philosophique* 1 (1): 71–86.

Perone, James E. 2009. *Mods, Rockers, and the Music of the British Invasion*. Westport, CT: Praeger.

Rahnema, Ali. 2000. *An Islamic Utopian. A Political Biography of Ali Shari'ati*. London: I. B. Tauris.

Rahner, Mechtild. 1993. *"Tout est neuf ici, tout est à recommencer …". Die Rezeption des französischen Existentialismus im kulturellen Feld Westdeutschlands (1945–1949)*. Würzburg: Königshausen & Neumann.

Rossanda, Rossana. 1987. Sartre e la sinistra italiana. In *Sartre e l'Italia*, ed. Ornella Pompeo Faracovi and Sandra Teroni, 251–263. Livorno: Belforte.

Rovatti, Pier Aldo. 1987. Viaggiatori senza biglietto. Note sul dialogo tra Enzo Paci e Jean-Paul Sartre. In *Sartre e l'Italia*, ed. Ornella Pompeo Faracovi and Sandra Teroni, 201–216. Livorno: Belforte.

Rowlandson, William. 2018. *Sartre in Cuba—Cuba in Sartre*. Cham: Palgrave Macmillan.

Sartre, Jean-Paul. 1985. *Critique de la raison dialectique*. Paris: Gallimard.

———. 2004. Preface. In *The Wretched of the Earth*, ed. Frantz Fanon, trans. Richard Philcox. xliii–lxii. New York: Grove Press.

———. 2006. Itinerary of a Thought. In *Conversations with Jean-Paul Sartre*, ed. Perry Anderson et al., 1–66. London: Seagull.

———. 2007. *Existentialism Is a Humanism*. New Haven: Yale University Press.

———. 2012. *L'être et le néant*. Paris: Gallimard.

Savignano, Alan Patricio. 2016. La recepción del pensamiento de Jean-Paul Sartre en Argentina: la generación existencialista del 25 y la nueva izquierda de *Contorno*. *Ideas* 4: 34–61.

Schaff, Adam. 1965. *Marx oder Sartre?* Berlin: VEB Deutscher Verlag der Wissenschaften.

Simons, Margaret A. 1999. *Beauvoir and the Second Sex: Feminism, Race, and the Origins of Existentialism*. Lanham: Rowman & Littlefield.

Slaymaker, Doug. 2002. When Sartre was an Erotic Writer: Body, Nation and Existentialism in Japan after the Asia-Pacific War. *Japan Forum* 14 (1): 77–101.

Song, Xuezhi, and Jun Xu. 2007. Sartre Studies in China: From the New Period to the New Century. *Frontiers of Literary Studies in China* 1 (2): 287–299.

Stern, Alfred. 1967. *Sartre. His Philosophy and Existential Psychoanalysis*. New York: Dell.

Suzuki, Michihiko, and Nao Sawada. 2011. An Intellectual Star Remembered: Sartre's 1966 Visit to Japan. In *Jean-Paul Sartre*, ed. Jean-Pierre Boulé and Benedict O'Donohue, 183–201. Newcastle: Cambridge Scholars Publishing.

Tessari, Roberto. 1987. Presenza ed assenza di Sartre nel teatro italiano. In *Sartre e l'Italia*, ed. Ornella Pompeo Faracovi and Sandra Teroni, 157–179. Livorno: Belforte.

Vargas Llosa, Mario. 1996. *Making Waves*. New York: Farrar, Straus and Giroux.

Werner, Juliane. 2017. Sartre in Austria. Boycott, Scandals, and the Fight for Peace. *Sartre Studies International* 23 (2): 1–18.

Woessner, Martin. 2012. Angst Across the Channel. Existentialism in Britain. In *Situating Existentialism. Key Texts in Context*, ed. Jonathan Judaken and Robert Bernasconi, 145–179. New York: Columbia University Press.

Zhang, Chi. 2008. *Sartre en Chine 1939–1976. Histoire de sa réception et de son influence*. Paris: Le Manuscrit.

Part I

North America

2

Sartre and the American New Left

Ronald Aronson

In the May 1965 issue of *Harper's* magazine, a little-known philosophy professor named Glenn Gray at a small college in Colorado published an article titled "Salvation on the Campus: Why Existentialism is Capturing the Students." In it he spoke about the mood of the current generation, born into relative affluence, lacking any compelling historical cause such as previous generations' experience of the Great Depression, the threat of fascism, or the struggle against Nazism. Gray's students found themselves alienated from a vastly expanded university system perceived as soulless, impersonal, and competitive. Influenced by Heidegger and Sartre, they were drawn to themes like Absurdity and Nothingness and sought to avoid bad faith and find authenticity. Rejecting the packaged lives awaiting them, they found themselves forced to choose between life paths pointing to absurdity on the one hand or tragedy on the other, yet sought to take responsibility for themselves by creating their own lives.

R. Aronson (✉)
Wayne State University, Detroit, MI, USA
e-mail: ac7159@wayne.edu

A. Betschart, J. Werner (eds.), *Sartre and the International Impact of Existentialism*,
https://doi.org/10.1007/978-3-030-38482-1_2

45

The author could not be aware that he was writing just after one historical turning point—the Free Speech Movement—at the University of California a few months earlier (which he fleetingly mentioned) and just before another—the April 17, 1965, March on Washington against the War in Vietnam sponsored by the Students for a Democratic Society. Nor did he know that, in a very important sense, Sartre was present at both.

II

These events marked the third phase of Sartre's reception in the United States. The first phase, described in detail by George Cotkin in *Existential America*, began with the public sensation caused by Sartre, and then Simone de Beauvoir and Albert Camus, that began in early 1945. Actually, already in December 1944, "The Republic of Silence," which had appeared in the first open issue of *Les Lettres françaises* in September just after the Liberation, was published in the *Atlantic Monthly*. In addition to its other strengths, I have described this article in my *Camus & Sartre* (Aronson 2004) as a brilliant piece of self-promotion—gathering Sartre and all those who sympathized with the Resistance alongside its active members—and so was publishing it in the United States just before he arrived in January 1945, sent as a journalist by his friend Camus, editor of *Combat*. Beyond the mainstream American media's fascination for the existentialists of newly liberated Paris, Sartre's arrival provoked articles by and about him, as well as receptions, meetings, lectures, and controversies.

Cotkin points to breathless articles in *Life*, *Time*, *Newsweek*, *The New York Times*, *The New Yorker*, and *The Atlantic Monthly* to demonstrate how the popular and middlebrow press was fascinated by the existentialists and the milieu from which they sprang—the bohemian French world of young people wearing turtlenecks, long hair, and beards, and inhabiting cafés during the day and jazz cellars at night. With his connivance the press also exaggerated Sartre's role in the Resistance—for example a compilation published in the United States in 1947 and entitled *The Republic of Silence* indicated Sartre's success in positioning himself. A quote from his article about the Occupation graced the book's title page and the article itself was introduced with the editor's comment that Sartre had been "fearless and active in the underground." Ironically and perhaps more appropriately, Camus, who had been editor of clandestine *Combat*, was represented in the collection anonymously—by his unsigned May 1944 piece on the massacre in Ascq.

Sartre visited the United States during the first half of 1945, and then again in 1946. Camus would spend two months there from March to May 1946, and Beauvoir several months in the first half of 1947. All of them attracted attention for being very French, openly irreligious, and authors of unconventional works generally regarded as seamy and pessimistic. Again, Sartre was the most scandalous: his works were placed on the Index by the Vatican during this time, he was attacked by Pravda, and the production of *The Respectful Prostitute* was prohibited by order of the Chicago police.

Leafing through the *New York Times* conveys another reason for the fascination with Sartre between 1945 and 1947: the incredible variety and quantity of his works—plays, novels, philosophy, engaged essays on the writer's responsibility, the first postwar discussion of the roots of anti-semitism, and a short exposition of existentialism. All of this poured forth from the editor of a new journal, *Les Temps modernes*. His promoter's flair was obvious: the publicist Sartre described France's "new writers" in a lecture published in a fashion magazine, *Vogue*, in June 1945 (*New Writing in France*). He began by asserting that after the experiences of war, defeat, occupation, resistance, and liberation, a new literature was arising in France. Its "best representative is Albert Camus who is thirty years old" (Sartre 1945, p. 85).

Listen to Sartre wrap himself and Camus in the Resistance: "In publishing a great many clandestine articles, frequently under dangerous circumstances to fortify the people against the Germans or to keep up their courage, they became accustomed to thinking that writing is an act; and they have acquired the taste for action" (Sartre 1945, p. 85). Sartre went on to focus on the books that had made Camus's reputation and cast them as wartime writings, connecting Camus's sense of absurdity with the horrors of the war. Living in an extreme situation, where the question "Would I talk if I were tortured?" was ever-present, Camus and other Resistance writers were concerned not only with man as a psychological or a social being but, Sartre said, "with the total, the metaphysical man" (Sartre 1945, p. 85). In so saying Sartre also recast his own prewar fiction, *The Wall* and *Nausea*, into politically committed works now relevant to the postwar era. In this remarkable lecture Sartre sounded a number of themes the two men shared: absurdity, a humanism without illusions, the necessity of struggle, willingness to face extreme situations, refusal of any escapism, rejection of heroic gestures, rejection of any scheme of understanding that did not center on human experience, and action.

No less gifted as a publicity agent was Simone de Beauvoir who, the following January, in another fashion magazine, *Harper's Bazaar*, painted a profile of "the most talked-about writer in France today." *Jean-Paul Sartre: Strictly Personal* begins as follows: "He hates the country. He loathes—it isn't too strong a word—the swarming life of insects and the pullulation of plants. At most he tolerates the level sea, the unbroken desert sand, or the mineral coldness of Alpine peaks; but he feels at home only in cities, in the heart of an artificial universe filled with man-made objects" (Beauvoir 1946). What follows are three breathless pages celebrating the man of no possessions who played "an active part in the Resistance movement," and his remarkable personal traits.

Cotkin tells another story about Sartre's reception during these years—by New York intellectuals, specifically the left-wing culturally sophisticated *Partisan Review* (*PR*) crowd. Looking at that journal between 1945 and 1948 we see numerous articles about existentialism including at least eight by or about Sartre in twenty issues. In short, until Sartre wore out his welcome *Partisan Review* was a kind of publicity bureau for existentialism. At first it seemed as if Sartre, and then Beauvoir, shared the outlook and interests of editors and writers like Philip Rahv, William Phillips, William Barrett, and Delmore Schwartz. But Sartre and Beauvoir rejected their anti-Communism. And his early love affair with American authors had been with writers mostly now considered passé—John Steinbeck, Ernest Hemingway and John Dos Passos for example—by those lovers of European high culture more interested in Marcel Proust. And the New Yorkers detested popular culture, mass popularity, and the mass media, where Sartre was clearly at home.

Formerly radical Jews who grew up in immigrant families speaking Yiddish, the *PR* editors had all been within the orbit of the Communist

Party in the early 1930s and then were spun out of it by the Popular Front strategy that favored proletarian literature and rejected high culture. They became attracted to Trotskyism and very early began to see Stalinism as the great evil—so much so that by the 1940s they had become early and ardent Cold Warriors, to the point of then championing such McCarthyite tactics as loyalty oaths and the firing of Communist professors. Only fleetingly interested in Sartre, they were not especially attracted to his existentialism and were critical of what they regarded as his and Beauvoir's literary crudeness. Philosopher William Barrett, a partial exception, reviewed *L'être et le néant* (*Being and Nothingness*) and wrote a longer study of existentialism in 1947—he was later the author of the immensely popular *Irrational Man*—but only demonstrated a partial understanding and appreciation of Sartre. And after Sartre's break with Camus in 1952, *PR*'s European editor Nicola Chiaromonte gave the journal's kiss of death to Sartre with a strong attack on him and an equally strong defense of Camus.

III

The second, much slower but longer lasting phase of the American reception of Sartre is the process of philosophers taking him seriously as a thinker. As described by Ann Fulton in *Apostles of Sartre*, at first Sartre was mostly read, and taught, by French professors at American universities because his philosophical works did not begin to be translated until 1947 (*Existentialism Is a Humanism*) and 1948 (*The Emotions* and *Psychology of Imagination*),[1] while his fiction and plays were almost immediately available.

Beyond analytic philosophers' discomfort with continental philosophy, and their skepticism toward a politically radical foreign thinker who rejected anti-Communism, was the obvious language barrier. And everything that made Sartre and Beauvoir famous to the wider public also

---

[1] Excerpts from *Materialism and Revolution* were published in the French-themed edition of former *Partisan Review* editor Dwight Macdonald's anarchist/humanist journal *Politics* that featured Camus's *Neither Victims nor Executioners* in 1947. Philosophers paid virtually no attention to Sartre's important philosophical attack on dialectical materialism.

repelled academics—their not specializing in philosophy but also writing plays, fiction, literary criticism, journalism, and essays, not having university employment, writing in cafés and living a very public life, their assertive atheism. Still, during the years 1948–1952, according to Fulton, "more American thinkers began to regard Sartreanism as a philosophical endeavor to be taken seriously" (Fulton 1999, p. 48). By 1952 the philosophers writing about Sartre included Maurice Natanson, Marvin Farber, Herbert Marcuse, Marjorie Grene, and Hazel Barnes. The journals discussing him included the *Journal of Aesthetics and Art Criticism, Journal of Philosophy, Kenyon Review*, and *Philosophy and Phenomenological Research*. As Fulton says, during these years "more philosophers were becoming aware of the centrality of human meaning and experience in their discipline, and they recognized that Sartreanism spoke to these concerns" (Fulton 1999, p. 82).

Between 1952 and 1956 "awareness of Sartreanism as a serious effort to formulate a solid doctrine of being finally became widespread among American philosophers" (Fulton 1999, p. 83). Hazel Barnes published sections of her translation-in-progress of *Being and Nothingness* as *Existential Psychoanalysis* in 1953 and they drew considerable attention. More books were published on Sartre (by Wilfred Desan and Alfred Stern), and above all in 1956 there appeared the student-oriented *Existentialism from Dostoevsky to Sartre* by Walter Kaufmann, which reached its sixteenth printing in only four years. During this time Sartre was discussed at least three times in presidential addresses to the American Philosophical Association (APA) and in more than one major APA symposium.

And then in 1956 Barnes's translation of *Being and Nothingness* appeared, and the key work of Sartre's philosophy was finally available in English. This was the turning point. Major universities now offered courses on Sartre and symposia on his work were frequent. Even if one disagreed profoundly, one could no longer ignore him—his work had to be taught and discussed. And more, in survey and introductory courses, Sartre was becoming an important drawing card. A search for meaning and a weariness with conformity seemed to be growing among American students—reflected by the growing awareness of the Beat poets, especially the poetry of Allen Ginsberg. Sartre's *Existentialism Is a Humanism* was guaranteed to provoke heated discussion wherever it was read and taught, especially among first-year students. Even if Sartre dismissed it as misleading and superficial, it was and still is a powerful introduction to existentialist thinking for millions of readers—especially among those raised according to the idea of personal responsibility so common in the United States.

IV

As she turns to the 1960s, then, it is appropriate that Fulton draws her study to a close by discussing the Glenn Gray article in *Harper's*. But as I said, although trying to grasp the current trends Gray missed something important happening in 1965. Here is where my own experience contradicts him and joins the story of Sartre's reception in the United States. As a graduate student and a new activist, I recall listening to one of the greatest of American speeches on the radio in early December 1964. It was by someone my own age, Mario Savio, leader of the Free Speech movement at the University of California Berkeley, standing on the steps of Sproul Hall the day before several hundred students sitting in at the president's office were dragged down those steps and arrested by campus police. He said: "There's a time when the operation of the machine becomes so odious, makes you so sick at heart that you can't take part! You can't even passively take part! And you've got to put your bodies upon the gears and upon the wheels, upon the levers, upon all the apparatus and you've got to make it stop! And you've got to indicate to the people who run it, to the people who own it that unless you're free the machine will be prevented from working at all!!" (Savio 1964).

Did Savio, a philosophy major, find this in Sartre—not only the alienation but the sense of individual responsibility, the need to act and not conform passively, the sense that one's own action matters, even if only to resist and not go along with evil? (Hatfield 1996). Such thinking, which might also have been found in Camus, was very much in the air at the time. It is what young people have always carried away from existentialism. It became the mood of the time, and it brought tens and then hundreds of thousands into the streets.

That April, I happened to be among the 25,000 mostly young people who descended on Washington, D.C., to make our presence felt against the escalating war in Vietnam. It was no surprise when Staughton Lynd, one of the speakers, said: "We are here to keep the faith with those of all countries and all ages who have sought to beat swords into ploughshares and to war no more." And then: "We are here on behalf of Jean-Paul Sartre" (Staughton Lynd, quoted in Pickus 1965, p. 38).

Why Sartre? Over fifty years later Lynd does not recall the exact meaning of his reference to Sartre. But thinking back to that time suggests several possibilities. We all knew that the great existentialist philosopher and playwright had just refused the Nobel Prize, and that his greatest fury was directed against people and systems that would oppress, dominate, and diminish others. We knew that he had written against torture, racism, colonialism, capitalism, and the Soviet invasion of Hungary, insisting that to not oppose an evil carried out in our name is to become its accomplice. This same Sartre wrote in support of the Cuban Revolution in 1960 in one of the first issues of *Studies on the Left*, and *Sartre on Cuba* was sold along with C. Wright Mills's *Listen, Yankee!* at *Fair Play for Cuba* meetings (Sartre 1960).

As we were coming to consciousness there was no contemporary quite like Sartre. He clearly seemed to live his principles. He had been the first writer after World War II to discuss the nature of antisemitism. In *Black Orpheus* he had explored how colonized and once-enslaved blacks sought to use poetry to find their voice. He had sided with the French Communist Party (PCF) when it was under siege in 1952, and he dramatically denounced the Soviet invasion of Hungary in 1956. He spoke at the first mass meeting against the Algerian war early that year and then wrote against government torture in Algeria—in an issue of *Les Temps modernes* that was seized by the authorities. Then he sided with the Algerian National Liberation Front (FLN) against his own government—this leading to his apartment being bombed twice during the struggle. In his introduction to Frantz Fanon's *The Wretched of the Earth* (1961) he dramatically described the colonized people's turn to violence as a mode of self-affirmation and struggle. All of this was known to us. And then in 1966 he would become president of the Bertrand Russell Vietnam War Crimes Tribunal and wrote its opening and closing statements. His insistence on solidarity with radical movements, and in 1968 with the French revolutionary youth, lifted many eyebrows among the older generation, but among many young radicals his militance intensified our connection with Sartre.

But Sartre's affirmation of radicalism did not go uncriticized. Already in 1961, *Dissent* had published an article by Lionel Abel accusing Sartre of "metaphysical Stalinism" (Abel 1961). More relevant for New Left activists was an article in *Liberation* after the March on Washington. It criticized Staughton Lynd—and Sartre—for being among those calling for the American withdrawal from Vietnam. This was the main demand of the bulk of the antiwar movement. The author cited Albert Camus's *Neither Victims nor Executioners*, which *Liberation* had printed as an independent booklet (and which had caused the famous dust-up between Camus and Maurice Merleau-Ponty twenty years earlier which Sartre had been unable to resolve; see Aronson 2004, p. 66). This was originally a series of articles in *Combat*—among Camus's last for the newspaper—which flatly equated Marxism with murder and called for abandoning all large-scale efforts for social transformation in the name of the "relative utopia" of creating peace between the major powers. In these articles Camus signaled a new direction from the one being taken by Sartre. As the article in *Liberation* demonstrated, the articles became a kind of bible of pacifists at the time of Vietnam, especially those who rejected the idea of outright American withdrawal. They saw that demand as one-sidedly blaming the United States for the war, failing to assign equal responsibility to the Communist side, and above all wishing for a Communist victory.

Camus had in fact become favorite reading for an important strand of American activists—Bob Moses wrote about being nourished by him, and Tom Hayden mentioned reading him while organizing in Newark (Cotkin 2003, pp. 225–251; Hayden 1965). Why Camus and not Sartre? With his Resistance credentials, his willingness to take lonely individual stands, and his primary concern for the morality of political choices, Camus had an irresistible appeal to many in the first wave of the New Left who were unmoved by Sartre's extreme, intellectual, and often rhetorical proclamations. Leaning on Camus was natural among many of those whose activist path embraced restraint, personal reflection, and a stress on morality, nonviolence, and respect for one's antagonists.

Sartre's violent Fanon preface could not have been further from this disposition, as was his support for the victorious Cuban Revolution or the Algerian FLN. Sartre's revolutionary commitment to the oppressed gave them a blank check to dramatically and violently overthrow their conditions; Camus, who had only slowly and painfully come to endorse violence against the German Occupation, always saw things as more complex both morally and politically. Applying *Neither Victims nor Executioners* in the 1960s meant: no victory to the Vietcong, no trying to bring the system to its knees.

V

Nevertheless, Sartre's core ideas of freedom and responsibility had helped shape an entire generation. But as political activism developed in the 1960s, one stream of the early New Left in the United States was clearly allergic to Sartre's radicalism, rejecting him as inspiration and example, while the other stream was eager to embrace him as one of its mentors. Then, as the New Left continued to broaden and deepen, Sartre made further contributions to many of the young radicals, specifically as a thinker. Above all, Sartre became important in the development of anti-racist thinking and in the new generation's absorption of Marxist theory.

Beginning early—and continuing into the present—Sartre influenced anti-racist thinking and activism. Starting with *Anti-Semite and Jew* and *Black Orpheus* in the 1940s, as Jonathan Judaken and Lewis Gordon separately discuss in *Race after Sartre* (Judaken 2008), Sartre contributed an impressive series of works explicitly exploring the dynamics of oppression; the ways in which the oppressed make themselves under constraint; the possibilities of a subjugated people finding its voice; patterns and systems of oppression such as antisemitism, white supremacy, and colonialism; and the role of violence in maintaining colonialism on the one hand and in resisting it on the other. Two specific examples may suggest Sartre's importance as an anti-racist thinker: his vehement endorsement of anti-colonial violence, and his role among theorists of Black Power.

If Frantz Fanon's *The Wretched of the Earth* became a kind of bible of black liberation, both in the United States and elsewhere, Sartre's ringing preface has become read as virtually indistinguishable from the book's message. Indeed, as Ronald Santoni points out, the many references to Sartre nearly ten years earlier in Fanon's *Black Skin, White Masks*, as well as the many implicit references to *Critique of Dialectical Reason* in *The Wretched of the Earth* show the significance of Sartre for Fanon. And conversely, his embrace of violence in the preface shows the significance of Fanon for Sartre (Santoni 2003, pp. 67–73).

Quite separately, in articulating the meaning of SNCC's, the Student Nonviolent Coordinating Committee's, turn to Black Power in 1966, its leader Stokely Carmichael began by mentioning Fanon, Camus, and Sartre, and went on to stress the Sartrean theme that we are all "born free." Then he dwelled specifically on a key theme from *Black Orpheus* (1949) first published in English in 1965: "anti-racist racism." As Rosie Germain points out concerning Sartre's role in SNCC's turn to Black Power, "Sartre reinforced black separatist aspiration by providing a language through which to express it" (Germain 2015).

Indeed, these two examples indicate, as Gordon says, that Sartre was "a constant ally of black existential thought and black liberation struggles throughout most of the twentieth century, since his emphasis on what it means to be a human being was a shared interest of people whose humanity has been denigrated in the modern world." Organically linked to a community in which he was not born, Sartre must be seen as "an insider to black existential philosophy … as a participant in its living debates, critical reflections, and political structure" (Gordon 2008, pp. 157–158).

VI

At the same time, Sartre was helping to revive Marxism and relay it to a new generation, overcoming what he called the sclerosis of Stalinism. The lesson learned by the New Left was that existentialism, the generation's powerful message of freedom and self-determination, was not opposed to systemic social change but *complemented* it. On the level of revolutionary social theory Sartre called for the end of the stifling Stalinist determinism, "dialectical materialism." He rejected it as a kind of a priori thought that pretended to have all the explanations needed for any given historical event before the event itself happened, and he called for its replacement by an undogmatic Marxism that studied events for themselves and took seriously human subjectivity. In 1960 *Ideology and Revolution* (in *Sartre on Cuba*) raised important theoretical questions by insisting on the specificity and originality of the Cuban Revolution, independently of any ideology.

The importance of Sartre's contribution to New Left thinking was that he made it acceptable to keep our regard for individual experience at the center while engaging in social critique and systemic analysis. A common critique of the 1960s has become that it legitimized and even glorified individual experience (see, e.g., Judt 2010, pp. 86–91), but this ignores the social commitment motivating a generation of political activists. Those influenced by Sartre may have rooted themselves in their personal experience of oppression, but in their political action, and helped by Sartre's theoretical influence, they sought in every possible way to join the individual and the social (see, e.g., Aronson 1971).

Of course, theoretical arguments followed immediately on the heels of Hazel Barnes's 1963 translation of *Search for a Method*. From *Dissent* to *Encounter* to *Studies on the Left* to a dozen other journals, articles appeared from every perspective, debating whether or not it was really possible to accommodate Marxism and existentialism. The best of these, by the great radical thinker André Gorz, appeared in *New Left Review* (NLR) in 1966. It described *Critique of Dialectical Reason* as explaining social action by beginning from individual praxis (Gorz 1966). This was paired in NLR's *Western Marxism* with my own critique of Sartre's *Individualist Social Theory* (Aronson 1978).

At the time, however, the specific arguments were less important than the fact that there was an argument. Many authors contributed to the discussion about Marxism and existentialism with book-length studies, including the signal contributions of Mark Poster and Thomas Flynn (Poster 1975; Flynn 1986; Aronson 1980). In my own first book, a New Left Marxist exploration of the key terms of Sartre's thought as they evolved over forty years, I concluded that Sartre was never able to philosophically bridge the gap between his Cartesian individualism and the plane of social analysis and action. But this analysis of unresolvable tensions wound up being less important than Sartre's own persistent drive to connect the individual and the social. Indeed, he posed the possibility with incredible drive and energy, in the process giving us the *idea* of an existential Marxism. This project informed the Freud screenplay (*The Freud Scenario*), *Critique of Dialectical Reason*, and the nearly 3000 pages of the Flaubert biography (*The Family Idiot*), along with essay after essay attempting to think the individual socially and the society individually (see Aronson 2018).

VII

Sartre's intersection with the American New Left dates back over fifty years. Although much of it is now forgotten, neither the man nor the movements can be safely relegated to the past. Sartre's example and ideas still contribute to larger trends and possibilities, and the New Left's issues refuse to be stilled today—about racism, about (post)colonialism, about foreign wars, about inequality, about power relations, about democracy. Indeed, like the Sartrean contribution to what has come to be called Critical Race Theory, the challenges of existential Marxism are still with us.[2] What Sartre said about Marxism remains true concerning his entire life-work: "We cannot go beyond it because we have not gone beyond the circumstances which engendered it" (Sartre 1967, p. 30). As long as these issues remain alive, Sartre will still be with us.

---

[2] Also under discussion today is the question of Sartre's possible contributions to the third essential area of radical thought emerging since the 1960s, namely feminism as articulated in Simone de Beauvoir's *The Second Sex*. Authors who have written about this include Dorothy McCall, Margaret Simons, Debra Bergoffen, Sonia Kruks, and "the riddle of influence" between Sartre and Beauvoir is very much under discussion today, including in a book edited by Christine Daigle and Jacob Golomb (*Beauvoir and Sartre: The Riddle of influence*, Bloomington: Indiana University Press 2009). It has become increasingly clear that Beauvoir's influence (although unacknowledged by him) is very much present in Sartre's understanding of the social nature of individuals and how they live their oppression, just as Sartre's influence (duly acknowledged by her) is very much present in Beauvoir's project. The goals of that project include understanding that "one is not born a woman but becomes one," in part through choices made under oppressive conditions, especially when one's life is structured under patriarchal social relations that cast women as the inessential Other to dominant males.

References

Abel, Lionel. 1961. Arms and the Man: Metaphysical Stalinism. *Dissent*, Spring.

Aronson, Ronald. 1971. Dear Herbert. In *The Revival of American Socialism; Selected Papers of the Socialist Scholars Conference*, ed. George Fischer. New York: Oxford University Press.

———. 1978. The Individualist Social Theory of Jean-Paul Sartre. In *Western Marxism: A Critical Reader*. London: Verso Editions.

———. 1980. *Jean-Paul Sartre: Philosophy in the World*. London: NLB.

———. 2004. *Camus & Sartre: The Story of a Friendship and the Quarrel that Ended It*. Chicago: University of Chicago Press.

———. 2018. The Philosophy of Our Time. *The Boston Review*. Accessed July 7, 2019. http://bostonreview.net/philosophy-religion/ronald-aronson-philosophy-our-time.

Beauvoir, Simone de. 1946. Jean-Paul Sartre: Strictly Personal. *Harper's Bazaar*, January.

Cotkin, George. 2003. *Existential America*. Baltimore: John Hopkins University Press.

Flynn, Thomas R. 1986. *Sartre and Marxist Existentialism*. Chicago: University of Chicago.

Fulton, Ann. 1999. *Apostles of Sartre*. Evanston: Northwestern University Press.

Germain, Rosie. 2015. Accessed July 7, 2019. https://blogs.history.qmul.ac.uk/philosophy/2015/08/11/french-existentialism-and-the-fight-against-paternalism/.

Gordon, Lewis R. 2008. Sartre and Black Existentialism. In *Race after Sartre. Antiracism, Africana Existentialism, Postcolonialism*, ed. Jonathan Judaken. Albany: State University of New York Press.

Gorz, André. 1966. Sartre and Marx. *New Left Review*, I/40, November/December.

Hatfield, Larry D. 1996. Mario Savio Dies; Free Speech Activist. November 7. Accessed July 7, 2019. https://www.sfgate.com/news/article/Mario-Savio-dies-free-speech-activist-3114627.php.

Hayden, Tom. 1965. Organizer's Notebook. *Studies on the Left* 5: 3.

Judaken, Jonathan. 2008. *Race after Sartre. Antiracism, Africana Existentialism, Postcolonialism*. Albany: State University of New York Press.

Judt, Tony. 2010. *Ill Fares the Land*. New York: Penguin.

Pickus, Robert. 1965. Political Integrity and Its Critics. *Liberation*, June–July. Accessed July 7, 2019. https://sites.duke.edu/robert-pickus/files/2016/01/20151231_Political-Integrity-and-its-Critics-Liberation-1965.pdf.

Poster, Mark. 1975. *Existential Marxism in Postwar France*. Princeton: Princeton University Press.

Santoni, Ronald E. 2003. *Sartre on Violence: Curiously Ambivalent*. University Park, PA: Pennsylvania State University.

Sartre, Jean-Paul. 1945. New Writing in France. *Vogue*, June.

———. 1960. Ideology and Revolution. *Studies on the Left* I: 3.

———. 1967. *Search for a Method*. New York: Knopf.

Savio, Mario. 1964. Sit in Address on the Steps of Sproul Hall. Delivered 2 December 1964 at the University of California at Berkeley. Accessed July 7, 2019. https://www.americanrhetoric.com/speeches/mariosaviosproul-hallsitin.htm.

3

The Absurd: Postwar Reception and Wartime Echoes at *Yale French Studies*

Julia Elsky

Camus defines the absurd in *The Myth of Sisyphus* as the realization of the world's irrationality resulting from a "confrontation between the human need and the unreasonable silence of the world" (Camus 1983, p. 28). As Sartre would put it in "*The Outsider* Explained," the absurd is part of the human condition of being-in-the-world; rather than an entity in man or in the world, "[i]t is nothing less than man's relation to the world" (Sartre 2010, pp. 153, 150. Text dated February 1943). Camus' and Sartre's explanations of the absurd as a condition and confrontation, rather than as an external force, would be received in vastly different ways in the first two decades of *Yale French Studies* (*YFS*). Reception of the absurd would

Published first as Julia Elsky, "The Absurd: Postwar Reception and Wartime Echoes at *Yale French Studies*", in *Yale French Studies* 135/136 (2019): 46–62.

I thank Lauren Du Graf, Clémentine Fauré, Diana Garvin, Christopher Davis, and Jennifer Row for their generous comments on this article. I am grateful to Zoe Egelman for her expertise on the Guicharnaud Papers. I am especially grateful to Alice Kaplan for her advice on this project.

J. Elsky (✉)
Loyola University Chicago, Chicago, IL, USA
e-mail: jelsky@luc.edu

© The Author(s) 2020
A. Betschart, J. Werner (eds.), *Sartre and the International Impact of Existentialism*,
https://doi.org/10.1007/978-3-030-38482-1_3

become the locus of memory of the Second World War and the center of discussions about the place of language in this history. The absurd in fact over time comes to be seen as an external force or the state of the world, a world fixed in the Occupation. The absurd itself in these discussions even began to stand in for existentialism as a whole. This article reviews postwar reception of the absurd in America over the course of three issues of *YFS*: number 1 (1948), number 16 (1955), and number 23 (1959). Articles in these issues by three major figures in French Studies from the mid-century through the early aughts, Henri Peyre, Jacques Guicharnaud, and Serge Doubrovsky, deal with the writings of Camus, Sartre, and Ionesco at the times when *YFS* was first introducing existentialism and the theater of the absurd to the American academy. In the very first issue, Peyre's article demonstrates how the specter of Vichy became tied to the absurd. Subsequently, in Guicharnaud's contribution, language and close reading take a central role in confronting the absurd to find meaning in language under the Occupation. However, Doubrovsky's article, the first scholarship on Ionesco in *YFS*' history, reverses Guicharnaud's approach to language and the absurd. Now we find a trope of criticism of the theater of the absurd that theorizes the meaninglessness of language in an absurd world in the aftermath of the Second World War. Tracing this reception reveals how the theater of the absurd not only began to be seen as part of existentialism in its earliest reception in America, but furthermore, it reveals how looking at existentialism through the lens of the theater of the absurd actually ended up distorting the teachings of existentialism.

1948: Communicating Anguish

The editor and contributors to the inaugural 1948 volume of *YFS* introduced existentialism to the American university.[1] Under the direction of Henri Peyre, chairperson and highly influential figure of the Yale

---

[1] Fulton (1999, pp. 22–23). The journal is not the first place to have published on the movement, but the devotion of an entire inaugural issue to the topic announced the importance of the journal for introducing existentialism. Other articles on the movement had appeared in previous years and at the same time. To name just a few, they include Herbert Marcuse's "Existentialism: Remarks on

University French Department from 1939 to 1969, and the editorship of Robert Greer Cohn, the journal in its early years aimed to introduce important topics in French literature, politics, and culture to non-specialists (Porter 1999, p. 13; Front Matter 1948, p. 1). It was first through French departments, as opposed to philosophy departments, that existentialism was taught in universities and treated seriously in academic journals and publications (Fulton 1999, p. 45). In a letter to Harry Levin on Nov. 17, 1947, Peyre boasted that existentialism was "a subject that we have been bold enough to treat here in a graduate course" (Peyre 2005, p. 241). Cohn perhaps taught the first course in the United States on existentialism at Yale in 1946 (Fulton 1999, p. 23). That same year Sartre visited Yale, preceding Simone de Beauvoir's own tour in the United States (Cohen Solal 1987, pp. 273–274). In the *YFS* issue, contributors including Peyre and Cohn were preoccupied with defending existentialism against criticism of the movement as a postwar fad that was only popular as a response to the war. Nevertheless, the specter of the Second World War lurks in many of the articles.

The war's presence in the issue can be felt in the opening articles that provide introductions to the movement. As each maintains that existentialism is not purely related to the Second World War, the reader senses its presence precisely in the argument of its absence. In "Existentialism—a Literature of Despair?," Peyre writes that it is a disservice to understand the movement "as a mere outgrowth of the Second World War and a reflection of the bad conscience felt by France in 1940 and since" (Peyre 1948, p. 28). In "French Existentialism before Sartre," Herbert Dieckmann, better known as a Diderot scholar, writing just one year before his death, studies French thinkers who preceded Sartre in order to ground the movement in an intellectually rigorous, interwar French academic milieu. Rather than looking to Kierkegaard, Husserl, Heidegger, and Jaspers, Dieckmann outlines the *Recherches philosophiques* group that in the 1930s studied these German philosophers, creating "in French a vocabulary for the new mode of thinking" (Dieckmann 1948, p. 34).

Jean-Paul Sartre's *L'être et le néant*" (Marcuse 1948), a three-part series of articles by Marjorie Grene in *The Kenyon Review* (Vol. 9, nos. 1–3), and Leo Spitzer's article "Man's Need for Faith in Man" in the special section of *The American Scholar* on The Humanities Today and Tomorrow (Spitzer 1947–1948).

Referring to scholars like André Koyré, Henri-Charles Puech, and Albert Spaier, Dieckmann adds weight to a movement led by Sartre whom some critics admonish "for having turned Existentialism into a literary fad or having distorted it into a nihilistic and atheistic doctrine" (Dieckmann 1948, p. 33). The City University of New York-Brooklyn College Marxist scholar Harry Slochower opens his article, "The Function of Myth in Existentialism," by stating that existentialism is not only a response to the conflicts and choices faced during the Second World War; it is not only a movement tied to an historic moment, but also one grounded in "absolute categories." Perhaps the war "provides the catalyst for its vogue. But only its catalyst. And only the mood and accent of the movement" (Slochower 1948, p. 42).

But what a mood. Despite these statements directed at critics of existentialism, the Second World War rattles throughout the 1948 issue, either directly or through oblique comments, as if an unavoidable aspect of the philosophy. *YFS* number 1 opens with an excerpt from Sartre's *Dirty Hands*, introduced by the editor Richard Greer Cohn who dates the section to just after that of the Battle of Stalingrad; Cohn describes the protagonist as "a young bourgeois intellectual, citizen of a certain Eastern European nation which is collaborating with Germany" (Cohn 1948, p. 3). Vercors' *The Silence of the Sea* and its conception under the Occupation is a key example in "The Case for 'Engaged' Literature," Charles G. Whiting's contribution (Whiting 1948, pp. 84–89). Madeleine Smith closes her discussion of *The Wall* and the character Lucien's involvement in *Action-Française* (in *The Childhood of a Leader*) by stating that despite the different histories of anti-Semitism and communism in France, Sartre's works still have relevance in American situations (Smith 1948, p. 83). This brief aside about communism and anti-Semitism seems to refer to recent history in France. And although Harry Slochower, as discussed above, sees the Second World War as only the catalyst of the movement, he contradicts himself by calling the movement "this German product" that "grew in the soil of the Vichy era" (Slochower 1948, p. 50). Moving from the language of chemistry to biology he sees existentialism as a plant that flourished among those (that is, the French) who were caught between "foreign and native systems"—Nazi occupation and Vichy rule—"both of which denied their individual existence" (Slochower

1948, p. 50). Slochower's article demonstrates that, despite all the arguments that date the movement's beginning to much earlier than 1940 or deny its reliance on the war for its importance, the war is an inescapable, almost organic topic of existentialism in this first issue.

Peyre, too, turns to the war despite his statements arguing that the movement is not only about the war. The Occupation is again the primary historical context for the development of the absurd, as Peyre relies on texts by Camus and Sartre that are explicitly about the war and the immediate postwar period. His primary aim is to demonstrate that existential anguish does not reveal a philosophy of quietism, fear, and inertia. He refers to despair in the article not in the existential sense or in the tradition of Kierkegaard, but rather in terms of the standard definition of losing hope. Existentialist writers for Peyre are not pessimists who ruminate on the negative, nor escapists, nor dilettanti who observe from the outside and get a kind of "Neronian comfort" from the historical disasters in which they live (Peyre 1948, p. 22). He calls existentialist writers "Frenchmen of 1940–48" who have been awoken by the events of the preceding decade to write engaged literature (Peyre 1948, p. 23).

To set up his argument that anguish does not lead to inaction, he draws on Camus' article *The Crisis of Man*, published in 1946 in *Vogue*,[2] in which Camus argues that what Americans might denounce as pessimism among young Frenchmen is actually an awareness of man's condition, which also allows him to strive to overcome it, even if he can never actually do so (Camus 1946a, b). Camus compares this to the necessity to diagnose your disease before being able to treat it. A state of inertia and fear that nothing makes sense comprises a crisis of man. However, because of their experience in the war, young French men and young Europeans have not lived with illusions, have not said that you cannot change man's nature, and instead have faced the harshest realities, that is, the Occupation. Peyre's use of Camus's text inscribes his argument into a political discussion about constructing a postwar order based on lived experience of the Second World War.

---

[2] Although Peyre refers to the article as it appeared in *Vogue*, it was also published in 1946 in Dorothy Norman's *Twice a Year* (Camus 1946b) in Lionel Abel's translation, directly followed by an article by Harry Slochower on Thomas Mann. I thank Lauren Du Graf for this reference.

Sartrean anguish begins to play an important role in Peyre's conception. Sartre distinguishes anguish from fear in part using the example of a soldier at war: fear is when a soldier in artillery preparation is afraid of dying; anguish relates to a change from within, an anxiety a soldier fears about his conduct or even of his being afraid of being afraid (Sartre 1956, p. 29). Yet this anguish is also "the consciousness of freedom," (Sartre 1956, p. 33) for it contains the realization that one is constantly choosing among possibilities and there is no external validity of these choices. For Peyre the primary questions that existentialists ask in their anguish regard their very existence and the existence of the universe, creating a close link between anguish, freedom, and the absurd. A sense of anxiety grows, writes Peyre, "when they [existentialists] realize that they are a paradox in this irrational universe, where, alone with his reason, man is 'de trop,' unwanted, unfitted, puzzled by the absurdity of his own presence, vainly applying his reason to explain a universe which baffles rationality" (Peyre 1948, p. 25). This contradiction between the rational individual who is searching for meaning and the irrational world that can offer none is the heart of the absurd.

Nevertheless, rather than true pessimists, escapists, or dilettanti, existential writers are, says Peyre, "metaphysical writers" (Peyre 1948, p. 23). Peyre is quoting from Sartre's fifth installment of "What is Literature?" in *Les Temps modernes* (Sartre 1947) which corresponds to a section of "Situation of the Writer in 1947." For Sartre, metaphysical writers of his period are not concerned with "a sterile discussion of abstract notions" but rather their literature "is a living effort to embrace from within the human condition in its totality" (Sartre 1993, p. 171). At the end of *Being and Nothingness*, he had explained his untraditional use of the term *metaphysical* in relation to "the study of individual processes which have given birth to *this* world as a concrete and particular totality" (Sartre 1956, p. 619). In the wartime context of "Situation of the Writer in 1947," the metaphysical writers focus on praxis, or "action in history and on history," (Sartre 1993, p. 184) and synthesize both historical relativity and absolute metaphysical morals in a hostile world. A writer does not choose his or her era but chooses how to act in it. For Peyre, this amounts to an austere heroism in the war, when writers did not shy away from their freedom to act.

Writing as a means of acting in history—and not an abstract idea of history—brings the absurd to the fore. Metaphysical writers in *What is Literature?* create "the literature of great circumstances" precisely in seeing their absurd condition:

> Forced by circumstance to discover the pressure of history, as Torricelli discovered atmospheric pressure, and tossed by the cruelty of the time into that forlornness from where we can see our condition as man to the very limit, to the absurd, to the night of unknowingness, we have a task for which we may not be strong enough [...] It is to create a literature which unites and reconciles the metaphysical absolute and the relativity of the historical fact (...). (Sartre 1993, p. 171)

Literature is like Torricelli's barometer, measuring the pressure of history—a history that brings man to the brink in which he sees his condition. Continuing with the language of weather, Sartre describes writers of 1940 as living in a "cyclone" that unhinged the stability of the position of the writer in the interwar period. Now more complex questions emerged, ones that require writers to be "in, by, and for history" (Sartre 1993, p. 171). "Forlornness" (the original French is "*la nuit du non-savoir*," and can also be read as abandonment (Sartre 1947, p. 1630)) Sartre later states is the "uncertainty and the risks of the present" (Sartre 1993, p. 172). Peyre himself would echo some of these ideas in his 1968 book on Sartre: "For Sartre ..., the absurdity stems from man's realization of his own contingency and of the facticity surrounding him. The world might very well not have been and I too might not have existed" (Peyre 1968, p. 15). The realization of not having chosen your situation, and of that situation not being in any way predetermined yet is subject to change, is the realization of the absurd. And this facticity is not abstract but very much linked to the particular historic situation.

Almost a decade later, in his study of *The Contemporary French Novel*, Peyre writes that if existentialists "delight in pointing out the absurdity of our lives" and "absurdity was rampant in the decade 1940–50," readers must keep in mind the brutality of the 1940s (Peyre 1955, p. 220). That is, anguish in confronting the absurd was drawn out by the historic pressures of the Occupation and the immediate postwar period. But in his

YFS article Peyre does not address the supposed joy of finding the meaninglessness of life, but rather how the existentialists communicated the absurd in writing. In the last section of his article, Peyre speaks of a new form of the novel that emerged and an urgent need to express the historical situation. If existentialist novelists turned to the style of American writers in 1940–1945, it was because it voiced "feelings of men lost and swamped in an immense continent" who are thrown into the incomprehensible conditions of the war. A "brutal means of communication" was necessary to convey the forsakenness of their country, like the forsakenness of Europe as a whole (Peyre 1948, p. 30). But the key here is a desire to convey, a desire to communicate and to act. Communicating the absurd through writing and the relationship between the absurd and language during the war would be a central issue in reception of the absurd, and a topic that Jacques Guicharnaud began to explore fifteen volumes later in *YFS*.

1955: Language in a Historical Situation

A new line of thought linked to language and the absurd emerges in Guicharnaud's article "Those Years: Existentialism 1943–1945" in the sixteenth issue of *YFS* (1955) that was devoted to the theme Foray Through Existentialism. Guicharnaud was another foundational figure of Yale's French Department, where he taught from 1950 to 1997 (In memoriam 2005). He actually calls his article a testimony, recounting his existentialist awakening as a student in wartime Paris as if it took place many years ago rather than a decade earlier, perhaps in a world that has already passed. His unpublished diaries from those years he discusses in the article, kept during his late teens and early twenties, provide a parallel account of his coming of age under Vichy and reveal a previously unheard immediate reception of the movement. In these diaries, he makes a rare explicit mention of his view of the Occupation: "Il y a la guerre, l'occupation. Je n'en parle jamais. Pourquoi? Il faudra un jour que je dise cette lassitude, cette incertitude qui me pèse" (There is the war, the Occupation. I never talk about it. Why? One day I will have to say this languor, this uncertainty that weighs on me).[3] He would draw out the philosophical implications of his life under the Occupation in the next decade in his *YFS* article. In that article, he discusses despair during Occupation years, and also mentions how he came to meet Sartre and Camus toward the end of the Occupation. As he used Sartre's teachings to confront the absurd, Guicharnaud recognized not only that understanding the absurd leads to rebellion and heroism, but also that words had to be understood in their historic situation to be used in meaningful communication of a political point of view.

And here we find a second thread of reception of the absurd: the importance of language itself. When Guicharnaud writes about the time just before he met Sartre, in his *prépa* studying for the competitive exams to enter the prestigious École normale supérieure, he states that there was no obvious connection at first between the *explication de texte* exercises he did and the deportation of his friend Levy; the implication after reading the rest of his article is that there is in fact a connection between close reading and his historical situation, but only when the words are historically situated and the absurdity is faced at an intellectual level. This could be read as one particular explanation of New Criticism, which was in its heyday and whose towering figures René Wellek, Cleanth Brooks, and Robert Penn Warren, were at Yale at the time. New Criticism has been disparaged for just being a form of *explication de texte* (Wellek 1986, p. 144), but here Guicharnaud proposes historically situated close readings as an alternative, perhaps thereby implicitly criticizing New Criticism. Guicharnaud wrote in his unpublished papers that he was worried about publishing this article for fear it would harm his position at Yale.[4]

Existential despair (as opposed to Peyre's use of the word *despair*), including in regard to his own speech, was Guicharnaud's way in to existentialism. In "Those Years: Existentialism 1943–1945," he lays out his existential path, in which dealing with the absurd as anchored in the war plays a crucial role. He aptly subtitles this section of the article "The Apprentice Existentialist (1943–44)." We find a kind of a four-step

---

[3] Jacques Guicharnaud Papers, Folder Notebook: 1943 Mar–1944 Apr, f. 22. Diary entry dated Jan. 12, 1943.
[4] Jacques Guicharnaud Papers, Folder 6: Notebook 1955–1956, ff. 3–4. Entry undated.

program about how to become a young existentialist in the early 1940s. Step one is despair. This despair neither refers to "spectacular manifestations of romantic despair" nor bitterness. Rather, for Guicharnaud despair means a kind of "uneasy conscience in connection with little things": "I was bursting with problems. Everything had become important, lighting a cigarette, stirring a cup of coffee, using certain words and intonations. The world had become an immense trap for catching crimes" (Guicharnaud 1955, p. 134). Despair as a concept in Sartre refers to the fact that although we live in a Godless world of different possibilities that are never certain and are out of our control, we act according to our own will and according to "the set of probabilities that enable action" (Sartre 2007, p. 34). For Sartre, man is nothing but his project, a project undertaken in despair; to leave this work to others would be to ignore despair. Guicharnaud's banal acts, which include his use of language, undertaken in a world of possibilities but devoid of answers, all seem to be weighted in despair.

In his diary entries from the episodes Guicharnaud discusses in his article, he actually describes this moment in the related term of *angoisse* rather than despair. Shortly before meeting Sartre for the first time, and just after his first ever mention of reading Sartre (*The Wall*), he writes: "Cet entre-deux terrible où il y a, derrière, ce que j'étais et, devant, ce que je serai, c'est-à-dire pour l'instant un néant, en tout cas néantisation future de tout ce que je suis actuellement" (This terrible interval where there is, in back of me, what I was and, in front, what I will be, that is to say for the moment a nothingness, in any case a future nihilation of all that I am right now).[5] In the context of his coming of age diary, this interval certainly seems to correspond to the intense three-year period of *prépa* full of failures between high school and entering the *Grande École*. But it also relates to a moment of intellectual growth in which words began to take form as something that could change the world. When Guicharnaud looks back at this time for *YFS*, he mentions the importance of words, specifically words spoken in the everyday just like coffee stirred in a quotidian moment.

---

[5] Jacques Guicharnaud Papers, Folder 1, Notebook: 1943 Mar–1944 Apr, f. 17. Diary entry dated Oct. 5, 1942.

This stage of despair ends when he first meets Sartre. Now we enter step two of the program, when "liberty was the root of the matter" (Guicharnaud 1955, p. 135). In January 1944, his friend Jean-Bertrand Lefèvre-Pontalis (the same J.B. he addresses at one point in the article) introduced Guicharnaud to Sartre. Sartre gave him a clue to confronting his problems; Guicharnaud writes that he "seemed to say" that "the world is yours," but yours to change. This liberty relates to a new approach to language itself. New words entered into the young existentialist's vocabulary—anguish, Dasein, nothingness, liberty, and commitment. Existentialism provided "great metaphors" that helped his generation understand their situation (Guicharnaud 1955, p. 132). Guicharnaud also began to show his writing to Sartre and Camus in the hope of publishing short stories. In his diaries, Guicharnaud describes Sartre as "le grand petit M. Sartre" (the great short Mr. Sartre) whose "hantise de l'honnêteté, de la propreté morale en face de lui" (obsession with honesty, with moral rectitude before him) intimidates Guicharnaud so that he can hardly speak and realizes that he should reread *Nausea*.[6] Later in his journal he refers to Sartre as the "maître" (master or teacher) and "la gentilesse même" (kindness itself) while Camus—"un grand monsieur brun, assez beau et excessivement sympathique. Mais on sent qu'il est profondément malade (ses yeux, et sa voix extraordinaire et extenuée)" (a tall, dark-haired man, rather handsome and excessively nice. But one senses that he is deeply ill [his eyes, his extraordinary and exhausted voice])—is more severe in his feedback on his writing.[7] Their generosity comes through in Guicharnaud's 1955 article as well, when he recalls how Sartre, Camus, and Beauvoir read and guided so many young writers, rising above snobbism at the Café du Flore. Sartre passed along Guicharnaud's writing to Camus, who published his short story "Quai de la Gare" in *Combat* (April 14, 1945), and perhaps also his collection of short stories, *Entre chien et loup* (*Between Dusk and Dawn*), that came out with Gallimard in 1946. The language of existentialism was also one linked to publication, for it was intimately tied to Guicharnaud's literary aspirations.

---

[6] Jacques Guicharnaud Papers, Folder Notebook: 1943 Mar–1944 Apr, f. 58. Diary entry dated Jan. 24, 1944.

[7] Jacques Guicharnaud Papers, Folder Notebook: 1944 Jan–1945 Jul, pages unnumbered. Entries dated April 14, 1944; May 22, 1944; May 12, 1944.

In step three, Guicharnaud addresses the absurd head on: "the world ceased to be absurd because we knew it was absurd" (Guicharnaud 1955, p. 136). In his 1955 article, like in his 1940s diaries, this absurd relates specifically to his situation in occupied Paris: Food shortages, the disappearances of Jewish friends and friends in the Resistance, the threat of bombardments, the contrast between the broadcasts of the collaborationist Radio Paris and those of the BBC, and even his own behavior. Simply accepting this absurd, writes Guicharnaud in 1955, would lead to "tears and sentimental outings" (Guicharnaud 1955, p. 136). Instead, spurred by his existentialist awakening, "the intellectual identification of the absurd leads to rebellion" (Guicharnaud 1955, p. 136). His own diaries demonstrate the trap of accepting the absurd in a sentimental sense. At the end of 1943, Guicharnaud expressed despondency that would lead nowhere, scribbling: "lassitude… s'en foutre. Cafard, cafard. Même pas le spleen" (lassitude … don't give a damn. Doldrums, doldrums. Not even spleen). But he finds J.B.'s suggestion to go to war "absurd."[8] He does not even feel a Baudelairean, poetic ill humor, but rather avoids existential despair, thus refusing to act.

Encountering the absurd on an intellectual level leads to step four, which is concerned with language as much as action. Once the absurd is accepted, language becomes part of the revolt. Young existentialists like Guicharnaud gave new meanings to words situated in this historical moment, and in particular the word 'hero' (one that Peyre also uses to describe the existentialists). This intellectual acceptance of the absurd historical situation of the Occupation, of his position as a student in Paris during the war, made him aware of how words were linked to a concrete, situated, historical moment: "heroism was not appraised according to its military importance, but placed in a historical situation. If this is not done, communication by means of language remains abstract and illusory" (Guicharnaud 1955, p. 138). Later he would analyze other terms like martyr, patriot, Communist, and fascist along these lines to find their meaning within the context of an absurd historical situation. Only through this facing of *angoisse*, and accepting the absurd on an intellectual

---

[8] Jacques Guicharnaud Papers, Folder Notebook: 1943 Mar–1944 Apr, f. 55. Diary entry dated Dec. 21, 1943.

level, did language become a means of communication. Guicharnaud gives us a window into what Peyre may have meant by existentialists turning to American writers (ones like Faulkner and Steinbeck whom Guicharnaud greatly appreciated) during the war to communicate a brutal historical situation.

1959: The Decomposition of Language

Peyre and Guicharnaud deal with topics that would become central to discussions of the theater of the absurd—namely, the role of language and communication in confronting the absurd—in journal volumes that either predate the movement or predate discussions of it. In 1948, Peyre was writing about the absurd a few years before what is considered to be the beginning of the theater of the absurd, the first performance of Eugène Ionesco's *Bald Soprano* in 1950 and Samuel Beckett's *Waiting for Godot* in 1953. It would not be until 1959 that the theater of the absurd made its way into *YFS*, save for one article by Edith Kern on Beckett in a volume entitled *Motley: Today's French Theatre* (No. 14, 1954). Serge Doubrovksy, known as a scholar of classical theater as well as the creator of the term *autofiction*, published the first article in *YFS* on Ionesco, "Ionesco and the Comic of Absurdity," in a volume devoted to Humor (No. 23, 1959). This volume included numerous articles on what we would now consider the theater of the absurd, although the term *theater of the absurd* had not yet been coined. That would come in 1960 in an article by Martin Esslin, and again in his book in 1961 (Esslin 1960, 2001). Just as the authors of the 1948 *YFS* volume were already revising existentialism in the 1940s, Doubrovsky calls Ionesco's plays classics of French theater only nine years since the first performance of an Ionesco play. Doubrovsky, like Esslin would one year later, opens a new phrase of reception of the absurd in America as he assimilates this theater into existentialism and the existentialist absurd. However, Doubrovsky changes the approach that Peyre and Guicharnaud took, arguing that Ionesco stages the 'decomposition' of language in an absurd world. Now language and the absurd are about meaninglessness and the war. Doubrovsky's reading seems to represent in many ways what Guicharnaud and Peyre wrote against years earlier. That is not to say that Doubrvosky's reading came from ignorance of the wartime situation; he survived the Shoah by living in hiding in France under the Occupation. Nor did he lack a deep understanding of Sartre's words; in a work of autofiction, *Le livre brisé*, Doubrovsky recalls his close relationship with Sartre and his veneration of *Nausea*, even discussing Sartre as his "père spirituel" (spiritual father).[9] Rather, he had a particular, and perhaps personal, reading of the absurd.

Doubrovsky reads Ionesco's absurd through the lens of existential absurd, tinted with a specifically postwar view of the movement. For Doubrovsky, Ionesco's theater has finally shown that literary expression has caught up with the philosophy of the absurd of the previous twenty years, as expressed by Camus and Sartre. It is an absurd anchored in the wake of the Second World War, as Ionesco is a writer situated in history who responds to "the agony of his century" (Doubrovksy 1959, p. 3). When asked directly in an interview in 1966 if he was influenced by the philosophy of the absurd, Ionesco responded that "the notion of the absurd was very much in the air at the time" (Bonnefoy 1970, p. 122). The time he refers to is the postwar period, rather than the war itself. Although Ionesco does not point to any particular texts by Camus and Sartre, he does acquiesce that he was influenced by what he read, and that the authors he read were influenced by the time in which they lived. Ionesco was also very much against Sartre's Marxist politics, and certainly never called himself an existentialist. He had a multifaceted understanding of the absurd that both converges and diverges from existentialism: he uses the absurd to describe what he does not comprehend, yet also his desire to comprehend it. Ionesco calls it "this situation of being here that I cannot recognize as being my situation," as well as "a kind of absurdity that is unreason, contradiction, the expression of my being out of tune with the world" (Bonnefoy 1970, p. 127). Ionesco himself would distance himself more and more from the movement and from Sartre in particular. But in his article, Doubrovksy reads Ionesco's approach as an elaboration of existential absurd in the postwar moment.

---

[9] Doubrovksy (1989, pp. 71–79). In this same work of autofiction, Doubrovsky also evokes traumatic memory of surviving the war.

Doubrovsky defines Ionesco's absurd as "the absurdity of a world where man is left alone to fill in the void of God, give a name and meaning to things and freely, but unjustifiably, create his own values" (Doubrovksy 1959, p. 3). According to Doubrovsky, Ionesco creates a comedy of circularity and a comedy of proliferation that illustrate both the desire to fill this void and the unrealizability of that action. The denouements of *The Bald Soprano* and *The Lesson* that bring the play back again to the beginning in an endless cycle show the negation of an individual character living in a linear progression. Circularity and proliferation also relates to a kind of "all-pervading presence of things" in Ionesco's theater; Doubrovsky includes examples of this proliferation such as the numerous chairs The Woman sets up for an empty audience in *The Chairs*, the overproduction of eggs in *The Future is in Eggs*, the unending moving in of furniture in *The New Tenant*, and the ever-growing corpse in *Amedée or How to Get Rid of It*. Doubrovsky recalls Roquentin's sense of "the essential emptiness of man before the monstrous kingdom of objects" in *Nausea* (Doubrovksy 1959, p. 6). He points out that anguish comes along with seeing the absurd; for Sartre this is the anguish of man's responsibility (Doubrovksy 1959, p. 10). But Doubrovsky maintains that Ionesco goes further in showing this anguish through evoking an absurd laughter. His theater holds up a mirror to the spectators, in which they see man's disintegration, and where tragedy becomes farce. This is a laughter directed at man rather than at the world, casting doubt on the "possibility of being a man" (Doubrovksy 1959, p. 10).

Through his use of language, Doubrovsky holds, Ionesco truly represents the absurd in more authentic ways than Camus or Sartre did in their theater. Unlike Camus and Sartre, who are conservative because they write coherent characters who speak rationally, Ionesco has launched a "perpetually renewed act of accusation against language" to demonstrate that it has always been a "systematic delirium" (Doubrovksy 1959, pp. 7–8). Language has been thinking for man, catching him in a false system, rather than man thinking through language. Ionesco's use of puns, meaningless sayings, clichés, and devolution of language into sounds is actually the disintegration of language. To write the absurd authentically, according to Doubrovsky, there must be a disintegration of both the personality of the characters and their language. This new language is invented by the experience of the absurd itself and goes against rational discourse. Rather than the not-yet-invented term of theater of the absurd, he calls it a theater of decomposition and a theater of irrationality. The world is a historically situated one, a world of decomposition, as Doubrovsky quotes the character Madeleine in *The Alma Impromptu* who characterizes the modern world in a "state of decomposition" (Doubrovksy 1959, p. 3). Ionesco's use of irrational, disintegrated language reflects the realities of his own postwar moment. Now that Ionesco has destroyed the illusion of language as a means to think, to communicate the truth, the Sartrean experience of nausea truly comes forth and the spectator sees the monstrosity of the world.

Doubrovsky's article represents a complete reversal of Peyre's and Guicharnaud's approach to the absurd. Peyre and Guicharnaud discuss Sartre's and Camus' absurd in terms of the war, showing that anguish and despair are part of the process of taking action. Peyre begins to discuss the role of communication, which Guicharnaud takes up through language as part of his existential awakening after confronting the absurd. Doubrovsky, writing later in the postwar years than his colleagues, instead sees the absurd historic situation as one of decomposition, in which language itself must be shown as disintegrated. The theater of the absurd, or the theater of decomposition, seems to draw out this view in particular. He concludes: "This determination to be gay in face of the utter confusion and final disappearance of all values offers no salvation, it does not conquer absurdity, it stresses it, it does not try to dodge it, it revels in it" (Doubrovksy 1959, p. 10). We hear the echo of Camus' famous statement that we must imagine Sisyphus happy, but at the same time Doubrovsky sets up the dichotomy of gayness and revelry on the one hand and utter confusion on the other. For Doubrovsky, Ionesco's decomposed language perfectly replicates this. Yet it also marks a departure from action and language in existentialism, and perhaps locates a moment in which the theater of the absurd ceases to be existentialist.

Viewed as a three-part series of reception, these central articles by Peyre, Guicharnaud, and Doubrovsky show a concretization of reading the absurd as one of the central concepts of existentialism, and one that anchors or even fixes the idea of France of the Second World War as the absurd world. Nevertheless, their depth of interest in this new movement indicates they were certainly not in the business of creating new clichés about existentialism. Rather, they reveal how a moment in time can be read into a movement. By tracing how an American understanding of the absurd to this day has been defined through postwar reception of these three scholars—who were French-born and educated but who worked in and introduced the concepts to the American academy—new readings of the absurd become possible.

References

Bonnefoy, Claude. 1970. *Conversations with Eugène Ionesco*. Translated by Jan Dawson. New York: Holt, Rinehart, and Winston.

Camus, Albert. 1946a. The Crisis of Man. *Vogue*, 86–87, July 1.

———. 1946b. The Crisis of Man. *Twice a Year*, 19–33, Fall/Winter 1946–1947.

———. 1983. *The Myth of Sisyphus: And Other Essays*. Translated by Justin O'Brien. New York: Knopf.

Cohen Solal, Annie. 1987. *Sartre: A Life*. Translated by Anna Cancogni. New York: Pantheon Books.

Cohn, Robert Greer. 1948. Introduction to "Scenes from *Les Mains Sales*". *Yale French Studies* 1: 3. Existentialism.

Dieckmann, Herbert. 1948. French Existentialism before Sartre. *Yale French Studies* 1: 33–41. Existentialism.

Doubrovksy, Serge. 1959. Ionesco and the Comic of Absurdity. *Yale French Studies* 23: 3–9. Humor.

———. 1989. *Le Livre brisé*. Paris: Éditions Grasset.

Esslin, Martin. 1960. The Theatre of the Absurd. *The Tulane Drama Review* 4 (4): 3–15.

———. 2001. *The Theatre of the Absurd*. Rev. updated ed. New York: Vintage.

Front Matter. 1948. *Yale French Studies* 1: 1–2. Existentialism.

Fulton, Ann. 1999. *Apostles of Sartre: Existentialism in America, 1945–1963*. Evanston, IL: Northwestern University Press.

Guicharnaud, Jacques. 1955. Those Years: Existentialism 1943–1945. Translated by Kevin Neilson. *Yale French Studies* 16: 127–145. Foray Through Existentialism.

In Memoriam: Jacques Guicharnaud, French theater scholar and associate of the Existentialists. 2005. *Yale Bulletin and Calendar* 33 (22), March 18.

Jacques Guicharnaud Papers. n.d. Beinecke Rare Book & Manuscript Library, Yale University, GEN MSS 883, Series II. Writings, Box 4.

Marcuse, Herbert. 1948. Existentialism: Remarks on Jean-Paul Sartre's *L'être et le néant*. *Philosophy and Phenomenological Research* 8 (3): 309–336, March.

Peyre, Henry. 1948. Existentialism—A Literature of Despair? *Yale French Studies* 1: 21–32. Existentialism.

———. 1955. *The Contemporary French Novel*. New York: Oxford University Press.

———. 1968. *Jean-Paul Sartre*. New York: Columbia University Press.

———. 2005. *Henry Peyre: His Life in Letters*. New Haven: Yale University Press.

Porter, Charles A. 1999. Celebratory Criticism: The First Dozen Years. *Yale French Studies* 96: 13–17. 50 Years of Yale French Studies: A Commemorative Anthology. Part 1: 1948–1979.

Sartre, Jean-Paul. 1947. Qu'est-ce que la littérature. *Les Temps modernes*, 1607–1641, June.

———. 1956. *Being and Nothingness: An Essay on Phenomenological Ontology*. Translated by Hazel E. Barnes. New York: Philosophical Library.

———. 1993. *What is Literature?* Translated by Bernard Frechtman. London: Routledge.

———. 2007. *Existentialism Is a Humanism*. Translated by Carol Macomber. New Haven: Yale University Press.

———. 2010. *The Outsider* Explained. *Critical Essays: Situations I*. Translated by Chris Turner. London: Seagull Books.

Slochower, Harry. 1948. The Function of Myth in Existentialism. *Yale French Studies* 1: 42–52. Existentialism.

Smith, Madeleine. 1948. The Making of a Leader. *Yale French Studies* 1: 80–83. Existentialism.

Spitzer, Leo. 1947–1948. Man's Need for Faith in Man. *The American Scholar* 17 (1): 93–94.

Wellek, René. 1986. *A History of Modern Criticism: 1750–1950*. Vol. 6. New Haven: Yale University Press.

Whiting, Charles G. 1948. The Case for 'Engaged' Literature. *Yale French Studies* 1: 84–89. Existentialism.

4

Walker Percy's *The Moviegoer,* a Signpost for Existentialism's Reception in the American South

Damon Boria

Introduction

The writings of Walker Percy are an underrecognized and underappreciated part of the reception of existentialism in the United States. They are not common inclusions in anthologies of existentialism, even when selections are drawn from American fiction. For example, Robert Solomon's *Existentialism*, which includes selections from Joseph Heller's *Catch-22*, Philip Roth's *The Human Stain*, and Arthur Miller's *Death of a Salesman*, excludes Percy. Gordon Marino's *Basic Writings of Existentialism*, which fittingly includes a selection from Ralph Ellison's *Invisible Man*, also excludes Percy. Nor are Percy's works commonly referenced in histories of or commentaries on existentialism.[1] For example, Kevin Aho's recent *Existentialism: An Introduction* ignores Percy despite making at least pass-

---

[1] An exception is the historian George Cotkin's *Existential America*, though Percy's presence is minimal and the view of existentialism is atypically broad.

D. Boria (✉)
Franciscan Missionaries of Our Lady University, Baton Rouge, LA, USA

© The Author(s) 2020
A. Betschart, J. Werner (eds.), *Sartre and the International Impact of Existentialism,*
https://doi.org/10.1007/978-3-030-38482-1_4

ing references to many American writers, including Chuck Palahniuk, Jack Kerouac, and Ellison. In fact, the scholarship on Percy's work frequently acknowledges and explores the influence of existentialism on Percy, whose work consistently engaged—sympathetically—the writings of Søren Kierkegaard, Fyodor Dostoevsky, and Gabriel Marcel, and—less sympathetically—the writings of Albert Camus and Jean-Paul Sartre. So, Percy's general exclusion from the set of existential literature cannot be defended by citing a lack of connection between him and existentialism. Rather, if the exclusion can be defended, it must be for lack of distinction or importance. This chapter attempts to show that Percy's work is a distinct and important part of the international reception of existentialism. More specifically, while neither an exhaustive overview of Percy's reception of existentialism nor a particularly close reading of his novel *The Moviegoer*, this attempt makes a case for Percy as a distinct and important signpost for the reception of existentialism in the American South.

Some Biographical Highlights of Walker Percy

Walker Percy spent most of his life in the American South. He was born 28 May 1916 in Birmingham, Alabama. After a brief stint in Athens, Georgia, in his early teens he moved to Greenville, Mississippi. He completed his undergraduate studies, receiving a degree in chemistry, at the University of North Carolina. In 1947, after an important half-dozen years in New York City, which included completing a medical degree from Columbia University, he moved to New Orleans, Louisiana. Three years after that, at the age of 34, he moved to the small town of Covington, Louisiana, where he would reside until his death from cancer in 1990.

Walker Percy's family tree is filled with people who were both privileged and troubled. Ancestors in the United States trace back to the eighteenth century and include figures of significance in the War of 1812, the Civil War, and World War I. Many were lawyers and influential in politics, including Percy's great-uncle, who was a U.S. senator from Mississippi (appointed by the state legislature, the last before the passage of the 17th Amendment of the U.S. Constitution). Percy's first name, Walker, traces to a family from which one person, John Williams Walker, a Princeton

University graduate and one of the first two U.S. senators from Alabama, married the sister-in-law of a Percy. The aforementioned sister, Maria Pope, was a relative of the British poet Alexander Pope. In short, the Percys were part of the aristocracy of the American South.

Troubling mental health problems were also common in the family. Charles "Don Carlos" Percy, the eighteenth-century ancestor who arrived in modern-day Florida in 1775, is said to have been overtaken by depression at the age of 90 and drowned himself in a creek. The problem intensified with Walker Percy's close relatives. When he was a baby, one of his grandfathers committed suicide. When he was 13 his father committed suicide. About three years later his mother died after her car drove off a bridge, an incident that has led to much speculation, including by Percy, that she too committed suicide. As noted above, Percy did not die by suicide. But he was no exception to the family history of mental health trouble. We know this from his own acknowledgment. From 1937 to 1940, it led him to pursue psychoanalytic treatment.

After their mother's death, the teenage Walker Percy and his two younger brothers were adopted by their older cousin. William Alexander Percy was a lawyer, planter, and bestselling poet and novelist with personal connections to many other writers including William Faulkner, Langston Hughes, and Robert Penn Warren. Percy leaves no doubt that his older cousin, who became his adopted father, had a tremendous impact on him, including his relationship with literature. This close relationship with literature and philosophy did not set Percy off on his writing career. As mentioned above, Percy successfully pursued a career in medicine. However, in 1942, he contracted tuberculosis after performing an autopsy. This led to some time at a tuberculosis sanatorium in upper New York. He read Kierkegaard and Dostoevsky extensively during this period. Also during this time he met a patient—a Catholic apologist—who catalyzed Percy's engagement with religion, ultimately resulting in his conversion to Catholicism in 1947. Despite occasionally self-identifying as a "bad" Catholic, he maintained and cultivated his Catholicism for the rest of his life. His distinctly Southern and Catholic reception of existentialism contributed significantly to his more than four decades of work in literature, philosophy, religion, and cultural commentary. The remainder of this chapter is a commentary on Percy's reception of existentialism that focuses on his novel *The Moviegoer*.

The Reception of *The Moviegoer*

In 1961 Percy published his first novel, *The Moviegoer*. The following year it won the National Book Award. The publisher, Alfred Knopf, was luke-warm on the novel and was not pushing it. But a writer for the *New Yorker* was intrigued after reading a review while in New Orleans. He read the novel and passed it on to his wife, Jean Stafford, who was on the selection committee for the award. She liked it and passed it onto others on the selection committee (Lacy 2011, p. 49). Among the novels considered that year were J.D. Salinger's *Franny and Zooey* and Joseph Heller's *Catch-22*. Robert Lacy notes that Percy's win was surprising but reasonable. He writes:

> In retrospect it's hard to argue with the NBA committee's choice. *The Moviegoer* captured the spirit of its time. Heller's book would go on to achieve cult status, in addition to adding a term to the language, but it had appeared ten years too late. America was no longer that interested in the problems of U.S. bomber pilots in World War II. And as for Salinger's little book, although it continues to have its partisans, history hasn't been especially kind. But *The Moviegoer* tapped into something that was beginning to be abroad in the land by 1961: a sort of is-this-all-there-is? disenchant-ment with the fruits of affluence. Sure, America was the greatest country on earth, but so what? How was that supposed to help a fella make it through the night? (Lacy 2011, p. 49)

In his acceptance speech for the National Book Award Percy compares his work in *The Moviegoer* with the work of a pathologist. Their shared "posture" is the "suspicion that something is wrong" (Percy 2000a, p. 246). He adds: "the pathology in this case has to do with the loss of individuality and the loss of identity at the very time when words like the 'dignity of the individual' and 'self-realization' are being heard more frequently than ever." The success of *The Moviegoer* has helped preserve an audience for Percy, especially among those reading twentieth-century literature from the American South. But fans are now taking more deliberate measures to keep Percy in the conversation. For example, an annual festival in St. Francisville, Louisiana, called Walker Percy Weekend, began in 2014.

The concern here, however, is the rare recognition among existentialism's readers and scholars of Percy, especially in *The Moviegoer*, as part of the international reception of existentialism and a noteworthy contributor to existentialist literature.

The Moviegoer as Reception

The Moviegoer is the result of Percy's Southern and Catholic-inflected reckoning with the works of Kierkegaard and Dostoevsky. The case for the influence of the latter was recently made by Jessica Hooten Wilson, who follows up on some perceptive but undeveloped insights by a couple earlier commentators. In *Walker Percy, Fyodor Dostoevsky, and the Search for Influence* (2017) she argues that Percy's novel reworks both the content and style of *The Underground Man* and the conclusion of *The Brothers Karamazov*. She cites as examples Percy's "aesthetic of incarnational realism and his polyphonic technique" (Wilson 2017, p. 43). Moreover, she observes that *The Moviegoer* and *Notes from Underground* share numerous similarities. The narrator for both communicates in the confessional mode, noting that the original title for the former was "Confessions of a Moviegoer," seen by an earlier commentator as an explicit reference to Dostoevsky (Wilson 2017, p. 44). Percy also suggested a subtitle that did not make it to publication, namely, "from the Diary of the Last Romantic." Wilson sees this too as a reference to Dostoevsky's *Notes from Underground*, though it could just as easily (also) be a reference to the Kierkegaardian scheme discussed later. Memory is a driving factor in the development of the two protagonists, who also share disillusionment with "modern scientists' reification of the human being" that contributes to their romantic retreat into books and movies, respectively (Wilson 2017, pp. 45–46). Both protagonists seek a third option, which results in a conversion (at least implied) for Percy's protagonist, Binx. Wilson suggests we may have seen the same result for the Underground Man had it not been for Dostoevsky's censors. Perhaps for this reason, the endings of *The Moviegoer* and *The Underground Man* are drastically different. As Wilson puts it, whereas the Underground Man only descends, Binx ascends (Wilson 2017, p. 44). To execute this, she contends that Percy turned to *The Brothers Karamazov*. Binx's conversion appears subtle or even ambiguous, but Wilson's identification of the numerous ways Binx's scene with his dying half-brother and other young relatives mirrors Alyosha's scene with children following the death of young Ilyusha (Wilson 2017, pp. 52–53), which for those who catch it make Binx's conversion into faith—from the Underground Man to Alyosha—significantly less subtle and ambiguous.

Meanwhile, the case for the influence of Kierkegaard has the benefit of an overt invitation from Percy. *The Moviegoer* has an epigraph, which is the following quote from Kierkegaard's *The Sickness Unto Death*: "the specific character of despair is precisely this: it is unaware of being despair." Given both Percy's and the fictional protagonist's geographical and cultural rootedness, this is an invitation not only to read the novel as a reception of existentialism but also to do so in connection to its particular place and time. Commentators have handled the epigraph in different ways. Some ignore it. Others acknowledge it as a convenient quote for Percy to make a narrow point. Many in both groups subsume the Kierkegaardian influence and read *The Moviegoer* as edifying for the Thomistic Catholicism already embraced by the author, who have the benefit of the fact that Percy planned an explicit Catholic conversion for Binx until a request from his editor (Wilson 2018, p. 32). But that has to be balanced against, first, Percy's claim that he is "not interested in edifying his readers" (An Interview with Walker Percy 1985, p. 64) and, second, his claim that Kierkegaard's essay "The Difference between a Genius and an Apostle" gave him the "basis" for the "whole structure" of Binx's search (Walker Percy Talks about Kierkegaard 1985, p. 113). In fact, that essay affected Percy far beyond *The Moviegoer*. He told an interviewer, "If I had to single out one piece of writing which was more responsible than anything else for my becoming a Catholic, it would be that essay of Kierkegaard's" (Walker Percy Talks about Kierkegaard 1985, p. 110). In the next section I provide an overview of the Kierkegaardian structure of *The Moviegoer* and then conclude with some brief reflections on the value of reading Percy as part of the international reception of existentialism.

The Kierkegaardian Structure of *The Moviegoer*

Kierkegaard's "The Difference Between a Genius and an Apostle" was written in 1847 and published in 1849 as one half of *Two Minor Ethical-Religious Essays*. The work is signed by H.H., the last pseudonym before Kierkegaard started using Anti-Climacus as the pseudonym and his actual name as the editor. At this point in Kierkegaard's authorship the triadic structure of modes of being-in-the-world had been communicated in, notably, *Stages on Life's Way* (1845) and *Concluding Unscientific Postscript* (1846). In the former the pseudonym Frater Taciturnus offers the following overview:

> There are three existence spheres: the esthetic, the ethical, the religious. ... The ethical sphere is only a transition sphere, and therefore its highest expression is repentance as a negative action. The esthetic sphere is the sphere of immediacy, the ethical the sphere of requirement (and this requirement is so infinite that the individual always goes bankrupt), the religious the sphere of fulfillment, but please note, not a fulfillment such as when one fills an alms box or a sack with gold, for repentance has specifically created a boundless space, and as a consequence the religious contradiction: simultaneously to be out on 70,000 fathoms of water and yet be joyful. (Kierkegaard 1988, p. 476)

An aesthetic existence is, as one commentator succinctly puts it, "reduced to the consumption of transitory pleasures and flight from the threat of pain and boredom" (Aho 2014, p. 86). The aesthete is wanting to not be a self and attempts this through externalization of oneself in a series of "interesting" moments. An ethical existence, meanwhile, commits to objective and universal duties. The ethical person chooses to be a self, but is inwardly "bankrupt." A religious existence, however, is elevated to authentic selfhood through the inward passion of risk-saturated faith.

In the "Difference Between a Genius and an Apostle" essay Kierkegaard emphasizes that the qualitative difference between these spheres is not a matter of degree. There is no bridge establishing continuity from one to the other. He writes in the essay, "As an Apostle St. Paul has no connection whatsoever with Plato or Shakespeare, with stylists or upholsterers, and none of them … can possibly be compared with him" (Kierkegaard 1962, p. 90). Perhaps Plato and Shakespeare were geniuses, as stylists, moralists, and the like. Perhaps St. Paul was a genius upholsterer. But genius is limited to the aesthetic and ethical spheres. Whereas geniuses are made, apostles are called by God. Herein lies the difference. As Kierkegaard puts it, "Divine authority is, qualitatively, the decisive factor" (Kierkegaard 1962, p. 93). He also notes here, consistent with his take on Abraham in *Fear and Trembling*, that empirical evidence of divine authority will not be available (Kierkegaard 1962, p. 95). The leap that is required to traverse the difference that separates geniuses from apostles must be difficult and risky since, as noted above, such inner turmoil is necessary for Christian faith—a faith that for several reasons he calls "paradox-religion."

To be clear, Kierkegaard's structure is not just about geniuses and apostles. It is about all people. Kierkegaard's other works make it abundantly clear that we find ordinary people—those who are neither geniuses nor apostles—becoming aesthetic selves, or ethical selves, or—ideally from Kierkegaard's perspective—religious selves. Percy read enough Kierkegaard to know this. So, even though he cited Kierkegaard's "Difference Between a Genius and an Apostle" essay as giving him the philosophical structure for *The Moviegoer*, we can view the novel's characters—who are neither geniuses nor apostles—through the "qualitative dialectic" of the three existence spheres.

The Moviegoer's protagonist, Jack "Binx" Bolling is the primary exhibit for the qualitative dialectic. He is an unremarkable 29-year-old stockbroker in late 1950s New Orleans. Nevertheless, he is the distinct presence in the story. Certainly this is based in the fact that, like Meursault in Camus' *The Stranger*, he provides first-person narration. But it is also based in the fact that Binx announces himself as the star of the qualitative dialectic. In his words, he is on a "search": "what," he says, "anyone would undertake if he were not sunk in the everydayness of his own life." He says the first time he became aware of the possibility of a search was while seeing, in what Wilson suspects is a link to Dostoevsky's Underground Man's occasional desire to become an insect, a dung beetle crawling near his nose as he lay injured on a Korean battlefield (Percy 1998, pp. 10–11).

He promised to undertake this search if he made it home. He did but forgot about the possibility until a morning years later in which he awoke tasting the war he dreamt that night. And with this Binx's search begins, prompting him to say—in an explicit reference to the novel's epigraph—that he is "onto something" and, as such, freed from the "despair" of not being onto something. Binx clearly does not suffer from unconscious despair, the most rudimentary type of despair presented in *The Sickness Unto Death*. But all is not well with Binx. His life is consumed by the pursuit of money, brief romances, spontaneous excursions, and moviegoing (Percy 1998, p. 41). He is an aesthete, living a mode of existence that is, in its own way, despair.

The novel's title suggests the importance of Binx's moviegoing. The moviegoing functions as a built-in symbol of the existential failure of the aesthetic life. On one hand, the moviegoing is successful. The main haunt of aesthetes is boredom. So they are in regular pursuit of the interesting, which is something movies can offer. Jerome Taylor notes Percy's frequent use of moviegoing (especially of American westerns) as an example of rotation—in the Kierkegaardian sense—due to "the change in feeling one achieves by going to a western movie where the process of aesthetic impersonation takes place in identifying with the hero. One escapes the ordinary everydayness of his life for a moment as he lives-over into the new and exciting life of the lonely plainsman" (Taylor 1986, p. 25). We have a readily available update on this point with Marvel Studios' ongoing run of hit superhero movies. One cannot impersonate in such a way without willing not to be oneself, which is one of the types of despair identified by Kierkegaard.

Perhaps unsurprisingly, then, Binx tells us that he finds the people on screen to be more real and their actions more meaningful than anything experienced in his daily life. The semi-conscious insight in this admission of the intrinsic existential failure of the aesthetic life is captured by Calvin Schrag writing on time in the aesthetic sphere: "The aesthete's experience of time is that of time and history externalized. The aesthete does not yet apprehend time as being constitutive of her/himself as *existing*, as being inserted in the world as a concretely becoming historical subject. Time for the aesthete is something external and objective, an orderly serial succession of nows" (Schrag 1995, p. 5). Intentional or not, Percy managed to reflect the serialized temporality of the aesthete's existence in the novel's plot. Set during Mardi Gras in New Orleans (with brief excursions out of the city), there are no significant events. The plot is essentially a series of occurrences, resembling what *The Stranger*'s *The Stranger* would look like if the murder was removed.

The most significant occurrence is late in the novel when Binx takes a trip to Chicago accompanied by his second cousin Kate Cutrer. Her mother justifiably thinks Kate is suicidal (Later, Kate denies this to Binx, saying that the thought of death is keeping her alive (Percy 1998, p. 194)). Early in the novel Aunt Emily tasks Binx with helping look out for Kate (Percy 1998, pp. 27–28). The request may not be out of love. As the novel's avatar of the ethical sphere (modeled on Percy's adopted father, William Alexander Percy), Aunt Emily is primarily concerned with Kate failing to fulfill her ethical duties, for which marriage is of prime concern. Kate is engaged to a clueless man who she does not love and, prior to that, was engaged to someone who died in a car accident. She did not seem to have loved her first fiancé either, given how she quickly fled the accident site and does not grieve afterward. Both cases of failed love fit within the Kierkegaardian structure. In the case of her first fiancé, Kate could not love him because through ordinary everydayness she lacked the subjective inwardness necessary for authentic love. In the case of her second fiancé, she could not love him because she—now jolted out of unconscious despair following the grave car accident—finds him and his krewe captain ways unbefitting of authentic love. In terms of Kierkegaard's qualitative dialectic, it is Binx and Kate who are aligned. As Kate says to Binx, pointedly capturing his inability to fulfill his aunt's order to care for her, "You're like me, but worse. Much worse" (Percy 1998, p. 43). Moreover, as she says in response to Binx's question of whether the car accident still bothers her, "it gave me my life. That's my secret, just as the war is your secret" (Percy 1998, p. 58).

In Chicago Binx is twice confronted with examples of his failure to love. First, he recalls a trip to the Field Museum with his father after the tragic death of Binx's brother. While looking at "a tableau of Stone Age Man," he realizes that his father is grieving and looking at him for an act of love. Binx recalls: "[I] turned him down, turned away, refused him what I knew I could not give" (Percy 1998, p. 204). Shortly after that,

Binx visits a friend who saved his life during the war and, more recently, who invited him to his son's baptism and designated Binx as the boy's godfather. But he is a day late, due to neither forgetfulness nor deliberate choice. Rather, it is the aesthete's apathy toward one's neighbors. These examples of Binx's failures to authentically love reach back through the story to reveal his other failures with the many vulnerable people in his life, such as his twelve-year-old half-brother who is disabled and dying, his other siblings, and, in particular, Kate.

In the end Binx qualitatively changes, similar to Meursault but without the dire circumstance. That is, Binx makes a leap of faith, out of the aesthetic sphere and into the religious sphere. However, both the fact and nature of Binx's self being transformed by faith are deeply ambiguous. The moment arrives shortly after returning to New Orleans. It is Ash Wednesday and Binx and Kate are chatting in her car. Then Percy writes: "A florid new Mercury pulls up behind us and a Negro gets out and goes up into the church" (Percy 1998, p. 233). And then several lines later:

> The Negro has already come outside. His forehead is an ambiguous sienna color and pied: it is impossible to be sure that he received ashes. When he gets in his Mercury, he does not leave immediately but sits looking down at something on the seat beside him. ... It is impossible to say why he is here. Is it part and parcel of the complex business of coming up in the world? Or is it because he believes God himself is present here at the corner of Elysian Fields and Bons Enfants? Or is he here for both reasons: through some dim dazzling trick of grace, coming for the one and receiving the other as God's own importunate bonus? It is impossible to say. (Percy 1998, pp. 234–235)

This ends the fifth and final chapter. The novel's last few pages are an epilogue in which Binx reveals that he and Kate are lovingly married, he is on peaceful terms with his aunt, and he is lovingly caring for his young siblings. The epilogue clearly communicates that Binx is now qualitatively different from Binx-the-aesthete. Some commentators have highlighted the connection between Binx's leap of faith and the novel's black characters. Throughout the novel the black characters—nearly all of whom are servants in the Cutrer household—are subjected to the patronizing racism expressed most explicitly by Aunt Emily. It is enough to encourage readers to suspect that she is the character truly speaking for the author. Such a conclusion, however, would fail to appreciate the novel's black characters. As David Crowe points out, during Aunt Emily's Ash Wednesday lambasting of Binx—a speech that is both an exquisite portrayal of the patronizing anti-black racism pervasive in the American South and a particularly pernicious example of a self in the ethical sphere (in the Kierkegaardian sense)—Binx's attention repeatedly diverts to the black servants, one of whom is sweeping ashes with palmetto leaves. Crowe, who follows Percy in viewing the novel as coherently based on Kierkegaard's "Genius and an Apostle" essay, writes, "The Christian imagery is unmistakable: palm leaves to greet the Lord with; ashes as the consequence of unredeemed death" (Crowe 2015, p. 200). Add to this the churchgoing black man at the very end of the conclusion of the main narrative (and several other clues throughout the novel) and there is a strong impression that Percy links Binx's salvation literally to loving his vulnerable family members and figuratively to consciousness of, and perhaps a religious response to, the plight of blacks in the United States.

Elsewhere Percy publicly sides with a religious response—the Catholic response in particular—to the plight of blacks in the United States. For example, in an article addressed to those like him and Binx—that is, to middle and upper-class white Southerners—he chides these self-identifying Christians (and especially Catholics) for defending racial segregation and dismissing the rights of labor. The situation for the article—titled "Stoicism in the South"—included the fact that Stoicism had become popular and ultimately entrenched among upper-class white Southerners following the Civil War. So Percy diagnoses white Southerners as more Stoic than Christian, with the result that such people are focused on inner tranquility rather than on loving their neighbors. He concludes, "We in the South can no longer afford the luxury of maintaining the Stoa beside the Christian edifice" (Percy 2000b, p. 86). Percy writes near the beginning of the article, "I only feel free to say this because no white Southerner can write a *j'accuse* without making a *mea culpa*" (Percy 2000b, pp. 83–84). In Percy's case, he was a segregationist until his Catholic faith helped catalyze a change that led to his public support for the Civil Rights Movement. This public support is documented in articles written for *Harper's* and *Katallagete*, though, as Paul Elie observes, Percy—a champion of Southern manners—was conflicted between gradualism and activism (Elie 2003, pp. 246–247). In the *Harper's* article, Percy himself admits to essentially staying on the sidelines instead of joining, for example, the marchers. As noted above, a significant catalyst for his conversion to Catholicism was his reception of existentialism. So, put together, we can say that, for Percy, Stoicism in the American South (and everyday aestheticism in the Kierkegaardian sense) was the problem, Christianity was the answer, and existentialism—especially of the theistic variety—was the gadfly catalyzing the qualitative progress of the self.

A noteworthy addendum here is the potential value of reading Percy alongside Sartre's *The Respectful Prostitute*. Sartre's play was written after his travels through the American South, which included New Orleans. Given both Binx's and Percy's Southern aristocratic identities, which in some ways mirror the identities of the racists in *The Respectful Prostitute*, one benefit of reading Percy is that it gives readers of Sartre's play a richer understanding of that identity with which they can then both (a) better appreciate Sartre's literary attack on anti-black racism in the American South and (b) see an example of how the Southern aristocratic identity is criticized by someone—Percy—who (in some ways) shared it.

In conclusion, though Percy embraced Thomistic Catholicism, he maintained a heavy appreciation for various existentialist philosophers: Kierkegaard for his dialectic of the self, Dostoevsky for his distinctly modern religious search, Ortega y Gasset and Marcel for their critiques of mass society, and the atheists Camus and (the early) Sartre for their respective descriptions of the modern world. As Percy once remarked, "I regard myself as more akin to the European existentialists than to the American novel. But I aim to Americanize the movement" (Walker Percy: He Likes to Put Protagonist in Situation 1985, p. 5). True to his aim, Percy's reception of existentialism was clearly situated in the author's specific time and place and inflected with the author's specific experiences. Moreover, the literary products of his reception were addressed to a fairly limited audience. That said, Percy's works, including but not limited to *The Moviegoer*, deserve to be read widely as part of the history of the international reception of existentialism.

References

Aho, Kevin Aho. 2014. *Existentialism: An Introduction*. Malden: Polity Press.

An Interview with Walker Percy. 1985. In *Conversations with Walker Percy*, ed. Lewis A. Lawson and Victor A. Kramer, 56–71. Jackson: The University Press of Mississippi.

Cotkin, George. 2003. *Existential America*. Baltimore: The Johns Hopkins University Press.

Crowe, David. 2015. Kierkegaardian Misreadings of Walker Percy's *The Moviegoer*. *Christianity and Literature* 64 (2): 187–204.

Elie, Paul. 2003. *The Life You Save May Be Your Own: An American Pilgrimage*. New York: Farrar, Straus and Giroux.

Kierkegaard, Soren. 1962. *The Present Age and of the Difference between a Genius and an Apostle*. Translated by Alexander Dru. New York: Harper & Row.

———. 1988. *Stages on Life's Way*. Translated by Howard V. Hong and Edna H. Hong. Princeton: Princeton University Press.

Lacy, Robert. 2011. *The Moviegoer*, Fifty Years After. *The Southern Review* 47 (1, Winter): 49–54.

Percy, Walker. 1998. *The Moviegoer*. New York: Vintage International.

———. 2000a. Accepting the National Book Award for *The Moviegoer*. In *Signposts in a Strange Land: Essays by Walker Percy*, ed. Patrick Samway, 245–246. New York: Picador.

———. 2000b. Stoicism in the South. In *Signposts in a Strange Land: Essays by Walker Percy*, ed. Patrick Samway, 83–88. New York: Picador.

Schrag, Calvin O. 1995. The Kierkegaard-Effect in the Shaping of the Contours of Modernity. In *Kierkegaard in Post/Modernity*, ed. Martin J. Matustik and Merold Westphal, 1–17. Bloomington: Indiana University Press.

Taylor, Jerome. 1986. *In Search of Self: Life, Death and Walker Percy*. Cambridge: Cowley Publications.

Walker Percy: He Likes to Put Protagonist in Situation. 1985. In *Conversations with Walker Percy*, ed. Lewis A. Lawson and Victor A. Kramer. Jackson: The University Press of Mississippi.

Walker Percy Talks about Kierkegaard: An Annotated Interview. 1985. In *Conversations with Walker Percy*, ed. Lewis A. Lawson and Victor A. Kramer, 101–128. Jackson: The University Press of Mississippi.

Wilson, Jessica Hooten. 2017. *Walker Percy, Fyodor Dostoevsky, and the Search for Influence*. Columbus: Ohio State University Press.

———. 2018. *Reading Walker Percy's Novels*. Baton Rouge: LSU Press.

5

The Reception of Sartre's Plays: *The Respectful Prostitute* and *Dirty Hands* During the Cold War Period

Adrian van den Hoven

The *Respectful Prostitute* was first performed on November 8, 1946, and *Dirty Hands* on April 8, 1948. We will deal with their reception in two stages. First, we will look at how they were viewed by the right- and left-wing press before Sartre became a "critical fellow-traveler." Next, we will deal with their reactions after Sartre decided to become a fellow traveler. In respect to this decision it is not difficult to argue that his ultimate interests always lay in reaching the French working class because he viewed it as his ideal audience. For example, in *What Is Literature?* he proclaimed "that the fate of literature is bound up with that of the working class," but he added: "Unfortunately in our own country they are separated from us by an iron curtain" (Sartre 1965, p. 247). At that moment he is very much aware of the power that the Party had over its adherents and, as a consequence, Sartre felt that he had readers but no public (Sartre 1965, p. 259).

His attitude changed in the early 1950s when he was asked by the Communists to write a preface for *L'Affaire Henri Martin*, the latter had

A. van den Hoven (✉)
University of Windsor, Windsor, ON, Canada

© The Author(s) 2020
A. Betschart, J. Werner (eds.), *Sartre and the International Impact of Existentialism*,
https://doi.org/10.1007/978-3-030-38482-1_5

protested against the war in Indo-China and received a five-year jail sentence. When, in May 1952, Jacques Duclos was arrested on trumped-up charges during a demonstration against the arrival of General Ridgeway as head of S.H.A.P.E., he was "overwhelmed with anger." As a result, Sartre stated: When I came back hurriedly to Paris, I had to write or I would suffocate. I wrote day and night, the first part of *The Communist and Peace*. In this article Sartre did proclaim that his "agreement with the Communists [pertained to] precise and limited subjects, [and that he would be] reasoning on the basis of [his] principles and not theirs" (Sartre 1964, p. 168). However, as he had already made clear some years earlier in *What Is Literature?*, the Party was not at all interested in "critical fellow travelers" and as a result he often found himself in untenable positions. One could say that now he had indeed found a "public" but it would only remain accessible to him as long as he followed the dictates of the Party. Therefore, it will not surprise anyone to discover that his new role as a "critical fellow traveler" of the French Communist Party ended up having a significant impact on these two plays.

To begin with *The Respectful Prostitute*, it is set in the Southern United States and deals with the racial conflict. Sartre's plot was inspired by the French translation of Vladimir Pozner's work *The Dis-United States*. In the chapter entitled "The Rape," it provided a detailed account of the Scottsboro Boys case which involved nine young blacks who were falsely accused of raping two white prostitutes while all of them were riding the rails in search of work during the Depression. The two women's testimony resulted in the young blacks being condemned to death. Although the alleged gang rape occurred on March 25, 1931, it was not until 1938 that a pardon was considered and it was not until the 1940s that they were freed (Pozner 1938. See also Linder n.d.).

Sartre's protagonist Lizzie is also a prostitute but she is from New York and she takes a train heading to the South in the hope of meeting three or four "gentlemen of a certain age who [will] look after her" (Sartre 2005, p. 211). She occupies the train compartment together with two black men and some members of the white Southern élite, however unlikely it would have been that blacks be allowed to occupy the same compartment with a white woman at the time of the segregated South. One member of the white élite, Thomas, attempts to abuse Lizzie sexually and, next, shoots one of the black men dead while the other manages to save his life by jumping from the train upon its arrival at the station (Sartre 2005, pp. 216, 218). This black man will later turn up at Lizzie's apartment and ask her to protect him. Initially, she promises to do so but after being pressured by Fred (who is in fact Thomas's cousin), the man she spent the night with after her arrival in the Southern town, and Fred's father, the senator whose sister is the mother of Thomas, she is forcefully made to sign a document falsely accusing the black man, who had fled, of having assaulted her and, finally, she resigns herself and accepts to become Fred's mistress.

Sartre was not unfamiliar with the American race problem. After his first visit to the USA, he published a two-part series in *Le Figaro*, June 15 and 30, 1945, entitled: "Return from the U.S. What I Learned about the Black Problem" (Contat and Rybalka 1974, p. 123). And in *Notebooks for an Ethics*, the editor, Arlette Elkaïm-Sartre, included as Appendix II an incomplete study Sartre wrote in 1945 which is entitled "Revolutionary Violence" (Sartre 1992, pp. 561–574) about the oppression of blacks in the USA.

In his commentary on the play in *Théâtre complet*, Gilles Philippe claims that *The Respectful Prostitute* (together with *No Exit*) is perhaps Sartre's "most 'existentialist'" play. But to avoid "that the evening's bill would be filled with a play from another author," Sartre decided to "immediately write another one-act play as the second part of the program" (Sartre 2005, pp. 1355–1356).

To that we can add the comment made by such an astute author as André Gide who considered the play a masterpiece and compared it favorably to the excellent stories of *The Wall* (Gide 1951, p. 275. See also Betschart 2018). It is difficult to comprehend that anyone could consider this play as exemplary of existentialism. After all, as Elena Galtsova commented "Lizzie barely evolves" (*Dictionnaire* 2004, p. 304) and, in addition, the black man is consistently portrayed as fearful and submissive. In other words, neither can be viewed as characters capable of making drastic and meaningful choices. As well, from a North-American point of view, the work contains some definite weaknesses. Firstly, it is highly unlikely that a New York prostitute would want to travel South to find some "sugar daddies"; after all, they would have been plentiful in

New York, and both Fred and his father, Senator Clarke, strike one as bombastic caricatures of Southern whites. In fact, it is fairly obvious that this hastily written play was the result of Sartre inspiring himself very much by his readings of Pozner's work and of Faulkner's *Sartoris* and *The Sound and the Fury*, novels which he had reviewed in the late 1930s (Sartre 1947, pp. 7–13, 65–75).

And, in addition, we should stress that nothing is more puzzling than the fact that Sartre viewed the play as a "comédie bouffe" in the vein of Mozart's *Le Nozze di Figaro*, Puccini's "opera buffa" *Gianni Schicchi* and Verdi's *Falstaff*. Of course, he may well have intended to use the play as an example of how the fake value system of the American South resulted in the victimization of gullible white women and especially of blacks. Nevertheless, it is obvious that any North American familiar with racial violence that still characterizes the USA can hardly see anything "comic" in a play in which one black man is shot, another lynched, and a third one has to run for his life.

As was the case with *No Exit*, Sartre relied heavily on the tradition of the boulevard theater ("théâtre du boulevard"), a kind of theater with which he had been familiar since childhood. This type of popular Parisian theater exploits the "fourth wall" convention which means that the play's action occurs as if it took place behind an invisible wall and it is limited to a single room, in the case of *The Respectful Prostitute*, Lizzie's living room. This creates the impression on the audience that everything takes place in a realm that is very much distant from theirs. However, it also means that the dramatist has to concentrate the action in this very limited space and, as a result, we only get a glimpse of Lizzie's bedroom, her bathroom, and even the street because all the action revolves around Lizzie while the black man, Fred, and his father Senator Clarke enter the room to interact with Lizzie, encounter each other sporadically and then disappear into the bathroom or go back into the street. However, given that the action takes place in the segregated Deep South, it also introduces the highly improbable situation of a black man seeking refuge in one of the town's better neighborhoods and of a senator visiting a prostitute unannounced in her room.

Then again, since all crucial events occur in this unique and private space, the dramatist was sometimes required to make use of flashbacks. To give just one example, in the opening scene Lizzie is vacuuming the room and then explains to Fred that she had just had a bath "in order to cleanse herself"; and then she refers back to their nightly tryst and attempts to solicit some favorable comments from him about her sexual prowess. Fred does not want to talk about what happened in the bedroom because this Puritan wants to keep such activities hidden in the dark. Subsequently, he also attempts to choke her because like the black man she is a "devil." Somewhat later, the black man will remark to Lizzie that when white folks who don't know each other begin talking together a black man will likely soon be lynched, and there we hear an echo of Faulkner's *Sanctuary* in which Goodwin is lynched because the crowd takes Temple at her word and ignores that she is lying because she is intimidated by Popeye. This same novel is also the source for Fred relating to Lizzie how he emptied his revolver on a black man being lynched because he saw an image of Lizzie in the flames.

Let us now turn to the play's original conclusion which is worth discussing in greater detail because, after 1952, it caused Sartre significant difficulties. When Fred opens the bathroom door, the black man who Lizzie had been hiding emerges. Lizzie explains: "I hid him because people want to hurt him. Don't shoot, you know very well he is innocent." Nevertheless, Fred pulls out his revolver but the black man manages to knock Fred aside and flees. Fred runs after him. Lizzie goes toward the door and yells: "He is innocent! He is innocent!"

Then two shots are fired; this provokes Lizzie to grab her revolver and confront Fred. Since she believes that Fred has managed to kill the black man, she wants to avenge his death and aims her revolver at him while proclaiming: "now it is your turn." In order to extricate himself from this difficult situation, Fred launches into a long speech about his family's historical importance and concludes: "Do you dare pull the trigger on all of America?" However, these arguments do not suffice to convince Lizzie and she keeps pointing her revolver at him. Therefore, Fred decides to try and belittle her by insisting that she is a nobody who probably does not even know her own grandfather while, as he says: "I, I have the right to live; there are still lots of things to do, and the world is waiting for me." Then he orders her to give him her revolver and when she complies, he confesses that "[a]s far as the black man is concerned, he ran too fast: I missed him."

Now he puts his arms around her and outlines his plans for her. He will put her up in a beautiful house on a hill with a park where she can take her walks but he will not let her go beyond the gate because he wants to keep her for himself. He will visit her three times a week and she will have black servants and be given lots of money but, in return, she will "have to give in to all [his] whims." The play concludes by him demanding Lizzie if "she really enjoyed herself" and Lizzie answering (*wearily*): Yes, it's true.

> Fred, (*tapping her on the cheek*): All right, then everything is back in order. (*After a moment.*) My name is Fred. (Sartre 2005, pp. 234–235)

Initially, the play was criticized by both right and left-wing critics. In the November 19, 1946, issue of *Le Spectateur*, Thierry Maulnier proclaimed that Sartre had depicted the "Americans with the face of the most repulsive ferocity, imposture and hypocrisy" and had there been "an American [...] in the theater, I would not have dared to look at him" (Contat and Rybalka 1974, p. 138). Sartre defended himself by insisting that he was not anti-American and that a "writer's duty [was] to denounce injustice everywhere. And this was especially the case if he love[d] the country which lets this injustice happen" (Contat and Rybalka 1974, p. 139). In *Force of Circumstances*, Simone de Beauvoir discussed the reaction of the left-wing press: "The Communists thought it a pity Sartre had shown his public a Negro trembling with fear and respect, instead of a real fighter" (Beauvoir 1968, p. 123). Sartre defended himself against this charge by stressing the fact that he considered that presently it was impossible to solve "the color problem in the U.S.A." (Contat and Rybalka 1974, p. 139).

We have already alluded to the play's lack of verisimilitude and that certainly pertains to the role the black man is made to play. We have also stressed the fact that it was very much influenced by the "boulevard theater," and that for his inspiration Sartre had been quite dependent on his various sources. But, nevertheless, below the surface, the play can also be seen as an analysis of the relationship between sexuality and violence in a society in which the white members of a patriarchal and feudal society dominate. In this world, blacks function as outsiders upon whom violence can be unleashed whenever whites feel impelled to practice it. It can also be said that they are viewed in a way similar to the manner in which Jews are depicted in *Anti-Semite and Jew*. Both are treated as being beyond the pale.

And, like blacks, women such as Lizzie are considered chattel; Lizzie will have to live by Fred's whims just like her black servants who, in turn, will at all times be treated as subservient. But then again, both prostitutes and blacks are also considered "diabolical"; Fred is tempted to strangle Lizzie whenever he sees her in daylight and she expresses herself in honest but critical terms about his mother while blacks can be lynched at will.

However, when Sartre changed position in the 1950s and drew closer to the Communist Party, the tenor of the play's ending also underwent a change. In 1952 Sartre gave his friend Marcel Pagliero permission to make a film out of the play and allowed him to give its ending an optimistic tone. In 1954 he also agreed to have the play produced in Moscow and once again he permitted the ending to be changed so that it ended on a positive note. In addition, the title was changed to *Lizzie Mackay*, which was more acceptable than the original title to the puritan Soviet regime.

In an interview he gave to *Libération*, July 16, 1954, Sartre justified the new endings which he claimed to have written by stating that his Moscow audience would have difficulty accepting that "the girl could have a glimmer of awareness and then be completely taken in" by the senator and his son. In *The Observer*, June 25, 1961, he justified himself once again but this time he focused on the young workers who, he claimed, had been discouraged to see the play end sadly and therefore he now realized that "those who hang onto life the best they can need to have hope." (Contat and Rybalka 1974, p. 140)

However, as Alfred Betschart points out[1] (and I translate):

Indeed, the movie and the Soviet version do end on a positive note but there is an essential difference between the two versions. In the movie version Lizzie and the black man succeed in fleeing in a police car. In this case, the police and therefore the functions of the state are treated as neu-

---

[1] Betschart (2018, pp. 7–8). I would like to thank Alfred Betschart for kindly sharing this article with me.

tral territory and they protect them from the masses who are obsessed with lynching. In the Soviet version Lizzie herself goes to the police because she bore false witness. This interpretation is very much in line with the Stalinist conception of the role of the state which requires that enemies of the people and spies must be denounced, even if the person is denouncing herself.

And he adds: "another difference concerns the treatment of sexuality and prostitution. ... Since 1929 ... in the U.S.S.R. [p]rostitution fits under the category of 'parasitic life styles.'" As a result, its title was changed from *The Respectful Prostitute* to that of *Lizzie MacKay*. As well, references to physical attributes were softened and Lizzie did not "enjoy" Fred; she liked him. And obviously under the Communist system a house can only be rented.

Let us quote the last lines of the film and the Moscow play version from Betschart's article to illustrate these changes. In the film when Fred discovers the black man in the bathroom, he yells out through the window to the waiting crowd: "He is here, people! He is here!" Lizzie picks up the revolver and tells Fred: "Set him free and be quiet!" Sirens are heard again. Fred: "You won't do that!" Lizzie: "Look at me! (Coolly). I didn't sleep with him, Fred. I only wanted to help him. But you louse, you lost. You really have lost me." Fred: "Lizzie ...."

> Lizzie (*to the black man*): "In the street there are cars. Let's go down!"
> *Lizzie and the black man show up on the street and run towards the police car, pursued by the crowd.*
> Lizzie yells: "He hasn't done anything. ... He is innocent. ... He is innocent."
> *They get into the police car which drives away. Lizzie hesitates, takes the black man's hand and smiles at him.*
> *Fred has also left the house and talks to an unknown person.*
> That person: "What kind of girl is that? She is crazy ...."
> Fred: "She's a whore."

Of course, the action in this final scene is extremely unlikely given that not too long before that the police had been colluding with Fred and had threatened to arrest Lizzie on the grounds that she had "accepted" money from Fred and therefore could be jailed as a prostitute!

In the Moscow play's final scene, after the black man manages to flee from the house and Fred, while pursuing him, aims two shots at him and then returns to Lizzie' room, she aims her revolver at him. Fred begs her not to shoot; he has a mother and offers to rent a house on the hill for her. Next, Fred attempts to persuade her of his family's importance and then, finally, admits that he did not shoot the black man. Lizzie retorts:

"Are you lying? He is alive?" Fred replies: "Please, Lizzie, he ran away!"
In turn Lizzie begins to ponder, walks back and forth, goes to the telephone, dials a number. She holds the phone in the left hand and the revolver in the right one while Fred looks on. "Hello! Hello! Is this the police?"
Fred (*in shock*): "What are you doing?"
Lizzie: "Hello? Is this the police? This is Lizzie MacKay. Yes, yes. This is me. I want to make an important statement."
Lizzie (*to Fred in a loud voice so that Fred will hear her*): "Now listen Mr. Clarke. Hello. Here is Lizzie MacKay! Today I bore false witness. Senator Clarke forced me to do so. He treated me like a piece of dirt." (*To Fred:*) "Don't shake, don't shake so much. It makes me sick to see you like that."
Fred: "You have gone completely crazy. When you give false witness, you will be the first to go to jail."
Lizzie (*to Fred, speaking loudly*): "Don't worry about me Mr. Clarke!" (*And into the speaker*). "Yes, please come and arrest me! But I swear that Senator Clarke forced me to do so. The black man is innocent. And the Clarke's, they are all so ...."
At the same time Fred, totally upset, is seen leaving the room.

The result is an odd mixture indeed. A play about the American South, written by a French playwright, whose uplifting ending now conforms to Soviet laws and its puritan mores.

Sartre's play *Dirty Hands*, a "why-did-he-do-it?" rather than a "who-done-it?" is a masterful and intricate portrayal of a young man's inability to deal with the cynical twists and turns of the Communist Party's *Realpolitik*. It deals with a reality that the higher echelons of the Party had been familiar with for a long time but which, nevertheless, had always remained an "unspoken" truth. The Party insiders knew that any and all policies could be changed at any moment depending on the orders received from the Kremlin and its almighty leader. Yet the Party's official stance was always proclaimed as invariable and sacred and consisted of such "eternal verities" as (1) the necessary overthrow of the capitalist system; (2) the unrelenting defense of the working class; and (3) the uncompromising struggle for the revolution to come. The contortions that the Communist Party's leadership had to perform to make these "eternal verities" comply with the arbitrary diktats from Moscow are at the heart of the play. Hugo ultimately falls victim to its latest change in policy after he has spent two years in jail for having assassinated Hoederer who the Party, unbeknownst to him, has since transformed into a posthumous hero.

But, nevertheless, this is not a political tract but a marvelous play in which contingencies and propitious moments combine with political opportunism to create a dramatic universe in which tensions remain high until the last moment. In addition, the play masterfully exploits such cinematic techniques as flashbacks and "flashforwards" that permit the dramatist to play with temporality and allow him to move the action back and forth in time, deal with the past as an unfolding present, and simultaneously leave the door open to the future. As well, the clever use of props (furniture, radio, revolver), the use of lighting—to signal a change from past to present—and the use of devices borrowed from popular theater, such as the surprise ending, illustrate the twists and turns of events in dramatic fashion. Nevertheless, it remains Sartre's most controversial play and, in a sense, one could "blame" Sartre himself. After all, in his 1944 lecture "On Dramatic Style," he had discussed the importance in a play of "the concept of distancing" and, as well, he had stressed that it was essential to "present the characters far away in time" (Sartre 1976, p. 15). However, the action of *Dirty Hands* is set in 1943 while it was first performed in 1948 when the tensions between Moscow and Washington were rapidly rising.

Consequently, and not surprisingly, the critics gave the play a political interpretation even before Sartre had become a "critical fellow-traveler." It was also Sartre's most successful play; the bourgeois audience appreciated its ostensibly anti-Communist theme and it identified eagerly with the young idealistic Hugo. It was performed at the Théâtre Antoine from April 2, 1948, until September 20, 1949, and was often performed in roadshows (Contat and Rybalka 1974, pp. 185–186).

Since Hugo is on the stage throughout the play and the long flashback retells his story up until the very moment he shoots Hoederer, it is of course not surprising that the audience identified with him. Additionally, even though his final decision not to compromise may strike one as the decision of an immature and inflexible young man; on the other hand, his willingness to go to his death in an attempt to preserve both his and Hoederer's principles makes him seem a martyr in contrast to the Party's ultimately strategic but cynical decision to submit itself once more to the orders of Moscow and change course once again.

And, of course, just like the right-wing press, the Communists were not capable either of appreciating Sartre's interplay between politics and principles. In the April 7, 1948, issue of *L'Humanité*, Guy Leclerc declared that "Sartre ha[d] dirty hands" and on top of that he considered him a "nauseating writer, scandal-mongering playwright, and third-rate demagogue." In December 1948, the Soviets also began to agitate against the play. They tried to persuade "the authorities in Helsinki to stop the performance of *Dirty Hands*," because they viewed it as "propaganda hostile to the U.S.S.R." The February 10, 1949, *Lettres françaises* published a similar attack by Ilya Ehrenburg (Contat and Rybalka 1974, pp. 187, 190).

However, Ehrenburg had already attacked Sartre earlier when *The Victors* came out. In *Force of Circumstance* Simone de Beauvoir describes what happened when Sartre first met Ilya Ehrenburg. The latter "reproached him bitterly" for the manner in which he had portrayed the members of the Resistance and accused Sartre of having "depicted them as cowards and traitors." When Sartre asked if he had actually read the play, he confessed that he "had merely skimmed through the first scene or two" (Beauvoir 1968, p. 123) but he stood by his first impressions!

Clearly, however, Sartre was quite willing to forgive because, years later, he and Ehrenberg became good friends. As he states in *It Is Right to Rebel* when discussing the Daniel and Sinyavsky trial with Philippe Gavi and Pierre Victor: "We in the West judged as individuals, and in the East they at all times represented their governments or their Party. ... We understood that their position was difficult; especially for me who had become towards the end a good friend of Ilya Ehrenburg's" (Sartre et al. 2018, p. 43).

However, something quite different occurred in the United States. To Sartre's dismay his publisher Louis Nagel had allowed a New York company to adapt his play under the title *Red Gloves* and as Sartre stated in an interview with J.-P. Vernet published in *Combat*, November 27–28, 1948: "They are Performing One of my Plays in America in a Version I have never Read" (Contat and Rybalka 1974, p. 189).

The changes in the actors' typescript of *Red Gloves* are indeed quite drastic. Instead of seven tableaux, this version features a Prologue, three acts, and an Epilogue. The names of several characters have been changed: Olga becomes Johanna; the two guards, George and Slick, are now called Kirtz and Marochek; other characters have been added, to wit, Loutec and Munster; and many parts of the plot and the dialogue have been modified. For example, Jessica hides the small revolver she had found in Hugo's bag (and not in his suitcase) as soon as she begins to unpack rather than at the moment when the guards enter their room to search it. But the biggest changes apply to the character of Hoederer, and, apparently, these changes had been made to satisfy the demands of the actor Charles Boyer who insisted on a starring role. Here are his comments to Hugo about the need to search the room:

> The matter of searching your room is not important. I'm sure you have nothing to hide. It's the idea behind the search—that's it, that's what we must observe. We are a tiny minority, hounded and abused and misunderstood. On all sides men distrust us because they do not want to know what we are. Everywhere we are stripped and questioned and searched. Perhaps this is good. There are so few of us; we are precious. We have to keep ourselves so clean, we have to be so pure and fresh. We are like apples in a barrel. Every so often we must empty them and look them over to pick out the ones that have a worm or have rotted. So that we will not taint the others. Yes, we must even search ourselves. … Barine, are you listening to me?
> Hugo: Yes—yes. Yes, of course.
> (As guards reach for the bag in which [Jessica hid] gun ….)[2]

---

[2] Taradash (1948, 1–19). I would like to thank Dennis Gilbert for locating the typescript and University of Windsor Librarian Maureen Souchuk for obtaining a copy of this typescript. The adaptation of *Dirty Hands* by Daniel Taradash and entitled *Red Gloves* can be found in The New York Public Library. The play opened on Broadway in December 1948.

In the original version Hoederer never spoke in laudatory terms about purity; on the contrary, he insisted that in politics "one must get one's hands dirty." And, in fact, in Act II he does indeed bring up the matter of political assassination and states: "In principle, I don't object to [it]." However, the remarks that follow differ significantly from those in the original:

> In certain circumstances it is almost inevitable. If your head is to be in the line of a bullet, there is no such thing as security. It will happen anywhere—a room, a garden, a street, even the theatre. You remember the American President, Lincoln? There he sat in a stage box in a rocking chair, watching the farce. What could be more deliciously innocent? And then. ... A moment in history. ... It always seems arranged that way. His head had to be in the line of the bullet. ... It is in the nature of power to be envied, misunderstood, stalked and hunted down, even by your own breed. (Taradash 1948, II, 16)

Rather than justifying assassination on political grounds, this Hoederer sees it as the fate that befalls all political leaders.

From a structural point of view the biggest flaw is that Hugo's reasons for assassinating Hoederer remain vague while, on the other hand, the portrayal of Jessica is much more convincing especially when she tries to persuade him not kill Hoederer.

The scene in which Hugo ends up shooting Hoederer has also been changed drastically. Hugo is convinced that Jessica left him the night before in order to spend the night with Hoederer. She is unable to convince Hugo that this was not the case and when Hoederer asks him to think before he acts he answers repeatedly: "I have stopped thinking." In a very emotional scene, the three struggle desperately but Hugo does manage to pull the trigger again and again. While dying Hoederer exclaims: "I slept with his wife. Waste—waste—and all that for a woman." And the stage instructions note: "*He dies. Jessica is sobbing. Hugo noticing the marks Jessica has left on his hands, rubs them distractedly*" (Taradash 1948, III, 19).

The Epilogue also contains drastic changes. After Johanna explains that the Party has changed policies on the orders of Moscow, Hugo exclaims: "Oh my God! It's too funny," and Johanna replies: "You are signing your own death warrant." The stage directions indicate: "*During the first part of next speech, Johanna raises the curtain at the window*" to signal to Munster, Reich, and Loutec to come in and "take care" of Hugo. Now Hugo explains his own position: "No, I'm already dead. You said so yourself. Hugo Barine must be eliminated." Then he proffers the same arguments as did the original Hugo but concludes: "As for the rest I am nothing but a plain murderer." The three guards having entered, Munster offers "a toast to Barine," but instead it is Hugo who offers a toast to them:

> Here's to you Johanna and you Munster, Reich, Loutec. All of you. You are the tough ones, the cold-blooded ones, I envy you all, I admire you but now it is all clear to me. We are not the same kind. I know what you're here for, and I shall go with you.

Johanna replies: "Take him, take him away." And Hugo rejoins: "Thank you gentlemen, I am ready." And the "*Curtain*" falls (Taradash 1948, E, 7).

It is not indicated what happens next to Hugo and, consequently, the ending lacks all the drama of the original. In addition, Hugo's remarks indicate that he sees himself not as a quixotic desperado but as a pathetic guilty murderer.

Of course, Sartre's attitude toward *Dirty Hands* changed after he became a "critical fellow-traveler of the Communist Party." He now realized that "his work [was being] used as a cold war weapon" (Contat and Rybalka 1974, p. 190). Of course, Sartre should not have been surprised by this fact since the play deals with politics and Hugo sacrifices his life in protest against the latest twist in the directions Moscow gave to the Party. And neither should he have been surprised that the anti-Communist right used the play as a propaganda tool against the "Machiavellian Stalinists?" However, as a result he decided to authorize the production of the play only in those countries where the local Communist Party agreed to have it performed. Hence it was banned in several countries such as Spain, Greece, and Indochina which at that time was still a French colony. Neither would he allow it to be performed in Vienna because he felt that it would be used as a weapon of propaganda during the Peace Congress. When in 1954 the Vienna Volkstheater decided to perform the play, Sartre gave a press conference there to denounce the performance. At that moment he declared that he did not disown the play but he objected to it being used as a political weapon and that in a time when tensions were running high, he did not think it would enhance the cause for peace (Contat and Rybalka 1974, pp. 190–191).

Clearly, Sartre's problematic stance was the direct result of his decision to commit himself and, in spite of the fact that he intended to maintain a "critical attitude," it illustrates clearly the risks that a writer runs when he attempts to align himself with a totalitarian regime.

Of course, Sartre never claimed that he "disowned" *Dirty Hands* but, in an article published in *Combat*, October 1–November 1, 1953, when asked "if he would rewrite it today" he added the following clarification: *No, I don't disown* Dirty Hands *and I am far from being sorry about the play. It expressed a position which was perfectly legitimate in 1948*" (Contat and Rybalka 1974, p. 286).

Sartre seems to have forgotten that in 1952 he had written an optimistic ending for the film version Marcel Pagliero's *The Respectful Prostitute* and we have also noted that two years later, in 1954, he wrote an optimistic ending for the Moscow play version. As well, he now limits the legitimacy of the positions expressed in *Dirty Hands* to the year it first appeared, that is 1948. In conclusion, politicians on the right or the left care little about the artistic value of a literary work but when a writer enters into their domain, they do not hesitate to use all the means at their disposal to call the author back to order. Sartre found that out before 1952 and he did again after that point in time.

References

de Beauvoir, Simone. 1968. *The Force of Circumstances*. Harmondsworth, Middlesex, UK: Penguin Books.

Betschart, Alfred. 2018. *Die ehrbare Dirne. Drei Versionen der 5. Szene im Zweiten Bild*. Accessed June 26, 2019. http://www.sartre.ch/Die%20ehrbare%20Dirne.pdf.

Contat, Michel, and Michel Rybalka. 1974. *The Writings of Jean-Paul Sartre, I, A Bibliographical Life*. Translated by Richard McCleary. Evanston, IL: Northwestern University Press.

Dictionnaire Sartre. 2004. Edited by François Noudelmann and Gilles Philippe. Paris: Honoré Champion.

Gide, André. 1951. *Journals. 1939–1949, 4.* Translated by Justin O'Brien. New York: Alfred A. Knopf.

Linder, Douglas O. n.d. *The Trials of "The Scottsboro Boys".* Accessed October 13, 2019. http://law2.umkc.edu/faculty/projects/FTrials/scottsboro/SB_acct.html.

Pozner, Vladimir. 1938. *Les Etats-Désunis.* Paris: Denoël.

Sartre, Jean-Paul. 1947. *Situations, I, Essais critiques.* Paris: Gallimard.

———. 1964. *Situations, VI.* Paris: Gallimard.

———. 1965. *What is Literature?* New York: Harper & Row.

———. 1976. *Sartre on Theater.* Edited by Michel Contat and Michel Rybalka. New York: Pantheon Books.

———. 1992. *Notebooks for an Ethics.* Translated by David Pellauer. Chicago: The University of Chicago Press.

———. 2005. *Théâtre complet.* Paris: Gallimard.

Sartre, Jean-Paul et al. 2018. *It Is Right to Rebel.* Translated by Adrian van den Hoven and Basil Kingstone. London and New York: Routledge.

Taradash, Daniel. 1948. *Red Gloves.* Manuscript in The New York Public Library.

Part II

Europe Outside France

6

Guéhenno in Gehenna. The English and German Translations of *La nausée*

Norbert Bachleitner

The Genesis of the Two English and German Editions

In a review of the first English translation of *La nausée* (*Nausea*) in *The New York Times*, Vladimir Nabokov lists some serious errors the translator committed (Nabokov 1949). The most curious example concerns the scene in which the central character, the 'Autodidacte', mentions a French writer who is dear to him as a major representative of humanism. In Jean-Paul Sartre's text, this author appears as "ce pauvre Guéhenno": "Il [l'Autodidacte] a quitté sans s'en apercevoir l'amour des hommes en Christ; il hoche la tête et, par un curieux phénomène de mimétisme, il ressemble à ce pauvre Guéhenno" (Sartre 1981a, p. 143). In the first English translation, we read "he resembles this poor man of Gehenna"

N. Bachleitner (✉)
Abteilung für Vergleichende Literaturwissenschaft, Institut für Europäische und Vergleichende Sprach- und Literaturwissenschaft, Universität Wien, Vienna, Austria
e-mail: norbert.bachleitner@univie.ac.at

© The Author(s) 2020
A. Betschart, J. Werner (eds.), *Sartre and the International Impact of Existentialism*,
https://doi.org/10.1007/978-3-030-38482-1_6

(Sartre 2013, p. 121): the translator interprets the phrase as an attribute to Jesus Christ who is mentioned in the previous sentence. But, as is common knowledge, Jesus Christ was not born in Gehenna, a valley near Jerusalem, nor is there any reason to associate him with hell (this is the usual connotation of the place's name, since the valley leads into the desert). Such a misleading error that radically distorts the meaning of the source text raises questions as to how a novel as important in literary history as *La nausée* was actually translated, who did it, how it came about, and what was its impact. In this article, we will try to answer these questions for the two English and the two German translations of the novel.

The first French edition of *La nausée* appeared in 1938. *La nausée* was not only Sartre's first novel, which due to its success paved the way for his career as a writer, but may be regarded—together with *L'être et le néant* (*Being and Nothingness*)—as a first summa of his philosophy. Michel Contat and Michel Rybalka, the editors of the Pléiade edition of Sartre's literary prose, consider it to be "l'œuvre fondatrice sur laquelle reposent tous les textes qui ont suivi—ou qu'en tout cas aucun n'a jamais démentie (...)" (Sartre 1981a, p. 1668) (the founding work which forms the base for all following texts—at least this has never been denied). Influenced not only by writers such as John Dos Passos, William Faulkner, Ernest Hemingway, Marcel Proust, Louis-Ferdinand Céline, and Franz Kafka, but also by Edmund Husserl's and Martin Heidegger's philosophy, the novel represents a perfect fusion of literature and philosophy. Representing a severe attack on the bourgeoisie and its values and norms, the book also describes the revelation of the truth about existence.[1] The plethora of references and the stylistic complexity render the translation of *La nausée* particularly difficult.

In 1949, two parallel editions of the novel, which we will analyze in the course of this article, appeared, namely, *The Diary of Antoine Roquentin* (London: John Lehmann; Sartre 1949a), and the same translation entitled *Nausea* in an edition for the USA (Norfolk, Connecticut: New Directions).[2] This translation was reprinted in 1961 by the publishing

---

[1] Cf. Vincent von Wroblewsky's afterword to Jean-Paul Sartre (1985).

[2] Sartre (1949b). The copyright page of the modern edition of this translation (Sartre 2013), contrary to most library catalogue entries, dates the first American edition to have appeared in 1952.

house of Hamish Hamilton in London, and by New Directions in New York in 1959, 1964, 1969, and so forth—the American edition is still available. A new translation, produced by Robert Baldick, appeared in 1965 with Penguin Books, was frequently reprinted, and is also still available today (Sartre 1965).

John Lehmann, the first publisher of the English *Nausea*, was educated at Trinity College, Cambridge, and went to Vienna as a journalist in the early 1930s, in order to serve as a political correspondent for the British government. He specialized in reports about the exploits of the socialist city government in the so-called Red Vienna and was impressed by Soviet Communism. His political commitment played an important role in his literary selection: in the mid-30s, he co-edited an anthology entitled *Poems for Spain* and founded the important book series "New Writing" that presented modern literature, including works by Christopher Isherwood, George Orwell, Federico García Lorca, Sartre, and many others (cf. Whitehead 1990). Having abandoned cooperation with Virginia and Leonard Woolf at Hogarth Press, he founded his own publishing house in 1946. He traveled extensively and may have met Sartre and/or the translator Lloyd Alexander in Paris, although there is no evidence of this.[3]

The American edition of *La nausée* was published by New Directions in Norfolk, Connecticut. The publishing house was directed by James Laughlin, originally a poet, who, from 1944—similar to John Lehmann—edited a book series entitled "New Classics Library" in which he (re-)published modernists such as Henry James, William Faulkner, F. Scott Fitzgerald, E. E. Cummings, Henry Miller, Gertrude Stein, Ezra Pound, William Carlos Williams, and Federico García Lorca (Dubinsky 2011).

The reception of the English *Nausea* seems to have been rather lukewarm. Many critics considered Sartre's predilection for conveying philosophical and political messages in his literary works to be detrimental to their aesthetics. Thus, Nabokov, in his review of the translation in *The New York Times*, makes fun of the "fashionable brand of cafe philosophy" that emerges from the novel. As already indicated, he finds blunders in

---

[3] Adrian Wright (Wright 1998, p. 187) writes laconically: "From Europe he had brought Sartre's *Diary of Antoine Roquentin* (...)".

the translation and deems the story to be unlikely, irrelevant, and—above all—badly written.

> When an author inflicts his idle and arbitrary philosophic fancy on a help-less person whom he has invented for that purpose, a lot of talent is needed to have the trick work. One has no special quarrel with Roquentin when he decides that the world exists. But the task to make the world exist as a work of art, was beyond Sartre's powers. (Nabokov 1949)

It may be worth mentioning that the New Directions publication series was used for pro-US propaganda in Europe, which was based on the conviction that the formal experiments of Modernism were a typical expression of a free society (see Barnhisel 2015).

Lloyd Alexander was in his early 20s when he translated *La nausée*. During the war, he had been stationed in Paris as an army member where he became acquainted with French language and literature. After the war, he attended the University of Paris. As a consequence of this French expe-rience, he also translated—in addition to Sartre—Paul Éluard (*Selected Writings*, 1952). The translation of Sartre's stylistically complex prose was his first literary publication, though he later made a name for himself as a prolific and successful author of fantasy novels and children and young adult's literature (including *The Chronicles of Prydain* and the *Westmark trilogy*) (Tunnell and Jacobs 2007, pp. 40–42).

Quite contrary to Alexander, Robert Baldick, who produced the new translation of *La nausée* which appeared in 1965, was already an accom-plished scholar of French literature and joint editor of the "Penguin Classics" series when he translated Sartre's novel. He wrote biographies of Joris-Karl Huysmans, Henry Murger, and the brothers Goncourt, and translated works by authors such as François-René de Chateaubriand, Gustave Flaubert, Joris-Karl Huysmans, Jules Verne, Henri Barbusse, and Georges Simenon.

If we turn to Germany and Austria, we have to take into account that the National Socialist rule, the Second World War, and its immediate aftermath were obviously not favorable times for the reception of Sartre's works. Compared to the English-speaking areas, only a few specialists of foreign literature and philosophy had any information on Sartre before the late 1940s. Only then did translations of his works into German begin to be published, and amongst them was the first German *La nausée* published by Rowohlt, the main distributor of Sartre's works in the German language.

Already before the war, Rowohlt was counted amongst the most active producers of books. After the war, the publishing house continued its extensive literary program and even set new standards with its famous popular paperback series "Rowohlts Rotationsromane" (1946–1949), which was the first of its kind in German publishing history. The series presented modern world literature from German (such as Anna Seghers, Kurt Tucholsky, and Erich Kästner) and foreign authors (such as Ernest Hemingway, John Steinbeck, William Faulkner, Sinclair Lewis, Jack London, Graham Greene, Joseph Conrad, Antoine de Saint-Exupéry, and Alain-Fournier). Rowohlt's bias toward foreign literature was in accord with the cultural policy of the occupying forces—the famous reeducation program. Rowohlt was the only German publisher who managed to get established in all four occupation zones, maintaining branches in Stuttgart (American), Hamburg (British), Berlin (Soviet), and Baden-Baden (French). In order to get a license in the French zone, Rowohlt promised in 1948 to publish at least two French authors in every number of the series "story. Erzähler des Auslands" (story. Narrators from abroad). Thus, Sartre's German popularity from the late 1940s onward is at least partly a result of the cultural politics of these years, or, to put it more bluntly, a consequence of pressure from the allied forces (see Ziegler 1997; Oels 2013).

The first German translation of *La nausée* was entitled *Der Ekel* and translated by Heinrich Wallfisch (Sartre 1949c). Since Rowohlt habitually counted the number of copies printed in each new print-run, we are able to ascertain the number of copies of *La nausée* produced over the following decades. Thus, between 1949 and 1952, only 1400 copies were printed, while in 1968, a total of 100,000 copies had been produced, in 1975, a total of 203,000, and in 1981, a total of 275,000. In 1981, the last copies of Wallfisch's text were printed. Rowohlt decided that 30 years after the first edition, a new translation was needed. It was produced by Uli Aumüller (Sartre 1981b) and based on the *Œuvres romanesques* edited by Contat and Rybalka in the "Pléiade" series in the same year. The output of approximately 130,000 copies per decade remained stable in the 1980s, but was reduced to some 50,000 in the 1990s: in 1990, a total of 409,000 copies had been printed, and in 2000, a total of 472,000. From this time onward, the output of the reprints slowed down to 5000 and even 2000 per year. We lack exact figures for the last two decades, but may still roughly estimate that the number of copies printed in the twenty-first century was approximately 30,000 to 40,000.

Unfortunately, information about Heinrich Wallfisch, the translator of Rowohlt's 1949 German edition, is extremely scarce; all we know is that he translated Sartre's early stories *Le mur* (*The Wall*, 1950, together with Hans Reisiger) and *L'enfance d'un chef* (*The Childhood of a Leader*, 1957), and Simone de Beauvoir's travel diary *L'Amérique au jour le jour* (*America Day by Day*, 1957). On the other hand, Uli Aumüller is a very productive professional translator who, in acknowledgment of her work, received the Paul Celan award. She holds a degree in Romance Studies and has produced translations of French and American literature, notably of works by Sartre, Albert Camus, Beauvoir, Milan Kundera, Jean Giono, Emmanuel Bove, Daniel Pennac, Jeffrey Eugenides, Toni Morrison, and Siri Hustvedt.

Comparing the Four Translations

Heinrich Wallfisch's version of 1949 bears many marks of the particular conditions in the literary market in the years after the war. The lack of printing paper and capital for purchasing books made publishers address the widest possible audience. In the case of the translation of *La nausée*, an explicative mode of translation was chosen, as Wallfisch obviously did not think that his readers were able to understand foreign words.[4] One can easily identify a remnant of Nazi ideology in this urge to avoid foreign words, which had virtually become translators' second nature (Wroblewsky n.d.).

---

[4] The same is true of the translation of Sartre's philosophical writing; see Vincent von Wroblewsky, "Traduire Sartre en allemand" (unpublished manuscript, read in 2005 at the Colloque de Cérisy "Jean-Paul Sartre: écriture et engagement").

Foreign terms that Wallfisch does not dare to leave untranslated include the word "aphrodisiaques" (42)[5]: in his text, the photographs stimulating Roquentin's memory serve as "Aufpulverungsmittel" (50), whereas the word is offered in its original ancient Greek as "Aphrodisiaka" (56) by Aumüller. The same applies to the word "extase" (155), which is translated in an explicative manner by Wallfisch ("Verzückung", 175), but transferred into the German text in its original form of a foreign word by Aumüller ("Extase", 203). To a lesser degree, Lloyd Alexander's 1949 English version shows the same impetus to explain foreign words: he renders the Autodidacte as "Self-Taught Man" (4), whereas this character simply remains an "Autodidact" (13) in Baldick's modern version.

In another passage taken from the beginning of the novel, Roquentin complains that he feels full of lymph or warm milk ("Il me semblait que j'étais rempli de lymphe ou de lait tiède", 9). Wallfisch decides on the phrase: "Ich hatte das Gefühl voller Pflanzensaft (...) zu sein" (14). In the case of "lymph", it is of course possible to think of vegetal fluids, but it seems certain that Sartre is referring here to human biology: let us briefly remind ourselves that "lymph" is a central concept in *La nausée*. In their notes on the "Pléiade" edition, Contat and Rybalka remind us that lymph, "comme tous les liquides organiques, est la métaphore privilégiée de la Contingence" (Sartre 1981a, p. 1729) (like all organic liquids is the main metaphor for contingency). Lymph counts amongst the liquids also characterized as "visqueux" (viscous) by Sartre; such liquids are, in particular, connected with the feeling or consciousness of existence (see Idt 1971, p. 42; Sartre 1981a, p. 1749). In any case, the term "Pflanzensaft" makes the passage sound rather burlesque. It goes almost without saying that Aumüller uses "Lymphe" (15) here, and so do Alexander (5) and Baldick (14) in their English versions.

Wallfisch's strategy, that recommends translating and "nationalising" as much as possible, also applies to the treatment of culturally specific realia such as proper names. Thus, he renders the name of Roquentin's favorite bistro "Rendez-vous des chéminots" (6) as "Eisenbahnerstübchen" (10). By explaining the semantics through the insertion of the fictitious

---

[5] In the following references, page numbers of the translations cited are included in brackets in the main text.

name of a similar pub in a German town, he pays the price of losing all local flavor. The name suggests a setting in Bremerhaven or any other comparable German town rather than Le Havre. Egon Vietta, a very accomplished translator who rendered a short extract from *La nausée* for the weekly *Die Zeit* in 1946, also chose to "nationalise" the bistro by calling it "Treffpunkt der Eisenbahner" (Sartre 1946). We may add that Alexander follows Wallfisch, at least half-way, by creating a hybrid "Railwaymen's Rendezvous" (2), which is very unlikely to have existed anywhere in an English- or French-speaking environment.

We observe an even more decisive exchange in the passage mentioning "le jeune dessinateur"—a young "designer" (Alexander, 45) or "draughtsman" (Baldick, 70)—looking like a "premier communiant" (57). Whereas Aumüller calls him "Erstkommunikant" (75–76) and the English translators refer to the First Communion, Wallfisch transfers the scene to a Protestant milieu by inserting a "Konfirmand" (67). It seems undisputable that the Catholic education and background is important for Roquentin's mental structure, and should, therefore, not be simply excluded in the translation.

The autodidact famously accumulates random knowledge by perusing the books in the city library in alphabetical order. The titles mentioned by Sartre show that this kind of knowledge is superfluous and useless. Pedantic titles such as *La Tourbe et les tourbières* and *Hitopadésa ou l'Instruction utile* (37), therefore, are telling, especially the second one: a translation from the Sanskrit, ironically promising useful instruction. In this case, Aumüller's decision to leave the French titles untranslated seems doubtful. Wallfisch deems it necessary to explain (*Torf und Moore* and *Hitopadèsa [!] oder der nutzbringende Unterricht*, 46), as do Alexander (*Peat-Mosses and Where to Find Them* and *Hitopadesa, or, Useful Instruction*, 29) and Baldick (*Peat and Peateries* and *Hitopadesa or Useful Instruction*, 48).

A further feature that distinguishes the early from the later translations is the loosening of taboos regarding the sexual vocabulary. Where Sartre uses the vulgar term "baiser" (24), Wallfisch exchanges it for the synecdoche "mit der Wirtin ins Bett zu gehen" (31) or the formula permitted in every salon "schlafen mit" (83). Alexander again joins Wallfisch by using the phrase "make love" (18), or even substituting it by a chaste "kiss" (59). Aumüller ("vögeln", 34) and Baldick ("fuck", 33) do not hesitate to employ the modern colloquial forms which might still be considered vulgar by a part of the readership. The male "sexe" (25) is rendered adequately by "Glied" (31), the feminine sex by the euphemism "Scham" (83) in Wallfisch's text. Alexander again joins the early German translator with a vague "in the sexual parts" (18), whereas Baldick decides for the more vulgar version "in my prick" (33), and Aumüller for "Genitalien" (34). During his surrealist daydream on the hill, Roquentin imagines "une forêt de verges bruissantes (...) avec de grosses couilles" (188): "a forest of rustling pricks (...) with big testicles" (226) in Baldick's translation. Wallfisch once again uses a sober, stylistically unspecific terminology: "in einem Walde von rauschenden männlichen Gliedern (...) mit dicken (...) Hoden" (211). Alexander censors the passage, entirely removing the genital character of this "wood", when he writes "a forest of rustling birch trees (...) with big bumps" (159).

The quota of errors and misunderstandings in the two early translations is high. In Wallfisch's translation—amongst many other similar cases—a misunderstanding regarding the alcohol consumption by the woman in the brasserie Vézelise is outstanding. According to Sartre's narrator, the woman drinks a bottle of wine together with her meal: "Elle siffle, comme un homme, sa bouteille de bordeaux rouge à chaque repas" (58) ("Like a man, she empties a bottle of claret at every meal"; Baldick 72). Wallfisch makes her empty a bottle with every single course: "Wie ein Mann, gießt sie zu jedem Gang ihre Flasche Rotwein herunter" (68). To offer another example, Anny reads the historian Michelet in the attic of her parents' house where they store old books: "dans un grenier" (173). Anny, however, appears as a farmer's girl when Wallfisch makes her read the book on a haystack ("Heuschober", 195), which makes little sense here—of course, the correct term would be "Dachboden" (Aumüller, 226) ("attic"; Baldick 209).

Alongside errors, we find also some stylistic slips in the early translations, especially in Wallfisch's German version. When Roquentin tries in vain to remember his past feelings and confesses "je n'y entre plus" (6), Wallfisch uses a very clumsy phrase: "ich finde keinen Kontakt mehr zu ihnen" (10) ("I can no longer enter into them"; Baldick 10). On the contrary, Aumüller remains idiomatic: "ich kann mich nicht mehr in sie hineinversetzen" (11). Moreover, Roquentin eases his nausea by making love with the patronne. He notes: "Je me purge ainsi de certaines mélancolies" (11) ("I purge myself in this way of a certain melancholy"; Baldick 17). Wallfisch's version of this sentence is entirely unidiomatic: "ich stoße eine gewisse Niedergeschlagenheit ab" (16); nobody would actually "abstoßen" their "Niedergeschlagenheit". Having dinner with the Autodidacte, Roquentin looks round the room: "Je parcours la salle des yeux" (132). Wallfisch lets his eyes literally hasten through the restaurant ("Meine Augen durcheilen den Raum", 150), a phrase that is reminiscent of a surrealist movie, with eyes wandering or rolling through the room.

Finally, we offer an example in which both early translations make the same error by taking a common metaphor literally. Sartre's Autodidacte indulges in his naive humanistic ideas about mankind and asks: "Qui peut épuiser un homme?" (142). For "épuiser", Wallfisch uses the verb "ausschöpfen" ("einen Menschen ausschöpfen", 162), while Alexander selects the equivalent verb "empty" ("empty a man", 120). Aumüller rightly chooses a metaphor which is familiar in this context, namely, to get to the bottom of something ("einen Menschen ergründen", 187), while Baldick, strangely enough, also remains in the lexical field of drying liquids ("drain a man dry", 173).

On the other hand, Alexander misconstrues the phrase "my life grew in a haphazard way" (Baldick, 124), rendering Roquentin's thoughts about his life ("Ma vie poussait au petit bonheur", 101) with the literal translation: "My life put out feelers towards small pleasures" (84). Alexander's most irritating error occurs in the novel's key passage with Roquentin's revelation about contingency, superfluousness, gratuitousness, and absurdity. "Tout est gratuit, ce jardin, cette ville et moi-même", he notes, and contingency is "la gratuité parfaite" (155) ("Everything is gratuitous, that park, this town, and myself … perfect gratuitousness"; Baldick 188). Alexander does not think twice about gratuité and translates "contingency is (…) the perfect free gift". And he goes on: "All is free, this park, this city and myself" (131).

Besides such faults, the early translations, and again especially Wallfisch's text, show all kinds of unmotivated errors that are due to careless handling by authors, editors, and typesetters, such as unintentional fallacies, misspellings, and typos. The golden tassels ("glands d'or", 54) hanging from the large archbishop's metal hat, with which a hatmaker tries to draw attention to his shop, are rendered (twice!) as "Goldtrotteln" by Wallfisch (64, meaning "golden blockheads") instead of "Goldtroddeln" (Aumüller, 72). The 1949 translator and/or his editor's linguistic insensibility is corroborated by a phrase he uses in Roquentin's long conversation with Anny. She maintains that after having left him, she has no more perfect moments ("moments parfaits"). Roquentin translates this remark as "Je suis ahuri. J'insiste. 'Enfin tu ne …'" etc. (169) ("I am astounded. I press the point. 'You mean at last you …'"; Baldick 204). Wallfisch—instead of "insistieren", "beharren", "nachfragen", or "weiter bohren" (Aumüller, 221)—uses the phrase "ich dringe in sie ein" (191) which clearly indicates penetration in sexual intercourse. Since it is hard to imagine that the translator actually wrote such a misleading phrase, we could alternatively suspect a hasty editor who did not grasp the idiom "in jemand dringen" (meaning to carefully read someone's mind or try to influence someone) and added the fatal "ein". Alexander's early translation bears the same marks of hasty and careless production ("his *lips* swayed gracefully", 75, instead of *hips*). In his case, the majority of minor errors and misspellings are due to factual ignorance rather than carelessness; examples are the disfigurement of the beer brand "Spatenbräu" (8) to "Spartenbrau" (17), or of "Neukölln" (34, a district of Berlin) to "Neuköln" (26), which suggests a non-existent suburb of Cologne.

Sometimes translators encounter inexplicable words or phrases. According to *Langenscheidt's French-German Dictionary*, a "censeur" is an assistant to the director of a high school who is mainly responsible for the conduct of the pupils. Roquentin remembers a strange man who—in the time when he was a child—used to sit in the Jardin du Luxembourg, eying and smiling at boys. In his former life, this man was such a "censeur" (14). Wallfisch simply translates "Zensor" (19; censor) which seems a clear case of a 'false friend' because censorship no longer existed in twentieth-century France. Àumüller comes closer to the man's profession by calling him a "Konrektor" (20). Alexander seems to find the exact English equivalent of a French "censeur" with his "proctor" (9): the *Oxford English Dictionary* explains that the word denotes a university officer with disciplinary duties and an invigilator at examinations. Baldick decides for "schoolmaster", which is a broader generic term. At least it conserves the adherence of the character to the educational system, which is important since he seems to be a prefiguration of the pedophile Autodidact.

Sartre describes the customers in the Café Mably who enjoy a coffee and playing cards after they have had lunch in their family residences ("des pensions de famille qu'ils appellent leurs popotes", 11) (boarding houses which they call their "messes"; Baldick 16). Wallfisch entirely drops the references to home-cooking and to military casinos implied in the term "popote", which both contrast with the freedom of choice in a bistro. Alexander leaves the word "popote" untranslated, which does not make much sense since hardly any English-speaking reader will have been able to interpret it. Aumüller dares to insert "Futterkrippe" (17), a word which implies rich and fast food rather than delicious meals. Baldick uses "writing messes" (16) which conserves the reference to the military environment associated with "popote".

When making love with the woman who runs the "Rendezvous des Cheminots" ("la patronne"), Sartre underlines the mutual interest in these intimate encounters which excludes any payment from his side: "Je ne la paie pas: nous faisons l'amour au pair" (11). Wallfisch again declines any translation and inserts a "sozusagen" in order to excuse this failure: "wir machen es sozusagen 'au pair'" (16). Aumüller drops the humorous aspect of the phrase, which reverts to the comparison with a nanny working for free and limits herself to the semantic core: "wir haben beide etwas davon" (17). On the other hand, Alexander—like Aumüller—chooses an explicative phrase ("our need is mutual", 6), whereas Baldick decides to retain the French phrase: "we make love on a *au pair* basis" (17).

Moreover, the comparative study of translation may also contribute to the demonstration of the inevitable dissemination of meaning in the process of reception and interpretation of a text. This spreading of meaning becomes most obvious in the case of idiomatic phrases such as "Je suppose qu'on ne peut pas 'faire sa part' à la solitude" (13). The inverted commas signal that the phrase is used metaphorically. The context makes clear that Roquentin is aware that being alone leads to defamiliarization from the average men around him—an experience that includes anxiety and certain whims. Wallfisch suggests "Vermutlich kann man aus der Einsamkeit keinen Vorteil ziehen" (18). Aumüller tries a colloquial phrase: "Vermutlich kann man mit dem Alleinsein nicht 'spaßen'" (19).

The inverted commas are, of course, reproduced from the French original, but they also signal uncertainty, a disclaimer for fuzzy semantics. Alexander proposes "I don't suppose you can 'take sides' with solitude" (8); Baldick, "I don't suppose you can 'make allowance' for solitude" (19). Another figure of speech occurs when Roquentin remembers Anny's employment of time: "Anny faisait rendre au temps tout ce qu'il pouvait" (69). The problem with interpreting this phrase reverts to the pronoun "il" which refers to "temps" and perhaps implicitly to the mythological god of time. The context makes clear that Anny tries to make events, mainly amorous encounters, more intense by compressing them into a very short time span. Wallfisch creates a phrase that is pure nonsense: "Anny hatte eine Gabe, die Macht des Zeitablaufes zu ermessen" (80). Aumüller is once again more to the point when she writes: "Anny holte aus der Zeit alles heraus was drin war" (92). In the same way, the phrase is interpreted by Alexander ("Anny made the most of time", 57) and Baldick ("Anny used to get the most out of time", 86).

The dissemination of meaning is most important in the translation of the key concepts of Sartre's existential philosophy. There is no patent translation for most of these key concepts; their rather undefined range of meaning is the object of discussions amongst philosophers and literary critics. Translators should, of course, know at least the outlines of these discussions and take them into account when translating. More often than not, the problem is the ambivalence between the physical and mental states of the protagonist that are inherent already in the title words "nausée", "nausea", and "Ekel"—the key concept par excellence of the novel and perhaps also of Sartre's existential philosophy. As Contat and Rybalka write in their commentary to *La nausée* in the "Pléiade" collection: "(...) le mot de nausée a en quelque sorte changé de sens grâce au roman de Sartre: il suffit aujourd'hui de lui mettre une majuscule pour qu'il évoque non plus le malaise physique ou les vomissements, mais l'angoisse existentielle" (Sartre 1981a, p. 1668) (thanks to Sarte's novel, the word nausée has in some respect changed its meaning: today it is sufficient to use a capital letter at the beginning of the word to make it mean existential anxiety rather than physical suffering or vomiting). We must, therefore, take into account that the translators, and especially the early ones, were not as well informed about the exact meaning of such terms.

Thus, "écœurement" (16) is translated both with terms stressing the mental aversion, such as "Abscheu" (Wallfisch, 21) and "disgust" (Baldick, 22), and terms clearly highlighting bodily revulsion such as "Übelkeit" (Aumüller, 23) or "sickness" (Alexander, 10). Another word used to describe Roquentin's nausea is "mélancolie": the first association is obviously Dürer's homonymous engraving which directs our imagination to rather delicate mental or even sublime spiritual states. Contat and Rybalka remind us, however, of the profane origin of Roquentin's nausea in their comments on the novel, calling it a euphemism for "un désir frustré de 'baiser'" (a frustrated desire to fuck) (Sartre 1981a, p. 1730). Frustration would be an anachronistically modernizing, but still possible translation in contrast to, for example, tristesse, depression, or weltschmerz. Wallfisch decides for "Niedergeschlagenheit" (16), Alexander for "nostalgia" (6), while, as we have already noticed, Aumüller and Baldick no longer shun away from introducing foreign words and use "Melancholie" (17) and "melancholy" (17), respectively.

Another central concept in *La nausée* is "la contingence" (155). In English, it is safe to use "contingency", and Aumüller also opts for "Kontingenz" (204), while, on the contrary, Wallfisch, as in other cases, avoided the foreign word and translated it with "das Zufällige" (175). We have already mentioned Alexander's funny mishap when interpreting "gratuité" and "gratuit" (155) as "free gift" (131). But the other translators also struggle with this term. Baldick chooses the English form of the words ("gratuitousness" and "gratuitous", respectively, 189), Wallfisch found "Zwecklosigkeit" and "zwecklos" (176) to be the adequate rendering, and Aumüller opted for "Grundlosigkeit" and "grundlos" (204).

Conclusion

Research on Sartre's international transfer and reception must take into account that his works were subject to all sorts of adaptation—an effect which is, of course, well known in cultural transfer studies. In the years of Cold War and reeducation, the German translation was a political statement of opening new horizons, but information about the development of foreign literature and philosophy was scarce, especially in the

German-speaking areas. It is little surprise, therefore, that in the years after the war, various English translations of Sartre's works were already extant, but hardly any German ones. In the case of *La nausée*, English and German translations were produced only in 1949. Both translations show certain marks of this epoch, for instance, in the reluctance to use colloquial or even vulgar words and phrases. The German version in particular reveals difficulties with philosophical terminology, which is partly due to the wish not to swamp audiences with foreign vocabulary. Both the English and American publishers of the novel were dedicated to Modernism and the literary avant-garde; at the same time, they were trying to reach a wider reading public. Thus, the early translators Wallfisch and—to a lesser degree—Alexander show a bias toward 'nationalising' the text by exchanging foreign names, book titles, tramway stations, and so forth with equivalents taken from their own cultures. In summary, we could call this mode of translating explicative.

On the whole, the early translations, and again, especially the German version, are characterized by superfluous production and abound with errors and misunderstandings, clumsy phrases, and stylistic slips. The publishers obviously did not check their translators' knowledge or linguistic capacity: Heinrich Wallfisch is a 'nobody' in literary and translation history, and Lloyd Alexander was very young and inexperienced when he translated *La nausée*. Thus, readers had to wait until 1965 for a reliable and stylistically adequate English version, and until 1981 for a German translation worthy of that name. Contrary to the early translators, Baldick and Aumüller stand for expertise and professional translation. What makes the study of the translations interesting (apart from questions of evaluation, the reconstruction of the role of mediators, and historical contexts) is the comparison of the use of ambiguous figures of speech and philosophical terms that are open to interpretation. A continuation of this kind of study including further translations into other languages would contribute to revealing the vast potential of meaning in a stylistically complex text such as *La nausée*.

References

Barnhisel, Greg. 2015. *Cold War Modernists. Art, Literature, and American Cultural Diplomacy*. New York: Columbia University Press.

Dubinsky, Alan. 2011. *Nausea by Jean-Paul Sartre. An Examination of Context and Physical Form*. Accessed February 5, 2019. https://alandubinsky.files. wordpress.com/2011/10/nauseabysartre1.pdf.

Idt, Geneviève. 1971. *La nausée. Analyse critique*. Paris: Hatier.

Nabokov, Vladimir. 1949. Sartre's First Try. *The New York Times*, April 24.

Oels, David. 2013. *Rowohlts Rotationsroutine. Markterfolge und Modernisierung eines Buchverlags vom Ende der Weimarer Republik bis in die fünfziger Jahre*. Essen: Klartext Verlag.

Sartre, Jean-Paul. 1946. Monolog über die Existenz. Aus der 'Nausée' frei über-tragen von Egon Vietta. *Die Zeit*, April 11.

———. 1949a. *The Diary of Antoine Roquentin*. Translated from the French 'La nausée' by Lloyd Alexander. London: John Lehmann.

———. 1949b. *Nausea*. Translated from the French by Lloyd Alexander. Norfolk, CT: New Directions.

———. 1949c. *Der Ekel*. Roman. Aus dem Französischen von Heinrich Wallfisch. Stuttgart and Hamburg and Baden-Baden: Rowohlt.

———. 1965. *Nausea*. Translated from the French by Robert Baldick, reprinted with an introduction by James Wood, 2000. Harmondsworth: Penguin.

———. 1981a. *Œuvres romanesques*. Édition établie par Michel Rybalka avec la collaboration de Geneviève Idt et de George H. Bauer. Paris: Gallimard.

———. 1981b. *Der Ekel*. Roman. Mit einem Anhang, der die in der ersten französischen Ausgabe vom Autor gestrichenen Passagen enthält. Deutsch von Uli Aumüller. Reinbek bei Hamburg: Rowohlt.

———. 1985. *Der Ekel*. Deutsch von Uli Aumüller. Nachwort von Vincent von Wroblewsky. Berlin, Weimar: Aufbau.

———. 2013. *Nausea* (La nausée). Translated from the French by Lloyd Alexander. Foreword by Richard Howard. Introduction by James Wood. Norfolk, CT: New Directions.

Tunnell, Michael O., and James S. Jacobs. 2007. The Remarkable Journey of Lloyd Alexander. *School Library Journal* 53: 40–42.

Whitehead, Ella. 1990. *John Lehmann's "New Writing". An Author-Index 1936–1950*. Compiled by Emma Whitehead. With an Introductory Essay by John Whitehead. Lewiston and Queenston and Lampeter: Edwin Mellen.

Wright, Adrian. 1998. *John Lehmann. A Pagan Adventure*. London: Duckworth.

Wroblewsky, Vincent von. n.d. Traduire Sartre en allemand. Unpublished manuscript.

Ziegler, Edda. 1997. Rowohlts Rotations Romane 1946–1949. Eine Programanalyse. In *Buch, Buchhandel und Rundfunk 1945–1949*, ed. Monika Estermann and Edgar Lersch, 125–136. Wiesbaden: Harrassowitz.

7

"Existentialist Hu-ha"?: Censoring the Existentialists in the British Theater

Jamie Andrews

This chapter will look at the censorship of playwrights associated with existentialist thinking in the British theater, from the opening up of the London stage to French writers after the Second World War to the end of theater censorship in Britain with the passing of the *Theatres Act 1968*. Consideration will be given to a range of writers but, inevitably, the focus will be on the plays of Jean-Paul Sartre, all of whose plays except one (ironically, *Kean*[1]) were performed on the British stage in this period.

Sartre's experiences with theatrical censorship date back to his first play, *Bariona*,[2] written and performed in December 1940 in the Stalag 12

---

[1] *Kean* was not performed in London until 28 January 1971, in an Oxford Playhouse production directed by Frank Hauser at the Globe Theatre.

[2] In the main text, I use the original French titles of plays to avoid confusion occasioned by multiple different English translations of the title of the same play, although I also note commonly used English translations in the main body of the text. In references, I use the English title as employed by the Lord Chamberlain's office.

J. Andrews (✉)
British Library, London, UK
e-mail: Jamie.Andrews@bl.uk

© The Author(s) 2020
A. Betschart, J. Werner (eds.), *Sartre and the International Impact of Existentialism*,
https://doi.org/10.1007/978-3-030-38482-1_7

D Prisoner of War Camp: "When I was a prisoner of war in Germany in 1940, I wrote, staged, and acted in a Christmas play which, while pulling wool over the eyes of the German censor by means of simple symbols, was addressed to my fellow-prisoners" (Sartre 1976, p. 39). Subsequent examples of censorship of Sartre's plays have been widely referenced, most especially the accommodation with German censors in occupied Paris (e.g. Ireland 2012, pp. 94–99), or the later self-censorship of productions of his own play *Les mains sales* (usually known as *Dirty Hands*, although the first UK productions were translated as *Crime Passionnel*, and the first production in the United States in 1948 was, despite Sartre's objections, titled *Red Gloves*) for over a decade during a period of escalating Cold War polarities (see e.g. O'Donohoe 2005, p. 117). However, the censorship of his work on the British stage has been barely recognized, either contemporaneously in France, or in subsequent criticism of his work.[3]

In this chapter, I intend to recover the forgotten history of the censorship of Sartre's plays on the British stage, and the fate of other playwrights often associated with existentialist thought. By looking at the process of censorship by the Lord Chamberlain's office (part of the Royal Household of the United Kingdom), we can gain new understanding of the ways that the British political/social establishment first responded to the plays of Sartre and his contemporaries, of the fears that the establishment had about them on behalf of the public whose morals they saw themselves as bound to protect, and the impact that this had on the plays' subsequent performance histories (or absence of).

I will firstly briefly summarize the background to, and processes of, theatrical censorship in Britain, and the documents that were left behind after its abolition in 1968. I will then look at how successive Lords Chamberlain and their Examiners responded to both the philosophy of

---

[3] A single, brief news story in *Le Figaro* reported the censoring of *Huis clos* in 1946: "Une pièce de J.-P Sartre interdite à Londres"; Benedict O'Donohoe also briefly references the banning of *Huis clos* in London (see O'Donohoe 2005, p. 74) but does not consider the broader impact of the official censor in his comprehensive review of the reception of Sartre's plays in London (O'Donohoe 2001). Steve Nicholson references the censorship of Jean-Paul Sartre and Jean Genet as part of a wider narrative of theatrical censorship in Britain between 1960 and 1968 (see Nicholson 2003–2015).

existentialism and its principal protagonists. Finally, I will look at two particularly rich case studies—the production and censorship histories of *Huis clos* (most commonly expressed in English as *Huis clos*, or, during this period, *In Camera* and *Vicious Circle*) and *La putain respectueuse* (correctly translated as *The Respectful Prostitute*, and often mistranslated as *The Respectable Prostitute*)—and examine the ways that these plays became caught up in a wider story of evolving ideological and social assumptions.

The Lord Chamberlain and Censorship of the British Theater

The history of theater censorship in Britain has been a recent focus of academic research, and the background is most clearly summarized in two publications that draw heavily on recently opened archives in the British Library (Nicholson 2003–2015; Shellard 2004). Statutory licensing of plays for performance by the Lord Chamberlain's Office dates back to the *Licensing Act 1737*, brought in by Prime Minister Robert Walpole in the face of increasingly satirical attacks by playwrights on his Government and the King. The *Theatres Act 1843* amended and clarified this legislation, allowing the Lord Chamberlain absolute discretion in making decisions, but for the first time providing a certain framework: the Act stated that "it shall be lawful for the Lord Chamberlain for the Time being, whenever he shall be of the opinion that it is fitting for the Preservation of good Manners, Decorum, or of the public Peace so to do, to forbid the acting or presenting any Stage Play" (An Act for Regulating Theatres 1843). This direction, subsequently confirmed by later interpretations, emphasized that the Lord Chamberlain's judgments were based to a great extent on how he considered an audience would respond to a play; the Office claimed not to be looking to restrict the expression of abstract opinion or beliefs, but to manage what Brigadier-General Sir Douglas Dawson—a Comptroller to the Lord Chamberlain—described as the "probable results consequent on the production of a play" (Report from the Joint Select Committee 1909). The Examiners liked to talk of an indulgent *examination* (rather than *censorship*) of plays, and characterized themselves as "guardians of dramatic good health and as protectors of audiences"

(Shellard 2004, p. 5), though this view ignored the roots of censorship in 1737 in blunting attacks on the political establishment.

The Lord Chamberlain's work overseeing the theater was just one part of his role as Head of the Royal Household, and his duties also included, amongst other tasks, looking after the Queen's swans and organizing royal pageantry. The degree to which the duties overlapped is amusingly illustrated by the files for Jean Genet's *Les nègres* (*The Blacks*), in which a note questioning Genet's text is written in hand on the back of the draft for the official invitation to the wedding of the Queen's sister, Princess Margaret, and Anthony Armstrong Jones (Draft note, in LCP CORR[4] 1961/1642, "The Blacks").

In the post-war period under consideration, practice dictated that a theater manager would submit a script and fee to St James's Palace, where the Lord Chamberlain was based. The Examiner of Plays would read the play and write a Reader's Report, and then recommend that the script be either licensed by the Lord Chamberlain for performance or not licensed (i.e. banned), or recommend cuts or changes to the work contingent on which the work should be allowed. The process often involved correspondence between the Palace and the management, who might barter over changes or even submit a new script. The Examiner's recommendations would usually be confirmed, but were sometimes passed up the hierarchy for approval from the Comptroller, or his Assistant, or in exceptional cases the Lord Chamberlain himself. During the period that we are considering, significant controversy was occasioned by a particular loophole in the law that tolerated private performances of disallowed plays in small members-only theater clubs. The provision was originally intended to allow obscure, challenging (and often foreign) work to be produced discretely for small and discriminating audiences, but in the post-war period, the policy was increasingly pushed to its limit as larger theaters self-declared as clubs in direct challenge to the Chamberlain's powers (Shellard 2004, pp. 155–157).

After a long campaign, theater censorship was rescinded by the *Theatres Act 1968*, and extant archival papers eventually transferred to the Manuscripts Department of the British Library. What remains in the

---

[4] LCP CORR refers to files that are part of The Lord Chamberlain's Correspondence archive, The British Library, London.

British Library are the original plays submitted (often, as not all performed plays are published, unique copies of scripts), the Reader's Report and list of eventual cuts or changes, a copy of the license issued, and, for more problematic or challenging works, records of official correspondence, private conversations, internal memos, newspaper clippings, legal papers, and so forth (The British Library 2019).

Perceptions of Existentialism and Existentialist Playwrights

Before examining two specific plays in detail, I intend firstly to survey the response of the official censors to plays by Sartre and associated writers, looking particularly at way that existentialism itself, and its leading personalities, were understood and perceived by St James's Palace.

The Lord Chamberlain's first attempt to understand existentialism followed the submission of Sartre's *Morts sans sépulture* (*Men without Shadows*) for performance at the County Theatre, Bangor, in 1947, and the response was brutal: "The play is steeped in unrelieved horror. We cannot believe in the nobility of the prisoners—nor, indeed, in their reality as human beings. Their sacrifice is in vain for vain ideals and even the dark powers have gained nothing. This, I understand, is pretty much what existentialism means!" (RR (= "Reader's Report") in LCP CORR 1947/7907, "Men Without Shadows"). The Examiner directly elides the horror of the German occupation depicted in the play with his identification of an underlying philosophy of nihilism (ignoring the positive ethical positioning that the character of Canoris brings, and that Sartre intended (Freeman 1998, S. 63)). Subsequently, as further plays were submitted for licensing, the official responses to the idea of existentialism tended more toward dismissal, or even outright ridicule; however, on occasion, the censors would make demonstrable effort to engage with the philosophical implications.

The Examiner reporting on *Le diable et le bon dieu* (*Lucifer and the Lord*) in 1957 professed himself exhausted by "pages and pages of existentialist hu ha"; clearly, too exhausted to try and explain the meaning of "an elaborate philosophical concept he [Sartre] has invented called existentialism, which is much too difficult to enter into at the end of a long report".[5] Conversely, when a new version of *Les mouches* (*The Flies*) was submitted the following year for an amateur performance at Cambridge University, the same Examiner demonstrated greater willingness to understand the implications of the work: "As it [*Les mouches*] is an expression of existentialist philosophy, which Sartre invented, in terms of the Greek Oresteian legend, both these must be explained briefly to give any comprehension of the play" (RR in LCP CORR 1958/741, "The Flies"). In his detailed report, the Examiner offered a measured, and relatively well-informed, summary of existentialism, although was unable to resist undercutting his assessment in the conclusion:

> By denying both morality in the sense of conduct based on conventional standards, and character, in the sense of predestinate or inherited traits, existentialism postulates man as a self-aware being with complete freedom of action, who projects himself towards his future not by what he may want that future to be, but by what it becomes from the aggregate of all his former freely determined actions. There is a great deal more, mostly nonsense, but the above is a not unfair definition of the basis of the concept. (RR in LCP CORR 1958/741, "The Flies")

The licensing of *Huis clos*, which will be the subject of more detailed analysis later in this chapter, offers an example of how the decision as to whether to license a play to be performed could be tied to the Examiner's own assessment of the value of the underlying philosophical truth that the work presented. Reporting on the 1946 of *Huis clos*, the Reader acknowledged that:

> It is a serious work of art by a writer with a large following among contemporary French intelligentsia, but it fails because it presents (however convincingly) only one side of a system of moral economy and totally ignores the possibility of redemption either by faith *or* works. This failure to develop completely a theme which must stand or fail by its metaphysical

---

[5]RR (= "Reader's Report") in LCP CORR 1957/WB 15, "Lucifer and the Lord". The Lord Chamberlain himself, Major-General The Right Honourable The Earl of Scarbrough, was clearly not put off by the absence of an attempt to engage with existentialism, pencilling a note at the bottom of the Reader's text: "What a good report!"

verity makes it easier to withhold permission on the obvious grounds … of eroticism and Lesbianism without feeling that an important work of art is being stifled. (RR in LCP CORR LICENCE REFUSED 1945/160, "Huis clos")

This underlines the subjectivity that the Examiners brought to their assessments, and also suggest that a stated concern for the public's moral health ("eroticism and Lesbianism") operated alongside more abstract judgments of philosophical worth ("this failure to develop completely a theme"). The report additionally offers the irony of the Examiner, the reactionary Charles D. Heriot—who, during the 1950s, would take up arms against almost all new writing—criticizing the author of *Forgers of Myths* (Sartre's essay was first published in *Theatre Arts* in June 1946) for not being sufficiently Cornelian; for not presenting, in Sartre's own terms, a more tautly balanced "conflict of rights" (Sartre 1976, p. 14).

Almost 15 years after first reviewing Sartre's work, the Examiner's response to the submission of *Les séquestrés d'Altona* (*Altona*) in 1961 for a production at the Royal Court demonstrated that understanding existentialism was still a challenge for the Palace: "Sartre is the trickiest of the notable French modern dramatists, because he invented an entire new philosophy called existentialism (which I had occasion to try to expound to the Lord Chamberlain more than once.)" (RR in LCP CORR 1961/1673, "Altona"). For all that the archives provide examples of Examiners mocking the complexities of "existentialist hu-ha" (RR in LCP CORR 1957/WB 15, "Lucifer and the Lord"), this statement does nonetheless reflect an acknowledgement of Sartre's status as a preeminent writer for the theater, albeit one whose philosophy (assumed here, and elsewhere, to be a wholly Sartrean invention) remains mysterious. We will now look at further responses to the existentialists themselves.

An addendum to the Reader's Report on *Les mains sales*, scribbled hastily by the Comptroller of the Household, suggests the low esteem in which Sartre was held within St James's Palace: "J-PS is *not* popular in this office". (RR in LCP CORR 1948/9305, "Crime Passionnel"). The main body of the report demonstrates a personal hostility on behalf of the Examiner as well ("I admit prejudice: I do not like Sartre"), and it is no surprise that he dismisses the play as "pretentious, with a sour, pessimistic irony that reduces any element of tragedy" (RR in LCP CORR 1948/9305, "Crime Passionnel"). On other occasions, however, the Office did acknowledge, and in some sense respond to, Sartre's perceived significance—at various times he is described as "very much a leading modern playwright" (RR in LCP CORR 1956/9493, "Nekrassov".), "a dramatist of much importance" (RR in LCP CORR 1957/WB 15, "Lucifer and the Lord)"), or "an eminent French author".[6]

The Reader's Reports also demonstrate the uncertain evolution of the understanding of Sartre's biographical background. Reporting the refusal of a license for *Huis clos* in London in 1946, an article in the French newspaper *Franc-Tireur* noted the post-war impatience of the English public to find out more about Sartre (Verney 1946), and the censors of St James's Palace were equally keen to find out more. In response to an enquiry from the Assistant Comptroller, in 1945, Stephen Thomas of the British Council Drama Panel explained (with only limited accuracy) that "Sartre has a tremendous reputation at this time in the French intellectual theatre. He is a professor at the Sorbonne and a leader of French Catholic philosophical thought".[7] In 1952, despite the growth in Sartre's reputation in Britain, the Examiner of Simone de Beauvoir's only play, *Les bouches inutiles* (*Useless Mouths*), for a French language production at Toynbee Hall, still appears a little uncertain when he speculates: "I'm told the play is by Jean-Paul Sartre's wife" (RR in LCP CORR 1952/4299, "Les bouches inutiles").

However unpopular Sartre's own work was, perhaps his greatest crime in the eyes of the Lord Chamberlain's Office was the responsibility that the playwright bore for Jean Genet. Genet—or, as he was described within St James's Palace, "the unspeakable M. Genet" (RR in LCP CORR 1957/WB19, "The Balcony")—provoked the ire of the censors to an almost unprecedented degree, and the blame was firmly assigned to Sartre. Refusing to license *Les bonnes* (*The Maids*),

---

[6] Norman Gwatkin, Assistant Comptroller, to the Chief Constable Liverpool Police, 18 November 1953, in LCP CORR 1947/7906, "The Respectable Prostitute".
[7] Stephen Thomas to Norman Gwatkin, 24 October 1945, in RR in LCP CORR LICENCE REFUSED 1945/160, "Huis clos".

the Examiner begins his report with a reference to Sartre: "Nobody had ever heard of Jean Genet until Jean Paul Sartre, founder of existentialism, wrote a short book saying that he was a blackguard, a ruffian and a pervert, but a writer of genius" (RR, in LCP CORR LICENCE REFUSED 1952/1, "The Maids"), while the report on *Les nègres* scathingly observes that "being a disciple and protégé of Sartre, Genet is not particular about being understood' (RR in LCP CORR 1961/1642, "The Blacks").

If Sartre was *not popular* at the Palace, Gabriel Marcel, a leading exponent of Christian existentialism, was remarkably respected. Examining *Le chemin de crête* (*Ariadne*) for a production in Cambridge in 1953, the Reader describes Marcel as "the most important living French dramatist", and this opinion was confirmed in the report of *Un homme de Dieu* (*A Man of God*), described as "the first play by the most important living French dramatist to be performed in this country" (RR in LCP CORR 1953/5990, "Ariadne"; RR in LCP CORR 1953/5126, "A Man of God".) In both cases, the Examiners identify the influence of Ibsen ("Like all good playwrights, Marcel derives directly from Ibsen" (RR in LCP CORR 1953/5990, "Ariadne")), an author who, in his time, had provoked fierce criticism from previous Lords Chamberlain, but now a reassuring reference point of approbation.

What about Albert Camus and Jean Anouilh, the other "Young Playwrights of France" referenced, alongside Simone de Beauvoir, in Sartre's outline of existentialist theater, *Forgers of Myths?* The Lord Chamberlain's Examiners Office does not explicitly link either of the two writers to Sartre, nor to existentialism, although the Examiner of the first production of Camus's *Caligula* at the Embassy Theatre in 1949 does place the play unenthusiastically within the recourse to ancient or mythic rituals that Sartre summarized in *Forgers of Myths*: "This is the sort of play for which I have no liking at all. Historical persons whose characters are twisted to fit the author's theories about life or art or politics are favourite subjects for contemporary French drama".[8] However, as was the case with Sartre, the Examiners tended to dismiss rather than engage: the report on Camus's Dostoyevsky

---

[8] RR in LCP CORR 1949/126, "Caligula". For "Forgers of Myths" see (Sartre 1976, pp. 33–44).

adaptation *Les possédés* (*The Possessed*) complains that "the plot is too complex, too interwoven, and too many-sided to be able to summarise. In fact if I were to attempt to summarise it all, even if I could, the summary would probably be nearly as long as the play itself, and equally confusing" (RR, in LCP1963/3631, "The Possessed").

Jean Anouilh, a star writer for the West End, was generally seen to be a more reassuring adapter of myths than either Sartre or Camus: the file for the first production of Anouilh's *Antigone* by Laurence Olivier's Old Vic Company in 1949 praised a "dignified and very moving" work; and the establishment status of the production is emphasized by amiable correspondence between the Lord Chamberlain's Comptroller, Lieutenant-Colonel Sir Terence Nugent, and Olivier.[9] Another production of *Antigone* in French language (hence required to be submitted again) at Toynbee Hall reflects the degree to which anticipation of audience reception guided the Palace's decisions. The verb *pisser* (to piss) would not be licensed under usual circumstances, but the elevated nature of the production by the French Society of Queen Mary College led to the Examiner to conclude that "in view of...the highbrow quality of the play, surely it would be rather silly to interfere...if the girls of Queen Mary are not over-prudish, we need not be so either" (Norman Gwatkin, note on RR in LCP CORR 1949/21, "Antigone").

This chapter has hitherto drawn on the documentation created during the licensing process to understand how the philosophy of existentialism, and its major protagonists, were received and understood within the Lord Chamberlain's Office. We will now consider in greater detail the examination of two of Sartre's plays that caused especial challenges within the system of theater censorship overseen by the Lord Chamberlain.

---

[9] RR in LCP CORR 1948/9837, "Antigone"; and Terence Nugent to Laurence Olivier, 10 January 1949. The tone of Nugent's correspondence is strikingly different from the language used elsewhere about Sartre: "I hope rehearsals are going well and that you are satisfied with everything. It was a great pleasure to see you the other evening and I wish I had more opportunity of discussing with you the rights and wrongs of Plum Warner being knighted for keeping cricket going through the two Wars".

Huis clos

The first suggestion of a production of *Huis clos* was made just a month after the end of the Second World War, when the visiting Vieux Colombier Company proposed a French-language production as part of a British Council cultural exchange endeavor. Given the importance of the Company, the play was sent to be read unofficially: a wholly unofficial parallel process to the established one, and a no less untransparent procedure. The play was read by Cynthia Carew Pole who, as was often the case, combined impeccable French language with equally impeccable establishment credentials (she was the wife of Sir John Gawen Carew Pole, 12th Baronet, later Lord Lieutenant of Cornwall, and a great-niece of John Pierpont Morgan). Carew Pole emphasized not the message of the play, but its Frenchness: "How typical it is of the French mentality and attitude". She also hinted at the element that would prevent its public performance for over 20 years: "I cannot see it having a successful run in London, as some of the action would have to be toned down and then there is little left" (Cynthia Carew Pole to Norman Gwatkin, 19 November 1945, in "Huis clos"). Thus, in late 1945, the Assistant Comptroller informed the British Council that the unofficial opinion was that it would not be passed if a license was requested; not officially banning it, because it was never officially submitted (Norman Gwatkin to Stephen Thomas, 23 November 1945, in "Huis clos").

The element that Carew Pole identified as likely to prove problematic was the character of Inès, and the explicit references to her lesbian relationships. The ban on portraying homosexual characters was long-standing, and when HM Tennent Ltd, the most important theater producers in London, followed up in December with a proposal to produce *Huis clos* alongside Lilian Hellman's *The Children's Hour* under a special license (acknowledging the problematic Lesbian themes in both plays) at the Lyric, Hammersmith, it prompted an internal debate. The Comptroller sent a "strictly confidential" memo to selected religious leaders, asking whether policy should change in light of the fact that "the present generation is outspoken on subjects which, previously, were not matters for open conversation. The subject of perversion occurs frequently in contemporary literature...it may be these facts or, indeed, it may be part of the aftermath of two major wars, but there is an impression that perversion is on the increase" (Norman Gwatkin, "Confidential Memo", February 1946, in "Huis clos").

The formal submission of *Huis clos* by Tennents would provide the answer to the Assistant Comptroller's question. The Examiner, like Carew Pole, saw the play as emblematic of national difference:

> The play illustrates very well the difference between the French and English tastes. I don't suppose that anyone would bat an eyelid over in Paris, but here we bar Lesbians on the stage. Some years ago we had quite a run of plays about Lesbianism, and of course we turned them all down. Our taboo is understood by informed opinion, and is accepted as reasonable; and I think that it would be extremely unwise to take any step which weakened our position. (RR, "Huis clos")

The Examiner's consideration of the play is focused almost entirely on the question of what he terms Inès's "abnormalities"; no reference is made to the philosophical framing of the work, nor, surprisingly, to the evident similarities of *Huis clos* to Sutton Vane's recently revived play *Outward Bound* (similarities that Jean Cocteau had identified at the time of the play's French premiere) (see Vane 1924; for Cocteau's comparison, see Sartre 2005, p. 142). Instead, consideration of the likely audience response is entirely focused on Inès's sexuality: "I am all for treating the claims of the high-brows (Sartre is all the rage amongst the intelligentsia at the moment) with as much consideration as those of the low…but it would need a clever advocate to persuade me that British culture needs the introduction of such queer themes from the Continent for its healthy life" (RR, "Huis clos"), and the decision was taken to refuse a license.

This did not entirely preclude a production, as the small Arts Theatre Club exploited the legal gray area and presented a Private Performance in August 1946. Over the succeeding years, the files show numerous requests to stage the play. The especial power of the theater, and consequent risk from the Chamberlain's perspective, are shown in correspondence with the Secretary of the Conference of Repertory Theatres, who made the case for *Huis clos* to be staged by emphasizing that it had already been broadcast on BBC Radio, but was rebuffed on the grounds of the theater's particular potency:

> I am sure that you understand that there is a difference between words coming over the air and the same words spoken in the more personal atmosphere of a theatre, by visible characters. It is interesting to note that many people who listened to the broadcast of this play did not notice the perversion of one of the characters, whereas this particular thing was quite apparent when produced in the theatre. (Norman Gwatkin to Patrick Henderson, 3 July 1947, in "Huis clos")

Over the years, while the ban on *Huis clos* was in force, opinion as to the desirability of overturning it differed. A steady stream of amateur and professional companies unsuccessfully requested permission; a drama group from Birmingham realized only after marketing a production that the play was banned; the *Birmingham Mail* saw "reason in the Lord Chamberlain's ban", while the *News of the World* deplored the inconsistency of the ban in light of its radio broadcast.[10] Commercially, Curtis Brown Agents lobbied again for "the finest work of one of the best modern French authors" to be licensed; while the Comptroller reported to the Lord Chamberlain that the producer Jimmy Smith told him that he did not think it should be licensed, as "quite apart from the rights and wrongs of the theme, he [Smith] could not see this particular play having a commercial success".[11]

In February 1959, another standard enquiry as to the status of *Huis clos* was received from a Sheffield amateur dramatic society. This time, however—14 years after the play was first refused a license—the Assistant Comptroller appended a note on the letter to be passed to the Comptroller: "Do you think this is now likely to be passed?"[12] The answer came a month later, when The Playhouse, Oxford, formally submitted the

---

[10] See CLW, *Birmingham Mail*, 22 January 1948; n.a., *Birmingham Mail*, 26 October 1949; n.a., "Vicious Circle", *News of the World*, 6 February 1955. These clippings, sent to the Lord Chamberlain, and all requests to stage the play are preserved in "Huis clos".

[11] Kitty Black to The Lord Chamberlain's Office, 3 February 1955 and Terence Nugent, note, 14 February 1955 in "Huis clos".

[12] Jean McKenna to the Lord Chamberlain's Office, 15 February 1959 and Norman Gwatkin, typewritten note, n.d., in "Huis clos".

translation by Stuart Gilbert. Gone was the rejection of "queer themes from the Continent", and in its place was an almost poetic evocation of the creeping revelation of the play's dramatic irony, and, with it, finally, a license for performance:

> Hell, to Sartre's mind, may be likened to a drawing room in Second Empire style…Knowledge of one another comes gradually, and with it the realisation that each is at the mercy of the others, that there is no need for torture-chambers, fire and brimstone, and all the paraphernalia of legend, for hell is … other people. There they are, for ever, without release; even without the release of murder or suicide … or sleep. (RR, in LCP CORR 1959/1888, "In Camera")

The explanation for the sudden reversal in opinion, and indeed the subsequent licensing of the French-language version in February 1960 for a performance at Goldsmiths College (see RR, in LCP CORR 1959/522, "Huis clos (French version)"), was a wider change in policy at St James's Palace. A year after the 1957 Wolfenden Report recommended the decriminalization of homosexual acts, the Lord Chamberlain had issued a "Secret Memorandum" that now permitted the licensing of "plays which make a serious and sincere attempt to deal with the subject [i.e. homosexuality]", though still banning "a play that was violently pro-homosexuality" (see Shellard 2004, p. 159). The adaptation of André Gide's *L'immoraliste* (*The Immoralist*) was the first play to have its ban overturned under the new recommendations, and *Huis clos* could also finally be performed two years later.

La putain respecteuse

If, during the long-running consideration of *Huis clos*, the Lord Chamberlain was chasing to keep up with public opinion, the narrative of the licensing of Sartre's *La putain respecteuse* was more complex. When first submitted in 1947, the Examiner accepted that it was "a violent play and if it is to be licensed at all, a lot of the violent language and implications will have to remain" (RR in LCP CORR 1947/7906, "The Respectable

Prostitute"). Though the original title, *Yankee Tart*, had to be changed to *The Respectable Prostitute*[13]—and one stipulation read: "Cut all the 'whores' on these pages. There's enough bad language already"[14]—the play was passed.

One of the reasons that theater producers were often at best ambivalent about (if not actively supportive of) stage censorship was that the Lord Chamberlain's licensing of a play was absolute, and shielded producers from subsequent civil action. So in 1950, when a production of *La putain respecteuse* at the New Cross Empire prompted a series of complaints from the Camberwell Borough Youth Committee to the Public Morality Council and the Chief Officer of the Public Control Department at London County Council, the Comptroller was obliged to defend the play as having been formally licensed for performance by his office. The complaint in this case was that such a play undermined "the work which Youth Organisations are endeavouring to carry on among young people to fit them to make the best possible use of their leisure time".[15] In fact, it was the sensationalism of the marketing, as much as the play itself, that was attacked, as was made clear in notes and diagrams appended to the letter sent to St James's Palace by Public Control Department at London County Council: 13 images of a woman in a negligee that, the Chief Officer emphasized, can be seen from across the street, and a lurid strapline also illustrated in the letter: "THE DARING VIVID TRUTH ABOUT A FORBIDDEN SUBJECT WHICH DEALS FRANKLY AND INTIMATELY WITH A TREMENDOUS HUMAN PROBLEM. The most talked about play of the century."[16] Whereas the first London production at the Lyric, Hammersmith, in 1947 was intended for a more discerning audience, it is apparent from this controversy that only three

---

[13] The accurate translation of *La putain respectueuse* is *The Respectful Prostitute* However, the title is consistently translated in the files as *The Respectable Prostitute* (the error is only noted in files for the later 1964 production), and in the main body text of this chapter, I refer to the play as *The Respectable Prostitute* for the sake of consistency with the sources.

[14] RR, "The Respectable Prostitute". In hand, the Assistant Comptroller has added: "Yes cut the lot".

[15] Camberwell Borough Youth Committee to Secretary, the Public Morality Council, 12 October 1950, in "The Respectable Prostitute".

[16] See attachments to Chief Officer of the Public Control Department, London County Council to the Lord Chamberlain's Office, 14 October 1950, in "The Respectable Prostitute".

years later, the play was being marketed very differently, to a very different South London audience (in fact, precisely the kind of popular audience that Sartre himself regretted he often failed to reach[17]).

Greater controversy was to come, however, when the play was produced in Liverpool in 1953. Observing the title of the play, the local police had visited the theater and asked to inspect the script licensed by the Lord Chamberlain. Having warned the actors to stick to the script, on 2 November, two undercover officers attended a performance, and observed unauthorized stage directions at the play's conclusion. In the words of Superintendent Hegg, from his Report presented to court:

> The final scene which, by the script, would appear quite reasonable, ends with the character Lizzie dressed in a nightdress and dressing gown (cut very low) being carried by the character Fred who was dressed in a brown suit and white shirt across the stage. He placed her on the bed, took off his coat, got on to the end with her and lay on top of her, at the same time making suggestive motions. (Superintendent C V Hegg, "Police Report", 3 November 1953, in "The Respectable Prostitute")

Intriguingly, given the Chamberlain's professed purpose to guard public morals, the report subsequently states that "the actions described were greeted with murmurs of resentment from members of the audience". As soon as the curtain came down, the police officers went backstage, and charges were brought against both the director and theater manager/ licensee on the grounds that the unauthorized ending was offensive to public morals and decency. Both men were found guilty and fined (see notes and press clippings in "The Respectable Prostitute"). In a final Sartrean irony, however, the theater licensee (but not the director) appealed to the High Court, and his conviction was overturned on what might be considered appropriately existential grounds. The licensee, James Lovelace, had been convicted on the grounds of "causing the play [in this case, the unlicensed version] to be presented"[18]; however, having

---

[17] See, for example, Sartre (1988), especially the chapters "For Whom Does One Write?" and "Situation of the Writer in 1947".

[18] "Lovelace v. Director of Public Prosecution: Judgment", 21 October 1954, in "The Respectable Prostitute".

heard evidence that Lovelace had explicitly warned the actors to stick to the authorized script—and perhaps remembering Sartre's emphasis on actions in *Existentialism is a Humanism* (Sartre 1948)—the presiding Lord Chief Justice of England overturned the original verdict, reasoning that "the fact is that if a man is charged with causing something or permitting something, it follows that that must come from some act of his which is equivalent to causing, a command or direction to do the act. There was no causing here" ("Judgment" in "The Respectable Prostitute").

The case of *La putain respectueuse* had suggested a dichotomy of reception (and assumed reception) of Sartre between arts theater audiences in London, and subsequent provincial touring. In correspondence with the Director of Public Prosecutions, the Assistant Comptroller suggested that the play was originally licensed with more high-minded aims, but that these risked being missed by provincial audiences: "In the original production, with the emphasis properly laid upon the social theme (the white man's inhumanity to the coloured man) and not the immoral setting, the play was allowed. The immoral setting is, however, an undoubted temptation, especially when the play goes on tour to audiences who might not be expected to be too interested in its social aspects".[19]

After the Liverpool production, *La putain respectueuse* continued to be a mainstay of repertory theater, during which time changes in public attitudes were reflected in the Chamberlain's responses. A challenge to the Palace from the Salisbury Watch Committee—whose members "were very concerned at the title given to the Drama 'The Respectable Prostitute' by J.P. Sartre, which was performed recently at the Playhouse in this City"— was countered with confidence by the Comptroller, for whom adherence to an agreed script was the only question: "The eminent dramatist Jean-Paul Sartre has been licensed ... [the play] has now been on tour in this country for some years and apart from one occasion when the licensed MS was departed from and the Lord Chamberlain instituted successful legal proceedings, the performance has been without general complaint".[20]

---

[19] Norman Gwatkin to Director of Public Prosecutions, 23 November 1953, in "The Respectable Prostitute".

[20] George Richardson, Town Clerk, to the Lord Chamberlain's Office, 29 December 1955 and Terence Nugent to George Richardson, 30 December 1955, in "The Respectable Prostitute".

For a new 1958 production for the more popular audiences of the Theatre Royal Stratford East, the Examiner regrets "the sexual flavour that made the piece into a scandalous attraction in the provinces instead of a serious comment on American injustice", but—"on the grounds that Canute [was] wrong"—felt unwilling to hold back the tide of increasing permissiveness and did not cut any of the heightened language in this new translation.[21] By 1964, and another new translation for Toynbee Hall, the Chamberlain's Office had given up any attempts to further cut the play, and was reduced to merely fussing that "one would have thought that a new translation of this play would have got the title right" (the new translation had been titled *The Respectable Prostitute*).[22]

Conclusion

The consideration of plays by Jean-Paul Sartre (and other related existentialist writers) by the Lord Chamberlain's Office is an intriguing part of the history of theater censorship in Britain as it drew to an end; in tracking developing attitudes to these writers, we have been able to chart the reception of the philosophy, and content, of their work in the context of shifting social and moral trends that the Office both resisted and grudgingly acknowledged.

The history of these performances, as recorded in the unmatched records of St James's Palace, also provides a unique record of theatrical performance. It emphasizes just how much new French existentialist theater writing was performed in Britain during the immediate post-War years: all but one of the plays of Sartre and Camus, but also lesser-known authors including Gabriel Marcel (one of his plays, *Un homme de Dieu*, toured the country in a mobile theater) and Emmanuel Roblès (Roblès, friend of Camus, had a huge hit with *Montserrat*, translated by Lillian Hellman).[23] The records also open up a regional perspective to the

---

[21] RR in LCP CORR 1958/995, "The Respectable Prostitute (Second Version)".

[22] RR in LCP CORR 1964/4652, "The Respectable Prostitute (Third Version)". Of course, the Office had itself consistently mistranslated the title.

[23] See RR "A Man of God"; RR in LCP CORR 1952/3926, "Montserrat".

reception of existentialist work in recording not the first London production (as conventional theater histories often do) but the very first pre-London openings. Thus, the first audiences to experience the plays of Sartre and others were not in London, but in places as apparently distanced from metropolitan theater as Bangor (*Morts sans sépulture*), the People's Theatre Newcastle (*Nekrassov*), The Century Theatre Worcester (Gabriel Marcel's *Un homme de Dieu*), or Merseyside Unity Theatre (Armand Salacrou's *Boulevard Durand*). The theater history recorded in the archives also emphasizes the centrality of Repertory, University, and amateur theater for sustaining this new work: pressure on the Lord Chamberlain to overturn the ban on *Huis clos* was received from amateur groups across the country, ranging from University of Edinburgh students to the Meteorological Office Drama Group, while the performance history of *La putain respectueuse*—from New Cross to Liverpool, where it was paired with a light comedy by Frederick Witney, *The Lady Elopes*—shows the way that challenging new work by Sartre was incorporated relatively easily into a classic English repertory model. With more diverse audiences came diverse reception, and the files have demonstrated the ways that these plays were received differently—and indeed framed differently—in these very different locations and contexts.

Finally, we can observe the particular challenge to the Lord Chamberlain that many of these plays presented in bringing together ideas of foreignness, sexuality, and an intellectual abstractedness. The "Frenchness" of the plays was often directly connected by the censors to the explicit depictions of sexuality (the "queer themes from the Continent" identified in *Huis clos* (RR, "Huis clos")), while the occasional efforts of the Office to understand existentialism were outnumbered by their outright rejection of its unfathomable intellectualism (or "existentialist hu-ha" (RR, "Lucifer and the Lord")). This reflected in microcosm the battle-lines that were already being drawn in the British theater in the post-war years; these were first theorized by Dan Rebellato, who reads the New Wave of British theater writing that emerged with John Osborne and others as an implicit "obliterating of the French" (Rebellato 1999, p. 147). John Osborne railed against those who promoted "a dollop of gynaecological metaphysic of Simone de Beauvoir, a trilogy from Sartre and a slice of melodrama from Camus" (see Rebellato 1999, p. 147) in favor of what Jimmy Porter (from his own breakthrough play *Look Back in Anger)* called "something strong, something simple…something English" (Osborne 1991, p. 39). In this, we may observe, the censors of St James's Palace were, paradoxically, closer to the avant-garde of new British playwrights—who were themselves battling to overturn theater censorship—than either side might have suspected.

References

An Act for Regulating Theatres 1843. (6&7 Victoria, c. 68). London: George E. Eyre and Andrew Spottiswoode Printers.

Freeman, Ted. 1998. *Theatres of War: French Committed Theatre from the Second World War to the Cold War.* Exeter: University of Exeter.

Ireland, John. 2012. Orality, Censorship, and Sartre's Theatrical Audience. *Sartre Studies International* 18 (2): 89–106.

Nicholson, Steve. 2003–2015. *The Censorship of British Drama, 1960–1968.* 4 vols. Exeter: University of Exeter.

O'Donohoe, Benedict. 2001. Dramatically Different: The Reception of Sartre's Theatre in London and New York. *Sartre Studies International* 7 (1): 1–18.

———. 2005. *Sartre's Theatre: Acts for Life.* Bern: Peter Lang.

Osborne, John. 1991. *Déjà Vu.* London: Dramatic Publishing.

Rebellato, Dan. 1999. *1956 and All That: The Making of Modern British Drama.* London: Routledge.

Report from the Joint Select Committee of the House of Lords and the House of Commons on the Stage Plays (Censorship). 1909. London: HMSO.

Sartre, Jean-Paul. 1948. *Existentialism and Humanism.* Translated by Philip Mairet. London: Methuen.

———. 1976. *Sartre on Theater.* Edited by Michel Contat and Michel Rybalka, translated by Frank Jellinek. London: Quartet.

———. 1988. *What Is Literature and Other Essays.* Translated by Steven Ungar. Cambridge, MA: Harvard University Press.

———. 2005. *Théâtre complet.* Edited by Michel Contat. Paris: Gallimard.

Shellard, Dominic, and Steve Nicholson with Miriam Handley. 2004. *The Lord Chamberlain Regrets: A History of British Censorship.* London: British Library.

The British Library. 2019. Lord Chamberlain's Plays. Accessed February 17, 2019. https://www.bl.uk/collection-guides/lord-chamberlains-plays.

Une pièce de J.-P Sartre interdite à Londres. 1946. *Le Figaro,* July 17.

Vane, Sutton. 1924. *Outward Bound.* London: Chatto & Windus.

Verney, Alain. 1946. Sartre à l'Index? *Franc-Tireur,* 14–15, July.

Bibliography of The Lord Chamberlain's Correspondence Archive[24]

The following files are part of the Lord Chamberlain's Correspondence archive, The British Library, London:
Anouilh, Jean:
LCP CORR 1948/9837, "Antigone".
LCP CORR 1949/21, "Antigone".
Camus, Albert:
LCP CORR 1949/126, "Caligula".
LCP1963/3631, "The Possessed".
De Beauvoir, Simone:
LCP CORR 1952/4299, "Les bouches inutiles".
Genet, Jean:
LCP CORR LICENCE REFUSED 1952/1, "The Maids".
LCP CORR 1957/WB19, "The Balcony".
LCP CORR 1961/1642, "The Blacks".
Marcel, Gabriel:
LCP CORR 1953/5126, "A Man of God".
LCP CORR 1953/5990, "Ariadne".
Roblès, Emmanuel:
LCP CORR 1952/3926, "Montserrat".
Sartre, Jean-Paul:
LCP CORR LICENCE REFUSED 1945/160, "Huis clos".
LCP CORR 1947/7906, "The Respectable Prostitute".
LCP CORR 1947/7907, "Men Without Shadows".
LCP CORR 1948/9305, "Crime Passionnel".
LCP CORR 1956/9493, "Nekrassov".
LCP CORR 1957/WB 15, "Lucifer and the Lord".
LCP CORR 1958/741, "The Flies".
LCP CORR 1958/995, "The Respectable Prostitute (Second Version)".
LCP CORR 1959/522, "Huis clos (French version)".
LCP CORR 1959/1888, "In Camera".
LCP CORR 1961/1673, "Altona".
LCP CORR 1964/4652, "The Respectable Prostitute (Third Version)".

---

[24] Files are part of The Lord Chamberlain's Correspondence archive, The British Library, London.

8

The Impact in Italy of Sartre and His Thinking

Francesco Caddeo

Sartre was an author who was present on the Italian intellectual landscape with quite some editorial success. In comparison to other nations—with the exception of France, of course—it is no exaggeration to say that Italy is the nation with which Sartre forged relations more considerable and longer lasting than anywhere else. In addition, the regular physical presence of Sartre on the Italian territory, especially for his holidays, allowed him to establish personal relationships of considerable depth with political figures and philosophers. Italy was a country wherein Sartre integrated himself into the cultural world on a personal level, particularly into the cultural world that was close to politics and that became a laboratory for ideas. In fact, Sartre's impressions of Italy were so important that he considered writing a monograph on Italy testifying his own change from the condition of a simple tourist to someone who had experienced the different aspects of life and Italian culture.

Existentialism as a whole gained a certain importance in the renewal of Italian philosophy and, with a focus on the era of liberation, in the

F. Caddeo (✉)
University of Lyon, Lyon, France

© The Author(s) 2020
A. Betschart, J. Werner (eds.), *Sartre and the International Impact of Existentialism*,
https://doi.org/10.1007/978-3-030-38482-1_8

151

opening up of Italian culture to what was beyond its narrow national borders. Although exerting certain influence, Sartre did not manage to make a lasting impression on the cultural panorama, and his thinking did not take root in universities.

First of all, to speak of Italian philosophy on the eve of the irruption of existentialism means to evoke the monopoly held by the idealism of Benedetto Croce and Giovanni Gentile. The former was a conservative hostile to fascism, the latter a minister and official philosopher of fascism for a few years. Idealist historicism was the dominant paradigm that stifled any other philosophical expression. When existentialism emerged between the early 1930s and the early 1940s, a sad period for Europe, it had to make its own path in the shadow of a philosophy that identified philosophy and history and made being a being of knowledge (on this point, see Limentani and Mondolfo 1985, pp. 103–124). Italian existentialism—mainly fed by the reading of Karl Jaspers and Martin Heidegger and the rediscovery of Søren Kierkegaard—developed in Turin, thanks to the work of Nicola Abbagnano and Luigi Pareyson, and in Milan, thanks to the contributions of Antonio Banfi and Enzo Paci. At least initially, it did not address French sources. Existentialism was about analyzing the relation of man to the world by focusing on the dimension of the possible and on human choices in a worldly existence with its unavoidable and effective materiality. It did not take refuge in an interior spirituality. Existence was considered in isolation and not reduced to a partial component of an absolute that overcomes it. Facing the tragedies of dictatorship, the triumphs of authoritarianism, and war on a European level, existentialism dealt with the problems of human failures, the wounds of history, and the issues of 'being-in-situation' that cannot refer to a historical rationality claiming to be the final realization of the absolute spirit. It is true that, at least as far as Italian culture is concerned, existentialism was a continuation of the prevailing idealism with regard to its mistrust of science and psychoanalysis, the limits and shadows of which it recognized.

As for the originality of the Italian contribution, we can focus on the existentialism of Milan, with Banfi and Paci at its center. Antonio Banfi has the merit of having begun the reinterpretation of Kierkegaard and the introduction of existentialist themes (Banfi 1953) in 1926. Banfi's understanding of existentialism centered on the ethical importance of individual responsibility, on the capacity to give oneself models of existence in a context where references are uncertain and without solid foundation. What Banfi progressively emphasized as the decisive aspect of existentialism was its focus on the aspects of the metaphysical crisis tied to the contemporary age, in which all traditional references were weakened—and in that sense, its cutting off all links to the idealism of nineteenth century—and on its proposal of an active component of transformation. Banfi's existentialism did not become an account of the individual's loneliness facing the dramatic aspects of life, but rather a dynamic reconstruction without confiding in the declining superstructures of metaphysics. The result was an anti-dogmatic philosophy that rejected both rationalism and irrationalism, affirming the limits of rationality and at the same time considering its presence to be necessary to start any discourse about responsibility (see Banfi 1941).

A few years later, Enzo Paci and Sartre began a discussion, both passionate and remote—passionate on a personal level, and remote because the two authors' theoretical nodes diverged. Paci found in Sartre themes on which Husserlian phenomenology, of which Paci was the great Italian interpreter, had not insisted enough, such as totalization and praxis. Paci presented an originality in his career that made him a real interlocutor and not an epigone of foreign existentialism. Drawing on the later Edmund Husserl, Alfred Whitehead, and Karl Marx, Paci proposed a philosophy independent from the gnoseological concerns that scrutinized the anxieties, finiteness, and temporality of human existence. Sartre entered the game not as an absolute model, but as a useful complement on specific points. For Paci, Sartre was the thinker who could effectively give another image of Marxism by reviving the notion of subjectivity that Paci interpreted as the action of the negative. In other words, subjectivity has a practical relationship with what exists because it denies what is contingent to transform it. Praxis thus operates as an opening to a horizon of meaning and presents itself as the irreversible action of change of an inherited reality. Therefore, with Paci, praxis emerges as negation as a result of incessant transformation (1973, pp. 3–4.). However, according to Paci, any consideration of praxis remains incomplete without a corresponding consideration of intersubjectivity.

Unlike Sartre, Paci completed the hard work of reading the unpublished Husserl and knew a series of texts Sartre never took in his hands. The Italian philosopher took advantage of this difference to juxtapose Husserl's idea of reference to lifeworld and Sartre's notion of totalization, which the German philosopher did not develop. For Paci, it was necessary to combine the Husserlian ideas of intersubjectivity that render the isolated individual a fiction with the idea of finality in human action conceived within the frame of totalization. Thus, any partial category of temporary worldliness and theoretical contingency is transcended. The horizon of finality, of *telos*, is dynamic and able to bring together—or, as Sartre would say, to 'wrap'—the various open relationships and to guide them. Paci's path toward the concrete meets Sartre at certain nodal points, for he shares with the French philosopher a dissolution of the metaphysical subject in the concrete of existence: in fact, Paci interpreted the concrete as an open relationship with the Other, as a connection through the gesture, the word, the sharing of practices that make the subject an entity in constitution through practices and not a master entity able to elude relationships with the Other (see Paci 1963). Thus, Paci's thinking detached itself from the existentialism of loneliness and the failure to lead to moral reflection on the construction of the world through the relationship with the Other—another who appears in a pre-categorial world.

Sartre as a Political Intellectual in Italy's Post-War Period

As far as relations with the broader cultural world are concerned, Sartre—and in particular his idea of engagement—burst into post-Fascist Italy together with other American and European writers who were read and disseminated to bring freshness after 20 years of dictatorial rhetoric and self-complacent nationalist propaganda. The culture that emerged through the rubble left by the war thus passed from the intellectual autarchy that had impoverished culture so much to the discovery of a series of foreign sources that had to be integrated in a culture in search of solid paradigms.

Indeed, the liberation in Italy had political (pluripartism was officially introduced after 20 years), economic (adherence to the Marshall Plan and the search for an economic policy allowing rapid reconstruction), cultural (free debate of ideas with the winners' ideologies being affirmed), and editorial meanings (with a policy of disclosures and education of the masses accompanied by an inflation of journals). Sartrean existentialism did not directly comply with the national narratives which were imposed after the liberation. Neither Catholicism nor the popular national culture promoted by the Italian Communist Party (PCI) found immediate consonance with Sartre's intellectual independence.[1]

The journals of the Catholic world armed themselves against the diffusion of Sartrean thought and warned their readers against any attention to an author who, as they told them, had no merit and 'speaks to an audience of amateurs, admirers of the absurd, the disoriented, the immoral, the corrupters of the human race' (Mondrone 1958, p. 252; trans. F.C.). Sometimes the tone was even more severe and invited the readers to forget Sartre and not to take his thoughts into consideration (Porcarelli 1948, p. 249).

On the progressive side, in the effervescence of the situation after the war, the development of left-wing thought could be witnessed, that led to the institutionalization of Gramsci's philosophy of history as an official philosophy of the PCI. However, that period was much more complex, with debates and statements. The most famous one materialized around the magazine *Il Politecnico*, directed by the writer Elio Vittorini. Although funded by the PCI, this magazine claimed independence from any editorial instruction. It emphasized the need to discuss the theses of bourgeois writers showing self-criticism and a policy of emancipation of the masses, including a wide dissemination of ideas not directly in line with the guidelines of the PCI. Vittorini's challenge was to avoid the double trap of intellectual isolationism in public debate and submission to Party directives that, in the short run, could only have stifled cultural aspirations.[2] Sartre's name and his claims were among the weapons that

---

[1] We take advantage here of Giovanni Invitto's rich fund of references in Invitto (1987).
[2] For an exhaustive summary of this controversy, see Faracovi (1987).

Vittorini aimed to use to defend himself against a party orthodoxy that progressively accused him of deviationism and cosmopolitanism.

However, it would be unfair and simplistic to reduce the Togliatti[3]-Vittorini conflict to a confrontation between a 'bad' political secretary of the PCI and the activist writer in favor of culture: we are well aware that Togliatti was also a man of culture and that his preoccupations were the result of a complicated balance between short-term and medium-term politics, between national requirements and international fidelity to Soviet Marxism, between participation in national reconstruction and the need to build an ideological line sheltered from confusion. On the other hand, it must be emphasized that Vittorini's valuable work was intended to capture the richness of the contemporary human and literary sciences without displaying a clear philosophical choice. Compared to Sartre, Vittorini lacked a theoretical work clarifying the foundations of his thoughts and preventing voluntarist eclecticism. Sartre was more courageous. He touched the delicate question of political activities by writers and rendered the clear division between intellectual and politician more complicated. Vittorini, in contrast, remained a prisoner of his own vision of culture as separate from political praxis, which he left to professional politicians (Faracovi 1987, p. 227) and which almost ended up sealing an inseparable divide between cultural production and political ideology.

It is widely known that Sartre harbored a certain sympathy for the PCI, which he considered a cousin more open and more inclined to debates than the highly dogmatic and Stalinist French Communist Party. He also appreciated the culture of the leaders of the PCI, starting with its leader Togliatti, and the cultural politics of the party that associated with intellectuals and writers without submitting them to stifling doctrinal pressure. Indeed, he did not cut his relations with the PCI until 1968, and considered the climate established by the PCI as favorable to sincere discussions. However, frictions were not lacking, as in 1962, after the release of Andrei Tarkovsky's film *Ivan's Childhood*. Sartre wrote an open letter to Mario Alicata, the director of the party newspaper *L'Unità*, to defend the film against the bitter and scornful judgments of the

---

[3] Palmiro Togliatti was the secretary-general of the PCI during two periods, 1927–1934 and 1938–1964.

newspaper's critics (Sartre 1972b). The exaltation of the film was accompanied by Sartre's call for freedom of expression and stylistic innovation against accusations of 'cosmopolitanism' and 'petty bourgeois' art. Sartre took the opportunity to reveal the simplistic categories used by the Party intellectuals and their lack of knowledge of cinematographic techniques (Sartre 1972b, pp. 290–291), and to reintroduce the theme of the tragedy of history that was not taken into account by the Soviet realism advocated by the communist officials in the field of art. Sartre covertly continued this controversy on cultural policy the following year in an interview with the PCI weekly *Rinascita* (Sartre 1972a, p. 313). During a period that the French philosopher defined as 'cultural expansion', Sartre claimed the need for debate, including non-Marxist bourgeois forces, because, in his opinion, Marxist analysis had to provoke an articulate response from opponents and the final result would be rewarding if the game of answers and criticisms continued progressively without shutting the discussion behind a doctrine.

From 1969 onward, Sartre showed his support for the leftists of *Manifesto*, who had been expelled from the PCI and with whom *Les Temps modernes* began a rich exchange of articles and contributions. The relationship with the PCI was thus interrupted: Togliatti had already died in 1964, and Sartre would never have the opportunity nor the will to get close to the new secretary-general Enrico Berlinguer, who moved away from leftist positions and pursued a program of rapprochement to power, culminating in the *Compromesso storico* (see Castellina 2015). To understand the change in Sartre's relationship with the PCI and, more generally, with cultural positioning, his last intervention on the Italian political scene has to be mentioned: it was about his signing a document in favor of the meetings of Italian leftists in Bologna in 1977—while France, during this same period, was in full anti-leftist swing—and against police repression and the axis of government of which the PCI had become a satellite. On this point, it is interesting to read Simone de Beauvoir's testimony:

> Sartre had signed a manifesto against repression in Italy: in doing so, he had raised a storm in the Italian press, especially in the communist press. *Lotta continua*, the far-left newspaper with which *Les Temps modernes* had

excellent relations, asked Sartre for an interview on this question. M.-A. Macciocchi insisted that he supported the Bologna meetings. Rossana Rossanda asked him not to support them: she foresaw a catastrophe. Sartre met several leaders of *Lotta continua* on 19th of September [1977] in the little cafe of which I have just spoken; they published the four-page interview in their September 15 issue under the title *Freedom and Power Do Not Go Together* (*Libertà e potere non vanno in coppia*). (...) He affirmed his solidarity with the young people, but wished that there was no violence in Bologna. His words pleased everyone, including Rossana Rossanda. (Beauvoir 1981, pp. 149–150; trans. F.C.)

This interview dealt with the questions of PCI, violence, the importance of dissent, Marxism, and the *nouveaux philosophes*.[4] A libertarian Sartre was emerging who claimed to have learned the lessons of Marxism and was looking for other horizons, an old philosopher who realized that the philosophical questions were changing. They no longer revolved around the question of the seizure of power, but rather the affirmation of freedom in relation to power that corrupts (Sartre 1977). The French philosopher showed his lucidity with regard to the authoritarian development underway in liberal countries, a development which the PCI henceforth joined. In his interview, Sartre also emphasized the different weights of the political parties in cultural life. In Italy, unlike France, the public intellectual was almost obliged to rely on a party he could relate to. This made the intellectual a critical figure, a man related to the functions of the state and the institutional machine.

Sartre between Marxism and Post-Marxism

The first conference in which Sartre participated at the Gramsci Institute in Rome in 1961 (the second would be three years later) was preceded a year earlier by the publication of essays by Sartre under the title *Che cos'é*

---

[4] Literally 'new philosophers'—i.e. André Glucksmann, Bernard-Henri Lévy, etc. They represented the anti-Marxist left at the end of the 70s, a sort of anti-totalitarian thinking about human rights and about the right of intervention to save democracy all over the world against communism and anti-colonial radicalism.

la letteratura? (*What is Literature?*; Sartre 1960). The essays were taken from the series *Situations* and included the contribution *Materialism and Revolution*, in which Sartre took stock of the inadequacies of the materialism preached by Marxism slipping back to dogmatism. According to Sartre, Marxism had moved away from the necessity of analyzing the situation in terms of its future transgression in order to place matter, with its self-founded mechanisms, at the center of its dialectics.

In addition, the effective question to ask throughout Sartre's writings was that of subjectivity: Sartre allows us not to choose between idealistic subjectivity and Marxist objectivity. His commitment remained a bet for the future without falling into historicist optimism: Sartre conceived a subjectivity that brings into play and immerses itself into the materiality of the world without returning to oneself.

The 1961 conference in Rome showed the intellectually open character of the PCI in comparison to the French Communist Party. The latter rather looked for experienced speechwriters repeating the established doctrine, and not for researchers questioning the foundations of Marxism. As well remembered by the two persons responsible for the publication of Sartre's speech (Kail and Kirchmayr 2013, p. 11), Sartre first highlighted the ontological distinction between subject and consciousness. With Sartre, the latter has a connotation quite different from György Lukács's class consciousness: according to the Hungarian philosopher, the path of consciousness is already established by the philosophy of history, and the movement of consciousness itself must conform to a being already thought beforehand. Sartre sketched his own vision of intentional consciousness—thus resuming his youthful ideas, at the time of writing the *Transcendence of the Ego*—and conceived intentionality as a bursting out, a 'going elsewhere' without interiority: therefore, consciousness is an element immersed in the world, an energy transcending its own positioning.

Subjectivity with Sartre is nothing fixed, no identity, nothing individual: it is at once a non-object—because it cannot position itself as an object without shifting its own intentionality—and a transparent element not to be considered as a mysterious and underlying vital force. This subjectivity is therefore not an interiority, a center of knowledge and reflection, but a movement toward targeted qualities: in other words, it is a response to instructions, and it can differentiate itself from these instructions by producing itself each time as an answer different from them. Consequently, the Sartrean text presents to us a subjectivity under construction, starting from needs, work, and desires: it is exactly this type of relation which brings to light the existence of subjectivity. In other words, subjectivity with Sartre is not an autonomous being opposed to matter, but is rather characterized by the intentional relations represented by needs, work, and desires. The subjectivity can be found when one asks the questions: who lives a need? Which entity works? Which intentional force desires? With Sartre, subjectivity emerges within a series of relations on which it is dependent, but without confusing its capacities for action with the intentional matter.

Unfortunately, the *Critique of Dialectical Reason* was ignored in Italy. As in France, Sartre fell victim to his own simplifications—we tend to read *Existentialism Is a Humanism* to escape *Being and Nothingness*, and stop at *Search for a Method* to avoid the overly complicated *Critique of Dialectical Reason*. The Italian philosophical landscape largely lost the opportunity for an in-depth reflection on rarity, the group-in-fusion, and impersonal praxis.[5] By limiting itself to the programmatic philosophy of *Search for a Method*, it considered the *Critique* one of the many expressions of Western Marxism—dedicated to eclecticism and making Marx an author 'to be completed with other philosophical contributions', of which the Frankfurt School would be the most widely read example of the time.

Simultaneously an exception and a confirmation of this tendency, the 1965 anthology by Franco Fortini, *Profezie e realtà del nostro secolo* (*Prophecies and Reality in Our Century*; Fortini 1965), integrated Sartre into the critical thought of the post-war period. It juxtaposed an excerpt from *Search for a Method* and one from the *Critique of Dialectical Reason* with texts by the heroes of anti-colonialism (Nelson Mandela, Malcolm X, Frantz Fanon, James Baldwin among others) Marxist leftist culture (Herbert Marcuse, Theodor Adorno, Mario Tronti), anthropology

---

[5] An exception to the understanding of the *Critique* was Sergio Moravia a few years later. Moravia fully understood how the Sartrean operation moved the sociological issue from class activity to group activity. Although Moravia rejected this notion as ahistorical and too vague in light of the inequalities of capitalist production, he acknowledged that this notion moved Sartre away from the classic view of Hegelian history as the unfolding of reason (Moravia 1983, p. 128).

(Claude Lévi-Strauss, Ernesto De Martino), and other specialists in sociology. Through that, Sartre was made the umpteenth critic of alienation provoked by mass society. However, the novelty of this anthology in terms of Sartre's presence is revealed in the choice of the passage of the *Critique*. Fortini emphasized Sartre's insights with regard to the latter's analyses of social ensembles (Fortini 1965, pp. 415–416), particularly of the processes of serialization and the formation of collectivity on an inertial and atomized basis. Unfortunately, the limitations of the anthology hampered a real theoretical discussion of the importance of the group in Sartre's concept. Sartre's theory of social ensembles would have allowed to relativize the notion of class and to show the versatility of the notion of the group, of which class is only a particular case. Indeed, it allows extension of the analysis by going beyond the historical time, in particular the social polarization in the industrial society, and avoids social dualism between proprietors and workers. The multiple nature of the notion of the group makes it possible to present an articulated vision of the social fabric and to leave behind the simple socioeconomic characterization in favor of a more complex understanding of the differentiations in society.

The same year, writer and translator Pietro Chiodi published *Sartre e il marxismo* (*Sartre and Marxism*; Chiodi 1965), a study synthesizing the thinking of Sartre, German existentialism, and Karl Marx. This text—which is an unavoidable critical reference in Italian studies, still read today, even if knowledge of the original texts is indispensable—is somewhat outdated from the point of view of interpretation. Praxis as conceived by Sartre was extended to a classic subject–object relation, and the connection between Marxism and existentialism—especially the complementarity of the two—was summed up around the theme of alienation. In this study, Sartre seems to be late in comparison to Heidegger's research and confined to a Hegelian idealism that Chiodi corrected by including Kierkegaard and the 1844 manuscripts of Marx (Chiodi 1965, particularly pp. 13–18, 48–50). Chiodi tended to emphasize the inadequacies of Sartrean thought, and he particularly denounced its alleged metaphysical dualisms (Chiodi 1965, pp. 84–85) and the pessimism vis-à-vis the possibilities of collectivities and of multiplicity (Chiodi 1965, pp. 136–139), which are subject to the law of the inevitable fall into alienation, according to Chiodi.

The reception of Sartre's thinking in Italy was highly complex. Philosophical interest in Sartre experienced a period of decline after the debates with the PCI in the early 60s. In 1967, in his large volume on existentialism, Santucci described Sartre's philosophy as dusty and as a secondary reference in intellectual research (Santucci 1967, p. 429). The reception of Sartre seemed to be transferred to the literary side—remember that the 1965 edition of *Nausea* sold 190,000 copies in the same year. A similar fate befell Sartre's theater: since 1945, his works had been inserted in the programming of the best contemporary theaters, together with a series of foreign authors who made their entry in Italy: a theater icon like Giorgio Strehler was particularly interested in *In the Mesh* (*L'engrenage*) in 1953; during the 60s, *No Exit, Dirty Hands*, and *The Devil and the Good Lord*) enjoyed valuable performances and aroused public interest—see, for example, the staging of *Dirty Hands* in Turin in 1964, with the explicit and public authorization of Sartre. However, Sartre was an eternal underdog in the theatrical landscape (Tessari 1987).

Here we share the questions posed by Eugenio Garin, who spoke about a passage by Sartre in Italian culture that was engulfed in the play of philosophical eclecticism between phenomenological exegesis, Heideggerian themes, and a Marx quoted without being discussed (Garin 1966, p. 546), all managed by a series of issues of academic rather than political character.

Existentialism never took root in Italian philosophy. Heidegger was read in the ontological and hermeneutic sense, thus leaving the centrality of *Dasein* from its first interpretations; Marxism was not to be renewed by existentialism, but overcome by its own internal crisis; Husserl and Maurice Merleau-Ponty, considered to be more rigorous than Sartre, would experience new fertile waves of studies; and the philosophical left would turn to postmodernism, relativism, and poststructuralism, thus sealing the transgression of Sartrean thought—Sartrean thought that was undoubtedly known, but not widely debated.

Leaving content aside, what could have produced appreciable results would have been a figure similar to that of Sartre, combining contributions on the level of a specialist and public debate, courage and competence, independence and presence in the news. There were two figures in Italian culture who had characters similar to that of Sartre's: Pier Paolo Pasolini and Franco Basaglia. The two figures were both characteristic of the social turn of the 60s and were victims of hostilities spread in a culture that saw in them a disturbance of the order of morals. They both followed a track similar to Sartre's—refusal of academic teaching, vision of the intellectual as doomed to intervention in society, political commitment as a necessary corollary of their personal work—and both were confronted by the immobility of a close-meshed Italian society. Pier Paolo Pasolini shared with Sartre only the idea of a polemist's writing capable of 'shaking heads' and awakening consciences, writing as denunciation, making the bourgeoisie face its hypocrisies and its faults, but without an effective thematic continuity. In his thought, the writer was entrusted with a historical and political role—effectively to change the society in which he was operating. Franco Basaglia, on the other hand, presented a real resumption of Sartrean themes and made Sartre his reference figure for his actions that included psychiatric care, criticism of the medical action and the structure of the hospital, and the need to link the social issue of marginality to the functioning of society as a whole.

Pasolini recognized the importance of Sartrean commitment, but he limited his own commitment to a production of essays, and he emphasized the lack of effective literary creativity accompanying engagement (Pasolini 1977b, p. 303). For the Italian writer, the presence of Sartre in culture was brilliant, but it did not translate into a discontinuity of literary forms that would have represented a real break with the past of the French academic tradition. Pasolini sarcastically concluded that the literary avant-garde of the 1950s would at least have spared Sartre from destruction and would have made him the only figure in the literary pantheon (Pasolini 1977b, p. 304). A few months earlier, Pasolini had already clarified his own idea of engagement in Sartrean terms: in fact, he declared that the committed writer had to participate in the workers' struggle and that this gesture had to be a choice, a free decision that came from his very culture (Pasolini 1977a, p. 236).

Basaglia found in Sartre his fundamental reference. Indeed, Sartre's thinking allowed him to take into account the specific issues of his discipline—a psychiatry that locks up and objectifies the patient, marginalizes the 'mad'—and to totalize this criticism at the politico-social level. Criticism of psychiatry could therefore not be confined to the hospital walls, but it had to question the social structures that made it possible (see Basaglia 1968, p. 7). Therefore, coercive medical action—confinement, the doctor's authoritarianism, the passivity of the patient subjected to drugs, and rigid protocols of the hospital—made the sick a body-for-others without autonomous existence. In addition, this gaze objectifying the patient's body was a look that the psychiatric structure conferred to relieve society of the patient's presence: the latter had left psychiatry the task of isolating the 'patient' and eliminating him from its view. Since he was not considered to be suitable for production processes, his body need not disturb the social functioning. On this point, the institution was the negation of the living body of the 'madman', of his ability to interact and express himself, and to be only a role, an existence confined to his 'sick' status (see Basaglia 2005, p. 103). According to Basaglia, the doctor had therefore to be destructive toward his own institution and his own role: across the Sartre of *Being and Nothingness*, it was a question of not giving in to the team spirit, to the *Mit-sein*, interpreted in a Sartrean way, that makes us acritical members of the group's functioning. More generally, it was necessary to make the inherited situation not an eternal and unsurpassable datum, but the product of an operation, of a large machinery that can be sabotaged, dismantled, and broken.

It remains to be seen what Sartre would have to say now in the face of the comeback of obscurantism, nationalist and chauvinist populism, reactionary Catholicism, and media and advertising politics. Would he succumb to the temptation of weak and fragile thought in front of an overflowing mediatization in which the intellectuals are devoured by the language of the TV set? His segmented journey prevents us from defining his role under an unequivocal label. Sartre was neither an academic professor (today in Italy, the intellectual is too withdrawn), nor a party intellectual (now nonexistent), nor a media character (today, this is reduced to a disgusting professional chattering and sterile repetition on TV sets).

We have thus summarized very different aspects that show how Sartre was an author who penetrated several domains of Italian culture. However, he did not manage to break through. Between his literature of engagement that could not enter the well-compartmentalized Italian culture and a political debate in which his philosophical ideas were reserved for specialists with open horizons, Sartre struggled to find an effective place in the Italian cultural landscape, away from the fluctuations of ephemeral fashions and trends.

References

Banfi, Antonio. 1941. Il problema dell'esistenza. *Studi Filosofici* 3: 170–192.
———. 1953. Il problema della filosofia contemporanea (1926). In *Filosofi contemporanei*, ed. Remo Cantoni, 75–95. Firenze: Parenti.
Basaglia, Franco. 1968. Presentazione. In *L'istituzione negata*, ed. Franco Basaglia, 7–9. Torino: Einaudi.
———. 2005. Corpo e istituzione (1967). In *L'utopia della realtà*, ed. Franco Basaglia, 100–113. Turin: Einaudi.
de Beauvoir, Simone. 1981. *La Cérémonie des adieux*. Paris: Gallimard.
Castellina, Luciana. 2015. Sartre in Italia. *Il Manifesto*, 31–32, December 5.
Chiodi, Pietro. 1965. *Sartre e il marxismo*. Milan: Feltrinelli.
Faracovi, Ornella Pompei. 1987. Intellettuali e impegno in tre riviste del dopoguerra. In *Sartre e l'Italia*, ed. Ornella Pompeo Faracovi and Sandra Teroni, 222–230. Livorno: Belforte.
Fortini, Franco. 1965. *Profezie e realtà del nostro secolo*. Bari: Laterza.
Garin, Eugenio. 1966. Quindici anni dopo. In *Cronache di filosofia italiana*, ed. Eugenio Garin, vol. II, 489–617. Bari: Laterza.
Invitto, Giovanni. 1987. Sartre e i filosofi italiani. In *Sartre e l'Italia*, ed. Ornella Pompeo Faracovi and Sandra Teroni, 181–199. Livorno: Belforte.
Kail, Michel, and Raoul Kirchmayr. 2013. Préface. Conscience et subjectivité. In *Qu'est-ce que la subjectivité?* ed. Jean-Paul Sartre, 5–25. Paris: Les Prairies ordinaires.
Limentani, Ludovico, and Rodolfo Mondolfo. 1985. Formes et tendances actuelles du mouvement philosophique en Italie (1936), trans. Pierre Schreker. In *Histoire intellectuelle et culturelle du XXᵉ siècle*, ed. Pierre Monzani, 103–124. Paris: Albin Michel.
Mondrone, Domenico. 1958. Il messaggio disperato di J.-P. Sartre. *Civiltà Cattolica*, 224–252, January.
Moravia, Sergio. 1983. *Introduzione a Sartre*. Bari: Laterza.
Paci, Enzo. 1963. Funzione delle scienze e significato dell'uomo, 364–367. Milano: Il Saggiatore.
———. 1973. La negazione in Sartre. *aut aut*, 3–12, 136–137, July–October.
Pasolini, Pier Paolo. 1977a. L'intellettuale impegnato (1964). In *Pasolini, Le belle bandiere*, ed. Pier Paolo, 235–238. Roma: Editori Riuniti.
———. 1977b. Le ragioni di un non amore (1965). In *Le belle bandiere*, ed. Pier Paolo Pasolini, 300–304. Roma: Editori Riuniti.
Porcarelli, Vanio. 1948. La Metafisica di Sartre. *Rivista di filosofia neoscolastica* 3: 249–257.

Santucci, Antonio. 1967. *Esistenzialismo e filosofia italiana*. Bologna: Il Mulino.

Sartre, Jean-Paul. 1960. *Che cos'é la letteratura?* Translated by Davide Tarizzo. Milano: Il Saggiatore.

————. 1972a. Coesistenza pacifica e confronto delle idee (1963). In *Il filosofo e la politica*, ed. Jean-Paul Sartre, 309–316. Roma: Editori Riuniti.

————. 1972b. Una perdita secca (1962). In *Il filosofo e la politica*, ed. Jean-Paul Sartre, 289–296. Roma: Editori Riuniti.

————. 1977. Libertà et potere non vanno in coppia. *Lotta continua*, 2–10, September 9.

Tessari, Roberto. 1987. Presenza e assenza di Sartre nel teatro italiano. In *Sartre in Italia*, ed. Ornella Pompeo Faracovi and Sandra Teroni, 158–177. Livorno: Belforte.

9

Toward an Ethics of Singularity: Temporality, Irreversibility, and Need in the Dialogue between Jean-Paul Sartre and Enzo Paci

Raoul Kirchmayr

I

In recent years, three posthumous texts by Sartre have been published concerning the problem of the foundation of a non-normative ethics. All of them have allowed us to discover an underground work that Sartre pursued between the end of the 50s and the beginning of the 60s. In many ways, that was a crucial time in his intellectual life, because, at that time, he was confronted with a new stage of continental philosophy, particularly in France, where structuralism started to compete with existentialism for cultural hegemony.[1] In the same period, he was breaking his

---

[1] Mainly after the publication of *The Elementary Structures of Kinship* by Claude Lévi-Strauss (Lévi-Strauss 1969), Levi-Strauss's book had been reviewed in 1949 by Simone de Beauvoir in *Les Temps modernes* and had been hailed as a pivotal work in contemporary ethnographic research (see Beauvoir 1949). Later on, in the last chapter of *The Savage Mind*, Lévi-Strauss declared that Sartre's interpretation of his masterpiece had been nothing but a misunderstanding: structuralism could not be referred back to a dialectical reason (see Levi-Strauss 1966, pp. 245–269).

R. Kirchmayr (✉)
University of Trieste, Trieste, Italy

© The Author(s) 2020
A. Betschart, J. Werner (eds.), *Sartre and the International Impact of Existentialism*,
https://doi.org/10.1007/978-3-030-38482-1_9

167

fairly brief companionship with the French Communist Party. This huge endeavor—that appears to the researcher's eyes like a real building site—corresponds somehow to the promised development of the *Critique of Dialectical Reason*, whose second volume was dedicated to comprehension of the 'concrete' in history and to a renewed philosophical anthropology. Nevertheless, the second volume was never completed by Sartre, even if—as we know following its publication in 1985—it achieved a substantial and ultimately consistent elaboration of its main themes.

The titles of the three posthumous texts are *What Is Subjectivity?* (published in French and English in 2013), *The Roots of Ethics* (original version in French *Les racines de l'éthique*, edited and published in 2015 in *Études sartriennes*; Sartre 2016) and *Moral and History* (the original version in French appeared as *Morale et histoire* in 2005, in a special issue of *Les Temps modernes*; Sartre 2005). They correspond, respectively, to the lecture given by Sartre in December 1961 at the Gramsci Institute in Rome, to the speech given in Rome three years later in 1964 and to the dialectical ethics developed for the lectures at Cornell University, in 1964–1965, that did not take place, because of Sartre's refusal following the American military escalation policy in Vietnam. What is now available is not the whole mass of pages written by Sartre or the complete discussion in which he got involved after his 1961 lecture, an edited version of which is still awaited.[2] In reference to the second speech, a short text was published in the proceedings of the conference by the Italian Communist Party publishing house, the Editori Riuniti, with the title *Determinazione e libertà* (*Determination and Freedom*, Sartre 1966), the original version showing a remarkable development of the subject of temporality in an ethical perspective, a topic debated three years earlier by Sartre. Finally, *Moral and History* represents just a part of the folder containing about 800 pages written to prepare the Cornell lectures.

In such a complex philosophical period, Sartre had a fruitful and quite long exchange with the Italian phenomenologist Enzo Paci.[3] I assume

---

[2] In fact, the typescript of the debate has been published only partially because of an editorial choice that preferred to offer just an abridged version of the long and dense discussion between Sartre and the Italian communist intellectuals (see Sartre 2013). The Italian edition offers a broad résumé of the debate (see Sartre 2015).

[3] Enzo Paci (1911–1976) was one of the most prominent phenomenologists in Italy. Following the path of the rationalist thinker Antonio Banfi, he studied Husserl's phenomenology, which he

here the hypothesis that the making of the Sartrean dialectical ethics, in its complex and rather contradictory foundations, can be seen as a result of some theoretical developments that, in a certain sense, represent a consequence of dialogue between the two philosophers. In particular, I will focus on the concepts of irreversibility, temporality and singularity that, considered together, form a peculiar constellation shared by Sartre and Paci.

The dialogue between Sartre and Paci was not limited to a careful tuning of a possible phenomenological reconstruction of dialectical reason, which was the common core of their respective researches during the late 50s and the early 60s. Moreover, Paci developed in an original way the philosophical principles and the methodological approach to the social and historical phenomena that Sartre had outlined a few years earlier in *A Search for a Method*. The theoretical perspective introduced by Paci, which he called "relationism" (Paci 1957), takes as its starting point the problem of the subject and the relationship between inside and outside, between the Same and the Other, connecting to it the issue of the dialectic between man and the world on the one hand, and man and history on the other. The most important result of this work is provided in the volume *Funzione delle scienze e significato dell'uomo* (*Function of Science and the Meaning of Man*, published in 1963): right from the title, the essay recalls the legacy of the *Crisis of the European Sciences* by Husserl and reflects on the immanent, concrete and historical possibility to overcome the crisis by means of a dialectic rationality reformed, thanks to a graft of phenomenology, into the Marxist theoretical body. In this way, Paci outlines the possibility of founding an open theoretical system that aims to ensure a methodological platform established for a new thinking of the Marxist concept of praxis.

Politically speaking, this operation cannot be considered as neutral. In fact, between 1956 and 1968, Paci fully endorsed instances of Marxism. Together with other Italian intellectuals, he shared the idea that Marxism

---

reinterpreted as an endless project of foundation of an encyclopedia of science. He taught theoretical philosophy at the State University of Milan and was the founder of the philosophical journal "Aut Aut". Among his most relevant publications are the essays *Tempo e verità nella fenomenologia di Husserl* (*Time and Truth in Husserl's Phenomenology*, 1961), *Funzione delle scienze e significato dell'uomo* (*Functions of Sciences and the Meaning of Man*, Bari: Laterza, 1963) and *Idee per una enciclopedia fenomenonologica* (*Ideas for a Phenomenological Encyclopedia*, Milan: Bompiani, 1973).

could offer the general framework for a historical understanding of economic and political processes. Therefore, it could also produce suitable conditions for the formation of a social subject resistant to the forces of neo-capitalism, embodying a historical and revolutionary project of disalienation and emancipation.

What was important in Paci's reappraisal of Marxist theory was a deep investigation of the topic of subjectivity. Paci considered it from a historical perspective as a practical foundation for values. In his theoretical approach, a concretely determined subjectivity can outline the human ends in an open horizon. For this reason, the ethical question has to be posed on the level of subjectivity: Paci made his philosophical move through a frank confrontation with Sartre, starting from the phenomenological perspective inaugurated by Husserl at the end of his career with *The Crisis of the European Sciences* and the collateral texts published posthumously. For Husserl, the subject has always to be considered as embodied. He called an embodied subject conceived as a monad *volle Konkretion* ("full concretion"). Because of the embodiment, every subject is "situated", as Sartre puts it in *Being and Nothingness*, and "being-in-situation" (*être en situation*) requires an analysis of the social, historical and political phenomena that condition the subject. Nevertheless, Sartre's existentialist *opus magnum* turns around the question of freedom of the *réalité humaine*, and the "situation" can, at most, describe a structural alienation which is not historical but ontological. During the 50s, the question of history became more and more clear to Sartre. For this reason, the problem of a subject seen in its material, practical and concrete dimensions started to be approached from a hybrid perspective that tried to put together phenomenology and Marxism, as the Vietnamese philosopher Trân Duc Thao did masterfully in his *Phenomenology and Dialectical Materialism* (Trân 2011).

Mentioning a decisive issue in the last Husserl, namely, the thinker that emphasized the "world-of-life" (*Lebenswelt*) as the last foundation for philosophical and scientific thought, Paci reinterpreted phenomenology in such a way to refer each theoretical construct back to a sociohistorical reality, thus focusing on the material determinations that affect the subjective existence in a social development marked by historical conflict. Paci primarily considers these references to subjectivity and to history as dialectical patterns based on conflict. They can be seen as many theoretical points tangential to the paths followed by Sartre in those years.

II

Sartre and Paci had met at least once before the 12 December 1961 lecture. In Paci's *Diario fenomenologico* (*Phenomenological Notebook*), published in the same year, two notes written by Paci and dedicated to Sartre can be found. The first dates back to 11 October 1960, shortly after the publication of the *Critique*. Paci tells that in his lessons given at the State University, he would simultaneously analyze Husserl's *Crisis of the European Sciences* and Sartre's *Critique*.[4] Then he adds: "what the contemporary thought seeks is precisely the concept of 'practical' ensemble" (Paci 1961, p. 109). Theoretically speaking, this note is significant because it calls into question both the philosophical and the political procedures for setting up a collective subject: the phenomenological issue concerning the foundation of the transcendental intersubjectivity, which is the philosophical center of Husserl's *Fifth Cartesian Meditation*. The issue is developed in an original way as the opening for a social theory built on phenomenological grounds. It should also be noted that investigations of *Being and Nothingness* in that regard had resulted in a theoretical cul-de-sac—as Sartre would later recognize (see Sartre 1965)—since his idea of the collective subject was defined in terms of a transition from one individual consciousness (the For-Itself) to a consciousness that is both unitary and plural (the We-subject) but constituted through the objectification/alienation that it incurs in relation to the Other. What was lost in the dialectic of conflict in *Being and Nothingness* was precisely the size of the historical and social concrete, in addition to its political determinations. The pattern elaborated by Sartre in *Being and Nothingness* could work at most as a description of an ontological relationship, but couldn't be linked to history (see Sartre 1985).

---

[4] See Rovatti (1987, p. 202) "The dialogue becomes fully explicit around 1960, in the horizon of phenomenology, when Sartre is, in Paci's eyes, the philosopher who rethinks Marxism critically by closely approaching the phenomenological themes of the subject and meaning, but without a complete awareness of them".

In Paci's eyes, the notion of 'practical ensemble' is crucial, to the point that in the note he develops an argument in which he stresses the progress achieved by Sartre in his research on the definition of practical ensembles. First of all, he emphasizes the phenomenological heritage in Sartre's dialectical thought:

> On the one hand, Sartre rightly formulated the problem of practical dialectics on 'ensemble': it is the center of his book. Undoubtedly, for this reason he has not been understood. On the other hand, Sartre himself does not know how much his position is a Husserlian one (…). Anyway, Sartre has deepened the dialectic beyond Husserl's point of view. So, phenomenology appropriates the problems of Marxism when, at the same time, existentialism reveals itself, to employ Sartre's terminology, as a 'parasitic' philosophy, although inevitable. (Paci 1961, p. 110)

In order to explain this passage, Paci defines the meaning of 'practical ensemble', which he links to the central concept of irreversibility. Later on, he defined the relationship between subjectivity, temporality and need in terms of the concept of irreversibility. This concept allowed him to describe how subjectivity is anchored in history. This anchorage, that is the mutual relationship between an inside and an outside, has to be defined as *ethical*. As Sartre puts both in his *Racines de l'éthique* and in *Morale et histoire*, need is the basis for a dialectical ethics, a 'radical ethics', as he terms it, in which need stands for the relationship itself. Adopting this perspective, praxis, in its philosophical status, depends upon irreversibility. But what is irreversibility, for Paci? In the same note, he says:

> Irreversibility is the essential and necessary mode of time: on it one can also build up its 'economic structure'. Time has an irreversible direction, but this direction can be transformed by man and can thus become meaningful, a meaning for history and reality. (Paci 1961, p. 110)

In order to explain this argument, he cites two quotations from the *Critique*, and he crosses irreversibility and totality:

> I can find confirmation in Sartre, who tends to see the sense as a transformation of the irreversible (a concept that was 'almost unknown' in Husserl)

in rationality and truth. For Sartre the 'individual and the group' acquire their sense in the 'raison intelligible de l'irréversibilité de l'Histoire'. 'L'Orientation de la totalisation, est ... le sens de l'Histoire et sa vérité'. (*Critique*, p. 156)[5]

The final link in the subjectivity-irreversibility-temporality chain is the dimension of history. Paci writes that history "can be understood as the product of a totalizing praxis", which is always, for him, an intentional totality. This requires the idea of a universal teleology and of a society based on phenomenological intersubjectivity. At the same time, it needs a foundation of science by means of phenomenology as a science of the *Lebenswelt*. The note ends this way: "I believe that Sartre agrees, although he doesn't set out these issues in a strict Husserlian way" (Paci 1961, p. 111).

In the note dated 11 January, 1961—that is eight months before the Rome conference—Paci reports a meeting between him and Sartre in Milan:

> It was a real joy to have Sartre here in Milan. We had breakfast with many friends. He insisted on the importance of the problem of subjectivity. He is perfectly conscious of the relationship between his concept of 'ensemble' with that of the mathematicians, while he evidently employs it in a differ-ent direction, I would say 'phenomenological'. He sees with favor a phe-nomenological reading of the *Critique*. (Paci 1961, p. 115)

How the note continues is particularly remarkable, since it refers to sub-jectivity as the center of gravity of his own philosophical research:

> On the problem of dialectic between internalization and externalization we begin a discourse that seeks to illuminate the relationship between an exte-rior not internalized and the unconscious. It seems possible to me, along this way, to see a very significant connection between what we call 'uncon-scious' and the exteriority of things, world and history. At one point the speech deals longer with the *Critique* and takes new directions (...). He insists on the fact that internalization is a work, a praxis. I feel myself

---

[5] "the intelligible reason of History's irreversibility". "The orientation of the totalization is... the sense of History and its truth" (Paci 1961, p. 110).

convinced about my hypothesis to investigate to what extent the unconscious is also a way of being within ourselves in the material world. A way
of being that has been remaining not conscious for such a long time that
we have assumed it. Although we are not aware of it, we are rooted in matter, which is within us. 'Internalized' by work, by the different kinds of
praxis, then it becomes one of the fundamental modes of subjectivity. (Paci
1961, pp. 115–116)

The ontological concepts presented by Sartre in the *Critique* are displaced
by Paci in favor of an ethical idea of the dialectic of both subjectivity and
praxis. Curiously enough, this philosophical displacement gained resonance with Sartre's own ethical investigations. In fact, Paci could not
know that Sartre had already tried to sketch an ethics based on phenomenological assumptions (the project entitled *Notebooks for an Ethics*,
which dates back to 1947–1949; Sartre 1992). What is also remarkable is
that the points concerning subjectivity, irreversibility and need, as presented in his autobiographical book, are the same that Paci developed in
his interventions during the debate which followed Sartre's lecture in
Rome in 1961.

III

As co-organizer, with the philosopher Cesare Luporini (Luporini 1974),
of the conference in Rome—which was held from 12 to 14 December
1961—Enzo Paci not only had the task of introducing Sartre's talk, but
also played an important role during the debate. In the morning session
of 14 December, Paci made quite a long statement, in which he set out
three main problems concerning the unconscious, temporality as irreversibility, and the subject conceived as 'unique'. All of these concepts
were rearranged in the idea of 'singularity'. Discussing the first problem,
Paci considered psychoanalysis as a proper method to investigate forms of
social and psychological conditioning. In his view, by analyzing the
deeper layers of conditioning, a fruitful combination of Freudism and
Marxism could be reached:

[...] with him [Marx] something really new appears in the world. I know that I've always been the world, and I know that the questions about the world are not 'what' or 'why' it is, but rather 'how I am in it?', 'What is my meaning in it?', and 'What we should do, me and the others, in order to give the world a historical sense, oriented toward the truth?'. These are the issues of materiality and of subjectivity seen as a journey. They are not solutions: it's a research I have been trying to conduct about the theme of the unconscious.[6]

What Paci calls the "unconscious" is the set of material forces that can be found, once internalized, in the subject. As a result, there is no subject that is not dependent on a social and historical genesis (DGI, tape 2, sheets 76–78; still unpublished). If, by means of analysis, the subject becomes conscious of his unconscious dimension, as it has been defined, what he gets is himself against the forces that constituted him: the transformation of oneself is a practice whereby conditionings are assumed and dialectically denied (DGI, tape 2, sheets 79–80). In this way, need turns into freedom, and recognizing necessity is the pivotal moment in a praxis of transformation (DGI, tape 2, sheet 80).

The second problem mentioned by Paci is irreversibility, which, in turn, is connected to subjectivity. The notion of irreversibility, as Paci specifies, should not be confused with that developed by contemporary physics (DGI, tape 2, sheet 80). In fact, Paci's aim was to describe the subjective experience as marked by the impossibility of overturning the course of time and so coming back to the past (DGI, tape 2, sheet 84). Humanity is conditioned by the structure of irreversibility—that is, by temporality. As he also says in the chapter of *Function of Sciences* dedicated to the "practico-inert" (Paci 1963, pp. 364–387), time is need because it is the consumption of the subject as a living body (the phenomenological *Leib*) and as a living organism. The material content of time is body and need. As a biological-material being, the human subject has the necessity to preserve his own subsistence through work and food. The discovery of this ontological-economic dimension must be traced

---

[6] Typewritten document of the Gramsci Institute in Rome (=DGI), sheet 77; see also Sartre (2015, p. 148).

back to Marx's 1844 economic-philosophical manuscripts which brought to light economic need as a fundamental structure of subjectivity (DGI, tape 2, sheets 82–83).

As an irreplaceable singularity marked by irreversibility, each subject is *einmal*—that is 'only once', since it is constituted by history and society, as well as by the modalities of subjective internalization (DGI, tape 2, sheets 85). The danger of a sociohistorical determinism—which could have brought this theoretical position back into the mainstream of ortho-dox Marxism, thus depriving it of its innovative power—can be avoided by resorting to the concept of subjectivation, which Paci draws from Sartre, as we can also see in the debate following the Rome conference. In Paci's interpretation of Sartre's theoretical position, subjectivation is both the dialectical negation of the social dimension produced by the subject, and a project for a future sociality. This implies a phenomenological con-sideration of intersubjectivity, whose starting point is the Husserlian *Fifth Meditation*: a human being cannot become human along with others, coming out of the condition of alienation in which he finds himself, that is, in our time, the alienation produced by the advanced capitalist society (DGI, tape 2, sheet 86).

The process of negation of being takes place with the prospect of the realization of a future humanity. Sartre calls this process "totalization in progress" (*totalisation en cours*) (DGI, tape 2, sheet 88). In it, according to Paci, the meaning of history must be recognized. In fact, Paci thinks phenomenologically about history—that is, in terms of an experience of temporality which, in turn, determines the structure of necessity that each subject shares with every other subject. The negation of need in the movement of praxis has its goal in an experience which is common to everyone, and in a freedom shared by all that results from totalization in progress.

It is here that we find the political consequence of Paci's argument. The task of the working class is to bring the totalization to an end—that is, to bring history itself toward its own end: neglected as a particular class and becoming a universal class, the working class brings upon itself the trag-edies and the mistakes of mankind. It must also take on the task of assert-ing the truth in history—that is, refusing the separation of humanity into social classes (DGI, tape 2, sheets 88–89).

If there is a universally human mission of the working class, and if this mission is the annihilation of the working class as a class by means of the return of sciences to their proper function, sciences and techniques are no longer neutral and they become necessary for the totalizing meaning of the concrete work of the subjects. For neo-capitalism science agrees with technical alienation and dehumanization (…). But for Marxism the original function of science is in its task of liberation from alienation. (Paci 1963, p. 378)

By means of this movement, Paci approaches Marxism in order to share its problems, prospects and themes. Yet it is also a kind of 'partial removal' (in a Freudian sense), involving the abandonment of any prospect of completion: the totalization processes described by Sartre are framed by Paci in such a way that the 'positivity' of the phenomenological categories is basically called into question. Driven by his studies on irreversibility of time and trying to outline a true philosophy of irreversibility, Paci reviews the methodological status Husserl attributed to the "pre-categorial" and to the "Lifeworld" as notions that "do not leave themselves handle—how often you have been led to believe—as positive keys to open the doors of knowledge: for Paci they remain always places for a hardworking return, a precarious balance, a constitutive insecurity of subjectivity" (Rovatti 1987, p. 211).

IV

The dialogue that Paci shared with Sartre in the debate following the Rome conference of 1961 resulted in an article, published in 1962, entitled *L'ultimo Sartre e il problema della soggettività* (*The Last Sartre and the Problem of Subjectivity*). The text served to Paci as the canvas for drawing up a critical point of view compared to the positions developed by Sartre in the *Critique*. Between the thesis of the essay and the second part of the *Function of Sciences*, therefore, there is just one step: for this reason, Paci's interventions contained in the typescript of the Gramsci Institute are precious in reconstructing the routes he followed during the development of his critical stance toward Sartre. In brief, the thesis of the second part of

Function of Sciences emerges from a living dialogue with Sartre that culminated in the debate at the Rome conference.

As a matter of fact, in *Function of Sciences*, we find some clear judgments on Sartre's thought. These judgments have their theoretical point in the statement according to which Sartre would not have understood the meaning of epoché. If, on the one hand, Paci saw in Sartre's thought an original elaboration of phenomenology, on the other he recognized its immanent limit: Sartre missed the methodological importance of the epoché, the operator, which permits us to reach for the level of consciousness, a reflexive description of the phenomena and, thereby, to move toward the *Sinngebung*, the donation of sense to the 'things in themselves'.

Phenomenology recognizes the epoché as a decisive step by which the subject leaves the *natürliche Einstellung*, the natural disposition, to get the *phänomenologische Einstellung*, the phenomenological disposition, the very possibility of a rational reconstruction of the lived experience. Sartre had taken leave of this perspective since the beginning of his career, in his (in many ways inaugural) essay *The Transcendence of the Ego*, where, in its final pages, he provided an existentialist version of the epoché, which is not alien to the influence of Heidegger's thesis (see Sartre 1960). If, of course, *Being and Nothingness* is entirely developed on the description of the ontological structure of consciousness as deeply divided in itself, in so far as it is located on both the unreflected and reflected levels, it is also true that during the 1950s, Sartre had advanced on a radical questioning of the human praxis, pursuing the project to bring Marxism on the level of the concrete, as it is firmly asserted in *Search for a Method* (See Sartre 1963, p. 9).

Nevertheless, according to Paci, Sartre had not been able to preserve the phenomenological movement of epoché, the "putting into brackets" of all those prejudices that shape our foreknowledge of the world. "Sartre missed the epoché, that is the return to the concrete subject and to its intentionality",[7] Paci writes in the chapter of *Function of Sciences* devoted to the practico-inert dimension and to irreversibility. First of all, this

---

[7] Paci (1963, p. 364). Rovatti comments on Paci's important quotation in this way: "Sartre rests still in debt toward Husserl: actually, he doesn't appear aware of the fact that his analysis of the subjectivity is wholly founded on this crucial theoretical difference that Husserl calls 'reduction'. Paci insists: it's not Heidegger's ontological difference. Rather, it's a matter of understanding the philo-

means that the operation consisting in a new description of the subjective structures as carried out by Sartre, and then the outside/inside/outside dialectic, can only be considered as phenomenologically accurate if they are conceived as depending on the reflective gaze of the phenomenological subject. It's only this subject that can grasp himself and clarify his own experience by moving toward a full assumption of the relationship between body, temporality and passive intentionality. These are also the central topics shown in Husserl's unpublished papers dedicated to the analysis of the *Lebenswelt*.

Thanks to this movement, some temporal stratifications of the living subject emerge as objects of investigation or as sociohistorically defined objects. Paci ascribes a political and an ethical value to this analysis, since the dialectic, seen as a concrete process, has to engage with the rational movement of living intentionality. Still, if the interpretation of Husserl's unpublished papers—especially those of the group 'C'—seems to bring Paci closer to Merleau-Ponty, and the phenomenologist makes his steps forward, thanks to an archaeology of subjectivity and a teleology of the community of 'concrete monads', it is also true that it is on the political ground that a countermovement occurs by which Paci—despite his criticism concerning the status of epoché—turns to Sartre in the name of a proposed immanent revitalization of Marxism.

What Paci emphasizes in Sartre is the dialectic of exteriority and interiority, by which Sartre himself defines the status of subjectivity and, in particular, the movement of *repetition* (*sursis*, in French) that is required in order to set up the relation between inside and outside as well as to define the "place" of subjectivity (according to a description that is a prelude to a real review of the ontological topology of *Being and Nothingness*). Paci openly shares with Sartre some theoretical points: first of all, the emphasis on the dynamic and temporal structures of subjectivity analyzed both in their living and passive intentionality; and secondly, the political nuance of that theme that outlines an idea of the constitution of the subject as concretely conceived (i.e., as socially and historically situated) and rooted in the practical field.

---

sophical revolution which is implicit in epoché as an 'artificial' exercise: the modification of thought that it requires" (Rovatti 1987, p. 208).

V

The pinnacle of the dialogue between Paci and Sartre can be seen in the essay that appeared in the review *aut aut*, in the same year (1964) as the Parisian conference dedicated to Kierkegaard, in which Sartre presented his *Singular Universal*.[8] Paci's essay is about the autobiographical novel *The Words*. The essay turns on the question of autobiography from a philosophical perspective. Here Paci finds in Sartre a phenomenological inspiration that led him to compare the dense pages of the novel in a kind of mirroring of the story of the author. The description of himself is a complex and difficult task that goes back to the problem of subjectivity.

From this point of view, from the beginning of the essay, Paci says that *The Words* must be read together with the *Critique*, since this allows us to think what a subject immersed in history is. It must also be acknowledged that the autobiography has a philosophical function in Sartre's work and that it must be understood in a horizon that is, again, philosophical, political and ethical, as if Paci had finally found in this horizon—during and after his conversation with the French thinker—the real point, that point of attack in which all thematic threads unraveled in conversing with Sartre converge.

This horizon is philosophical: what emerges from the problem concerning the phenomenological constitution of the subject is the issue of the singularity translated on the level of a materialist dialectic. Moreover, this horizon is at the same time also political: there can be no constitution of the concrete subject that does not call into question a social dimension. That is why Paci underlines this issue as follows:

---

[8] Rovatti quotes some unpublished pages taken from Paci's *Journal* about the meeting that took place with Sartre after the end of the conference: "'This morning I met Sartre at the bar Pont-Royal...'. Paci and Sartre start to discuss the situation of the Italian left, then Sartre goes on to speak about the translation of his anthology of political writings (he does not like the choice of the title that has been chosen: *Il filosofo e la politica* [*The Philosopher and Politics*]; the discourse then shifts to the next conference at the Gramsci Institute dedicated to the moral, to which Sartre has been invited, but Paci has not. There is a gradual approximation to philosophical themes, a long round, a *politesse* that makes them hesitate: they speak at length about Merleau-Ponty, then about Heidegger, on whom they share their criticism; finally, they discuss *ideology*. It is only at the end of their talk that some essential points seem to emerge: 'but then comes out the discourse on Husserl: Sartre confesses that he knows him thanks to *Ideen I* and the existentialist versions. I give a real lecture about the last Husserl" (Rovatti 1987, p. 210).

Sartre stands today in front of himself as before the problem of identification and singularity. We realized by reading the first volume of the *Critique* that the story is a movement in progress toward an open totalization; however, only individuals, subjects, are real. We know that here a genuine collectivism is not forbidden: on the contrary, socialism seems to be the only option not to oppose to an abstract society an abstract, or a subject become an object. (Paci 2012, p. 107)

It is not just a shift in Paci's investigations leading to a heterodox Marxism through the dialogue with Sartre. In fact, a socialist perspective regards a *possible* society made of *concrete subjects* living in a net of plural and practical relations.

In *Search for a Method*, Sartre had denounced that analytical thinking was the main philosophical and cultural enemy. Methodologically and from the beginning, this way of thinking could only lose the concrete and historical dimension of the social bond. Paci resumes such criticism by adding to it the theme of a rational need to bring the philosophical activity into the social and relational living experience. No subject could be thought of as *living present* (*Lebendige Gegenwart*), but in terms of a mere abstraction.

In consideration of the common battle against the abstract and calculative thinking that both Sartre and Paci fought, it is also necessary to emphasize the way Paci slightly changed his perspective on Sartre in terms of the description of the individual as a concrete subject. In fact, Paci acknowledged a major shift in the Sartrean approach to the question of the subject, as Sartre leads his philosophical research project more as a writer than as a philosopher, and particularly when his autobiographical writing follows an oblique path that unravels the concrete and historical forms of the constitution of a subject. This is what Sartre, in *The Family Idiot*, later calls "personalization". After discussing the dialectic between subjectivation and alienation, Paci stresses the importance of Sartre's writing, but also its limitations. Toward the end of the essay he writes:

We are conditioned in every moment and we recreate ourselves in every moment: at any moment we can reveal or hide ourselves again, deny us in the image, dress up in it and then, having abandoned the disguise, rediscovering ourselves once again. This 'living' dialectic is the philosophy of Sartre—is both his theatre, his criticism, his literature. Above all, it is a 'pre-categorical dialectic': not crystallized in objectification and not evaporated in an abstract conceptual scheme. It is the dialectic that interweaves the dynamic watermark of *The Words* and it is even, if you will, the limit of Sartre. (Paci 2012, p. 115)

Later in the text, Paci offers an extraordinary definition of the novel, also underlining the common area between Sartre's philosophical project and his literary one. More precisely, *The Words* is for Paci an account of a reflexive movement whereby the writer is recognized as a philosopher because, as philosopher, he poses the problem of truth, that truth of the self that coincides with the questioning of himself. This truth, which is not eternal because it is situated in time, is called intelligibility of history: first of all of the individual story, which acquires its meaning solely through its constant interplay with the history of the world. There is no biography that does not weave an individual life with and in the universal history. At the same time, there is no singularity which, through language, does not articulate itself in the dimension of universality. At the intersection of these questions, we find the instance of the subject and its relationship to itself, on the one hand, and to history, on the other hand, through the medium of language. To question this intersection is the task of philosophy.

In this way, Sartre finds the source of the meaning and direction of his philosophical research. "*The Words* is a phenomenology of the errors of the writer. Dialectically, it is precisely this phenomenology that allows Sartre to be writer and philosopher when he tries to rebuild his life, to make sense of the 'stories' of his own life", as Paci writes (Paci 2012, p. 115).

If the path of self-seeking is the route followed by Sartre, we cannot fail to recognize that it is a journey toward truth, and that it has its proper place in the history as horizon for truth. The conclusion of the text, then, does nothing but witness Paci's gratitude for Sartre and his work, highlighting the complex gesture that Sartre was able to accomplish an analysis of the Self based on self-distancing, on an objectification of himself and a self-reflexive description. Paci says:

> *The Words* seems to be, therefore, an introduction to phenomenological man and to the meaning of the truth about man. We know now that this

point was already in us—although we did not know before and it was not recognized. Sartre warns against the danger of reducing the man and the meaning of truth to mere words. And, in fact, there is required a praxis, an exercise, a set of operations. Isn't also *The Words* such an exercise? And couldn't it be the beginning for other exercises, an arrival which also becomes a starting point, an "awareness", a making of our life in the totalization in progress of history, not of an abstract history, but of that history which is always individual and universal, if each of us is 'all a man, made by all people'? (Paci 2012, p. 116)

Paci found in Sartre, as a novelist and an autobiographer, that phenomenological attitude that Sartre succeeded in taking, but only intermittently, along his philosophical path. It is in the happy moments of this intermittency that Sartre can embody phenomenology as a practice and an exercise, as a questioning of the Self that requires *immer wieder* (time and again) to be resumed and restarted. This is also the task Sartre himself assumed during the 60s, trying to sketch the main lines of a 'dialectical ethics'.

References

de Beauvoir, Simone. 1949. Compte-rendu des Structures élémentaires de la parenté. *Les Temps Modernes* 49: 943–949.

Levi-Strauss, Claude. 1966. *The Savage Mind*. London: Weidenfeld & Johnson.

Lévi-Strauss, Claude. 1969. *The Elementary Structures of Kinship*. Translated by J.H. Bell, J.R. Von Sturmer, and R. Needham. Boston: Beacon Press.

Luporini, Cesare. 1974. *Dialettica e materialismo*. Rome: Editori Riuniti.

Paci, Enzo. 1957. *Dall'esistenzialismo al relazionismo*. Messina and Florence: D'Anna.

———. 1961. *Diario fenomenologico*. Milano: Bompiani.

———. 1963. *Funzione delle scienze e significato dell'uomo*. Bari: Laterza.

———. 2012. Le parole. aut aut, 1964; re-published in *Il coraggio della filosofia. Aut aut 1951–2011*, ed. Pier Aldo Rovatti, 107–116. Milano: Il Saggiatore.

Rovatti, Pier Aldo. 1987. *Viaggiatori senza biglietto. Note sul dialogo tra Enzo Paci e Jean-Paul Sartre*. In *Sartre e l'Italia*, ed. Sandra Teroni and Ornella Pompeo Faracovi. Livorno: Belforte.

Sartre, Jean-Paul. 1960. *The Transcendence of the Ego. An Existentialist Theory of Consciousness*. Translated by F. William and R. Kirkpatrick. New York: Hill & Wang.

————. 1963. *Search for a Method*. Translated by Hazel E. Barnes. New York: A. Knopf.

————. 1965. *Merleau-Ponty*. Translated by B. Eisler. In Jean-Paul Sartre, *Situations*, 227–326. London and New York: Hamish Hamilton and Braziller.

————. 1966. *Determinazione e libertà*. In *Morale e società. Atti del convegno di Roma organizzato dall'istituto Gramsci, 22–25 maggio 1964*, ed. Galvano Della Volpe, Roger Garaudy, Karel Kosik, Cesare Luporini, Mihailo Marković, Howard L. Parsons, Jean-Paul Sartre, and Adam Schaff, 30–43. Rome: Editori Riuniti.

————. 1985. *Merleau-Ponty* (first draft). Edited by Pierre Verstraeten. *Revue Internationale de Philosophie*, 3–29, 152–153.

————. 1992. *Notebooks for an Ethics*. Translated by D. Pellauer. Chicago: University of Chicago Press.

————. 2005. *Morale et histoire. Les Temps Modernes*, no. 632–633–634. Paris: Gallimard.

————. 2013. *What is Subjectivity?* London: Verso.

————. 2015. *Marxismo e soggettività. La conferenza di Roma 1961*. Milan: Marinotti.

————. 2016. *Les racines de l'éthique*. Edited by Gregory Cormann and Jean Bourgault. *Études sartriennes*, 19. Bruxelles: Ousia.

Trân Duc Thao. 2011. *Phenomenology and Dialectical Materialism*. Translated by Daniel J. Hermann and Donald V. Morano. Boston: Springer.

10

Sartre in Germany—Even in the East

Vincent von Wroblewsky

I had the 'privilege' of living the history of the German Democratic Republic (GDR) from May 1950 until November 1989, so almost from its beginning on 7 October 1949 until its end. On this journey of 40 years, Sartre accompanied me for more than 30 of them. I remember one of the first encounters: the *Volksbühne* (People's Theater) in Rosa Luxemburg Square, the popular theater built before the Nazi era with the money collected by the Berlin workers, presented Sartre's play *Nekrassov* in 1958. This story of an impostor, a supposed Soviet dissident, of whom the anti-communist press took advantage, was perfectly compatible with the prevailing ideology in the GDR in 1958. Its anti-anti-communist message was welcome. The play was published in East Germany in 1955, a year before *Rowohlt* published it in West Germany. This was one of the few examples, but not the only one, where Sartre was published first in the East. I do not remember what fascinated the Kant High School student in Berlin-Rummelsburg that I was then: Sartre's play, Fritz Wisten's

V. von Wroblewsky (✉)
Sartre Society, Berlin, Germany

© The Author(s) 2020

A. Betschart, J. Werner (eds.), *Sartre and the International Impact of Existentialism*,
https://doi.org/10.1007/978-3-030-38482-1_10

staging, Roman Weyl's set, Alexander Hegardt's performance in the leading role, or that of Franz Kutschera as chief editor ...?

The first Sartre text published in the GDR was *The Henri Martin Affair*, translated by Karl Heinrich. Two years after its release in France, the publishing house *Volk und Welt* offered the East German readers this documentation with a commentary by Sartre. They thus became acquainted with the French communist sailor sentenced to five years of forced labor for writing and distributing leaflets against the Indochina War in 1949. *Rowohlt* in Hamburg, West Germany, presented a translation of this text by Eva Moldenhauer only in 1983. In its bibliography, on page 276 of this first West German edition, the East German edition of 1955 is mentioned. This did not prevent the publishers of *Rowohlt* from pointing out on the first page that it was a "Deutsche Erstausgabe"— the first German edition. This was a contradiction only seemingly: from the official West German point of view, there was Germany, whose correct name was the Federal Republic of Germany, and then, further east, not recognized as a legitimate state, this other unspeakable thing called the GDR. Since the GDR was not Germany, an edition published in this country, this region, was not German, so it could not be the first German publication. From a logical point of view, there was nothing to say—provided you accepted the assumptions. This example shows that Sartre's reception in Germany sometimes obeyed formal logic, but it especially obeyed the political and ideological logic of the Cold War. What followed proved the relevance of this thesis with a few exceptions.

As to *The Henri Martin Affair* and *Nekrassov*, the GDR had no ideological obstacles to overcome. For *The Childhood of a Leader*, published by the *Aufbau-Verlag* in 1957, the choice was less clear. Admittedly, this short story, one of the five published in *The Wall*, showed how the son of an entrepreneur, of a boss, and therefore a capitalist and exploiter, became himself a boss after many hesitations and temptations—a beautiful illustration of social determinism! However, a more attentive look quickly revealed that instead of determinism, there is freedom in action. The young hero of history makes a choice, makes choices. He is not a leader, but he is made, he chooses himself as a leader, and at the same time, he chooses himself as an anti-Semite. However, the underlying philosophy of Sartre, which had provoked passionate debate, was not the reason for this text being withdrawn from public libraries shortly after. Without my good relations with the mother of my best friend at the time, who ran a library, I would have been deprived of reading it. The argument was neither ideological nor political nor philosophical: Sartre's story was, as far as I remember, ... pornographic! It was necessary to protect the readers from its harmful influence.

Let us go back to the beginnings of Sartre's influence on the well-protected citizens of the new Germany. After his first stays in Germany—in Berlin in 1933/34, to become acquainted with the philosophy of Husserl and Heidegger, and in 1940, as a prisoner of war in Stalag XII D near Trier—Sartre returned to this country, invited as a famous author. At the end of 1947, Gustav Gründgens had staged *The Flies* in Düsseldorf, where Gründgens himself played Orestes. At the beginning of 1948, Jürgen Fehling presented his interpretation of the play at the Hebbel Theater in West Berlin. Supported by the sets of Heinrich Kilger, he confronted the public with a staging of the society of Argos, barbaric, bloodthirsty. This presentation, barely three years after the end of the war, provoked enthusiasm and rejection, sometimes both in the same critique. In the *Tägliche Rundschau*, a daily newspaper published in the Soviet sector of Berlin under the control of the Soviet military administration, the young philosopher Wolfgang Harich enthused over the production by Fehling. He described the play itself as a "seminar on Heidegger in the flaying house". On 1 February 1948, a Sunday, Sartre and Simone de Beauvoir, having come to Berlin for the occasion, watched the production. The evening after the performance was one of the great cultural and intellectual events in post-war Berlin, invited by the Hebbel Theater and the satirical newspaper *Ulenspiegel* of East Berlin. At the round table—in reality a long rectangular table—were well-known intellectuals from the West and East such as Gert H. Theunissen, Pastor Zimmermann, Walter Karsch, Günther Weisenborn, and Professor Alfons Steininger. Felix Lusset, head of the French cultural mission in Berlin, also participated in the discussion on 'What is existentialism?' Thus, the staging of *The Flies* was the origin of the last great East-West intellectual debate in Berlin, an open, high-level debate, the last before the Cold War turned dialogue into mutual polemics, into a dialogue between the deaf where each side defended its unshakable truth by trying to impose it on the other, where

arguments were replaced by convictions. Together with other intellectuals from the East and West, Sartre and Beauvoir strove to counteract the
instrumentalization of culture in the Cold War.[1] This was all the more
remarkable, as in contrast to Konstantin Fedin, Anna Seghers, Bertolt
Brecht, Louis Aragon, and Elsa Triolet, well-known intellectuals such as
Georg Lukács and Ernst Bloch proved to be rather Stalinists in their
polemics against Sartre in the 1950s, before the 20th Party Congress of
the Communist Party of the Soviet Union (CPSU) in 1956.[2]

Let us not idealize this farewell evening to East-West dialogue or
Sartre's controversial but civilized perception of this already divided
Germany that had not yet taken the paralyzed form of states. It is not
about the perception of Sartre in the GDR proper; however, future interpretations were already on the horizon at this time anticipating the future.
The argumentative structures, the demagogic *topoi* that characterize a
good, rather bad part of the reception of Sartre's thought in the GDR,
can already be recognized.

Fritz Erpenbeck, the most famous and influential theater critic of the
time in the East, was editor of the *Theaterdienst—Eilnachrichten—
Informationsblätter für Bühne, Film und Musik*, an information service
about theater, film, and music. On 7 January 1948, three weeks before
the discussion with Sartre, he sketched in his newsletter the prolegomena
of any future pseudo-criticism. The essential was the introduction and
the punchline of his article. He declared that existentialist philosophy—
not only that of Sartre—was decadent, that it was the culminating point
of subjective idealism and thus to be rejected. However, a theater critique
cannot prove this. Stating it was sufficient; proving it was not necessary.
Especially since existentialism would remain 'with us', even more than in

---

[1] Gesine Bey has extensively researched and comprehensively presented this meeting (see Bey
2000).

[2] As to the relationship between Anna Seghers, Bertolt Brecht, and Sartre, they showed mutual
respect to each other. A few weeks before his death in 1956, Brecht proposed to appoint Sartre as a
Corresponding Member of the Academy of Arts of the GDR (see Wroblewsky 1983). As to Georg
Lukács's criticism of Sartre, see his books *Existentialismus oder Marxismus* (*Existentialism or
Marxism*, 1951) and *The Destruction of Reason* (1954). On Bloch's polemic against Sartre and in
particular his role in the conference "The Problem of Freedom in the Light of Scientific Socialism",
organized in 1955 by the *Section Philosophy of the German Academy of Sciences in Berlin*, to whose
head Bloch had been appointed, see Wroblewsky (2003).

France, the affair of a limited circle of intellectuals of 'particular intellectual (mis)education'. Finally, Erpenbeck declared that Sartre remained
incomprehensible to the masses, whereas the theater, more than any other
art, was an art for the masses.

This elitist and demagogic attitude would be found until the end of the
GDR. Fortunately, there were intellectuals (Erpenbeck) who understood
(in the name of the Party) what the masses (led by the Party) could not
understand, but what they, the intellectuals, understood, and these intellectuals could explain to the masses that it was better not to try to understand what in any case was not worth understanding, because it was
decadent, absurd, idealistic, too complicated, chimeras invented by a
minority for a minority, and anyhow would soon be forgotten.
Nevertheless, it was necessary to fight these chimeras (this was one of the
functions of the intellectuals), because they were commanded by the big
capital, imperialism, and other harmful powers to divert the masses from
the good path. A year earlier, the newspaper *Tägliche Rundschau* had set
the tone in an article by politician and political writer Ernst Niekisch,
published on 10 January 1947 under the title "Existentialism, a post-war
neo-fascist fashion" (Niekisch 1947). It would be easy to multiply the
examples. The communists were not alone in rejecting Sartre's philosophy: Christians reproached him for not respecting the human person, the
creature of God, for being a cynical nihilist. The Vatican decree of 30
October 1948 encouraged them—it had put all of Sartre's (and Simone
de Beauvoir's) works on the index of prohibited books.

The retrospective reveals not only rejections but also misunderstandings of all kinds. Sartre was not very convinced by the staging of *The Flies*
in Berlin. Simone de Beauvoir wrote in a letter to Nelson Algren:

> Finally—oh, what an ordeal!—there was the representation of the *Flies.* ...
> pure shame. [...] The director had deliberately distorted it into a nihilistic
> work, cutting entire scenes, directing the actors so that it meant exactly the
> opposite of what Sartre had wanted. And everything was so ugly, the cos-
> tumes, the gestures, the decorations, everything. No one can do things as
> ugly as Germans when they are going about doing something. The actors
> never stopped bellowing, sweating, rolling on their backs, tumbling up and
> down stairs: a veritable asylum for lunatics. The French unanimously

considered it a scandal, but the Germans applauded for half an hour, a real triumph, which in their eyes made the arrival of Sartre an event. (Beauvoir 1999, pp. 229–230)

Of the evening at the club *Die Möwe*, Simone de Beauvoir wrote, without mentioning the debate between intellectuals of the East and West:

It was crowned by a long dinner at the Russian club, bad food but vodka afloat .... It was gratifying to speak with Russian and German communists, they were really friendly, made friendly speeches, while the French Communists, you know, are tearing us apart. We were able to explain ourselves on a lot of things. (Beauvoir 1999, p. 230)

A year later, nothing was left of the sympathy of the Russian and German communists. The premiere of *Dirty Hands*, staged by Otto Eduard Hasse, had taken place at the *Renaissance Theater* in West Berlin on 15 January 1949. This piece, which the communists always considered as being anti-communist, was warmly welcomed. In the East, Sartre was once again one of the privileged ideological targets. From 18 to 23 May 1949, a large conference was held at the House of Soviet Culture. It had been prepared by an *Initiative Committee of Soviet and German Comrades* to showcase Lenin's book *Materialism and Empirio-Criticism* published 40 years earlier. The conference was meant to be an 'ideological offensive', a 'general offensive of dialectical materialism against the forms of current idealism most hostile to progress'. For the initiators, Sartre was at the forefront of these enemies of progress.

Times passed, and three of the four occupation zones turned into a state: in February 1948, the Federal Republic of Germany was created. The German Democratic Republic followed in October 1949. The Cold War intensified, and then Stalin died in 1953. Between his death and the 20th Congress of the CPSU in February 1956, which became famous for Nikita Sergeyevich Khrushchev's confidential speech on the crimes committed under Stalin, a certain uncertainty reigned. It resulted in a partial liberalization in the GDR, which benefited the publishing houses. Hence, the publication of Sartre's first texts in 1955, texts which, like *The Henri Martin Affair* and *Nekrassov*, did not run counter to the dominant ideology.

In 1956, the publishing house *Aufbau-Verlag* in Berlin published a small volume with three plays by Sartre, *The Flies, The Respectful Prostitute,* and *Nekrassov.* In 1957, another prominent publisher, *Reclam Publishers* of Leipzig, published three pieces, almost the same, but they replaced *Nekrassov* with *The Condemned of Altona* and added an afterword by Werner Mittenzwei, best known for his work on Bertolt Brecht. A few years of silence followed. In 1961, the Cold War produced its most visible symbol: the Berlin Wall. On the East side, the reception of Sartre's work remained limited to this choice of plays for theater. But in 1965, a *coup de theatre* on the stage of reception! A year earlier—Gallimard had published *The Words* in 1963—Sartre had refused the Nobel Prize. Does this explain why the two Germanies—that is to say the publishers *Rowohlt* in Hamburg and *Aufbau-Verlag* in Berlin—published simultaneously, in the same translation by Hans Mayer, this famous story of Sartre's childhood? This anticipated literary unification of Germany would remain an exception.

In the East, readers relying on the internal market were able to read more of Sartre's plays, and they could also see them performed. However, they still did not have access to much of Sartre's work. To know his philosophical texts, his literary critiques, his aesthetic or political essays, they must have recourse to the scientific libraries where they could borrow the writings of Sartre, often on the condition of having a special authorization. The books in question, like many others, were marked on the back by a red circle. One strange exception to this was that while the German version was marked with a hot iron, the original version could be borrowed without restriction!

For many potential readers, the language barrier was insurmountable. They had to find other solutions. And many of them wanted to read Sartre. They were artists and teachers, researchers, but also members of the scientific and technical intelligentsia. They were interested in literary, philosophical, and political works that were not limited to what was offered to them by the 'Marxist-Leninist basic studies', the Party press, the propaganda books, and the novels of socialist realism. They looked for a more differentiated, more complex, aesthetically richer view of the world, other answers to their questions. They found them, among others, in texts of the eighteenth and nineteenth centuries and in more contemporary authors, in Nietzsche, Freud, Proust, Kafka, Camus, Simone de Beauvoir, ... and Sartre. Retirees who had the privilege of passing through the Berlin Wall quite freely took the risk of being smugglers; pocketbooks crossed the border in a slip or a bra.

There were easier ways to get to know these authors, at least by proxy. Not all the specialized intellectuals thought that it was their role to prevent the so-called non-specialists from getting to know these works and to warn them, to protect them from the danger of ideological intoxication. After the publication of some articles in cultural journals and thereafter of a part of my doctoral thesis under the title *Jean-Paul Sartre—Theory and Praxis of an Engagement*, I was invited by various clubs and cultural centers created on the initiatives of universities in Dresden, Leipzig, and Rostock, and by centers of municipalities and the Cultural Association of the GDR (*Kulturbund*) in Frankfurt (Oder) or those on the border of the Baltic Sea. Even a big company had the idea of putting Sartre on the program. Peter Knopp, a mathematician working at the Computing Center of *Kabelwerk Oberspree* (one of the largest companies in East Berlin producing cables) and at the same time responsible for culture with the trade union, a man of great literary and musical culture, invited me to talk to interested engineers and workers about Sartre on the occasion of the author's 70th birthday in 1975. Knopp had noticed in my articles and reports published, among others, by the philosophical journal *Deutsche Zeitschrift für Philosophie* (*German Journal for Philosophy*) that the information available to me was not limited to that officially accessible in the GDR. It was a fine example of a counter-finality difficult to understand for those who today have a ready-made image of the GDR: a monolithic block, homogeneous, without contradiction. My thesis, published in 1977 in the collection *Critique of Bourgeois Ideology* (*Zur Kritik der bürgerlichen Ideologie*), directed by Manfred Buhr, had certainly an official function to criticize the subjects treated—like all the 100 titles finally published in this collection. However, there were different ways to criticize and different ways to read these reviews. The readers in the GDR had a great experience: they could read between the lines, read the innuendos, allusions, the unsaid; they could read criticism critically and extract the information they were looking for. Reactions to my publications, the echo I encountered during discussions with different circles in different parts of the GDR, gave me an idea of the real interest in Sartre. The director of my Institute of Philosophy at the Academy of Sciences, Manfred Buhr, was not fooled by it. In 1981, probably after having read the part of my thesis published in 1977, *Kiepenheuer*, the publisher in Leipzig, addressed me, proposing that I make a choice among the essays published by Sartre in *Situations* and write a postface. I obviously had to ask permission from my institute director. He told me about Sartre: "You have to criticize him, not propagate him." As I had taken care to support my request with an official letter from the editor of the publishing house, Manfred Buhr could hardly refuse. But he took precautions by demanding that the publisher took ideological responsibility. Neither the choice of Sartre's essays nor my afterword published in 1982 as number 39 of *Gustav Kiepenheuer Bücherei* under the title *Jean-Paul Sartre—Situations, Speeches, Essays, Interviews about Literature (Situationen. Reden, Aufsätze, Interviews zur Literatur)* shocked the guardians of ideological purity: they probably preferred to be open-minded. For me, it was a welcome precedent. I later published several postfaces to editions of Sartre's works, this time without asking permission.

Also in 1982, the publishing house *Aufbau-Verlag* published the novel *Nausea* and the five short stories of the volume *The Wall*. In 1985, *Nausea* was published in paperback, then in 1987 *War Diaries: Notebooks from a Phony War*, and finally, from 1988 to 1990, the three volumes of the trilogy *The Roads to Freedom: The Age of Reason, The Reprieve,* and *Troubled Sleep*. Thus, the writer Sartre was finally almost completely present in the GDR through his theater, his works of fiction, and some of his literary critiques. On the other hand, his philosophical work remained entirely absent, whether his major texts—*Being and Nothingness* and *Critique of Dialectical Reason*—or his numerous essays, interviews, polemics, prefaces, along with his biographical work, from Mallarmé to Flaubert. I had unsuccessfully suggested *Reclam* in Leipzig to publish *Anti-Semite and Jew*. This proposal was found to be very interesting, but it was deeply regretted that no department of the publisher could handle this publication. The text was unclassifiable; it did not fall into the category of fiction nor into what the Germans call a *Sachbuch*, an untranslatable term normally translated into English simply as nonfiction.

No text of philosophy by Sartre was published during the 40 years of GDR. But it was not possible to ignore him completely, especially when the verdict of subjective idealism became more and more difficult to maintain. The situation became particularly complicated for the leaders in charge of the citizens' ideological health when Sartre tried to integrate his existentialism into Marxism. Criticism of the *Critique of Dialectical Reason* was first left to foreign authors. In 1965, VEB Deutscher Verlag der Wissenschaften, an important publishing house of scientific texts in the GDR, printed a German translation of *Marx or Sartre—Essay on a Philosophy of Man* by the Polish Marxist Adam Schaff, two years before a West German translation was published by *Rowohlt*. Shortly thereafter, Schaff was accused of revisionism. Although he wanted to demonstrate the superiority of Marxism in the face of existentialism, the subtitle of his book betrayed an unacceptable intention: to prove that Marxism was also a philosophy of man. Although he criticized Sartre's subjectivism and idealism, it nonetheless meant revising Marxism from a reprehensible angle by replacing the classes and their struggle with a theory of the subject, a shift toward the individual. In my copy, I found some handwritten sheets reminding me of what, very early, fascinated me about Sartre. They quote from the chapter "On moral responsibility" (Schaff 1965, pp. 88–100). Schaff spoke of Sartre's reception in Poland, and he could have said the same thing about the GDR: "the milieu of Marxist intelligentsia, especially the young Marxist intelligentsia, enthusiastically accepted the set of problems treated by existentialism like a revelation" (Schaff 1965, p. 89). And he added—the task of criticism obliges— "unfortunately frequently together with the subjectivist way of its solution" (Schaff 1965, p. 89). Having distanced himself, Schaff recognized the *raison d'être* of the existentialist set of problems: "[...] it is the result of the *experiences* of men who perceived the political difficulties of the past years above all as a problem of moral responsibility for their own acts, for the approval of the acts of others" (Schaff 1965, p. 89). It is needless to recall what was very present to the readers of the time—the 20th Congress of the CPSU, the intervention of the Russian troops in Budapest ... Schaff did not beat about the bush:

What interests us here is a situation of a particular type, which triggered in the years 1955 to 1957 the moral indignation of a wide range of people and continues to distress them. We are thinking of the question of moral responsibility for a *political act* performed in conflict-ridden situations. (Schaff 1965, p. 90)

Let us quote again Schaff, who deserved the accusation of revisionism, because what he tried to review was the reigning dogmatism of the time:

Personally, I consider as one of the great theoretical merits of existentialism to have revealed the importance of morally ambiguous situations in life. (...) Here, the individual is really condemned to choose, and the experiences of the past period show that neither public opinion nor the opinion of the group relieve us from such moral responsibility. (Schaff 1965, pp. 91, 98)

So no predominance of the group, that is, the Party. This idea developed by Schaff was perfectly in line with what I thought, and it was also consistent with the experiences I had as a teenager with the particularly rigid forms of Prussian socialism in the GDR, especially during the years mentioned by Schaff, 1955–1957, which I had spent at Wiesenburg in a boarding school where calls for the flag and other militaristic survival exercises were celebrated under the sign of discipline. I was therefore dazzled by Sartre's thought, his valorization of the individual, his freedom, and his responsibility. From there on, Sartre was my faithful companion during my crossing of the GDR.

Let us go back to the end of the GDR. *Reclam* had refused me *Anti-Semite and Jew*, but at the beginning of the year 1989, I could present to the readers in the GDR, thanks to the same publisher, a new edition of Sartre's theater. For the first time, this volume also contained *Dirty Hands* as well as Sartre's texts on the theater, taken from the volume published by *Rowohlt* under the title *Myth and Reality of the Theater*. This publication should have caused a sensation. It did not. It was buried under the fall of the Berlin Wall in autumn of the same year. I was not sad. I had won freedom!

References

de Beauvoir, Simone. 1999. *Eine transatlantische Liebe*. Reinbek: Rowohlt.

Bey, Gesine. 2000. Das Schriftstellertreffen in Knokke het Zoute (April 1954)— Ein unbekannter Ost-West-Dialog mit Bertolt Brecht und Jean-Paul Sartre. In *Peter Weiss Jahrbuch für Literatur, Kunst und Politik im 20. Jahrhundert, Bd. 9*, ed. Michael Hofmann et al., 130–150. Röhrig: St. Ingbert.

Niekisch, Ernst. 1947. Der Existentialismus. Eine neofaschistische Nachkriegsmode. *Neues Deutschland*, January 10.

Schaff, Adam. 1965. *Marx oder Sartre? Versuch einer Philosophie des Menschen*. Berlin: VEB Deutscher Verlag der Wissenschaften.

von Wroblewsky, Vincent. 1983. Brecht, Sartre and Marxism. In *Brecht 83— Brecht and Marxism—Documentation, Minutes of the Brecht Days 1983, 9 to 11 February*, 283–289. Berlin: Henschelverlag Kunst und Gesellschaft.

———. 2003. Sartre and Bloch between the Fronts of the Cold War. In *Die Freiheit des Nein: Jean-Paul Sartre Carnets 2001/2002*, ed. Peter Knopp and Vincent von Wroblewsky, 165–183. Berlin: Philo Verlag.

11

French Cultural Policy and the Transfer of Existentialism in Allied-Occupied Austria

Juliane Werner

To explore the reception of existentialism in Austria is to first of all explore what the French allied authorities perceived to be the country's specific needs after 1945. The Austrian readership existed in a vacuum, having been disconnected for seven years from international literary and philosophical developments, the latest of them being French existentialism. This chapter outlines how political reasons led French cultural officials to take a different approach toward existentialism in Austria than in Germany, first and foremost by ignoring Sartre's play *The Flies* and the accompanying debates surrounding remorse and responsibility. Their aim was to reestablish the culture of the interwar years instead, promoting mostly those French contemporary movements that merged with already existing views in Austria, such as *Renouveau Catholique*. Straying from this official policy, however, journalists and translators working for allied periodicals act as powerful agents who help transmit existentialist thought to a young and artistic audience. With Sartre becoming a 'fellow

J. Werner (✉)
University of Vienna, Vienna, Austria
e-mail: juliane.werner@univie.ac.at

© The Author(s) 2020   **197**
A. Betschart, J. Werner (eds.), *Sartre and the International Impact of Existentialism*,
https://doi.org/10.1007/978-3-030-38482-1_11

traveler' of the Communist Party in 1952, they too cease the coverage of existentialism almost entirely, in adherence with the radical anti-communist stance of the Western Allies.

Austria, *pays ami*

The crucial historical context within which cultural artifacts were imported into Austria after World War II is what historian Tony Judt calls the country's "stroke of doubly unmerited good fortune" (Judt 2005, p. 2): its victim status as "the first free country to fall victim to Hitlerite aggression" (United States Department of State 1943, p. 761), agreed upon by the British, Soviet, and American governments at the Moscow Conference in 1943, and its assignment to the Western side, as a nation whose independence was essential for stability and peace owing to its geographical position adjacent to communist Eastern Europe. The so-called Mitschuldklausel (co-responsibility clause) in the Allies' "Declaration on Austria"—the mention that Austria should take responsibility for its involvement in the crimes of Nazi Germany—was felt to be a burden by the public and was eventually dismissed in the State Treaty of 1955.[1]

French cultural policy in Austria after 1945 relied heavily on the victim theory, which has been linked to the French Resistance due to a similar downplaying of the extent of the nation's collaboration during wartime and a certain willingness to continue as if nothing had happened thereafter. This view is held by Manès Sperber, who, born in the Austro-Hungarian Galicia, experienced, like Sartre, the 'Phoney War' on the

---

[1] It is only in 1991 that Chancellor Franz Vranitzky (Vranitzky 1991, p. 3282) takes up the 'Mitschuldklausel' and admits Austrian guilt, ultimately dismantling the victim theory. Leading to this are several years of public debate, inspired by the presidency of former SA member Kurt Waldheim in 1986. In the National Assembly, Vranitzky presses for the acknowledgment of "the other side of our history" ("zu der anderen Seite unserer Geschichte"), namely, that "there was no small number of Austrians who, in the name of this regime, have brought much suffering upon others, participating in the persecutions and crimes of this Reich" ("daß es nicht wenige Österreicher gab, die im Namen dieses Regimes großes Leid über andere gebracht haben, die teilhatten an den Verfolgungen und Verbrechen dieses Reichs").

All unattributed translations are mine.

French side, and afterward worked for the French government in Southwestern Germany. France's traumatic defeat in 1940—which, according to Sartre, caused a "formidable inferiority complex" (Sartre 1988, p. 284)—led to a comparable distortion of the past: "One met people who told in detail how they had, gun in hand, chased the Germans out of Paris. In their braggadocio they were encouraged by nationalistic legends according to which France had from the very beginning offered active resistance to the occupation and the Pétain regime (...)."[2] As Austria was now to be officially considered a victim of German troops in 1938, this experience was taken as a connecting factor, a singular bridge for future understanding, that had to be rebuilt after seven years of Francophobia instilled by Nazi Germany. For Raoul de Broglie of the French Forces in Austria, both countries had yet more in common: Catholicism, a grand history, a self-image of being a beacon of culture and civilization, humanistic ideals like "respect and independence of the human person", and even the "cult of true democracy, whose high principles hail from France and have found an echo in the Austrians' minds" (De Broglie 1948, p. 174). Many cultural officials used this kind of imagery to describe France as Austria's big sister, who has offered novel impulses and inspirations since the Middle Ages. After World War II, the French Allies—lacking material resources—again concentrated on transferring cultural assets, creating a bilateral *accord culturel* in 1947 that stipulated plans to promote French culture in Austrian schools, universities, libraries, theaters, and media. This cultural agreement applied primarily to their own sector, which, besides the interallied Vienna, consisted of the two western states of Vorarlberg and Tyrol, taken over from the United States Forces in July 1945, with roughly 18% of the Austrian territory and 8.4% of the country's population, around 590,000 people (cf. Haut Commissariat 1948, pp. 7–9).

In their aim to permanently secure Austria's separation from Germany, French cultural policy focused on establishing a feeling of togetherness and strengthening Austria's self-esteem. This was to be achieved by

---

[2] Sperber (1994, p. 223f). Ute Weinmann (Weinmann 2009, p. 90) notes that in its coverage on Austria from 1945 to 1950, the French newspaper *Le Monde* avoids terms such as 'National Socialism', using 'problem' or 'impasse' instead.

emphasizing the Habsburg cultural heritage, despite it being rather cosmopolitan than national in character (cf. George 2014, p. 73), and additionally by praising France as a role model, not one that is enforced but, as High Commissioner Émile Béthouart states, one voluntarily accepted. In a classified directive, Charles de Gaulle in July 1945 argues that, while a rigorous purge of pro-German elements was indispensable, Austria should be handled with a spirit of tolerance and courtesy, which is why members of the French Army generally didn't speak of 'occupation' but simply of 'presence'.[3]

Denazification is rather brief and benevolent, leaving not much room for allied intervention, says Béthouart. While the German people had to relearn democratic principles with the help of a foreign culture, the basis of the Austrian rehabilitation was its own culture. A whole ensemble of preexisting political, social, and ethical structures had to be taken into consideration: "Organisms in a state of lethargy have to be brought back to life, avoiding all overly abrupt gestures, all overly radical actions, which risk stopping their life's very principle."[4] Strikingly, the allied reasoning was that Austrians needed to be woken from a seven-year slumber—sleep being a metaphor compatible with the victim theory (and in frequent use alongside the image of National Socialism as an infectious disease). A gentle awakening is hardly the effect existentialism has on its average recipients—quite the contrary, as Béthouart notes in January 1946: "(…) when it comes to literature, it would be careless to approach contemporary currents at once (the few Austrians, who have read Sartre, are scared or shocked)."[5] The shock Sartre causes can be either negative or positive, adds Armand Jacob, a key journalist within the framework of Franco-Austrian cultural transfers:

---

[3] Cf. De Gaulle (in Klöckler 1996, p. 12): "Une épuration rigoureuse des éléments pro-allemands est indispensable, car l'Autriche a subi fortement l'influence hitlérienne et son économie a même profité, dans une large mesure, des avantages que lui a procurés le réarmement intensif du pays. Il convient donc d'éliminer soigneusement de l'administration aussi bien que des postes dirigeants de l'économie toutes les personnalités qui pourraient en raison de leur attitude passée, combattre ou gêner notre influence, et s'opposer à la réalisation de notre politique."

[4] Haut Commissariat (1948, p. I): "*Il faut rappeler à la vie des organismes en état de léthargie, en évitant tout geste trop brusque, toute intervention trop radicale, qui risquerait d'arrêter en eux le principe même de la vie.*"

[5] Béthouart (in Porpaczy 2002, p. 73): "(…) was die Literatur betrifft, wäre es unvorsichtig, sofort die zeitgenössischen Strömungen anzugehen (die wenigen Österreicher, die Sartre gelesen haben, sind verschreckt oder schockiert)."

"He has thrilled some, exasperated others, but he has astounded all and thrown everyone off the beaten track."[6] This, however, is the opposite of what the French military authorities had in mind for Austria. Even more counterproductive from their viewpoint would have been a debate created by existentialism's philosophical considerations of freedom and responsibility, which is exactly what they were actively promoting in their zones in Southwestern Germany. There, they included existentialism in their measures of democratization by organizing theater tours of French ensembles and by supporting public discussions about the necessity of remorse, turning the play *The Flies* (staged in Duesseldorf and Berlin) into one of the major cultural exports and an immense success (cf. Lusset 1981, p. 99), with Sartre being invited to Berlin and treated like a statesman.

Skipping *The Flies*

Sartre's famous 1947 comment on the sterility of remorse—referring to the German performances of *The Flies*—spoke to the heart of contemporary debates in West Germany:

> After our defeat in 1940 all too many Frenchmen gave way to discouragement or yielded to remorse. I wrote *The Flies* and tried to show that *remorse* was not an attitude Frenchmen should choose after our country's military collapse. Our past no longer existed. (…) The problem is the same for the Germans today. I believe that for the Germans, too, remorse is sterile. I do not mean that the recollection of past faults should be expunged from their memory. No. But I am convinced that complacent remorse is not the way for them to obtain whatever pardon the world may grant them. The better course is a total and genuine commitment to a future of freedom and work, a determination to build that future, the presence among them of the greatest possible number of men of good will.[7]

---

[6] "Jean-Paul Sartre un[!] der Existentialismus," (1947, n.p.): "Er hat die Einen begeistert, die Anderen zur Verzweiflung gebracht, alle aber hat er in Erstaunen versetzt und aus ihrer gewohnten Bahn geworfen."

[7] Sartre (1976, p. 191f). The Austrian reader could come across Sartre's text "Après notre défaite…" (originally in *Verger*, no. 2, June 1947) in mid-1948 in the theater magazine *Komödie* ("Der Un-Mut der Selbstverleugnung").

Most controversial was the universalization of the historical situation (comparing France 1940 with Germany 1945). Even though Sartre explained that his words did not imply that bygone faults should be forgotten, many criticized his philosophy for permitting its recipients to move on from their pasts all too quickly by readjusting their lives to the future. His future-oriented perspective, at odds with Austria's new focus on looking backward, is already clearly visible in Sartre's war diary from March 1940: "It's of no importance to have this or that past. For it to exist, we have to throw ourselves through it towards a certain future: we have to adopt it as our own *for* some future end or other. Each time, it's some act of freedom which decides its efficacy—and even its meaning" (Sartre 1999, p. 335). In this sense, *The Flies* was now understood as an artistically conveyed absolution, heroizing Orestes's crime as an act of freedom: "I have done *my* deed, Electra, and that deed was good. I shall bear it on my shoulders (…). The heavier it is to carry, the better pleased I shall be; for that burden is my freedom" (Sartre 1989, p. 105). Among the few Austrian critics to comment on this, the theologian Johann Fischl warns about the dangers of the Sartrean equivalency of all acts: "How should we behave? Sartre answers: Do as you please! Decide out of freedom only and stand by your deed! Don't take life all too seriously: life is absurd. So he solves the serious question of life's meaning with the Frenchmen's frivolity: 'It comes down to the same thing if you quietly get drunk or if you're the leader of nations.'"[8] Notwithstanding that Orestes's vengeful murder of his mother and her husband (representing Hitler und Pétain) may be interpreted as "an elegant parallel to the political situation of France under German rule" (Wilkinson 1981, p. 41), philosopher Günther Anders, who was to become Sartre's main contact person in Vienna, finds remorselessness as "a general ethical proposition" highly problematic:

---

[8] Fischl (1954, p. 315): "Wie sollten wir uns verhalten? Sartre antwortet uns: Tue, was du willst! Entscheide dich nur aus Freiheit und stehe zu deiner Tat! Nimm das ganze Leben nicht allzu wichtig: das Leben ist absurd. So löst er die ernste Frage nach dem Sinn des Lebens mit der Frivolität des Franzosen: 'So kommt es auf das gleiche hinaus, ob man sich im stillen betrinkt oder ob man Führer von Völkern ist.'"

Just imagine a German war-criminal reading the play; a man steeped to his neck in what has been called "collective guilt": He will gladly renounce contrition before even starting on it; he may even distort or misinterpret the war against the flies in a way to justify the ruthlessness of his own past. The similarity between Hitler's unswerving identification of his decision with morality, and Orest's killing of the flies is certainly superficial: but for superficial readers it may be puzzling; and for hypocritical ones tempting, or even inviting. (Anders 1947, p. 16)

Even as an invitation to collective repression, the play was not embraced in Austria where the topic of guilt was to be avoided at all costs. Reactions were negligible primarily because stagings of *Die Fliegen* (*The Flies*), otherwise the first step of transfer in the German-speaking countries, were practically skipped. Its first Austrian production in the Viennese theater *Kammerspiele* premiered on 7 May 1948 (Director: Karl Wessel, Set Designer: Gustav Manker), with neither success nor noteworthy media response. Only one of the mainstream papers, the social democratic *Arbeiter-Zeitung*, published a short review, not mentioning the notion of remorse at all, but being all the more outraged by the repulsiveness of what they had witnessed: "(…) a naked, brutal pile of people whimpering with fear, screaming mythological criminals, howling Erinyes, and cold-blooded gods, from which the rotting spiritual intestines are taken out with an expert hand and spread out steaming in front of us. An evident expression of a generation which mauls itself and gives up."[9] Such depictions were no exception in the early years: the Socialists in Austria found Sartre's works as appalling as did most of the communists and the Catholic critics. Consequently, the French cultural officials felt vindicated in their assertion that Sartre's fiction was basically 'too much' for the public and still 'too exotic' in 1950, when stagings of *No Exit* brought about clear signs of readiness on the part of the audience, as one Tyrolean reviewer writes: "Sure enough, Sartre shows dirt and filth, perversity and the most fervent lust (…). The audience, however, gave a strong applause. Certainly,

---

[9] "Orgie des Flagellantismus," (1948, p. 3): "(…) eine nackte, brutale Aufeinanderhäufung angstwinselnder Menschen, schreiender mythologischer Verbrecher, heulender Erynnien und kaltblütiger Götter, aus der die verfaulenden geistigen Eingeweide mit kundiger Hand hervorgeholt und dampfend vor uns ausgebreitet werden. Sinnfälliger Ausdruck einer Generation, die sich selbst zerfleischt und aufgibt."

some could not relate to the piece, which may provoke fierce reactions both for and against it. In any case, it was a courageous act to put this topical, enthralling drama up for discussion."[10]

While cultural officials didn't open up toward existentialism on a larger scale, there have been a handful of journalists of the allied press who reported on Sartre in allied (*Wort und Tat, Europäische Rundschau, Österreichische Rundschau*) or independent (*Plan, Der Turm*) cultural magazines, regardless of the general orientation of French cultural policy. In doing so, they played a major role in the circulation of existentialist thought early on, especially via the German-language weekly bulletin of the French Documentation Center in Vienna, *Kulturelles* (later renamed *Geistiges Frankreich*), which represented the biggest source of information on French culture for all Austrian media. These journalists shows how processes of intercultural transfer are often the work of specific individuals who act as multipliers. One of them is Armand Jacob, whose biweekly reports briefly covered new texts by Sartre and Camus, and occasionally also by Gabriel Marcel, Simone de Beauvoir, and Maurice Merleau-Ponty. Like Jacob, a French specialist in German studies, most of the key transfer agents for existentialist thought stood in one way or another between cultures (Lilly von Sauter, P. A. Stéphano, Jean Hyppolite, Jean Daniélou, Pierre Seguy, René Ferriot), a famous example being the Austrian-born French author André Gorz. Under the name Gerhard Horst, Gorz was one of the first to introduce the actual philosophy of existentialism to the Austrian readership through Sartre's still untranslated *Being and Nothingness* in early 1946 ("Der Existentialismus bei Jean-Paul Sartre", *Der Turm* 2, no. 1, 12). Such accounts were of the utmost importance, since—except for the controversial *Existentialism Is a Humanism*—most of Sartre's original works weren't translated until 1949/1950. In the early postwar years, translation rights were expensive enough to yet increase the preference for canonized and salable books, mostly from Catholic literature, as the French bulletin *Kulturelles* notes:

---

[10] "Sartre-Premiere in Innsbruck," (1950, p. 4): "Gewiß, Sartre zeigt Schmutz und Unrat, Perversität und brünstigste Lust (…). Das Publikum spendete starken Beifall. Sicherlich konnten manche keine rechte Beziehung zum Stück finden, das ebenso heftiges Für und Wider auslösen dürfte. Jedenfalls war es eine mutige Tat, dieses zeitnahe, packende Drama zur Diskussion gestellt zu haben."

"Admittedly, the specific Austrian literary taste, which, for example in Vienna, offered a reserved response to a play by Jean-Paul Sartre that was extraordinarily successful in Berlin, will continue to prefer entertainment and the Christian-based social novel: the collected works of François Mauriac are being prepared in Vienna (…)."[11]

Catholic Criticism or a Believer in Spite of Himself

Progressive Catholicism, as represented by the *Renouveau Catholique* authors such as Georges Bernanos, Paul Claudel, and François Mauriac, was culturally the main point of contact between Austria and France after 1945. Special attention was being paid to the so-called Christian existentialist Gabriel Marcel and the *Esprit* editor and proponent of personalism Emmanuel Mounier, to whom the Austrian critics took an unanimous liking. Jacob notes: "Among today's French philosophers there is probably no one as well-known in Austria as Gabriel Marcel. More is being said about Sartre, but Gabriel Marcel is really being read."[12] Contrary to Marcel—whose popularity is evident from separate Austrian translations (while almost all German translations of texts by Camus and Sartre first arrive in Austria via Germany or Switzerland)—Sartre and Camus were not read so much as philosophers by the general readership, but as novelists and dramatists.[13] Camus' *The Plague* (1947), in particular, was highly praised by readers and critics alike, even though he is "the farther away of the two from Christianity, since Sartre is merely anti-Christian, while Camus is un-Christian, pagan", as Serge Doubrovsky argues in 1960 in

---

[11] "Französische Autoren auf der österreichischen Buchausstellung" (1948, n.p.): "Freilich wird der spezifisch österreichische Literaturgeschmack, der z. B. einem in Berlin ausserordentlich erfolgreichen Stück Jean-Paul Sartres in Wien eine zurückhaltende Aufnahme bereitete, auch weiterhin die Unterhaltung und den christlich fundierten Gesellschaftsroman vorziehen: eine Gesamtausgabe François Mauriacs wird in Wien vorbereitet (…)."

[12] Armand Jacob (Das Geheimnis des Seins von Gabriel Marcel 1952, n.p.): "Unter den französischen Philosophen der Gegenwart gibt es wohl keinen, der in Österreich so bekannt wäre, wie Gabriel Marcel. Von Sartre wird zwar mehr gesprochen, aber Gabriel Marcel wird wirklich gelesen."

[13] Cf. Collins (2002, p. 765): They are part of a newly constructed canon, together with authors from the Austrian tradition, kindred "literary writers of heavily philosophical content", especially the belatedly discovered Franz Kafka.

Yale French Studies: "Sartre and the Christians alike burden the individual with the weight of his original guilt and the sinfulness of his existence. Many Sartrean themes, such as responsibility, guilt, anguish, hatred of the flesh, (…) often seem to be inverted Christian themes. Camus, on the contrary, proclaims the value of sensuousness and the right to happiness (…)" (Doubrovsky 1960, p. 91). Among the so-called existentialists, Camus as a fiction writer is perceived to be "not the greatest of his generation, but well the most needed and essential",[14] mainly because in Austria and elsewhere he has been labeled a moralist, whose honesty and humbleness pose no danger to Christianity.

Unlike Camus, whose philosophical works have barely been registered, Sartre caused strong polarization due to his inescapable presence in several fields (prose, drama, politics, philosophy), soon making it impossible not only for his supporters, but also for his adversaries and rivals not to state their position on his views (cf. Boschetti 2016, pp. 193–198). Most opponents belonged to communist and Catholic circles, seeing themselves in rare accord over their judgment of Sartre's thinking ("a bold and boring mishmash of misanthropic philosophy, abnormal pathology and pornography"[15]). The latter group, however, had much more power than the communists, who could hardly be compared to their intellectually dominant French brothers in the second half of the 1940s. Catholicism's main answer to existentialism was in most cases not strictly theologian in nature, but an almost mechanical reaction against its alleged nihilistic tendencies (cf. Hoff 2010, p. 133). With Sartre's notoriety ever increasing, the allied press tried to soften his reputation as a nihilist, whose bottomless pessimism endangered the young: "Is Sartre's diagnosis pessimistic or nihilistic? A thermometer showing degrees of cold when it's freezing would be equally pessimistic or nihilistic. Whoever scolds Sartre holds the stenographer liable for an insulting speech."[16] The *Wiener Kurier*, a paper issued by the American Forces, which featured articles by journal-

---

[14] Jacob (1952/1953, p. 193): "nicht der Größte seiner Generation, aber wohl der Notwendigste und Unentbehrlichste."

[15] "Eine Verzerrung des Menschen" (1947, n.p.): "ein wildes und langweiliges Gemengsel misanthropischer Philosophie, krankhafter Pathologie und Pornographie."

[16] "Die Jungen" (1950, n.p.): "Ist Sartres Diagnose pessimistisch oder nihilistisch? Ebenso pessimistisch oder nihilistisch ist ein Thermometer, das bei Frost Kältegrade zeigt. Wer Sartre schilt, der macht den Stenographen für eine beleidigende Rede haftbar."

ists such as Jean Prieur and Claude Roy working for the French Forces, also came to Sartre's defense: The "friendly and gentle" philosopher was gathering more and more followers around him, who appreciated his "philosophy of courageous responsibility and austere morals": "His talks have been as well received in Switzerland, Italy, Sweden, and England as in the United States, and in each of these countries the existentialist school enjoys a growing clientele."[17] The *Weltpresse*, published by the British Information Service, struck a similar note, calling France the center of the European mind, but drawing contradictory and somewhat peculiar conclusions about Sartre and his play *Huis clos*: "Sartre's message is simple: No one can escape their own personality, therefore it is of no use to revolt against oneself. (…) Only, Sartre adds that everyone must atone for their sins in the end, so there's a need for a biblical hell. Everybody carries their own hell in them…."[18]

Intended or not, these remarks are good examples of how audience preferences may lead to shifts in meaning during the transfer process. Atheistic existentialism has usually been presented in relation to Catholicism, some authors went to quite some lengths in order to ease Sartre's reception for the Catholic readership. Owing to its elasticity and openness to interpretation, existentialism can be linked to religion or even merged into it. The Styrian theologian Gotthold Hasenhüttl, who translated Sartre's Christmas play *Bariona, ou le Fils du tonnerre* in 1972, insisted that Sartre's thought was continuously moved by the question of God: "No atheistic philosopher of our time has spoken so much about God as has J.-P. Sartre. No one has linked the search for life's meaning as closely with theodicy as he has."[19] Hasenhüttl was not alone in selling

---

[17] "Philosophie der Verantwortung und Moral" (1946, n.p.): "freundliche und weich veranlagte," "Philosophie der mutigen Verantwortlichkeit und strengen Moral": "Seine Vorträge wurden in der Schweiz, Italien, Schweden und England ebenso gut aufgenommen wie in den Vereinigten Staaten, und in jedem dieser Staaten erfährt die existenzialistische Schule einen immer größeren Zulauf."

[18] "Stefan-Zweig-Roman in London verfilmt" (1946, n.p.): "Sartres Botschaft ist einfach: Niemand kann seiner eigenen Persönlichkeit entrinnen, und es nützt deshalb nichts sich gegen sich selbst aufzulehnen. (…) Sartre fügt hinzu, daß jeder letzten Endes für seine Sünden büßen müsse und daß dazu eine biblische Hölle notwendig sei. Jeder trägt seine eigene Hölle in sich…."

[19] Hasenhüttl (1972, p. 11): "Kein atheistischer Philosoph unserer Zeit hat so viel von Gott gesprochen wie J.-P. Sartre. Keiner hat die Sinnfrage unseres Lebens so stark mit der Gottesfrage verbunden wie er."

existentialism as a kind of a secular religion, or Sartre as a believer in spite of himself. Metaphorically, many transformed him into a religious leader, the head of a European "sect of intellectuals, who call themselves 'Sartrists'",[20] the "Pope of Existentialism",[21] an admired deity, a man worshipped "like a God from foreign lands".[22] Still, the fact that Sartre, contoured with such absolute terms, was able to somehow subdue "the whole intellectual universe" (Bourdieu 1980, p. 11), stayed a thorn in the side of most Catholic thinkers. After the pope decided to put Sartre's works on the *List of Prohibited Books* in 1948, a good part of the community of Catholic readers—the group that initially showed the greatest interest in him—was irrevocably lost, while Catholic journalists continued to monitor his development.

Cold War Disinvolvement

In the early 1950s, Sartre attracted positive attention from a new group, the formerly hostile Austrian communists, who, however, were a political *quantité négligeable*. Since their arrival, the French Allies had cooperated with Christian as well as with communist politicians, groups who had proved to be the most reliable partners against Nazi Germany during the war. When the Cold War conflicts intensified in the late '40s, Vienna's position on the fault line between opposing spheres made the French join the British and American forces in their radical anti-communism. This is why, when Sartre publicly turned into a *compagnon de route* by attending the communist *World Congress of People for Peace* in 1952 (cf. Werner 2017, pp. 1–18), they remained silent, as did all of the Western press who were asked to boycott the unwelcome event by government order. In the weeks leading up to the congress, Sartre managed to cancel what was to be the first Viennese production of the allegedly anti-communist play *Dirty Hands* on short notice, explaining: "I disavow neither 'Les mains Sales' nor any other of my writings. But I don't want it to be used for propaganda purposes … If people of all nations and, as I hope, of all

---

[20] Fischl (1954, p. 315): "eine Sekte von Intellektuellen, die sich selbst 'Sartristen' nennen."
[21] Knilli (1961, p. 41): "Existentialistenpapst Jean-Paul Sartre."
[22] Kräftner (1950, p. 120f): "wie einen Gott aus fremden Ländern."

political opinions make an effort to understand one another, the moment to take up old fights is badly chosen" ("Sartre besteht auf Zurückziehung seines Stückes," 1952, n.p.). Two years later, while on holiday in Salzburg with Simone de Beauvoir, Sartre returned to Vienna to stop the next attempt to stage *Dirty Hands*, this time without success (cf. de Beauvoir 1978, p. 324). Although he was certainly not too eager for gatherings with representatives of the allied forces, at least during his second stay, it is nevertheless remarkable—especially when compared to the French Allies' hospitality toward Sartre in 1948 in Berlin—that one of the world's most famous thinkers visits Vienna twice without meeting with any cultural officials and without being invited to the *Institut Français*, which otherwise welcomed almost every French intellectual, scientist, and artist at the time.

From *The Flies* to *Dirty Hands*, Austria's role changed from the frail victim that had to be spared the troubling philosophy and provocative literature of existentialism to being the outrider of the anti-communist West, to whom the 'fellow traveler' Sartre had come to be a *persona non grata*. Yet, before the allied transfer—ambivalent as it was in its attempts first to ignore an unavoidable phenomenon and then to adapt it to the expectations of an allegedly over-traditionalist Austrian audience—came to a sudden halt in the early '50s, the commitment of individual young magazine editors and journalists and venturesome theater directors in the late '40s had already been sufficient to ensure existentialism's impact for later more open-minded decades.[23]

References

Anders, Günther. 1947. On Sartre [The Illusion of Existentialism (Sartre's "Les mouches")]. Literaturarchiv der Österreichischen Nationalbibliothek, Wien (LIT), Sign.: 237/W74.

de Beauvoir, Simone. 1978. *Force of Circumstance*. Translated by Richard Howard. Harmondsworth: Penguin.

---

[23] For an in-depth analysis of the impact of existentialism on Austrian literature, philosophy, and (youth) culture, see my forthcoming book *Existentialismus in Österreich. Kultureller Transfer und literarische Resonanz* (Berlin: De Gruyter, 2020).

Boschetti, Anna. 2016. Sartre au centre des querelles. In *La vie intellectuelle en France, no. 2: De 1914 à nos jours*, ed. Christophe Charle and Laurent Jeanpierre, 193–198. Paris: Seuil.

Bourdieu, Pierre. 1980. Sartre. *London Review of Books* 2 (22): 11–12.

de Broglie, Raoul. 1948. *Souvenirs français dans le Tyrol*. Innsbruck: Selbstverlag des Verfassers.

Collins, Randall. 2002. *The Sociology of Philosophies. A Global Theory of Intellectual Change*. Cambridge, MA and London: Harvard University Press.

Das Geheimnis des Seins von Gabriel Marcel. 1952. *Geistiges Frankreich*, December 29.

Die Jungen. 1950. *Welt am Montag*, January 23.

Doubrovsky, Serge. 1960. Sartre and Camus: A Study in Incarceration. *Yale French Studies* 25: 85–92.

Eine Verzerrung des Menschen. 1947. *Österreichische Zeitung*, November 15.

Fischl, Johann. 1954. *Idealismus, Realismus und Existentialismus der Gegenwart. Ein Beitrag zur Aussprache über die Weltanschauung des modernen Menschen*. Graz: Styria.

Französische Autoren auf der österreichischen Buchausstellung. 1948. *Kulturelles*, September 13.

George, Marion. 2014. Encore une Querelle des Anciens et des Modernes—quelques remarques sur la perception française de l'identité culturelle autrichienne après 1945. In *Eclats d'Autriche. Vingt études sur l'image de la culture autrichienne aux XXᵉ et XXIᵉ siècles*, ed. Marion George and Valérie de Daran, 67–80. Bern: Lang.

Hasenhüttl, Gotthold. 1972. *Gott ohne Gott. Ein Dialog mit J.-P. Sartre*. Graz, Wien, and Köln: Styria.

Haut Commissariat de la République Française en Autriche (Division Information, Centre de Documentation). 1948. *Deux ans et demi de présence française en Autriche*. Notes documentaires et études no. 870 (Série européenne—CXIV).

Hoff, Gregor Maria. 2010. *Stichproben: Theologische Inversionen. Salzburger Aufsätze*, Salzburger Theologische Studien 40. Innsbruck: Tyrolia.

Jacob, Armand. 1952/1953. Albert Camus oder die Bemühung um einen Generalnenner. *Perspektiven*: 191–205.

Jean-Paul Sartre un[!] der Existentialismus. 1947. *Kulturelles*, June 17.

Judt, Tony. 2005. *Postwar. A History of Europe Since 1945*. New York: Penguin.

Klöckler, Jürgen. 1996. *Quellen zu Österreichs Nachkriegsgeschichte in französischen Archiven. Tirol, Vorarlberg und Wien nach dem Zweiten Weltkrieg*. Dornbirn: Vorarlberger Verlagsanstalt.

Knilli, Friedrich. 1961. Saint Genet—Komödiant und Märtyrer. *Wort in der Zeit* 7 (3): 40–42.

Kräftner, Hertha. 1950. Aus dem Pariser Tagebuch 1950. *neue wege* 6 (60): 120–121.

Lusset, Félix. 1981. Un épisode de l'histoire de la Mission Culturelle Française à Berlin (1946–1948): Sartre et Simone de Beauvoir à Berlin à l'occasion des représentations des *Mouches* au théâtre Hebbel (Janvier 1948). In *La dénazification par les vainqueurs. La politique culturelle des occupants en Allemagne 1945–1949*, ed. Jérôme Vaillant, 91–104. Lille: Presses universitaires de Lille.

Orgie des Flagellantismus. 1948. *Arbeiter-Zeitung*, May 11.

Philosophie der Verantwortung und Moral. 1946. *Wiener Kurier*, December 5.

Porpaczy, Barbara. 2002. *Frankreich—Österreich. 1945–1960. Kulturpolitik und Identität*. Innsbruck, Wien, München, and Bozen: StudienVerlag.

Sartre, Jean-Paul. 1976. *Sartre on Theater*. Edited by Michel Contat and Michel Rybalka, translated by Frank Jellinek. New York: Pantheon.

———. 1988. The Nationalization of Literature. In *"What Is Literature?" and Other Essays*, trans. Jeffrey Mehlman, 271–288. Cambridge, MA: Harvard University Press.

———. 1989. The Flies. In *No Exit, and Three Other Plays*, trans. S. Gilbert. New York: Vintage.

———. 1999. *War Diaries. Notebooks from the Phoney War 1939–1940*. Translated by Quintin Hoare. London and New York: Verso.

Sartre besteht auf Zurückziehung seines Stückes. 1952. *Österreichische Zeitung*, November 19.

Sartre-Premiere in Innsbruck. 1950. *Tiroler Tageszeitung*, May 15.

Sperber, Manès. 1994. *Until My Eyes are Closed with Shards*. Translated by Harry Zohn. New York and London: Holmes & Meier.

Stefan-Zweig-Roman in London verfilmt. 1946. *Weltpresse*, August 10.

United States Department of State. 1943. Declaration on Austria. In *Foreign relations of the United States Diplomatic Papers, 1943. General*, vol. I. U.S. Government Printing Office.

Vranitzky, Franz. 1991. 35. Sitzung Nationalrat, XVIII. Gesetzgebungsperiode—Stenographisches Protokoll, July 8.

Weinmann, Ute. 2009. À propos de l'image politique de l'Autriche en France. Le 'problème autrichien' dans le journal *Le Monde* de 1945 à 1950. In *"Au nom de Goethe!" Hommage à Gerald Stieg*, ed. Marc Lacheny and Jean François Laplénie, 79–90. Paris: L'Harmattan.

Werner, Juliane. 2017. Sartre in Austria. Boycott, Scandals, and the Fight for Peace. *Sartre Studies International* 23 (2): 1–18.

———. 2020 [forthcoming]. *Existentialismus in Österreich. Kultureller Transfer und literarische Resonanz.* Berlin: De Gruyter.

Wilkinson, James D. 1981. *The Intellectual Resistance in Europe.* Cambridge, MA: Harvard University Press.

Part III

Asia, Latin America, and Africa

12

The Journey of Sartrean Existentialism into Turkey

Ayşenaz Cengiz

This paper describes the migration of existentialist philosophy to Turkey by means of translation, here focused mainly on Sartrean existentialism. "Theory does not travel on its own, but under the name of a well-known writer" (Susam-Sarajeva 2006, p. 1), as is the case with the migration of existentialism through the import of Jean-Paul Sartre's work into Turkey, where Sartre's name is invariably associated with existentialism. In the 1960s and 1970s especially, Sartre and his work had a profound influence on Turkey's intellectual community, as the number of his works translated into Turkish indicates.

Texts relating to theories and intellectual movements move across language boundaries through translation. However, the crucial role played by translation in the migration of theories and intellectual movements has been greatly neglected. Edward Said does not even provide room for the word 'translation' in his writing on traveling theories, and thus

A. Cengiz (✉)
Bogazici University, Istanbul, Turkey
e-mail: aysenaz.cengiz@boun.edu.tr

© The Author(s) 2020
A. Betschart, J. Werner (eds.), *Sartre and the International Impact of Existentialism*,
https://doi.org/10.1007/978-3-030-38482-1_12

neglects the close link between translation and the movement of ideas and theories from one place to another (Said 1991).

This tendency to overlook the relationship between theory and language is also underlined by Lawrence Venuti, who states that "in philosophical research widespread dependence on translated texts coincides with the neglect of their translated status, a general failure to take into account the differences introduced by the fact of translation" (Venuti 1998, p. 106). Nevertheless, when a theoretical text is translated, when it crosses borders, it makes a new place for itself in a new territory and language. In this new environment, the theory may serve other purposes it never originally intended, at the same time transforming the culture it enters (Miller 1996, p. 219). According to J. Hillis Miller, "to translate theory is to traduce it, to betray it", for theory is the result of "one particular place, time, culture, and language" (Miller 1996, pp. 209–210).

Likewise, Pierre Bourdieu states that the misunderstandings in international exchanges of ideas stem mainly from the fact that "texts circulate without their context" (Bourdieu 1999, p. 221). As a result, these texts are re-interpreted "in accordance with the structure of the field of reception"—that is, a field of production different from that of which they are a product (Bourdieu 1999, p. 221). Consequently, "the field of reception" and "the field of origin" play a role in determining "the sense and function of a foreign work", as the transfer of a foreign text from its source field to a target one is the outcome of a set of social operations, generally on the target side (Bourdieu 1999, p. 222). A foreign text moves across linguistic and cultural boundaries, not on its own but through cultural mediators, including translators, editors, publishers, and critics who contribute to its 'rewriting' for its new destination. Thus, the translation process, as seen in a wider field of cultural activity, embraces the translated text's existence, reception, and consumption in the receiving cultural milieu. The process starts with the very selection of the text to be translated into a specific linguistic culture at a specific time. It does not end, however, with the publication of the translated text, but continues with the reading process; the text which will be read by a new public will become part of local realities and interpreted with the dominant ideology of the target culture. Thus, it is in this way that the cultural good, a philosophical theory in this case, is 'rewritten' for its new destination.

At this point, referring to André Lefevere's concept of "rewriting" (Lefevere 1992, p. 9; Lefevere 1985, pp. 234–235), it is necessary to examine together the translations and accompanying indigenous writings, as different channels through which Sartrean existentialism has been received in Turkey. As translations and accompanying indigenous writings represent various forms of rewriting through which a philosophical theory travels from one country to another, examining them as observable aspects of the rewriting process will provide us with some clues about the discourse generated around this philosophy and its reception in the target culture. This study will thus dwell on the patterns of translations (text selection and the time factor) and indigenous writings on Sartre and existentialism, such as reviews, statements, and comments by critics, writers, translators, or editors, which help "determine the response towards this imported theory" (Susam-Sarajeva 2006, p. 23).

The reception of Sartrean existentialism in Turkey is based largely on translation; so far, 70 translations (and retranslations) of Sartre's works have been published in book form in Turkish since 1950, whereas the number of indigenous works in book form on existentialism and/or Sartre is only ten, two of which appeared in the 1980s, the other eight in the 2000s. In exploring the role of translation in this migration, the translation of both Sartre's fictional and nonfictional works is taken into account, for certainly Sartre used his novels and plays as a medium to communicate his philosophical themes. Normally, one would expect that the key philosophical treatises by Sartre would be translated first to pave the way for the traveling of existentialism; however, his fictional works were accorded higher preference, while his nonfiction was relatively neglected for a rather long period of time. As mentioned above, the indigenous critical pieces on existentialism and Sartre will also be granted space, since "research on translations yields more fruitful results when it is carried out in conjunction with research on other forms of 'rewriting'" (Susam-Sarajeva 2006, p. 22).

My main source of reference for the Turkish translations of Sartre's works, along with translated and indigenous texts on Sartre and existentialism, is the bibliography prepared by Asım Bezirci (2002). I collected additional data from ideefixe.com, nadirkitap.com, and the Turkish national library's internet website mkutup.gov.tr. I also inspected almost all the published issues of several prominent Turkish periodicals on literature, translation, and philosophy.[1]

Sartrean Existentialism in Turkey

Since World War II, existentialism as a philosophical movement has been extremely popular in France, Germany, and Latin America; shortly thereafter, it became influential in the English-speaking world as well (Popkin and Stroll 1993, p. 302). Existentialism continued to develop in different forms after World War II. It was after 1945 that existentialism became very popular. Numerous articles on this philosophy appeared in journals; it was discussed in the cafés of Paris as well as outside France. There is a general consensus that existentialism became a shout of despair following World War II, at a time of frustration when all conventional values had been turned upside down. This philosophy was a way through which those who had fought against the Nazis could develop a new system of values and a new humanism inspiring hope. This wide popularity of existentialism, especially in France, was largely due to the personality of Sartre, who took philosophy from textbooks and placed it in the heart of everyday life (Aksoy 1981, pp. 316, 320). It is, as Kaufmann states, "mainly through the work of Jean-Paul Sartre that existentialism has come to the attention of a wide international audience" (Kaufmann 1956, p. 40).

As in the rest of the world, existentialism was primarily influential in Turkey from the 1950s to the 1980s (Direk 2002, p. 441). Following World War II the echoes of existentialism also resounded in Turkey,

---

[1] These are: *Birikim* (1975–1980), *Cep Dergisi* (1966–1969), *Hisar* (1964–1980), *May* (1967–1970), *Metis Çeviri* (1987–1992), *Felsefe Dergisi* (1977–1988), *Felsefe Yazıları* (1981–1983), *Papirüs* (1966–1971), *Tercüme* (1940–1966), *Türk Dili* (1951–2019), *Varlık* (from 1946 to 2019), *Yapraklar* (1964–1965), *Yazko Edebiyat* (1980–1985), *Yazko Çeviri* (1981–1984), *Yeditepe* (from 1960 to 1970), *Yelken* (1957–1980), *Yeni Dergi* (1964–1975), and *Yeni Ufuklar* (1953–1976). *Varlık*, one of the groundbreaking journals of the Turkish literary scene, has been inspected from 1946 (when translations and indigenous pieces on existentialism began to appear) to the present date, and *Yeditepe* from 1960 to 1970 when the popularity of existentialism was on the rise in Turkey.

bringing about translations and introductory articles on the subject in Turkish periodicals (Bezirci 2002, p. 16). The Turkish reader's interest in existentialism can be traced back to the second half of the 1940s, when translated and indigenous pieces on this philosophy began to appear in various periodicals with an aim of introducing it.

The following is an overview of the journey of Sartrean existentialism to Turkey on the basis of three periods.

From 1946 to 1959

Prior to 1960, no nonfiction works by Sartre had been published in Turkey in book form, and all but one of the pieces published in periodicals had been either essays on existentialist philosophy of an introductory nature or excerpts from his famous lecture *L'existentialisme est un humanisme* (*Existentialism Is a Humanism*). Furthermore, only three of Sartre's fictional works—*Huis clos* (*No Exit*), *Les jeux sont faits* (*The Chips Are Down*), and excerpts from *Le mur* (*The Wall*)—had been translated into Turkish before 1960. Most of the early translations (and retranslations) on existentialism appeared in the 19 May 1946 special issue of *Tercüme*, the journal of the Translation Office, a state institution established to promote translation. The aim of this issue, as explained in the preface, was to introduce to the Turkish readership a contemporary intellectual movement by presenting texts by its followers (*Tercüme* 1946, pp. 30, 34–36).

As for the first indigenous publication on existentialism of note in this early period, it was a series of articles written by Hilmi Ziya Ülken, published in 1946 in three subsequent issues of the literary magazine *İstanbul* (Direk 2002, p. 441). In the first part of his article, Ülken refers to Kierkegaard, Heidegger, and Jaspers, referring to Sartre as the principal representative of the movement (Ülken 1946a, p. 2). He devotes the second part of his article to Sartrean existentialism, with special emphasis on *L'être et le néant* (*Being and Nothingness*) (Ülken 1946b, pp. 3–4). In another article, Oğuz Peltek complains about the scarcity of translations and indigenous works on philosophy in Turkey, and concludes that he has attempted to summarize the basic themes of existentialism by referring only to Sartre's *Existentialisme est un humanisme* and not to the more complicated philosophical treatise *L'être et le néant* (Peltek 1954, p. 21). Another endeavor aiming to introduce existentialism to the Turkish readership was undertaken in 1950 by the German scholar Professor Joachim Ritter, who had taught in the Philosophy Department at İstanbul University. This was a series of conferences entitled *Zum Problem der Existenzphilosophie* (*About the Problem of Philosophy of Existence*) (Direk 2002, p. 441). The proceedings of the conference were later translated into Turkish by Hüseyin Batuhan and published in 1954 by the İstanbul University Press under the title *Varoluş Felsefesi Üzerine* (*About Philosophy of Existence*).

According to Zeynep Direk, the year 1956 was crucial to the reception of existentialism in Turkey. In the literary magazine *Yücel*, Nusret Hızır, a prominent philosopher and historian, published a series of articles on existentialism that initiated both conflict and consensus on existentialism in leftist and rightist circles (Direk 2002, p. 442). The first two install-ments are introductory articles to the philosophies of Kierkegaard and Heidegger, respectively. In the following three articles, Hızır discussed Sartre's existentialism, and in the last, Sartre's literary career, claiming that Sartre's philosophy derived from his literary works (Hızır 1956, p. 128). In another article published in the literary magazine *Türk Düşüncesi*, Peyami Safa summarizes the basic themes of existentialist philosophy (Safa 1957, p. 26) and shows a clear prejudice against the atheist aspect of existentialism and Sartre's understanding of freedom (Direk 2002, p. 444). In Direk's opinion, Safa's harsh criticism of atheist existentialism reflects the general attitude of conservative rightist *intellectuals* of the time, caught up in nostalgia for the Ottoman past (Direk 2002, pp. 445–446). A piece of critical writing by the leftist Şerif Hulusi appeared in 1956 in the literary magazine *Yeditepe*. In this article, Hulusi associates Albert Camus' views with existentialism, claiming that existen-tialism aimed at undermining science. Hulusi argues that what Turkish revolutionists need is an optimistic outlook on life rather than a "litera-ture of despair" (Hulusi 1956, pp. 3, 7). Another publication showing the interest of Turkish intellectuals in existentialism is a special issue in 1959 devoted to existentialist philosophers and existentialism of the liter-ary magazine *A Dergisi*, launched by a group of intellectuals (Günyol

1986, p. 62). As far as Direk is concerned, nearly all these early criticisms reduce existentialism to mere individualism and pessimism: "what was discussed at that time was not the existentialist philosophy itself, but rather its popular image" (Direk 2002, p. 448).

From 1960 to 1970

Although both translated and indigenous pieces on Sartre and on existentialism had continued to appear, it was not until the 1960s that the works of Sartre himself became popular and influential in Turkey. Selâhattin Hilâv argues that a parallelism exists between the popularity of Sartrean philosophy in France after the devastation and frustration of World War II and its popularity in Turkey in the 1960s among Turkish writers who had suffered under the dismal political regime during the 1950s (Hilâv 1995, p. 203). In a similar vein, in the preface to *Çağımızın Gerçekleri* (1961; *The Truths of Our Age*), a collection of essays by Sartre, the editor notes that the aim of the translation is to initiate discourse on Sartrean thought in a country long starved of freedom (Sartre 1961, *Çağımızın Gerçekleri*, p. 7). The Turkish writers and intellectuals of the 1960s were thus drawn to the main concepts of Sartre's philosophy—the meaninglessness of life, responsibility, freedom, and political commitment—by their tendency to revolt against something not clearly defined. According to Hilâv, however, much of Sartre's thinking was lost on them because they had not been brought up in the tradition of Western thought (Hilâv 1995, p. 203).

Let us look more closely at the sociopolitical background of Turkey in the 1960s. The new world order introduced after World War II necessitated a change of regime in Turkey, and indeed the process for the change from a single-party to a multiparty system began as early as 1945. In 1950, the Democrat Party (right wing and conservative) won the election and ended the long single-party regime of the Republican People's Party (CHP). During the subsequent ten-year rule of the Democrat Party (1950–1960), Turkey became increasingly aligned with the non-communist Western world. This did not, however, entail any further integration of contemporary Western philosophy and culture into the intellectual climate of Turkey; the cultural policies of the Democrat Party "were more geared towards reviving the religious sentiment in the country" (Tahir Gürçağlar 2002, p. 255). In fact, from the 1950 program of the Democrat Party, one sees that freedom of thought was scarcely tolerated at all (Kaplan 1999, p. 217). Especially in the final years of the Democrat Party's hegemony, such factors created an environment in which the intelligentsia, the youth, and those officials in favor of "social reform and modernization (...) sought refuge in political radicalism" (Landau 1974, p. 5). Following so much unrest, a military coup d'état took place on 27 May 1960, and was generally well-received throughout the country (Turan 2002, p. 17). After only one year, a new constitution was in force. This new constitution of 1961 respected nearly all the freedoms guaranteed by contemporary counterparts, aiming to reconcile the rights and freedoms of both individuals and society as a whole (Turan 2002, p. 61). It was, therefore, not surprising that "the 1960s saw a lively intellectual debate about all kinds of political and social issues" (Zürcher 1993, p. 267). With the liberal period initiated by the new constitution, Turkish culture of the 1960s became increasingly receptive to new foreign authors and literature (Landau 1974, p. 21). Jacob M. Landau emphasizes that the 1960s showed a steady increase in the publication of books on the social sciences, a trend that gained momentum in 1962 and 1963 with liberalization in government censorship (Landau 1974, p. 21). This period thus witnessed "a flourishing of leftist thought in Turkey", partly nourished by "the translation of political and especially left-wing writings and their publication in cheap editions" (Tahir Gürçağlar 2002, p. 260).

Under the above-mentioned sociopolitical conditions, the import of existentialism into the Turkish intellectual system in the 1960s was part of a translation effort to expose the Turkish intellectual world to the West. As the Turkish historian Zafer Toprak states, "in the 1950s, Turkey tried to get to know herself, whereas in the 1960s she was mainly interested in getting to know the world" (Tahir Gürçağlar 2002, p. 260). Thus, translation was resorted to "as a major way of filling the gaps" (Toury 1995, p. 27); many prominent Turkish writers and intellectuals opened publishing houses to provide translations of philosophical and critical works still nonexistent in the Turkish intellectual milieu of the time (Doğan 1997, p. 63).

Consequently, the 1960s saw the translation of a number of works on existentialism and Sartre,[2] and of the majority of works by Sartre. Nearly all of the earlier translations of Sartre's works were fiction, and what is common to all of them is that they were all translated into Turkish more than once, and mainly in the 1960s. The real 'boom' in the translation of nonfiction works by Sartre came between 1960 and 1970: 13 of Sartre's nonfiction books were published in the 1960s.

In Afşar Timuçin's opinion, *Varoluşçuluk* (1960), the Turkish translation of Sartre's lecture *L'existentialisme est un humanisme* (*Existentialism Is a Humanism*) that enjoyed a large number of editions, is concrete evidence of the wide interest in existentialism in Turkey (Timuçin 1985, p. 88). This interest is later reflected in the number of translations of Sartre's works into Turkish, most especially after 1960. In the 1960s, he was a one of the favorite philosophers and a must-read for Turkish intellectuals; his works were printed over and over again (Kakınç 1983, p. 34). Beginning in the 1950s, nearly all the texts written in Turkish on existentialism regarded Sartre as the principal representative of existentialism. We can, therefore, say that the reception of his work is closely linked to the introduction and reception of existentialism in Turkey.

The introduction of existentialism into the Turkish system in the 1960s generated debates and initiated new discourse. There appeared some indigenous writings that criticized either existentialist philosophy or Sartre himself rather sharply. For instance, Orhan Duru criticized existentialism for foregrounding individualism and found this semi-mystical philosophy irrelevant to the Turkish intellectual tradition, which attaches

---

[2] Translations on existentialism are Roger Garaudy's *Marxisme et Existentialisme* (1960)/*Jean-Paul Sartre ve Marxisme* (İstanbul: Sosyal, 1962), Roger L. Shinn's *The Existentialist Posture* (1959)/*Egzistansiyalizmin Durumu* (İstanbul: Amerikan Bord Neşriyat Dairesi, 1963), Jean Wahl's *A Short History of Existentialism* (1949)/*Existentialisme'in Tarihi* (İstanbul: Elif, 1964), Walter Kaufmann's *Existentialism from Dostoevsky to Sartre* (1956)/*Dostoyevski'den Sartre'a Varoluşçuluk* (İstanbul: De, 1964), and a collection of essays by Adam Schaff and Piama P. Gaidenko under the title *Marxism, Varoluşçuluk ve Birey* (İstanbul: De, 1966). Translations on Sartre are Iris Murdoch's *Sartre. Romantic Rationalist* (1953)/*Sartre. Yazarlığı ve Felsefesi* (İstanbul: De, 1964) and an excerpt from Charles Moeller's *Littérature du XXe siècle et Christianisme 2. La Foi en Jésus-Christ* (1954), *Jean-Paul Sartre ve Tabiatüstünün Bilinmemesi* (İstanbul: Remzi, 1969).

paramount importance to solidarity (Duru 1964). Other pieces criticizing existentialism were written by Erol Güngör and appeared in the literary magazine *Hisar*. Güngör attempts to analyze the intellectual phases of Sartre's philosophy and belittles him for confusing art with politics (Güngör 1964b). In another article, he condemns the literary tradition of "despair" in Turkey inspired by existentialist ideas; in his opinion, the interest shown in existentialism by Turkish intellectuals is absurd, because this intellectual movement is based upon social realities of the West and not those of Turkey (Güngör 1964a). Meanwhile, several Turkish novelists attempted to write works under the impact of this philosophy (Timuçin 1985, p. 89). This literary tradition was popularly called "literature of despair"; it incited much criticism for provoking despair among the youth of the time. According to Timuçin, these Turkish novels have remained ineffectual because their authors did not understand what existentialism really was. Timuçin also suggests that the original conditions under which existentialism had been introduced in France were nonexistent in Turkey at the time (Timuçin 1985, pp. 89–90).

Timuçin argues that, in spite of its popularity, existentialist philosophy is not properly understood in Turkey because no holistic study on this subject has ever been undertaken by Turkish scholars (Timuçin 1985, p. 5). Another reason for this rather superficial knowledge stems from the characteristics inherent in existentialism itself, which embrace numerous contradictions on essential matters, making the philosophy difficult to conceptualize (Timuçin 1985, pp. 5–6). Particularly fashionable in the metropolis, according to Timuçin, existentialism was an intriguing topic for Turkish intellectuals, generally much closer to romantic and mystic schools of thought than to rationalistic ones (Timuçin 1985, p. 86). Like Timuçin, Hilâv argues that Sartrean philosophy was not properly digested by the Turkish intellectual circles of the 1960s (Hilâv 1995, p. 203). Similarly, Ferit Edgü, a Turkish author who wrote under the impact of existentialism in the 1960s, has suggested in an article that his contemporaries had not grasped the real meaning behind mottos such as "human beings are free", "freedom is anguish", "existence precedes essence", and "you must make your own sense out of the world" (Edgü 1976, p. 10).

From 1970 to 2019

In the 1970s, the popularity of existentialism began to dwindle in the intellectual circles of Turkey due to an increasing interest in Marxism and structuralism (Hilâv 1995). The fact that only two translations were published in the 1970s on existentialism[3] illustrates this waning interest. As is the case with translations, indigenous writings on Sartre decreased in number during the 1970s. In 1972 and 1973, the journal *Felsefe Dergisi* gave place in each of its first three issues to a piece related to existentialist philosophy. Another publication related to existentialism, however, was a special issue of the literary magazine *Milliyet Sanat* devoted to existentialism in 1976. Three indigenous articles on existentialism appeared in this issue, published "to introduce to the readership the different aspects of existentialism that have become a source of debate" (*Milliyet Sanat* 1976, pp. 3, 202).

After 1980—the year the military coup d'état imposed a temporary silence on Marxist and socialist thinkers and activists—a relative increase can be observed in the number of new translations and indigenous studies on existentialism and Sartre, as well as republications of earlier translations. As Susam-Sarajeva notes, after 1980, Turkish intellectuals who had been working mainly within the socialist and Marxist paradigm began to search for alternatives (Susam-Sarajeva 2006, p. 188), and existentialism was one of the alternatives. It might be argued that existentialism was a way out for Turkish leftist circles at that time, allowing them to criticize the social system with a discourse other than Marxism or socialism.

Arguably, the recent interest in existentialism does not stem from an attempt to keep abreast of fashionable movements, but from an endeavor to understand this philosophy properly. In an article published in 1981 in a special issue of the journal *Türk Dili* on literary movements, Ekrem Aksoy outlines existentialism once again, referring particularly to Sartre, Albert Camus, and Simone de Beauvoir. *Niçin Varoluşçuluk Değil* (*Why not Existentialism?*; 1985), a slim volume on existentialism by Afşar

---

[3] These are Paul Foulquié's *L'existentialisme* (1946)/*Varoluşçu Felsefe* (İstanbul: Gelişim, 1976) and a selection from Frank N. Magill's *Masterpieces of World Philosophy* (1963)/*Egzistansiyalist Felsefenin Beş Klasiği* (İstanbul: Hareket, 1971).

Timuçin, aimed to contextualize this philosophy within other schools of thought and explain it from a critical point of view. Furthermore, in the 1980s—most particularly upon the occasion of his death in 1980—numerous articles on Sartre appeared in Turkish newspapers and periodicals. In 1982, the journal *Yazko Felsefe* devoted an entire issue to Sartre, in which appeared three indigenous studies on his philosophy, and a piece by Demir Özlü recounting his own first exposure to existentialism (Özlü 1982). Interestingly enough, in the 1980s, there also appeared two articles on the Turkish translations of Sartre's works (Kakınç 1983; İnce 1987).

From the 1980s to 2019, 16 works on Sartre and/or existentialism appeared in Turkish translation[4] as well as six seminal philosophical works by Sartre himself. Almost all of the translations (and retranslations) of Sartre's fiction were republished in the 1990s. All these translations, especially those published in the 2000s, are indications of the prevailing interest in Sartrean existentialism in Turkish cultural circles.

Almost all of the latest book-length indigenous works related to existentialism and Sartre are academic studies[5] and are, in this sense, indicative

---

[4] These are Walter Biemel's *Sartre* (1983)/*Sartre* (İstanbul: Alan, 1984), George Michel's *Mes années Sartre. Histoire d'une amitié* (1981)/*Sartre Yıllarım. Bir Dostluğun Öyküsü* (İstanbul: Adam, 1985), Paul Strathern's *Sartre in 90 Minutes* (1998)/*90 Dakikada Sartre* (İstanbul: Gendaş Kültür, 1998) and *Kierkegaard in 90 Minutes* (1997)/*90 Dakikada Kierkegaard* (İstanbul: Gendaş Kültür, 1999), an excerpt from Frederick Copleston's *A History of Philosophy* (1999), *Sartre. Çağdaş Felsefe* (Cilt 9 Bölüm 2b) (İstanbul: İdea, 2000), an excerpt from Alasdair MacIntyre's work *Varoluşçuluk* (İstanbul: Paradigma, 2001), Bernard-Henri Levy's *Le siècle de Sartre* (2000)/*Sartre Yüzyılı. Felsefî Bir Soruşturma* (İstanbul: Doruk, 2004), an edited book by Hakkı Özdal, *Bilim ve Düşünce 1. Varoluşçuluk ve Sartre* (İstanbul: Evrensel, 2004), Ronald Aronson's *Camus and Sartre. The Story of a Friendship and the Quarrel that Ended it* (2004)/*Camus-Sartre. Bir Dostluk ve Onu Bitiren Çekişmenin Hikayesi* (Ankara: Bileşim, 2005), Claudine Monteil's *Les amants de la liberté. L'aventure de Jean Paul Sartre et Simone de Beauvoir dans le siècle* (2000)/*Özgürlük Aşıkları. Jean Paul Sartre ile Simone de Beauvoir'ın 20. Yüzyıl Serüveni* (İstanbul: Can, 2005), Annie Cohen-Solal's *Jean Paul Sartre. A Life* (2005)/*Jean Paul Sartre. Doğumunun Yüzüncü Yıldönümünde* (Ankara: Dost, 2005), Jacques Colette's *L'existentialisme* (1994)/*Varoluşçuluk* (İstanbul: Dost, 2006), Denis Bertholet's *Sartre* (2000)/*Sartre. Biyografi* (İstanbul: İthaki, 2009), a collection of short articles on Sartre edited and translated by Kenan Sarıalioğlu, *Sartre: Felsefeye Adanmış Bir Yaşam* (İstanbul: Omnia, 2013), Oscar Zarate and Richard Appignanesi's *Introducing Existentialism. A Graphic Guide* (2001)/ (*Varoluşçuluk. Çizgibilim* (İstanbul: Say, 2018), and Thomas E. Wartenberg's *Existentialism. A Beginner's Guide* (2008)/*Yeni Başlayanlar İçin Varoluşçuluk* (İstanbul: Say, 2018).

[5] *Jean Paul Sartre'in İnsan Anlayışı* (İstanbul: Üniversitesi Edebiyat Fakültesi Basımevi, 1984) by Nejat Bozkurt, *J. P. Sartre Ateizmi'nin Doğurduğu Problemler* (Ankara: Kültür ve Turizm Bakanlığı Yayınları, 1987) by Kenan Gürsoy, *Jean Paul Sartre'in Özgürlüğün Yolları'nda Anlatı Kişisi ve*

of a new concern with existentialism that differs significantly from that of the 1960s, when works related to existentialism were hastily read, almost consumed, with little serious critical evaluation. It can be argued that translations of Sartre's works, most probably of his nonfiction, contributed to a rise in scholarly interest in his work.

On the occasion of Sartre's centenary, indigenous writings on Sartre increased in number in 2005 and 2006. Two literary journals devoted a portion of an issue to existentialist literature (*kitap-lık* no. 86) and Sartre (*Varlık* no. 1178) in 2005. In 2009, there appeared four indigenous writings on the occasion of the publication of the Turkish translation of *L'être et le néant* (*Being and Nothingness*). In almost all of these pieces, there is an emphasis on the delayed arrival of the translation into Turkish. In one of these articles, Özdemir İnce, referring to the 1950s and 1960s, ironically states that "despite our love of Sartre almost none of his philosophical and intellectual works have been translated into Turkish in our youth" (İnce 2009). Earlier in 2005, this was also stressed by Gaye Çankaya, the co-translator of *L'être et le néant* (Çankaya 2005).

Summary and Concluding Remarks

This study is concerned with the question of how and why a philosophical theory travels from one cultural and linguistic system to another, with a special focus on the role of translation. The role 'rewriters' play is crucial to this journey because theory does not move across linguistic and cultural boundaries on its own but through cultural mediators who contribute to the rewriting of this theory for its new destination. In this travel the theory is often personified, coming to be represented by a single person, here Sartre in the import of existentialism into Turkey. Consequently,

---

Toplumsal Özne Olarak Birey (Ankara: Kültür Bakanlığı Yayınları, 2000) by Mehmet Emin Özcan, *Varoluşçuluk ve Eğitim* (İstanbul: Siyasal, 2001) by Sabri Büyükdüvenci, *Sinema ve Varoluşçuluk* (İstanbul: Altkırkbeş, 2003) by Hakan Savaş, *Sartre Felsefesinde Varlık Sorunu* (İstanbul: Elis, 2004) and *Jean Paul Sartre ve Varoluşçuluk* (İstanbul: Elis, 2004) by Talip Karakaya, *Jean-Paul Sartre: Tarihin Sorumluluğunu Almak* (İstanbul: Metis, 2010) by Zeynep Direk and Gaye Çetinkaya, *Varlık Tutulması. Jean-Paul Sartre Tiyatrosunda Varlık ve Hiçlik* (İstanbul: Ayrıntı, 2012) by Ahmet Bozkurt, and *J. P. Sartre'da Yabancılaşma Fenomeni* (İstanbul: Pales, 2017) by Emel Binbirçiçek Akdeniz.

translation profiles and indigenous writings on Sartre and existentialism helped to create a domestic understanding of existentialist philosophy.

Among other rewritings, translation played an important role in the reception of Sartre's work in Turkey. In the first place, due to nonchronological and partial text selection, the overall development in Sartre's writings remained unclear. "When compared to the translation of literary texts, the nonchronological text selection and partial representation in the translation of theories may carry greater significance" (Susam-Sarajeva 2006, p. 207). While literary texts usually carry unity in themselves, theoretical texts tend to reflect the ideological phases of their writers (Susam-Sarajeva 2006, p. 207). In the Turkish case, Sartre's texts carrying a political significance and related to his political stance as a committed writer attracted most attention first in the 1960s. Turkish intellectuals concentrated at that time on only a small part of Sartre's texts, mainly his manifesto-like essays and lectures. Almost all of Sartre's works of fiction have been translated into Turkish beginning from the 1950s. It is important to note that most of the translations of his fiction appeared in the 1960s when Sartre was enjoying his greatest popularity in Turkey. However, this is not the case with his works of nonfiction. Firstly, except for *Varoluşçuluk* (*Existentialism Is a Humanism*), *Baudelaire*, and *Yahudilik Sorunu* (*Anti-Semite and Jew*), the translations in book form of Sartre's nonfiction works, which appeared in the 1960s, are not complete translations; they are rather collections of essays by or interviews with him. It was only after the 1980s that Sartre's nonfiction works of a philosophical nature started to appear in Turkish.

The nonfiction works by Sartre that have not been translated are generally critical studies of certain French writers and collections of essays published posthumously. However, *La critique de la raison dialectique* (1960; *Critique of Dialectical Reason*), a voluminous philosophical work very significant for Sartre's intellectual development, is among those left untranslated. His voluminous philosophical treatise including the basic themes of Sartrean philosophy, *L'être et le néant* (1943, *Being and Nothingness*), appeared in Turkish translation in 2009, with a 66-year delay. It is indeed a remarkable fact that most of the translations of Sartre's philosophical works have appeared in Turkish only in the last sixteen years, and yet since the 1950s, Sartre's name was evoked whenever existentialism was discussed in Turkey. Normally one would expect that key philosophical treatises by Sartre would be translated first to pave the way for the migration of existentialism; however, his fictional works received higher preference, while his nonfiction was relatively neglected.

In spite of the crucial role played by translation in the migration of theories, once these imported theories have become part of domestic debate in their new destinations, their 'translated' status is often forgotten—as was true of existentialism in Turkey in the 1960s (Venuti 1998, p. 106). This tendency expressed by Venuti may apply to the meta-discourse on existentialism as imported into Turkey, but minimally, for a number of pieces written (especially after the late 1970s) on the reception of existentialism in Turkey, emphasized the 'imported' status of this philosophical theory (cf. Hilâv 1995; Timuçin 1985; Edgü 1976; Direk 2002). In almost all of these contributions, it was pointed out that existentialism had not been properly digested by Turkish intellectuals, and that it had been received merely as a 'fashion'. In some articles, concerns about unfamiliarity with the intellectual heritage underlying Sartre's work were also expressed (cf. Timuçin 1985). On the other hand, the fact that Sartre's main philosophical treatises had never been translated did not receive mention as one of the reasons that existentialism had not been properly digested in Turkey. In one sense, the close relationship between the migration of existentialism and translation of related works was overlooked.

I think more studies on the traveling theories which have shaped Turkish intellectual life should be undertaken with a special focus on the crucial role played by translation, because it is in this way that translation will receive its due credit in these journeys.

References

Aksoy, Ekrem. 1981. Yazın ile Felsefenin Eylemde Buluşması. *Türk Dili Aylık Dil ve Yazın Dergisi*, Yazın Akımları Özel Sayısı, 314–321.

Bezirci, Asım. 2002. Önsöz. In *Varoluşçuluk*, ed. Jean-Paul Sartre, 7–20. İstanbul: Say.

Bourdieu, Pierre. 1999. The Social Conditions of the International Circulation of Ideas. In *Bourdieu: A Critical Reader*, ed. Richard Shusterman, 220–228. Oxford: Blackwell.

Çankaya, Gaye. 2005. Sartre Düşüncesinin Radikal Dönüşümü. *Radikal,* June 24. Accessed July 31, 2019. http://www.radikal.com.tr/kitap/sartre-dusuncesinin-radikal-donusumu-857167/.

Direk, Zeynep. 2002. Türkiye'de Varoluşçuluk. In *Modern Türkiye'de Siyasi Düşünce. Modernleşme ve Batıcılık,* ed. Uygur Kocabaşoğlu, 441–451. İstanbul: İletişim.

Doğan, Erdal. 1997. *Edebiyatımızda Dergiler.* İstanbul: Bağlam.

Duru, Orhan. 1964. Varoluşçuluk Üzerine Aykırı Düşünceler. *Yeni Ufuklar* 150: 12–17.

Edgü, Ferit. 1976. Varoluşçuluğun Türk Edebiyatına Etkisi. *Milliyet Sanat,* 10 and 29, 202.

Güngör, Erol. 1964a. Bunaltı Edebiyatı ve Türkiye. *Hisar* 6: 6–7.

———. 1964b. Sartre'ın Değişen Dünyası. *Hisar* 4: 12–14.

Günyol, Vedat. 1986. *Sanat ve Edebiyat Dergileri.* İstanbul: Alan.

Hızır, Nusret. 1956. Jean-Paul Sartre'ın Edebî Tecrübesi. *Yücel* 9: 127–128.

Hilâv, Selâhattin. 1995. Sartre'ın Düşünce Dönemleri ve Sartre Felsefesinin Ana Çizgileri. In *Felsefe Yazıları,* ed. Selâhattin Hilâv, 200–204. İstanbul: Yapı Kredi. (first published in 1975 *Milliyet Sanat* 137).

Hulusi, Şerif. 1956. Veba ve Eksistansiyalizma. *Yeditepe,* 3 and 7, 98.

İnce, Özdemir. 1987. Bir Çeviri Anlayışı ve Çevirmenin Sorumluluğu. *Yeni Düşün,* 8–11, November.

———. 2009. Jean-Paul Sartre'ın 'Varlık ve Hiçlik'i. *Hürriyet,* July 19. Accessed July 31, 2019. http://www.hurriyet.com.tr/jean-paul-sartre-in-varlik-ve-hiclik-i-12101590.

Kakınç, Tarık Dursun. 1983. Sartre'cılık Oynadık!…. *Çağdaş Eleştiri* 6 (2): 34–35.

Kaplan, İsmail. 1999. *Türkiye'de Milli Eğitim İdeolojsi.* İstanbul: İletişim.

Kaufmann, Walter. 1956. *Existentialism from Dostoevsky to Sartre.* New York: Meridian.

Landau, Jacob M. 1974. *Radical Politics in Modern Turkey.* Leiden: E.J. Brill.

Lefevere, André. 1985. Why Waste Our Time on Rewrites? In *The Manipulation of Literature. Studies in Literary Translation,* ed. Theo Hermans, 215–243. Manchester: St. Jerome Publishing.

———. 1992. *Translation, Rewriting, and the Manipulation of Literary Fame.* London and New York: Routledge.

Miller, J. Hillis. 1996. Border Crossings, Translating Theory: Ruth. In *The Translatability of Cultures. Figurations of the Space between,* ed. Sanford Budick and Wolfgang Iser, 207–223. Stanford: Stanford University Press.

Özlü, Demir. 1982. Bir Tanıklık. *Yazko Felsefe: Felsefe Yazıları* 2: 122–127.

Peltek, Oğuz. 1954. Existentialisme Üzerine. *Kültür Dünyası Dergisi* 5: 19–21.

Popkin, Richard H., and Avrum Stroll. 1993. *Philosophy Made Simple*. New York: Broadway Books.

Safa, Peyami. 1957. Egzistansiyalizm (Existantialisme) II. *Türk Düşüncesi* 35: 22–26.

Said, Edward W. 1991. Traveling Theory. In *The World, the Text and the Critic*, ed. Edward W. Said, 226–247. London: Vintage.

Susam-Sarajeva, Şebnem. 2006. *Theories on the Move. Translation's Role in the Travels of Literary Theories*. Amsterdam: Rodopi.

Tahir Gürçağlar, Şehnaz. 2002. Translation as Conveyor. Critical Thought in Turkey in the 1960s. *Works and Days* Special Issue. *Vectors of the Radical Textual Exchange and Global Political Struggle in the 1960s*, ed. Michael Sell, vol. 20, 252–273.

Timuçin, Afşar. 1985. *Niçin Varoluşçuluk Değil?* İstanbul: Süreç.

Toury, Gideon. 1995. *Descriptive Translation Studies and Beyond*. Amsterdam: John Benjamins.

Turan, Şerafettin. 2002. *Çağdaşlık Yolunda Yeni Türkiye (27 Mayıs 1960–12 Eylül 1980)*. *Türk Devrim Tarihi V*. Ankara: Bilgi.

Ülken, Hilmi Ziya. 1946a. Existentialisme'in Kökleri. *İstanbul* 66: 2–4.

———. 1946b. Existentialisme'in Kökleri. *İstanbul* 67: 3–4.

Venuti, Lawrence. 1998. *The Scandals of Translation. Towards an Ethics of Difference*. London: Routledge.

Zürcher, Erik J. 1993. *Turkey. A Modern History*. London: I.B. Taurus.

Bibliography of Sartre's Book-Length Works in Turkish

1950 Gizli Oturum, trans. Oktay Akbal. Ankara: Milli Eğitim Bakanlığı Yayınları. [Huis clos, 1945]

1955 İş İşten Geçti, trans. Zübeyr Bensan. İstanbul: Varlık; 13th ed. in 2009. [Les jeux sont faits, 1947]

1960/2002 Varoluşçuluk Bir İnsancıllıktır. Varoluşçuluk, trans. Asım Bezirci. İstanbul: Ataç; latest ed. in 2016 by Say. [L'existentialisme est un humanisme, 1946]

1961 Saygılı Yosma, trans. Orhan Veli Kanık. İstanbul: Ataç; 2nd ed. in 1965. [La putain respectueuse, 1946]

1961 Kirli Eller, trans. Berrin Nadi. İstanbul: Cumhuriyet; 2nd ed. in 1965 by İzlem. [Les mains sales, 1948]

1961 Bulantı, trans. Selâhattin Hilâv. İstanbul: Ataç; 9th ed. in 2008 by Can. [La nausée, 1938]

1961 Çağımızın Gerçekleri, trans. Sabahattin Eyüboğlu and Vedat Günyol. İstanbul: Çan; 2nd ed. in 1963; 3rd ed. in 1973; 1st ed. in 1982 by Onur; 7th ed. in 1996 by Say.

1962 Saygılı Yosma, trans. Selâhattin Demirkan. İstanbul: Artun Tiyatro Yayınları. [La putain respectueuse, 1946]

1962 Mezarsız Ölüler, trans. Adalet Ağaoğlu. İstanbul: Meydan Sahnesi; 2nd ed. in 1964 by İzlem. [Morts sans sépulture, 1946]

1962 Materyalizm ve Devrim, trans. Emin Eliçin. İstanbul: Düşün; 2nd ed. in 1964 and 3rd ed. in 1967 by Ataç; 4th ed. in 1998 by Toplumsal Dönüşüm. [Matérialisme et révolution, 1946, and L'existentialisme est un humanisme]

1963 Sinekler, trans. Tahsin Saraç. İstanbul: Dönem [Les mouches, 1943]

1963 Siyaset Çarkı, trans. Güzin Sayar. İstanbul: Ataç; 2nd ed. in 1969. [L'engrenage, 1948]

1964 Şeytan ve Yüce Tanrı, trans. Eray Canberk. İstanbul: Ataç. [Le diable et le bon dieu, 1951]

1964 Altona Mahpusları, trans. Mahmut S. Kılıççı. İstanbul: Dönem. [Les séquestrés d'Altona, 1960]

1964 Akıl Çağı. Özgürlüğün Yolları, trans. Gülseren Devrim. İstanbul: Nobel; latest ed. in 2016 by Can with the title Yaşanmayan Zaman. Özgürlük Yolları 1. Kitap. [L'âge de raison, 1945]

1964 Uyanış, trans. Necmettin Arıkan and Engin Sunar. İstanbul: Altın; 9th ed. in 1992. [L'âge de raison]

1964 Bekleme, trans. Hayri Esen. İstanbul: Ak. [Le sursis, 1945]

1964 Ruhun Ölümü, trans. Hayri Esen. İstanbul: Ak. [La mort dans l'âme, 1949]

1964 Çark, trans. Tahsin Saraç. İstanbul: Toplum. [L'engrenage]

1964 Baudelaire, trans. Bertan Onaran. İstanbul: De; 2nd ed. in 1982 by Yazko; 3rd ed. in 1997 by Payel. [Baudelaire, 1947]

1964 (with Roger Garaudy, Jean Hyppolite, Jean-Pierre Vigier, Jean Orcel) Dialektik Üzerine Tartışma. Marksizm Eksiztansializm, trans. Necati Engez. İstanbul: İzlem. [Marxisme et existentialisme, 1962]

1965 (with Francis Jeanson and Albert Camus) Sartre-Camus Çatışması, trans. Bertan Onaran. İstanbul: İzlem.

1965 Yahudilik Sorunu, trans. Emin Türk Eliçin. İstanbul: Ataç; 2nd ed. in 1995 by Toplumsal Dönüşüm with the title Hür Olmak, and 3rd ed. in 1998 again by Toplumsal Dönüşüm with the title of Özgür Olmak. Antisemit'in

Portresi; 4th ed. in 2008 by Salyangoz with the title Yahudi Düşmanı.
Antisemitin Portresi [Réflexions sur la question juive, 1946]
1965 Yabancının Açıklaması, trans. Bertan Onaran. İstanbul: De; 2nd ed. in
1997 by Payel. [Excerpts from Situations I]
1965 Gizli Oturum, trans. Bertan Onaran. İstanbul: De. [Huis clos]
1965 Kirli Eller, trans. Samih Tiryakioğlu. İstanbul: Varlık; 2nd ed. in 1975.
[Les mains sales]
1965 Sinekler, trans. Selâhattin Hilâv. İstanbul: Dönem. [Les mouches]
1965 Erteleme. Yaşanmayan Zaman, trans. Gülseren Devrim. İstanbul: Nobel;
latest ed. in 2015 by Can with the title Yaşanmayan Zaman. Özgürlük Yolları
2. Kitap [Le sursis]
1965 Bekleyiş, trans. Nazan Dedehayır. İstanbul: Altın; latest ed. in 1992. [Le
sursis]
1965 Tükeniş, trans. Nazan Dedehayır. İstanbul: Altın; latest ed. in 1992. [La
mort dans l'âme, 1949]
1965 Yıkılış, trans. Gülseren Devrim. İstanbul: Nobel; latest ed. in 2015 by Can
with the title Yıkılış. Özgürlük Yolları 3. Kitap. [La mort dans l'âme]
1965 Sözcükler, trans. Bertan Onaran. İstanbul: De; 3rd ed. in 1989 by Payel.
[Les mots, 1964]
1967 Edebiyat Nedir?, trans. Bertan Onaran. İstanbul: De; 2nd ed. in 1982 and
3rd ed. in 1995 by Payel; latest ed. in 2015 by Can. [Excerpts from Qu'est-ce
que la littérature?]
1967 Gizlilik, trans. Eray Canberk. İstanbul: Habora; 7th ed. in 1981 by
Gözlem; latest ed. in 2006 by Can with the title Duvar. [Le mur]
1967 Bulantı, trans. Samih Tiryakioğlu. İstanbul: Varlık; 2nd ed. in 1983; 5th
ed. in 1994. [La nausée]
1967 Bir Şefin Çocukluğu, trans. Eray Canberk. İstanbul: Habora. [L'enfance
d'un chef, 1939]
1968 Jean-Paul Sartre Küba'yı Anlatıyor, trans. Şahin Alpay. Ankara: Anadolu.
[Ouragan sur le sucre, 1960]
1968 Sanat, Felsefe ve Politika Üstüne Konuşmalar, trans. and ed. Ferit Edgü.
İstanbul: Çan.
1968 Akıl Çağı, trans. Samih Tiryakioğlu. İstanbul: Varlık; 4th ed. in 1996 by
Oda. [L'âge de raison]
1968 Oyunlar Oynandı, trans. Ferdi Merter. İstanbul: Damlacık. [Les jeux sont
faits]
1969 Komünistler Devrimden Korkuyor. Jean-Paul Sartre'ın Fransız
Komünistlerini İthamı, trans. Şiar Yalçın. İstanbul: Öncü. [Les Communistes
ont peur de la révolution. Le "j'accuse" de Jean-Paul Sartre, 1969]

1973 Duvar, trans. Erdoğan Alkan. İstanbul: Altın [Le mur]
1973 Bulantı, trans. Erdoğan Alkan. İstanbul: Altın; 2nd ed. in 1995 and 3rd ed. in 1999 by Oda. [La nausée]
1974 Duvar, trans. Nihal Önal. İstanbul: Varlık; 7th ed. in 1995. [Le mur]
1981 Yöntem Araştırmaları, trans. Serdar Rıfat Kırkoğlu. İstanbul: Yazko; 3rd ed. in 1988 by Alan, 4th ed. in 1998 by Kabalcı. [Questions de méthode, 1960]
1983 Sözcükler, trans. Alp Tümertekin. İstanbul: Ada. [Les mots]
1984 Yazınsal Denemeler, trans. Bertan Onaran. İstanbul: Payel. [Excerpts from Situations I]
1985 Aydınların Savunusu, trans. Serdar Rifat Kırkoğlu. İstanbul: Alan. [Plaidoyer pour les intellectuels, 1972]
1993 Ruhun Ölümü, trans. Fuat İstanbullu. İstanbul: Morpa. [La mort dans l'âme]
1994 Sartre Sartre'ı Anlatıyor. Filozofun 70 Yaşındaki Otoportresi, trans. Turhan Ilgaz. İstanbul: Yapı Kredi; 2nd ed. in 2004. [Autoportrait à soixante-dix ans, Situations X, 1976]
1994 Duvar, trans. Eray Canberk. Istanbul: Can. [Le mur]
1994 Bulantı, trans. Metin Celâl. Istanbul: Can; latest ed. in 2016 [La nausée]
1995 Hepimiz Katiliz. Sömürgecilik Bir Sistemdir, trans. Süheyla N. Kaya. İstanbul: Belge; 2nd ed. in 1999. [Excerpts from Situations V, 1964]
1996 Bulantı, trans. Mustafa Özcan. Ankara: Yeryüzü. [La nausée]
1997 Aydınlar Üzerine, trans. Aysel Bora. İstanbul: Can; 2nd ed. in 2000. [Plaidoyer pour les intellectuels]
1997 Sözcükler, trans. Selâhattin Hilâv. İstanbul: Can; latest ed. in 2015. [Les mots]
1997 Çark, trans. Ela Güntekin. İstanbul: Telos. [L'engrenage]
1999 Estetik Üstüne Denemeler, trans. Mehmet Yılmaz. Ankara: Doruk; 2nd ed. in 2000. [Excerpts from Situations IV, 1964]
2003 Ego'nun Aşkınlığı, trans. Serdar Rifat Kırkoğlu. İstanbul: Alkım; 2nd ed. in 2016 by Hil. [La transcendence de l'ego, 1936]
2003 Baudelaire, trans. Alp Tümertekin. İstanbul: İthaki; latest ed. in 2017. [Baudelaire]
2005 Yahudi Sorunu, trans. Işık M. Noyan. İstanbul: İthaki. [Réflexions sur la question juive]
2005 Yahudi Sorunu, trans. Serap Yeşiltuna. İstanbul: İleri. [Réflexions sur la question juive]
2005 Altona Mahpusları, trans. Işık M. Noyan. İstanbul: İthaki. [Les séquestrés d'Altona]

2006 İmgelem, trans. Alp Tümertekin. İstanbul: İthaki [L'imagination, 1936]

2006 Tuhaf Savaşın Güncesi, trans. Z. Zühre İlkgelen. İstanbul: İthaki. [Carnets de la drôle de guerre, 1983]

2007 Jean-Paul Sartre Toplu Oyunlar, trans. Işık M. Noyan. İstanbul: İthaki. [Huis clos, Morts sans sépulture, Les mouches, Les mains sales, Le diable et le bon dieu, La putain respectueuse]

2009 Varlık ve Hiçlik, trans. Turhan Ilgaz and Gaye Çankaya Eksen. İstanbul: İthaki. [L'être et le néant, 1943]

2015 Öznellik Nedir?, trans. İnci Malak Uysal. İstanbul: Can. [Qu'est-ce que la subjectivité?, 2013]

2015 Jean-Paul Sartre Toplu Oyunlar 2, trans. Şehsuvar Aktaş and Mine Olgun. İstanbul: İthaki. [Nekrassov, 1955; Adaptation de Kean d'Alexandre Dumas, 1954; Adaptation de Les troyennes, 1965; Bariona, ou le fils du tonnerre, 1940]

2018 Heyecanlar Üzerine Bir Kuram Taslağı, trans. Kenan Sarıalioğlu. İstanbul: Kırmızı Kedi. [Esquisse d'une théorie des émotions, 1939]

13

Middle Eastern Existentialism

Hamid Andishan

What is Middle Eastern existentialism? In answering this question, one must consider a couple of other, related questions: (1) how did Middle Eastern philosophers adopt existentialism, and, more importantly, (2) *why* did they adopt existentialism? I will argue that existentialism was deeply effective in reviving the spirit of humanistic philosophical thinking in the Middle East. Philosophers such as Jean-Paul Sartre were a kind of reminder for Middle Eastern philosophers to recapture the essence of philosophical thinking.

I will argue that, first and foremost, adopting existentialism was a philosophical need. Middle Eastern political activism or literary inspiration, such as literature of commitment or absurdist literature, can be interpreted as a consequence of a philosophical humanism revived with the help of existentialism in the Middle East.

H. Andishan (✉)
University of Ottawa, Ottawa, ON, Canada
e-mail: handisha@uottawa.ca

© The Author(s) 2020
A. Betschart, J. Werner (eds.), *Sartre and the International Impact of Existentialism*,
https://doi.org/10.1007/978-3-030-38482-1_13

Political and Literary Influence was Ubiquitous but Not Deep Enough

Considering the acceptance of existentialism by Middle Eastern thinkers and social activists, indicative of the idea that existentialism was a weapon against colonialism and local despotism, may be a fair interpretation, but it is not the whole story. One must dig deeper in order to discover the philosophical roots of that political and literary acceptance. But before explaining those philosophical roots, I must mention some literary and political movements, because without referring to these Arab, Turk, and Iranian political figures and artists who were inspired by existentialism, our picture would not be complete.

In this section, I will provide a summary of what we will call the political and literary influences of existentialism in the Middle East. Through the 1960s and 1970s, introductory articles, translations, and works of poetry inspired by existentialist philosophers were a ubiquitous part of intellectual (mostly literary) journals from Egypt to Turkey to Iran. In terms of literary influence, we see a similar story in various countries. Literary magazines started to publish introductory articles and translations on existentialist philosophers and novelists. Sartre is the dominant figure here. After this stage of introducing existentialist themes and translating existentialist works, we see an upsurge of novelists and poets who take the further step of producing their own original works inspired by existentialism.

In the Arabic world, the political and literary influence of existentialism is very colorful. There is, on the one hand, intense fervor for Sartre due to his support for Algeria's independence, but also dismay due to Sartre's silence on the Israel–Palestine issue. Arab intellectuals have been deeply influenced by Sartrean existentialism, and the influence begins with some translations and introductory essays in literary magazines. In 1952, Suhayl Idris launched the publication *al-Adab*, a literary journal that became, quickly, a place to publish existentialist ideas in literature.

The prolific Taha Husayn was one of the first Arab intellectuals who grasped the idea of *Qu'est-ce que la littérature?*, although he was against the idea of committed literature. In response, it was Salama Musa who published *Literature to the Masses* (Musa 1956), in defense of committed literature.

In other areas, we see some literary productions such as the novel *The Latin Quarter* (Idris 1953), in which Suhayl Idris adopts existentialist themes and describes his own individualistic anxiety and his predicament as an Arab intellectual stuck between East and West, tradition and modernity. Another similar novel is Ahdaf Soueif's *In the Eye of the Sun*. (Soueif 1992). Asya, the protagonist, despite her marriage obligations, commits adultery. She knows that according to her society's culture, sleeping with a man other than her husband is immoral; she even feels uneasy betraying her husband, but a powerful desire to cross the borders of cultural obligation pushes her to do it again and again. She feels liberated and fulfilled, a defiant *femme de plaisir*; therefore, nothing can stop her from going further, despite her internal unease.

Even in Iraq we see Ali Bader, who, in 2001, published *Papa Sartre* (Bader 2001). The protagonist is "the Sartre of the Arabs" who wishes Baghdad would become the Arab capital of existentialism. In Lebanon, we see Layla Ba'albakki who writes *I Live* (Ba'albakki 2010). It is similar to Ahdaf Soueif's novel. Lena, a 19-year-old girl, experiences individual freedom, giving no attention to the cultural or political concerns of her nation.

However, all this fervor for Sartre dried up suddenly with Sartre's silence on the Israel–Palestine problem. Arab intellectuals were desirous to have Sartre's support on the issue, but Sartre was reluctant to speak out against Israel. After the Six-Day War, the depressing defeat, and losing Sartre's support, Arab writers were drawn into a period of nihilism and national depression. An upsurge of absurdism in Arabic literature is the fruit of this period. It is not surprising that *The Waste Land* of T. S. Eliot has been translated and cited more than any other poem in Arab intellectual circles. Arab poets have been repeatedly influenced by the idea of a wasteland in which nothing grows. They were seeing their own dry and hopeless lands represented in the poem. The wasteland has no water for drinking or creating a life. It is entirely covered by sand and rock, and no one can stop or rest in this dry land (Eliot 2010, V. 331–340). The poem was a good metaphor to show Arabs' despair and exhaustion.

In Turkey, the literary magazine *Yucel* published a series of influential introductory articles on existentialism by Nusret Hızır (Direk 2002, pp. 441–451). Hilmi Ziya Ülken wrote the first article on existentialism and referred to Sartre as "the principal representative of this movement" (Ülken 1946, pp. 2–4). In 1954, the literary magazine *Kültür Dünyası* again referred to Sartre as the principal representative of existentialism.

In the 1960s, several Turkish novelists attempted to write works popularly called *bunalım edebiyatı* (literature of despair). Asking why Turks took notice of existentialism, Selahattin Hilâv argues that there is a similarity between France after the devastation of the Second World War and Turkey under the dismal political regime during the 1950s. In a similar comment, *Çağımızın Gerçekleri*, the editor of a collection of essays by Sartre, explains that the aim of translating Sartre was to initiate a discourse in a country long starved for freedom.[1]

With respect to academic works on Sartre, there are two noticeable studies in Turkish. The first is *Jean-Paul Sartre'ın İnsan Anlayışı* by Nejat Bozkurt. The book was published in 1984. It is on man's place within Sartrean existentialism. The second book is *J. P. Sartre Ateizmi'nin Doğurduğu Problemler* by Kenan Gürsoy. It was published in 1987. Gürsoy analyzes the problem of atheism in Sartrean existentialism.

In Iran, one sees a similar story. A few magazines, such as *Kitab-I Jon'eh*, were pioneers in translating Sartre's works for the first time. Again, like in Turkey and the Arab countries, Sartre is the first existentialist philosopher to be translated. Sadiq Hedayat, the predominant Iranian novelist, is the first to translate a work by Sartre: *Le mur*. Another influential leftist author, who translated *Les mains sales* and Camus' *L'étranger* and *Le malentendu*, was Jalal Al-Ahmad. Hedayat was interested in Sartre from a nihilistic point of view (and here nihilism, in my view, is not considered negatively). Al-Ahmad, who was a social activist, was interested in Sartre in relation to committed literature. In a famous quotation, Al-Ahmad admires Sartre as a political barometer that alerts us to wherever there is political pressure or oppression; it does not matter whether the pressure comes from western colonialism, American imperialism, Stalinist

---

[1] Ayşenaz Koş (Cengiz) has written a comprehensive MA thesis on the Migration of Sartrean Existentialism into Turkey through Translation (Koş 2004).

communism, or Eastern despotism (Rasekhi Langeroudi 2018, 64). Both of these figures were very influential in promoting Sartre's thought in Iran.

In the case of the 1979 revolution against the Shah regime in Iran, Sartre was involved in person. A group of Iranian students in Europe, who were revolutionaries against the Shah, visited Sartre and asked him to be the head of a group called 'The Community for Defending Political Prisoners in Iran.' Sartre accepted the suggestion with two conditions. First, these students should always update him about Iranian news; second, there should be no discrimination in defending political prisoners. Any political prisoner with any religious or political orientation must be entitled to receive support from this community. Sartre also issued three statements, on three occasions, defending Ayat-allah Khomeyni. In one specific case, Sartre also sent a telegram to Tehran in defense of a young revolutionary who had been sentenced to death. He entreats the Shah regime to respect the rights of prisoners to have public hearings.

Now, after more than half a century since the first translations in Iran, one can see that most of the major existentialist works by various philosophers have been translated into Persian. Daryoush Ashouri is one of the scholars who has translated the main works of Nietzsche and is still working on the relation between Nietzsche's philosophy and philosophical problems in Iran. With respect to Heidegger, there are at least two reliable translations of *Being and Time*, translated by academic scholars Abdul-Karim Rashidian (Heidegger 2014) and Siyavash Jamadi (Heidegger 2010). Another Iranian intellectual who has published very comprehensive introductions to Heidegger and Sartre is Babak Ahmadi (Ahmadi 2001a, b, 2005). Although the works of these scholars have been very helpful for introducing Iranian society to existentialist philosophers, they have not created a new Iranian philosophy inspired by existentialism. Therefore, I will end my survey of the political and literary influences of existentialism in the Middle East and proceed to the next step: explaining two genuine philosophical adaptations of existentialism by Middle Eastern philosophers.

Philosophical Adaptation

Any political or literary movement in the Middle East inspired by existentialism—whether inspired by existentialist thoughts against colonialism, in favor of Marxism, following absurdist literature, or challenging traditional values and trying to create new values—must be regarded as a consequence of something more fundamental: a rebirth of the human in philosophical discourse in the Middle East. If a nation can revolt against external oppression, if it endangers its own life to stand up politically, if a woman stands face to face against patriarchal hierarchy in an Islamist society, if some so-called nihilist poets and novelists appear all over the region from Egypt to Iran, if "God is dead" becomes a slogan for the youth to protest against old and outdated values, then all of these need a philosophical explanation. Any demonstration needs an internal motivation. I argue that, amidst these grand political and literary changes, there is a Middle Eastern by-itself consciousness that has stood on its feet again judging the world for-itself. These changes are due to the rise of a humanistic sensibility inspired by existentialism.

If the activists, philosophers, and poets were protesting against oppression, it was because of the rebirth of the human. Yusuf al-Khal mentions this priority of the human over any political action in his poem: "I do not write poetry for Jamila or for protesting despots, I do poetry for Humanity in me and you" (al-Salesi 2004, p. 149).

I will argue that existentialism was very effective in contributing to this rebirth of humanism in the Middle East. I say *rebirth* because philosophers from the Islamic lands have always been accused of being humanistic, but under the domination of a religious judiciary that condemned such humanism. It is not an accident that the most translated work by Sartre into Arabic, Turkish, and Persian is *Existentialism is Humanism*.

Philosophy in the Middle East has a long history. The so-called Islamic philosophy has been an effort by Muslim rationalists to defend and justify philosophy and rationalism in an Islamic context. From the beginning, most of these philosophers have been denounced for their rationalism, humanism, or atheism. It was in response to this kind of accusation that Sohrivardi, Farabi, Avicenna, and many of their successors tried, over centuries, to prove that philosophy can be aligned with or work in parallel to Islam. Were they atheists at heart but tried to soften the tension between philosophy and Islam? No, we cannot say that; they were Muslims, but perhaps, philosophers first.

Thinking philosophically and questioning everything, even religion, within the limits of reason, is quintessentially humanistic. Questions such as how humans can be free to choose their own way of life under divine providence, the rational possibility of resurrection, and arguments for proving God's existence all have a humanistic aspect.

Over the whole history of philosophy in the Islamic lands, and even now, doing philosophy is directly, sharply, and immediately accused of atheism. In such a situation, even if you are a faithful and pious person and at the same time you have some philosophical approach to finding answers to your questions, you are essentially atheist, even if you do not know it.

Defending rationality means humans as humans have nothing except reason to understand whatever they encounter in the world. Reason and only reason is available to humans. This means that we are human; we live in a human situation; whether God exists or not, it is us who should decide who we are, to build our lives, and to take our responsibility. This emphasis on human rationality over anything else, including revelation, means a philosopher in an Islamic context wants to limit everything within the bounds of reason, or as Kant put it: *Religion within the Bounds of Bare Reason.*

If we accept this, then what the philosophers in the Islamic lands were defending was rationality, and this rationality had an implicit humanism hidden within it. For some historical and societal reasons, that I have no room here to address, Islamic countries have been suffering a long period of degeneration and downfall, almost since the fifteenth century. When, in Europe, philosophers were awakening from their dogmatic slumber, in the Middle East, philosophers were falling into the slumber of ignorance and infertile thinking. These countries have been suffering from religious fanaticism, scientific infertility, and philosophical decline across all these centuries. It was only at the end of this period, after a multi-century slumber, that Middle Eastern intellectuals encountered for the second time European philosophy (the first time was in the eighth century with Greek philosophy).

Looking at European achievements in health, economy, transportation, agricultural industry, social equality, and political power, a group of intellectuals in each Middle Eastern country, who all studied at European universities, started to awaken their people back home. They were learning an array of European modern sciences—natural and human sciences—including modern philosophy. In Iran, for instance, it was Mohammad-Ali Foroughi who discovered Descartes as the founder of modern philosophy. Therefore, he thought that Iranians must learn from him how to use their own rationality to solve their modern problems. Foroughi translated *Discourse Touching the Method of Using One's Reason Rightly and of Seeking Scientific Truth* in the hope that his people could learn this lesson.

Since the beginning of the twentieth century, Middle Eastern philosophers have been discovering different branches of European modern philosophy, from Kantian and Hegelian modernism, to British utilitarianism, Marxism, linguistic/analytic philosophy, continental philosophy, and even postmodernism. They have been furiously translating and learning modern European philosophies. In each variety of philosophy, they have been also looking for familiar themes to make the process of adaptation (or even criticism, in some cases) more meaningful. For instance, there is a similarity, as well as an asymmetry, between some linguistic inquiries in analytic philosophy and a branch of Islamic philosophy called *elmi kalam*, which literally means "science of language."

Among these investigations, I believe nothing was more rousing than existentialism. It emphasizes the social dimension of life enough to address societal problems in Middle Eastern countries, but also individualistic enough to touch personal, emotional, and private problems of Middle Eastern poets, novelists, and philosophers. (I mentioned some cases in the previous section.) However, I believe that the core of inspiration that Middle Eastern philosophers took from existentialism is its attention to humanism. Existentialism reminded philosophers in Islamic countries of the missing concept of humanity. Islamic philosophers were struggling with many confusions and malfunctions that had arisen in the philosophical apparatus in Islamic countries and were questioning why it was unable to deal with hundreds of new questions—questions concerning moral issues in modern life, concerning leaving traditional lifestyles and getting used to urban life, concerning modern life, concerning the cause of weakness in the face of colonialism, concerning the absence of divinity, and loneliness of men of faith in the modern era. Considering all of these problems, it was existentialism that reminded philosophers in the Middle East of the cause of this philosophical paralysis: the lack of attention to humanity in philosophy.

Sartre was the most influential in this retrieval of humanity. *Existentialism is Humanism* has been the most translated, the most discussed, and the most interpreted of Sartre's works by Middle Eastern thinkers, compared to other existentialist philosophers. Specifically the doctrine of precedence of existence over essence was very welcome, because the humanism implicit within it was very much needed. Middle Eastern philosophers were able to conjoin it with a similar doctrine from Islamic philosophy (although by mistake)[2]; the Hegelian–Sartrean idea of freedom as the only essence of human being was very inspirational for them. Many Middle Eastern poems such as those of Ahmad Shamlou in Iran—in his poem titled Abraham in Fire—or al-Khal in his poem says: "Be whatever you want, this is your humanity. The essence of human is undetermined, his definition, if ever, is the very glorifying freedom" (al-Khal 1979, p. 97). In what follows, I discuss two Middle Eastern philosophers who were inspired by the idea of humanism in existentialism, one from Egypt, and the other from Iran.

---

[2] I mean the theory of *isalat vojoud* in Islamic philosophy. Many scholars have compared this theory with the theory of the precedence of human existence to human essence in Sartre's philosophy. The theory in Islamic philosophy is not at all about human existence, and comparing it with Sartre's is wrong. It is a metaphysical question concerning that which constitutes the core of beings, the existence of a being, or its essence. For instance, in response to "what is the main aspect of being an apple," some philosophers believe that the essence of being apple is the main part, like having sweet taste and red color; some others think that the existence of it is the main part, and essence is an accident to it.

Abdel Rahman Badawi

Among Arab philosophers, Abdel Rahman Badawi is the most prominent one who tried to offer a meaningful adaptation of existentialism, combining it with some Islamic-Sufi ideas. By meaningful adaptation, I mean he used existentialist ideas to reshape and revive philosophical discourse in Islamic philosophy. It was not sufficient for him to just teach existentialism to his Arab students or to translate the relevant European texts into Arabic. He tried to offer a meaningful combination, and I think that this is the true meaning of adapting a philosophy by philosophers with another cultural background. Through this adaptation, he became the pioneer of existentialism in Egypt. In 1937, he was the first Arab philosopher working on "Death in Existential Philosophy" (Badawi 1964) and "Existential Time" (Badawi 1955) under the supervision of Alexandre Koyré.

Over his life, he published several books on existentialism including his course notes that cover the main existentialist philosophers (Badawi 1973). The important book in which he compares existentialism with Islamic philosophical topics is *Humanism and Existentialism in Arabic Thought* (Badawi 1947). It might be the most technical comparative work in this field. He focuses mainly on Kierkegaard and Heidegger, trying to translate existentialism into a Sufi language to formulate an Arab existential philosophical school.

According to Badawi, the shared idea between existentialism and Sufism is the priority of the single individual. In both, it is the individual who must make each moral decision. In a back and forth between these two doctrines, Badawi explains some similarities that might be noticeable. He mentions this idea that because the individual is the starting point of any judgment, the existence of humans precedes their essences, and we can see this idea both in Sufism and existentialism. He even compares the concept of *qalaq* in Sufism with the existentialist concept of anxiety or anguish (Badawi 1947, pp. 87–97).

Another concept, in which he found a certain asymmetry between Sufism and existentialism, is the concept of the "perfect man." He offers the concept, describing human existence as an encompassing existence that addresses everything in the universe. It is a ubiquitous idea in Islamic philosophy that human existence is a mirror for the rest of the world. One can see the heavens by looking into the human head and human thoughts. The human body is a reference to the material and the mundane. Human sleep is a symbol for the night, and human happiness is a symbol for spring. Therefore, human existence is the mirror for everything, from mortality to eternity, necessity, and contingency. Badawi compares this human situation with Kierkegaard's definition of man as a pendulum between necessity and possibility, eternity and mortality. He claims that the idea of the "perfect man" in Islamic Sufism is a good equivalent for *l'unique* in Kierkegaard (Badawi 1947, p. 75).

Badawi also compares the notion of the loneliness in front of God in Kierkegaard and Sufism. Independent from any mediator such as church, mosque, prophet, or leader, a Sufi must encounter God on his own. Nobody can or should help him. Badawi thinks that this is exactly what Kierkegaard means by a "true Christian" (Badawi 1947, p. 76).

Regardless of the correctness of these comparisons, what is important in this book is the inspirational adoption of the idea of humanism and the idea that in both Islamic Sufism and existentialism, humanism plays a key role. *Al-insaniyah* in Arabic means humanism (الإنسانية). Badawi thinks that *al-insaniyah* is the reliance on human reason and nothing else, in every judgment. Then he gives some examples from ancient Iran, the book of *Kelileh and Demnih*, showing that humanism has deep roots in Arabic civilization (Badawi 1947, pp. 28–29). He even claims that one can doubt faith, but not rationality.

The main problem that one can find in his comparative study is that his efforts to combine existentialism with Sufism had no practical results. Living in an era of war and defeat (specifically the 1967 defeat of Arab countries by modern Israeli army, a defeat by which all Arab intelligentsia were affected), and also an era of political depression and the revolt against colonialism, his philosophy suffered from a lack of real-life application and political or ethical consequence. The irony is that, in his personal life, he was heavily involved in political activities. What is dismaying is that Badawi was pro-nationalist with semi-fascist orientations (Di-Capua 2012, p. 1069).

Ali Shariati

Jumping from the west of the Middle East to the east of the Middle East, one can see Ali Shariati in Iran who was very influential in promoting existentialist humanism in 1970s. He received his PhD in sociology from the Sorbonne in Paris, in 1964. Over the course of his graduate studies, he was exposed to many aspects of the western philosophy and political thought, especially Sartre's thought. When he was in Paris, he collaborated with the Algerian National Liberation Front. He was the first philosopher who introduced Frantz Fanon to Iran by translating *The Wretched of the Earth*. When he came back to Iran, he became a very influential revolutionary lecturer against the Shah's regime and religious authorities in Iran.

Shariati was a prominent Islamic philosopher who was deeply inspired by existentialism and Marxism. Almost all of his highly emotional lectures were about reviving the degenerated Islamic society, letting fresh blood flow in the veins of his society in thinking critically against any religious prejudice. He was always moving between Islam, existentialism, and Marxism. The youth were very interested in this combination that he was offering, made up of Islamic-revolutionary ideas and existentialist concepts such as freedom, anxiety, and responsibility. Unfortunately, he died two years before the pivotal Islamic Revolution in Iran, in 1979. He could have been more influential if he had lived longer and seen all the positive and negative results of the revolution.

It is a fact that, among all the European philosophers, Sartre was the most influential for him. In most of his works, he refers to Sartre as the biggest philosophical figure of the West. It seems that Sartre had also heard about him. Ahmad Rasekhi Langeroudi, the author of the book titled *Sartre in Iran* (Rasekhi Langeroudi 2018), recently published in Iran, tells a story. Apparently, in a secret session on Algeria's independence, an Iranian named Mohammad Molavi was present and Sartre talked to him about Shariati. He described Shariati as a "star that is rising from the East" (Rasekhi Langeroudi 2018, p. 60).

Shariati has many opponents as well as followers in Iran. Some Iranian philosophers, such as Daryoush Shaygan, criticize Shariati for ideologizing the tradition. They mean Shariati offers a meaningless amalgamation of Islamic tradition and modern philosophies such as existentialism and Marxism. However, nobody can deny that Shariati was very influential on the next generation of philosophers in Iran. His attention to existentialism, and his focus on the humanism implicit in existentialism, was a gateway for him to offer a philosophy that is inspired by existentialism but addresses local problems in Islamic countries.

To explain his view on the importance of existentialism for Middle Eastern thought, and the way in which it is able to have meaningful answers for contemporary issues, I will focus on volume 24 of his complete works. This volume, titled *Man* or *Human Being* (انسان), is a collection of papers on the relation between Islam and the western philosophies with respect to anthropology. In these papers, he repeatedly returns to existentialism, and one paper, specifically, has the title of *Existentialism*.

In these papers, the reader finds that Shariati is fascinated by Sartrean existentialism because he thinks that, compared to the other Western philosophies, this type of thinking can bring true freedom for human beings. Humanism for Shariati means asserting human dignity (Shariati 2014) and converging all efforts to emancipate human beings from the limits of religious prejudice, as well as other chains such as capitalism or materialism. For Shariati, Marxism has accomplished half of this liberation, but it is unable to bring ultimate freedom for the human being because, despite all its beautiful slogans, Marxism arrests itself in materialism.

Evaluating Shariati's claims on existentialism and Marxism is beyond my scope here. I only want to shed light on his interest in existentialism and his belief that Sartre has been able to articulate the most meaningful description of human freedom. Shariati refers to the theory of the precedence of human existence over human essence. He thinks that this theory is compatible with what Islam means by human freedom. Again, I should repeat that I do not want to evaluate this claim. What is important here is that the commensurability between these notions was something that Shariati, perhaps idealistically, wished to demonstrate. He was trying to present a reasonable harmonization of Islam and existentialism, and he used humanism as the pivotal concept in this project. He even talks about

Islamic humanism, in which the human is in an equal and friendly relation with God.

At several points, he admires Sartre for creating such a fantastic theory of human freedom that gives humans primary status. However, he thinks that this theory is deficient. In terms of morality, this theory does not work. If man is the criteria of everything, if the burden of responsibility is only on men's shoulders to create their own values and ways of life, morality is the weak point of Sartre's philosophy. Morality needs a social criterion. One cannot tell the people to choose whatever they want because there is no recourse outside of themselves to show them what is right and what is wrong. Here, Shariati thinks that Islam can help existentialism to complete its project to usher in true human freedom and human responsibility within morality.

Whether he is successful or not, Shariati's effort to combine Islam and existentialism was earth-shaking and revelatory for Iranian society. In other areas of his work, areas in which he explains our existential crisis and the concerns of human life in the era of collapsing traditional values and the struggle with modern life, he was very effective at spreading existentialist concepts among the Iranian youth.

Future Young Existentialists

Western philosophy and Middle Eastern philosophy have been exchanging their ideas since ancient times. The first time, in the eighth century, the adaptation and translation of Greek philosophy by Muslim philosophers created a prosperous philosophical discourse in the Islamic lands. Afterward, in the thirteenth century, the Muslim scientists and philosophers rather helped jump-start the scientific and philosophical development in the thirteenth century. For instance, Ibn Sina (Avicenna) was very influential in philosophical and scientific (medicine) revival in Europe. In the twentieth century, it was Europe's turn to help Middle Easterners awake from the slumber of dogmatism, despotism, and degeneration. Existentialism was very helpful in this project. Offering a variety of humanist approaches to philosophy—including the approaches of religious philosophers such as Kierkegaard, Jaspers, or Gabriel Marcel, and atheist philosophers such as Sartre—existentialism helped Middle Eastern philosophers to evaluate their traditions more critically. Self-criticism was a pressing need for people in the Middle East, according to Sadiq al-Azm,[3] and I think that existentialist humanism could aid in this attempt at self-criticism.

In learning that, beyond all religious authorities, beyond all social traditions, beyond all political oppression in the name of colonialism or local despotism, it is the individual who must take up responsibility for her/his choices and emancipate herself/himself from any nonhuman limitation, Middle Eastern consciousness may stand again on her feet. Because of this need, Middle Eastern philosophers, poets, and novelists have been furiously adopting existentialism over the second half of twentieth century. The youth in the contemporary Middle East are digesting existentialism in order to mature healthily and become what Nietzsche calls *Übermenschen*. After having lived for a long time under the pressure of *good and evil*, now young girls all over the Middle East, from Iran to Egypt, are breaking traditional boundaries. In Iran, women are experiencing one of the harshest forms of oppression by a religious judiciary in human history. They cannot even enjoy the basic right of movement. They cannot participate in many public sporting activities, such as riding a bicycle. However, they know that nothing can diminish their essential freedom. The Iranian Women's Soccer Team is one of the best in Asia. So far, they have twice taken second place in the Asian championship. This would appear to have nothing to do with existentialism, but philosophers may know what underlies this achievement.

References

Ahmadi, Babak. 2001a. *Heidegger va Porsishi Bonyadin*. Tehran: Nashr-i Markaz.
———. 2001b. *Heidegger va Tarikh Hasti*. Tehran: Nashr-i Markaz.
———. 2005. *Sartre ki Minevesht*. Tehran: Nashr-i Markaz.
al-Azm, Sadiq Jalal. 2013. *Critique of Religious Thought*. Berlin: Gerlach-Press.

---

[3] Leftist Syrian philosopher. He has interesting ideas about the causes of degeneration and defeat in the Middle East, criticizing religious orientation (al-Azm 2013).

al-Khal, Yusuf. 1979. *al-A'mal al-She'riyah Kamilah*. Beirut: Dar al-'udau.

al-Salesi, Jak Ama-Taees. 2004. *Yusuf al-Khal va Majlate Shi'r*. Beirut: Dar al-Nahar.

Ba'albakki, Layla. 2010. *Ana Ahya*. Beirut: Dar al-Adab.

Badawi, Abd al-Rahman. 1947. *al-Insaniyya wa-l-Wujudiya fi-l-Fikr al-Arabi*. Cairo: Dar al-Seqafat.

———. 1955. *al-Zaman al-Wujudi*. Cairo: Maktab al-nihzat al-misriyah.

Badawi, Abdurahman. 1964. *Le problème de la mort dans la philosophie existentielle*. Cairo: Institute Francais d'Archeologie Orientale.

Badawi, Abd al-Rahman. 1973. *Drasat fi-l Falsafah al-vojoudiyah*. Cairo: Dar al-Seqafat.

Bader, Ali. 2001. *Papa Sartre*. New York: American University in Cairo Press.

Di-Capua, Yoav. 2012. Arab Existentialism: An Invisible Chapter in the Intellectual History of Decolonization. *The American Historical Review* 117 (4): 1061–1109.

Direk, Zeynep. 2002. Türkiye'de Varoluşçuluk. In *Modern Türkiye'de Siyasi Düşünce Modernleşme ve Batıcılık*, ed. Uygur Kocabaşoğlu, 441–451. Istanbul: İletişim.

Eliot, T.S. 2010. *The Waste Land and Other Poems*. London: Faber & Faber.

Heidegger, Martin. 2010. *Hasti va Zaman*. Translated by Siavash Jamadi. Tehran: Qoqnous.

———. 2014. *Hasti va Zaman*. Translated by Abul Karim Rashidian. Tehran: Nashr Ney.

Idris, Suhayl. 1953. *Al-Hayy al-Latini*. Beirut: Dar al-Adab.

Koş, Ayşenaz. 2004. *An Analytical Study on the Migration of Sartrean Existentialism into Turkey Through Translation*. MA diss., Boğaziçi University. Accessed July 14, 2019. http://www.transint.boun.edu.tr/html/tezler/AysenazKos.doc.

Musa, Salama. 1956. *Adab lel-Sha'b*. Cairo: Dar al-Moharir al-Adabi.

Rasekhi Langeroudi, Ahmad. 2018. *Sartre dar Iran*. Tehran: Akhtaran.

Shariati, Ali. 2014. *Insan*. Volume 24 of his Complete Works. Tehran: Elham.

Soueif, Ahdaf. 1992. *In the Eye of the Sun*. London: Bloomsbury.

Ülken, Hilmi Ziya. 1946. Existentialisme'in Kökleri. *İstanbul* 66: 2–4.

14

Arab Existentialism: What Was It?

Yoav Di-Capua

Welcoming Jean Paul Sartre to Egypt in late February 1967, writer Ahmad ʿAbbas Salih went straight to the point:

> Your influence in this region is deeper and wider than that of any other writer. We have known you for a long time, and from the first contact with your ideas … their appeal grew deeper until our publishing houses were working daily to translate and print your work … You are the only Western writer that all Arab newspapers follow closely. (Salih 1967, p. 25)

Unlikely as it sounds, it was true. For about two decades (1950c–1970c), Arab intellectuals drew on Sartre's ideas in order to devise a local existentialist tradition that would meet the formidable challenges of

---

Published first as Yoav Di-Capua, Arab Existentialism: What Was It? *Yale French Studies* 135/36 (2019): 171–188. This chapter is based on my book *No Exit: Arab Existentialism, Jean-Paul Sartre and Decolonization* (Di-Capua 2018).

Y. Di-Capua (✉)
University of Texas, Austin, TX, USA
e-mail: ydi@austin.utexas.edu

253
A. Betschart, J. Werner (eds.), *Sartre and the International Impact of Existentialism*,
https://doi.org/10.1007/978-3-030-38482-1_14

decolonization and carry them forward into a new era. Even Sartre was surprised at his fame. Indeed, with the exception of the dead Karl Marx, no other European thinker was so venerated, engaged and translated in the Arab lands as Sartre was. This warm reception cannot be reduced to Sartre's stance on Algeria, where, in the heat of battle, intellectuals were scarce and existentialism made very little sense. Rather, it is the story of the Arab East and its energetic intellectual centers: Beirut, Cairo, Baghdad and Damascus. It is also the story of a new cadre of Arab intellectuals who forged a concrete two-way relationship with Sartre and hoped that the French philosopher will fully enlist on behalf of what they began to call "the Arab cause."

As it were, in terms of its scope, goals, actual influence and eventual reach, the phenomenon of Arab existentialism is an episode in global intellectual history whose brave beginnings were optimistic and whose aftermath marks a painful setback to the cause of Arab liberation. But how so? How could a French intellectual tradition that was saturated in a narcissistic scene of sex, caffeine and alcohol was supposed to usher the Arab world into a post-colonial era? How was existentialism put to work, by whom and on which terms? To answer these questions, we need to untangle the cultural specificity of Arab decolonization and make sense of the creative ways in which the local intellectuals reinvented existentialism as an emancipatory response to the problem of liberation. As Egyptian philosopher and literary critic Mahmud Amin al-ʿAlim succinctly put it: "When we discuss existentialism, we do not discuss French or German philosophy but an intellectual movement with roots in Arab culture" (al-ʿAlim 1970, p. 228). Reinvented as "their own," Arab existentialism no longer adhered to its European provenance and could not be comfortably positioned within a European intellectual genealogy. It became Arab and this is how it happened.

The Challenge

Entering the era of decolonization, the territorial liberation of Arab lands constituted only a small part of the overall liberation project. A more significant challenge than securing territory was the quest for social justice in order to overcome extreme levels of poverty, low literacy rates, poor hygiene, low life expectancy and the general destruction of the socio-economic fabric. These important tasks are more obvious than the momentous and elusive question of *being* in the wake of empire or, for lack of better terminology, the question of identity. What does it mean *to be* a person after colonialism? After decades during which Arabs were struggling objects in the closed world of European consciousness, who and what dominated the definition of the self and the political community to which it belonged? From an ontological standpoint, the question of being touches on three sub-aspects, namely authenticity (*asala*), sovereignty (*siyada*) and freedom (*hurriyya*). Being authentic and sovereign meant owning the ability for self-determination and for finding one's own place in the world. In this constellation, authenticity and sovereignty function as preconditions for freedom.

Local philosophers such as the Palestinian refugee Fayiz Sayigh and the Egyptian were quick to understand the challenge. Here is Badawi:

> We, the Egyptian and Arab youth …, are unable to bear our situation and surrender to our wretched fate … We find ourselves in the same state of destruction of Eastern youth from India, Japan and China … In our minds we live the tribulations of European youth and we became spiritually pre-occupied by them … (but when attached) to our own actual painful experiences, enormous charges of revolt, anxiety, spiritual confusion, and psychological disorder generated in us an exceptional sensitivity. (Badawi 1946, p. 135)

Equally concerned, Sayigh wrote:

> The key to the character of Arab youth is … dissatisfaction: our dissatisfaction with the way our leaders, or our rulers, look upon things in general, manage our affairs, and run our lives … Our dissatisfaction has transformed itself into rejection. We have lost respect for our traditional values, virtues, and way of life. We have become a generation at odds with its world. We no longer belong to our immediate world: We are no longer at home. (Sayigh 1955, pp. 9–10)

Given the absence of authenticity, sovereignty and freedom and the prevalent sense of alienation and anxiety that this lack had created among the youth, a phenomenological approach to this crisis began to be considered. Indeed, among a very small circle of intellectuals, the cure for the troubling feeling of not being at home in your own home was a new philosophy but also an engagement with psychology.[1]

An Abstract Engagement

Phenomenology arrived to an Egyptian academic environment that was dominated by Bergsonian philosophy to the exclusion of all other traditions. It was an unexpected arrival. In June 1940, as the German army closed in on Paris, Russian émigré philosopher Alexander Koyré escaped to Cairo and took a teaching position that critically influenced a young generation of Egyptian philosophers; chief among them was Badawi. In the annals of French philosophy, Koyré is credited for bringing Husserl and Heidegger to the attention of Sartre's and Merleau-Ponty's generation. He did the same in Cairo and added to the mix the works of Max Scheler, Karl Jaspers, Martin Heidegger, Gabriel Marcel, Jean Wahl and Emmanuel Levinas. Badawi immediately connected to this new frame of reference and began working on various aspects of existentialism relating to questions of time and death. Working from within this newly minted existentialist tradition, he accepted its most basic premises: namely *existence precedes essence* (i.e. who a human being is [his essence] is the result of his or her choices [existence]), *time is of essence* (i.e. human beings are time-bound and they experience lived time in a dissimilar way to measured clock time), *radical individualism* (i.e. humanistic focus on the individual's quest for meaning and identity) and *freedom* (i.e. the only guarantee for individualistic self-reflection and responsibility).[2] Explaining existence in such terms and understanding it from a circumstantial perspective in which culture, or for that matter any subject, is not historical, linear or continuous, but fragmented, ruptured and synchronic, opened great post-colonial possibilities.

---

[1] On this point see the original work of Omnia El Shakry (El Shakry 2017).
[2] Characteristically immodest, Badawi preferred to think of his work as "complementary to that of Heidegger" (Badawi 2000, pp. 179–180; see Badawi 1964, pp. 1–7).

Thus, from the perspective of the colonized, existentialism announced the possibility of rejecting the Cartesian dictum "I think, therefore I am" for its radical separation of the individual from the surrounding world of human beings. They were no longer required to be subjected to a universe of sharp ruptures between object and subject, true knowledge and daily experience, body and mind which were the bread and butter of colonial Enlightenment. Authored by *Husserl* and Heidegger, the philosophical propositions of phenomenology automatically discredited a host of existing colonial ideas about Oriental people: about how the essence of Islam, to cite one famous example, is fundamentally incompatible with reason, science and democracy. That is, how Islam was essentially incompatible with the contemporary modern world. Indeed, the Arab experience of colonial Enlightenment was often referred to in terms of a critique of the Cartesian cogito. Among other things, Arab thinkers like Badawi were bothered by the way in which the philosophical proposition of sharp rupture marginalized Islamic categories of knowledge and hence furthers cultural inauthenticity.

And so, long after Koyré already left, Badawi found himself in the same position of Chinese and Japanese intellectuals who broke with colonial Enlightenment by attempting a synthesis between Heidegger and Eastern philosophies in the service of increased cultural authenticity.[3] Specifically, Badawi embarked on an ambitious project to synthesize Islamic mysticism with Heidegger in a fashion that would potentially heal the fragmented Arab self and create a new form of subjectivity which is both contemporary and authentically Islamic. If achieved, the project would heal the schism that made the tradition and heritage of Islam (*turath*) culturally redundant and would thus allow the post-colonial Arab generation to join the modern world on equal, authentic and unified philosophical terms.[4] Badawi poured an enormous amount of energy into this project and traveled extensively to spread his new creed. Yet, for all its brilliance, as the 1950s began, and political, social and economic problems mounted, the youth wanted concrete action. Though they

---

[3] Sandford (2003, pp. 11–22). For influence in Vietnam, see Gadkar-Wilcox (2014).

[4] In Badawi's words: "(the goal is to) … establish a comprehensive philosophy for our generation" (al-Badawi 1947, p. 103).

venerated Badawi, they wanted to see a sweeping change that would reshuffle "everything" and not a promising philosophical abstraction. Against this background, Sartre's new philosophy was much more appealing than that of Husserl and Heidegger.

Commitment

With the 1952 revolution in Egypt and the beginning of active and at times aggressive decolonization, the political and cultural structures of Egypt and much of the Middle East were about to be radically changed. Against this background, the young intellectuals of the 1950s (all born in the 1920s) had shifted to a post-colonial mode of being in which active decolonization of one's culture was a main preoccupation. Acting intuitively, they sought to replace the established class of cultural leaders (*the udaba'*) for their profound association with colonial Enlightenment. The main intellectual vehicle for the accomplishment of this task was a local take on Sartre's notion of commitment (*engagement*). Known in Arabic as *iltizam*, this notion came to politically determine the viability and legitimacy of any new idea that was introduced into the public sphere during decolonization. However, regardless of the common urge to decolonize, the politics of *iltizam* did not yield intellectual homogeneity as Marxists and pan-Arab nationalists traded in contending visions of *iltizam*.

Tough Sartre's philosophy was still important, the most important text which represented him in the Middle East was not his major philosophical oeuvre *Being and Nothingness* (1943) which was translated to Arabic only in 1966, but his 1947 essays in *Les Temps modernes* which were later delivered publicly and published as *Qu'est-ce que la littérature?* (*What Is Literature?*).[5] Taha Husayn, the doyen of Arab letters, introduced these essays to Egyptian readers shortly after their publication in France. In doing so he also coined the Arabic term for commitment (*iltizam*). Taha Husayn was a polyglot renaissance man with an incredible mind and an enormous capacity for work. Blind since childhood, he nonetheless

---

[5] However, in a series of critical essays on Sartre's existential philosophy, Najib Baladi accounted also for *Being and Nothingness* (Baladi in April 1946; see also follow-ups in June and July 1946).

studied French, graduated from the Sorbonne and returned to Egypt with a mission to bring Arab culture closer to that of France. Closely attuned to Paris, his journal began writing about Sartre as soon as he became a Left Bank phenomenon. He asked Didier Anzieu, an existentialist with credentials, to explain the French mystique of post-war existentialism to Arab readers (Anzieu 1946). Anzieu and several others did, but when Husayn encountered Sartre's *Qu'est-ce que la littérature?* he began to have second thoughts. He must have realized that he was going to become *iltizam*'s principal victim.

Qu'est-ce que la littérature? critically examined the relationship between the writer and society, and argued that since writing is a consequential form of acting/being, intellectuals should assume political responsibility for their work and the circumstances that condition it. This call for responsibility-*cum*-professional action was conjoined in Sartre's concept of commitment. Though the philosophical concern of commitment was human freedom and authentic existence, its practical application was "something for which (one) is prepared to die." This "something" was widely understood as a political cause. Even though often understood in this way, Sartre's notion of commitment was far from a straightforward call for politics. In fact, it was just one essential element in a quest for authenticity or, in his words, the "complete consciousness of being embarked" (Cooper 1990, pp. 172–177). Nonetheless, since Sartre himself led a politically engaged life, his example of action overrode the complexity of his philosophy to the degree that the notion of commitment as total submersion in the political became a mainstay of Sartrean existentialism. At least this is how young Arab intellectuals understood it. Against them, from the other side of the divide stood Husayn and his generation with an apolitical sense of literature as "art for art's sake" (Mahmud 1947).

The Lebanese literary critic Suhayl Idris was one of the young intellectuals who championed *iltizam* as a new template for post-colonial culture. Living in Paris during the early 1950s he witnessed the revolutionary potential of existentialism to engender meaningful cultural change. His vision was to do something similar in the Arab world by means of adopting the model of Sartre's *Les Temps modernes*. By 1953 *al-Adab* was up and running with a mission statement that was tantamount to a revolutionary call to arms:

The present situation of Arab countries makes it imperative for every citizen, each in his own field, to mobilize all his efforts for the express object of liberating the homeland, raising its political, social and intellectual level. In order that literature may be truthful it is essential that it should not be isolated from the society in which it exists … The kind of literature which this Review calls for and encourages is the literature of commitment (*iltizam*) which issues from Arab society and pours back into it. (Quoted in Badawi 1972, p. 868)

Under the skilled stewardship of Idris and his wife, ʿAida Matraji-Idris, the magazine grew into a busy publishing house and a translation hub for much of the existentialist cannon and contemporary French culture more generally. By the late 1950s, it became the most important and widespread cultural magazine in Arab lands. Loyal to the new creed of *iltizam*/ commitment the magazine insisted that words can and should change the world. Early theoreticians of committed literature (*al-adab al-multazim*) declared that "commitment should be the essence of each work of literature and the mission of each writer." That was the purpose of the "existentially committed" writer, one who is "connected to his surroundings, close to the people and their feeling," and never separated from the big "questions of his generation" (al-Maʿdawi 1953, p. 12). And so, since its early articulation, *iltizam* emerged as a doctrine of cultural action and a framework of thought that could organize, systematize and rationalize the quest for post-colonial culture. As one committed commentator boasted: "The idea of committed literature dominates the Arab world now."[6] But this dominance was somewhat misleading as two different ideological camps bitterly fought to control it.

Propelled forward by the unmistaken post-colonial character of the 1952 Revolution in Egypt and by Nasserism's many early political successes (for instance in nationalizing the Suez Canal in 1956), Idris harnessed the culture of *iltizam* on behalf of pan-Arab nationalism and the vision of a unified regional culture. Concomitantly, on the other side of the ideological divide, opposition thinkers like Mahmud Amin al-ʿAlim,

---

[6] Indeed, Iraqi writers who published in Beirut at about the same time confirm this diagnosis. See for instance the commentary of Iraqi literary critic Nahad al-Takarli (1953a, b, 1954) and al-ʿAzmi (1952).

who were in fact victims of Nasserism, made a deliberate attempt to appropriate Sartrean *iltizam* and submerge it in a Marxist-Leninist schema and the aesthetics of Socialist Realism. At stake was the sphere of individual freedom. While Suhayl Idris and his group wanted the writer to stay "connected to his surroundings, close to the people and their feeling," and never separated from the big "questions of his generation" (al-Maʿdawi 1953, p. 12). Communist theoreticians envisioned a writer that acts on behalf of the party and its doctrine. These were fundamental differences with regard to the function, purpose and scope of artistic and intellectual freedom. Indeed, they spoke of different intellectual models of action and responsibility. With both groups claiming ownership of *iltizam* and struggle to establish some measure of control over its reception and usage, the culture of commitment became forever divided between these two opposing camps and their opposing sources of inspiration: Paris and Moscow. The only thing they shared was a critique of Taha Husayn and his generation.

Between these two poles, *iltizam* was articulated as a moral imperative that divided the entire Arab intellectual field to good versus bad, just versus unjust, true versus false and progressive versus reactionary. Thus, drawing on Sartre's basic question *What do we write, why do we write, and to whom do we write?*, Arab intellectuals narrowed the act of writing down to a political act. In doing so they defined literature and literary criticism as the symbolic field of cultural decolonization. In the long run, the authoritarian post-colonial Arab state was able to appropriate pan-Arab *iltizam* as a tool of civic cooptation and, simultaneously, liquidate communist-style commitment.

Counter-Culture

The 1950s rise of the trans-regional pan-Arab state of Egypt, the most hegemonic state in the Arab world, ushered in the tendency to monopolize culture and buy the loyalty of intellectuals in whatever means possible. This pan-Arab state was predicated on a collective notion of freedom that overrode personal rights and minimized individual freedom. In that context, the notion of *iltizam* as political work in the field of culture was appropriated as a form of commitment, in fact a demand, to sacrifice without reservations on behalf of any state-led cause. This was a far cry from Sartre's original idea and in due date, when visiting Cairo, he would directly comment on this problem (Al-Kutab yunaqishun Sartar 1967, p. 12). But the hegemonic drive to rectify the individual in the body of the state did not pass without the response of intellectuals who draw on existentialism as philosophy of freedom in order to point out the dangers of authoritarianism. In Baghdad, which was known at the time as the capital of Arab existentialism, poets, writers and artists forged an informal, and largely oral, counter-culture that declared its skepticism toward any collective project. Dissenting and non-committed voices were also heard elsewhere in the region.

One famous incident of defiance took place in Cairo. During the 1958 Congress of Arab Writers President Gamal ʿAbd al-Nasser presented the quest for pan-Arab unity as a truthful cause that demands total compliance (al-Nasir 1958, p. 3). Embraced by the champions of *iltizam* this message dominated the circulation of print (Idris 1958, p. 1). By that point, the tendency to delegitimize the opposition and minimize the various political freedoms that enabled it became a political norm. Indeed, the general mood in the Congress did not welcome disagreements and critical reflection on the means and ends of pan-Arabism. The guests came to celebrate the will to sacrifice or what Suhayl Idris described as "the right kind of *iltizam*" (Idris 1958, p.2). Clearly, the top tier of Arab thinkers voted for intellectual syndicalism. That is, all except one, the Tunisian externalist playwright Mahmud al-Masʿadi whose commitment to individual freedom could not be undone by the collective drive toward national liberation and the syndicalist culture of thought. Drawing on his training in phenomenology and his experimentation with existentialist play writing, he produced a dramatic rebuke of pan-Arab urges and a courageous validation of freedom and radical individualism (Omri 2006, p. 42).

Standing out among the non-committed was the Lebanese female writer Layla Baʿalbakki, who at age 22 released her debut teen-angst novel *Ana Ahya* (*I Live!*) whose 19-year-old girl-woman Lena exhibits an insatiable thirst for freedom. Lena's female radical individualism is a counter-point to the collectivist spirit of pan-Arab nationalism:

Frankly, I do not have the mind to find a solution to the problems of Palestine, Kashmir, or Algeria … What worries me … is how to walk for the first time with my high-heeled shoes that raise me seven centimeters above the ground. Will they break as I rush into the street? (Baʾlabakki 1963, p. 45)

Known at the time as the "*Françoise Sagan* of the Arabs,"[7] she was blamed for nihilism, radical individualism and egoism. Eventually, her tirade against patriarchy and her call for sexual liberation became an all-encompassing Arab affair, when, for the first time in Lebanese history, the state brought charges against an author for "offending public morality" (she was acquitted) (Aghacy 2001).

There were many others too. Yusuf al-Khal and Adonis (ʿAli Ahmad Said) published *Shiʿr*, or *Poetry*, a new journal that followed an unapologetic anti-*iltizam* agenda that was wrapped around the freedom of the individual and the condition of his or her existence. They paid significant attention to a prevailing, yet denied sense of alienation (*ghurba*), anxiety (*qalaq*), rejection, (*rafd*), disintegration (*tamazzuq*) and loss of identity (*dayaʿ*).[8] Responding to the internal needs of decolonization as well as to those of state authority, existentialism became dominant in much of the poetry, prose and theatre of the late 1950s and 1960s. Thus, classic existentialist themes such as anticipation of death, absurdity, angst, estrangement and revolt were proven to be very effective in addressing the concerns of the time. In addition to Mahmud al-Masʿadi, who published *The Dam*, a work that cast doubt on the hubris of human economic and technological development (Ostle 1977), one can also find established writers such as Naguib Mahfouz, Mustafa Mahmud and, much later, Sonallah Ibrahim.[9] Syrian writers and playwrights such as Hani al-Rahib with *Mahzumun* (*The Defeated*), Jurj Salim with *Fi-l-Manfa* (*In Exile*) and Saʿd Allah Wannus with *al-Maqha al-Zujaji* (*Glass Café*) followed

---

[7] Sayigh (1958, p. 59). The Arabic translation of Segan's *Aimez-vous Brahms* was published by *al-Adab* in 1961.

[8] See for instance: Saʿid (1961) and Habashi (1957). For an elucidating take on *Shiʿr*'s intellectual environment see Creswell (2012) and Giordani (2010).

[9] For a standard literary survey see: Gordon (1990), Jad (1983, pp. 295–307), Mehrez (1994, pp. 39–57), Meyer (2001, p. 16), al-Musawi (1991, pp. 202–227).

suit.[10] The Palestinian writer Ghasan Kanafani published *Men in the Sun* (*Rijal fi-l-shams*), a short novella that drew on themes such as "anxiety" and "facing death" in order to achieve authentic clarity and account for the traumatic expulsion from Palestine and their continuous estrangement by fellow Arabs. Collectively, they explored questions of alienation and estrangement as a counter-point to the dominant culture of state-*iltizam*.

However, above all forms of critique was Baghdad's existentialist carnival. There, beginning in the late 1940s, a vibrant, if small, artistic scene of writers, poets, painters, students and teachers began to address the problem of freedom in multiple terms, some of which were decidedly existentialist. In this environment, "existentialism competed with Marxism, and the two ways of thinking intersected … Yet, the troubling awareness of freedom, the freedom of the body and of opinion, were associated here with the intellectual desire to achieve romantic isolation from society or the desire to confront society in words and deeds" (Mohsen 2012, p. 12). Feeling estranged in the midst of a collective nationalist drive, this young and diversified community insisted on "doing its own thing."[11]

Casting themselves as social rebels, bohemians, misfits and politically indifferent individuals whose lives were saturated in alcohol, tobacco and sex, Baghdadi existentialists were alienated from the established order and exhibited a profound distaste for authoritarianism. Seeing society at large with its values, codes of behavior and cultural expectations as the alienator, they mirrored this established order by spontaneously forming an amorphous community of alienation. Especially in comparison with the discipline and passion of Iraqi Communists, they were politically disengaged, yet artistically active and innovative. Thus, withdrawing to the artistic, they insulated themselves from the prevailing moral climate and created something of a counter-culture in which rather than reading and engaging philosophy, the prime emphasis was on "performing existentialism" in the service of everyday freedom. Undeniably, for this small and

[10] Other important playwrights were Walid Ihlasi, Farah Bulbul and 'Ali 'Uqla 'Ursan (Machut-Mendecka 2000, pp. 86–96; Muhammad 1982, pp. 62–165).
[11] For other treatments of this theme see Hanoosh (2012) and Davis (2005, pp. 82–147).

informal community of alienation to be free meant to be determined neither by national causes nor by social norms but only by the ability think and act for oneself. This was Baghdad's spirit and echoes of it could be found in the literature and conduct of intellectuals all over the region.

As some novelists later joked, Baghdad's carnivalesque allowed many of these disengaged artists and intellectuals to pretend that they were living in Paris. They could easily imagine themselves listening to Sartre delivering his passionate defense of freedom in a packed and smoky cinema where, along with hundreds of others, they crowded out to hear his foundational lecture "Existentialism Is a Humanism" (a text, by the way, which was translated to Arabic in 1954 but almost for certain Baghdadis never read). Sadly, as the political violence of the 1950s and early 1960s repeatedly and dramatically reminded them, they were not living in Paris. However, they owned the point about humanism and freedom which they embraced as hard, and as desperately, as they could.

Universal Emancipation

Intellectually connecting to the cause of the Global South was another significant domain that was profoundly influenced by existentialism. During the 1950s, Arab public speech was characterized by a fiery rhetoric of sovereignty, sacrifice and armed resistance. It paired nicely with politics but its one-dimensional outward orientation (physical liberation) did reduce decolonization to the power-play of anti-colonial politics, thus falling short of addressing the inner sphere of self and culture. Furthermore, while the language of anti-colonial nationalism was enough in order to meaningfully tie the Arab world to the international collective that formed in Bandung, it was not enough in order to connect it to the more sophisticated spirit and struggles of the 1960s. For that connection to happen, Arab publics needed to revisit the ways in which phenomenology and existentialism were processed by like-minded allies from the French colonies.

Mostly, they needed to familiarize themselves with the accumulative work of anti-colonial humanism which began with Sartre but included writers such as Frantz Fanon, Aimé Césaire and Léopold Sédar Senghor.

This body of work went beyond the obvious politics of anti-colonial nationalism to expose the process by which epistemic racism dehumanized groups, rendered them subhuman and pushed them into a hopeless zone of nonbeing where they were routinely suppressed, tortured and violated.

Initially, Sartre's anti-colonial humanism was not so much about activism as pure thought. As such, it consisted of texts such as *Anti-Semite and Jew* (1946) and *Black Orpheus* (1948) which introduced key post-colonial notions such as Otherness, authenticity and alienation.[12] In the context of decolonization, these notions became critical in "Spelling out the relationship between existential freedom and political freedom" (Arthur 2010, p. 69). "Black Orpheus," for example, "represents a clear shift in Sartre's politics in this period: In it, he synthesized ideas on freedom, collective Otherness, and the concrete situation that had been brewing since *Being and Nothingness*" (Arthur 2010, p. 30) This text was a result of his close collaboration with the Négritude movement of Aimé Césaire and Léopold Sédar Senghor as well as with the Black American writer Richard Wright who introduced Sartre to American racism and slavery. By virtue of this collaboration the notion of Otherness developed from being a problem which nests in outcast individuals (as Sartre theorized in *Anti-Semite and Jew*) to a problem that infects entire communities and is hence collective in nature as in slavery and colonialism. Drawing on this body of work, intellectuals from the French colonies published key anti-colonial texts such as *Fanon's Black Skin, White Masks* (1952) and Césaire's *Discourse on Colonialism* (1955). Beginning in the early 1960s, these foundational ideas about the link between race, Otherness, humanism and decolonization were taken very seriously. Though many Arab intellectuals read these works in French, by the mid-1960s, available material in Arabic showed the many ways in which Sartre "recognized outright the legitimate subjectivity of colonized peoples—not as a potential, but as a fact. His arguments in support of their right to self-determination were analogous to existentialist arguments concerning individual freedom" (Arthur 2010, p. XIX).

---

[12] Another critical text, *Notebooks for an Ethics, was written during 1947–8 but was published* posthumously and hence was not available.

At play too was the connection between dehumanization and torture in Algeria. Illustrating how Otherness, alienation and race coalesce to make the subhuman, Sartre went on to show that once stripped of its very humanity, the Algerian is subjected to the most inhumane forms of torture. The fact that Sartre, Beauvoir, and the French left committed themselves fully and publicly to an Arab struggle with universal implications made a huge and long-lasting impact on Arab audience (see for instance: Shukri 1960). It also encouraged the Arab left, and with it the public as a whole, to move toward a more universal position in which the fight in Algeria constitutes an important battle in an otherwise long war for Third World liberation in areas such as Congo, Cuba, Rhodesia, Vietnam and, most importantly from an Arab perspective, Palestine. Inspired by Sartre, intellectuals began writing about the big ideas of the 1960s, such as racism, neo-colonialism, settler colonialism, Otherness, subhuman existence, human dignity, hegemony, justice and the emancipating possibilities of guerilla warfare. By adopting this global system of meaning making, the revolutionary Arab world acquired the ability to understand, connect and identify with distant and seemingly irrelevant events.

Against this background, intellectuals like the Syrian Jurj Tarabishi made a serious effort to reconcile existentialism and Marxism as two locally practiced traditions that prepare the ground for a Third World socialist revolution; a revolution that was itself informed by these two traditions.

> every revolutionary is in need of a theory ... and the only possible revolutionary theory today is Marxism. But this does not at all mean that we need to understand Marxism as orthodox Marxists want. The contemporary Arab revolutionary needs to discover the living Marxism rather than the dogmatic and frozen one. The prime virtue of Sartrean existentialism is that it achieved this re-discovery of Marxism. (Tarabishi 1964, pp. 13–14)

Thus, for Tarabishi's revolutionary generation, Sartre embodied the promise of a global humanistic left, a movement that was to deliver them from the post-colonial state of being to that of global citizenship. In order to be able to participate in this project from an Arab standpoint it was crucial to dispel any doubts about the incompatibility of Marxism and existentialism (Tarabishi 1964, pp. 11–12). Tarabishi's work did precisely that. Drawing on the rich tradition of Arab existentialism that the previous generation had laid, revolutionary theoreticians like the Syrian Muta^c Safadi envisioned a new ethical subject of the left whose horizons of action were global (Safadi 1961). This new subject was not a peaceful and law-abiding bourgeois citizen but a revolutionary whose scope of analysis and action far surpassed the geographical limits of the Arab nation-state. Thus, by the early 1960s, Arab thinkers created an intellectual web that, in conjunction with concrete political engagements, allowed the inhabitants of the region to see themselves in a new universal light not simply as Arab subjects but as universal citizens who are committed to a global struggle against injustice and, following that, true liberation. They soon asked Sartre to recognize this development by supporting the cause of Palestine, something which much to their distress he failed to do.

Conclusion

So, what was Arab existentialism? Reflecting on this unique phenomenon one can say that it was an extended and hopeful experiment in intellectual *bricolage* that registered the intellectual specificity of Arab decolonization, thus showing how diverse, multi-layered and even contradictory the process really was. Within the immense cultural effort of decolonization, Arab existentialism took a central place as a variation on the influential theme of self-liberation. Serving as a major tool for individual and communal retrospection and self-fashioning, the ethos of Arab existentialism revolved around the key issues of authenticity, sovereignty and freedom. In that, Sartre's work was constitutive of the effort to forge a new Arab self, or as they called it, "A New Arab Man;" authentic, free and sovereign.

Authenticity was indeed a main cultural concern. Quite urgently, there was a fragmented and inauthentic cultural self to heal and because the colonial Arab self also contained within it the European Other, the potential of existentialism was immediately recognized as a possible bridge between these two badly coordinated lobes. The project of authenticity was and still is on the minds of Arab intellectuals. The arcane philosophical experiments were indeed so arcane that authenticity was submerged in the seemingly general culture of pan-Arabism.

Initially, it was believed that addressing the challenges of authenticity, sovereignty and freedom would suffice in order to rehabilitate Arab life. The hegemonic notion of commitment, or *iltizam*, was foundational to this effort. No other concept during this era proved as versatile and applicable to a host of situations and political constellations as that of *iltizam*. Its tasks were significant. The Arab revolutionary scene of the 1960s was a young one. And if there were no men of the nineteenth century calling the shots, it was partially, because the politics of *iltizam* aggressively retired these men. The phasing out of the *udabaʾ*, against their own will, was the work of young intellectuals who invoked *iltizam* in order to expose the degree to which the *udabaʾ* heavily relied on colonial humanism, especially in its French version.

Iltizam was also implicated in the battle for and against radical individualism. To whom is the new Arab Man committed, to society or to itself? Because it was entangled in the question of freedom and sovereignty this became a major question of the day. With the rise of the authoritarian Arab state and its sacrificial politics, *iltizam* assumed the properties of sacrifice on behalf of the nation as means of regaining collective sovereignty. Being an existential effort that seeks to alter Arab ontology, the state defined the notion of *iltizam* as commitment to the sacred politics of collective sacrifice and rebirth. In this way, *iltizam* became the subject of pan-Arabism. Emptied of its original meaning of intellectual commitment to freedom as such, it gradually slipped into the traitorous trap of self-referential commitment to commitment. In this new role, it was used to justify horrendous acts of political terror against a long list of real and imagined internal enemies. Though existentialism equipped the authoritarian nation-state with an effective tool for the suppression of freedom, it also endowed the opponents of this state with a rich intellectual repertoire with which to resist this oppression. In this role, it was especially useful for marginal groups and individuals who declined the reduction of decolonization to state sovereignty and imagined alternative venues toward freedom.

Another notable aspect of Arab existentialism was its smooth interface with Third Worldism and the revolutionary culture of the 1960s. If until the 1950s the main Arab perspective on world order was that of "East versus West," the 1960s vertically reconfigured this order as one in which the "South" fights the "North." Via the prevalence of existentialism, an actual political link was made to Sartre and his ethics of global action. Here what mattered was not lofty philosophy, but on-the-ground political action against racism, settler colonialism, neo-colonialism, imperialism and so on. The ethics that followed from this action were all-encompassing as they pertained to state, society and the self. Most importantly, they pointed toward humanity at large and hence toward a new form of universality. Subscribing to the idea that Middle Eastern battles were merely one front in a global war, the Arab Left developed an expectation that the difficult heritage of colonialism would find its resolution via its attachment to a universal framework. Unfortunately for them, that did not happen as on the eve of the 1967 war Sartre appeared to be siding with Israel instead of with the Arab revolutionary project that was predicated on his thought. In what follows, Arab regimes lost the war and the slow process of cultural reckoning that started in its wake pointed to a future that was free of the universal message of Arab existentialism.

References

ʿAbd al-Nasir, Jamal. 1958. Hajatuna ila al-taharrur al-fikri. *Al-Adab*, 3, January.

Aghacy, Samira. 2001. Lebanese Women's Fiction: Urban Identity and the Tyranny of the Past. *International Journal of Middle East Studies* 33: 503–523.

al-ʿAlim, Mahmud Amin. 1970. Al-Hurriyya wa-l-iltizam ʿinda Sartar. In *Maʿarik fikriyya*, 226–237. Cairo: Dar al-Hilal.

al-ʿAzmi, ʿAwad Majid. 1952. al-Nuzha al-wujudiyya. *Al-Adib*, 27–31, January.

Al-Kutab yunaqishun Sartar hawla Brecht wa tatawwur al-masrah al-Misri. 1967. *Al-Jumhuriyya*, 12, March 8.

al-Maʿdawi, Anwar. 1953. Al-Adab al-multazim. *Al-Adab*, 12, February.

al-Musawi, Muhsin. 1991. The Socio-Political Context of the Iraqi Short Story, 1908–1968. In *Statecraft and Popular Culture in the Middle East*, ed. Eric Davis and Nicholas Gaverieldes, 202–227. Gainesville: Florida University Press.

al-Takarli, Nahad. 1953a. Al-Masrah al-wujudi. *Al-Adib*, 3–6, January.

————. 1953b. Simun di Bufwar wa mushkilat al-mawt. *Al-Adib*, 33–34, July.

————. 1954. Al-nitaj al-jadid. *Al-Adab*, 33–39, August.

Anzieu, Didier. 1946. Al-wujudiyya. *Al-Katib al-Misri*, 119–148, October.

Arthur, Paige. 2010. *Unfinished Projects: Decolonization and the Philosophy of Jean-Paul Sartre*. London: Verso.

Badawi, ʿAbd al-Rahman. 1946. *Humum al-shabab*. Cairo: Maktabat al-Nahda al-Misriyya.

————. 1947. *Al-Insaniyya wa-l-wujudiyya fi-l-fikr al-ʿArabi*. Cairo: Maktabat al-Nahda al-Misriyya.

Badawi, Abdurahman. 1964. *Le Problème de la Mort dans la Philosophie Existentielle*. Le Caire: Institute Français d'archéologie Orientale.

Badawi, M. Mustafa. 1972. Commitment in Contemporary Arabic Literature. *Cahiers d'histoire mondiale* 14 (4): 858–879.

Badawi, ʿAbd al-Rahman. 2000. *Sirat hayati*, Vol. I. Beirut: al-Mu'assasa al-ʿArabiyya li-l-Dirasat wa-l-Nashr.

Baʾlabakki, Layla. 1963. *Ana ahya*. Beirut: Dar Majallat Shiʿr.

Baladi, Najib. 1946. Jan-Bul Sartar wa mawaqifuhu. *al-Katib al-Misri*, 427–434, April 1946, 50–59, June 1946, 277–283, July 1946.

Cooper, David. 1990. *Existentialism: A Reconstruction*. Oxford: Blackwell.

Creswell, Robyn. 2012. *Tradition and Translation: Poetic Modernism in Beirut*. PhD diss., New York University. http://ezproxy.lib.utexas.edu/login?url=http://search.proquest.com.ezproxy.lib.utexas.edu/docview/992988836?accountid=7118.

Davis, Eric. 2005. *Memories of State: Politics, History and Collective Identity in Modern Iraq*. Berkeley: University of California Press.

Di-Capua, Yoav. 2018. *No Exit: Arab Existentialism, Jean-Paul Sartre and Decolonization*. Chicago: University Press of Chicago.

El Shakry, Omnia. 2017. *The Arabic Freud: Psychoanalysis and Islam in Modern Egypt*. Princeton: Princeton University Press.

Gadkar-Wilcox, Wynn. 2014. Existentialism and Intellectual Culture in South Vietnam. *Journal of Asian Studies* 73 (2): 377–395.

Giordani, Angela. 2010. *Shiʿr and the Other Revolution of the Arab Fifties*. Unpublished Seminar Paper, University of Texas at Austin.

Gordon, Hayim. 1990. *Naguib Mahfouz's Egypt: Existential Themes in his Writings*. New York: Greenwood Press.

Habashi, René. 1957. Al-Shiʿr fi maʿrakat al-wujud. *Shiʿr*, 88–95, January 1.

Hanoosh, Yasmeen. 2012. Contempt: State Literati vs. Street Literati in Modern Iraq. *Journal of Arabic Literature* 43 (2/3): 372–408.

Idris, Suhayl. 1958. Mu'tamaruna al-adabi al-thalith. *Al-Adab*, 1–2, January.

Jad, Ali. 1983. *Form and Technique in the Egyptian Novel, 1912–1971*. London: Ithaca Press.

Machut-Mendecka, Ewa. 2000. *Studies in Arabic Theatre and Literature*. Warsaw: Dialog.

Mahmud, Husayn. 1947. al-Fann min ajl al-fann. *Al-Katib al-Misri*, 66–73, January.

Mehrez, Samia. 1994. *Egyptian Writers Between History and Fiction*. Cairo: The American University Press.

Meyer, Stefan. 2001. *The Experimental Arabic Novel*. Albany: State University of New York Press.

Mohsen, Fatima. 2012. Debating Iraqi Culture: Intellectuals between the Inside and the Outside. In *Conflicting Narratives: War, Trauma and Memory in Iraqi Culture*, ed. Stephan Milich et al., 5–24. Wiesbaden: Reichert.

Muhammad, Nadim Ma'alla. 1982. *Al-Adab al-masrahi fi Suriyya: Nash'atuhu, tatawwuruhu*. Damascus: s.n.

Omri, Mohamed-Salah. 2006. *Nationalism, Islam and World Literature: Sites of Confluence in the Writings of Mahmud al-Masʿadī*. Abingdon: Routledge.

Ostle, Robin. 1977. Mahmūd al-Masʿadī. *Journal of Arabic Literature* 8: 153–166.

Safadi, Muta'. 1961. *Al-Thawri wa-l-ʿArabi al-thawri: Dirasa fikriyya qawmiyya li-namadhij al-thawriyyin al-gharbiyyin wa-l-ʿArab*. Beirut: Dar al-Taliʿa.

Saʿid, Khalida. 1961. Bawadir al-rafd fi-l-shiʿr al-ʿArabi al-jadid. *Shiʿr*, 88–95, July 19.

Salih, Ahmad ʿAbbas. 1967. Risala ila Sartar. *Al-Katib*, March 25.

Sandford, Stella. 2003. Going Back: Heidegger, East Asia and 'The West'. *Radical Philosophy* 120: 11–22.

Sayigh, Fayiz. 1955. *Self-Examination and Arab Youth* (address given at the fourth Annual Convention of the Organization of Arab Students in the United States, University of Wisconsin, Madison, September 6, 1955), 9–10. Stored in Box 267 Folder 6 It1. FSC, J. Willard Marriott Library's Aziz A. Atiya Library, University of Utah, Salt Lake City, Utah, USA.

Sayigh, Anis. 1958. *Al-Adab*, May.

Shukri, Ghali. 1960. Nakarazuf: Faylusuf al-azma al-faransiyya. *Al-Adab*. 22–25, 74–77, May.

Tarabishi, Jurj. 1964. *Sartar wa-l-Marksiyya*. Beirut: Dar al-Taliʿa.

15

Sartre's Presence in Israeli Literature: The Case of Hanoch Levin

Rony Klein

Jean-Paul Sartre's introduction in Israeli literature has to be placed in its precise context. Let us remember that the Israeli literature of the first years of the state was heroic. The new state had to use all its energies to survive, facing at the same time the dangers of war—the War of Independence had ended in 1949—and the challenges of domestic policies, such as the integration of a very large wave of immigration from Arab countries. In such a situation, literature could only be a text accompanying the Zionist epos on its way. The writers and poets of the 1950s, like Natan Alterman, S. Yizhar, and Haim Gouri, are known for their novels and poems on the War of Independence and the sacrifices it required. We can thus describe this age as the heroic age of Hebrew literature: the hero of the young Israeli literature was usually a soldier or someone whose place within society was well defined. Those were the most ideological years of the state, a state whose model was the Soviet Union. Israel was a country entirely mobilized for its struggle to survive.

R. Klein (✉)
Tel Aviv University, Tel-Aviv, Israel

© The Author(s) 2020
A. Betschart, J. Werner (eds.), *Sartre and the International Impact of Existentialism*,
https://doi.org/10.1007/978-3-030-38482-1_15

It is only with the generation of the 1960s—that of Amos Oz and A.B. Yehoshua—that Sartre could enter Israeli literature. Indeed, this generation opened literature up to questions concerning the individual as such and not only the young soldier or the member of a kibbutz. The ideological dilemmas were not forgotten or erased, but more latitude was given to individual preoccupations. In this context, the Israeli society discovered the existence of identity and moral questions of the Self, and writers such as Sartre or Albert Camus. However, we have to recognize that even then, Sartre's influence as a writer is not easy to define. He is translated and read, but not for its own sake. He is read with other writers such as Camus and Franz Kafka and is associated with them in a current which bears the vague name of 'literature of the absurd'. Thus, *Nausea* is read together with *The Stranger* and *The Process* without really distinguishing what belongs to each one of them. On the theater scene alike, authors like Samuel Beckett and Eugène Ionesco played a bigger role than Sartre and Camus that was somehow still very classical in comparison with the so-called Theater of the Absurd. The situation advantaged authors aiming to present their ideas through theater instead of through prose or poetry. Finally, to close this short introduction to Sartre's influence on Israeli literature, let us remember that from the 1950s onward, Sartre was considered more a public figure and engaged intellectual struggling for justice and peace than a writer. This was the case in Israel like everywhere else. It is very striking when one reads the testimonies of Sartre's visit to Israel in 1967, shortly before the Six-Day War (see Ben-Gal 1992). Although he was received by the great poet Avraham Shlonsky at the airport in Tel Aviv, most of the people who attended the ceremony were small bureaucrats of the Workers' Party *Mapai*, maybe with the exception of the anti-conformist journalist Uri Avnery. Ben Gal perfectly depicts Sartre's image in Israeli opinion when he speaks of him as "the high priest of the peace camp and of socialism" (Ben-Gal 1992, p. 13). When Sartre came to Israel, it was not primarily for the writers, but for two things of high interest for him: the kibbutz experience and the question of the Israeli-Arab conflict. As to the first matter of interest, he went to visit the historical kibbutz leader Meir Ya'ari, with whom he had an important discussion on socialism. He also visited the kibbutzim and center of the leftist movement *Hashomer Hatzair*. As for his interest in the Israeli-Arab conflict, he published an important review on this topic in his review *Les Temps modernes*, as soon as he came back to France from Israel and Egypt, which he visited just before Israel. That sums up Sartre's influence in Israel: it was more political than literary. Let us add that his influence can also be perceived in philosophical circles in Israel: the philosopher Menahem Brinker translated major pages from Sartre's philosophical work in these years.

I would like now to focus on literature and on one specific case: the theater of the dramatic author Hanoch Levin (1943–1999). Beyond any doubt, Levin is Israel's most important theater dramatist, author of many plays, from political satires to romantic comedies, from dramatic comedies to more 'serious' and sometimes dark tragedies, like *Job's Passion*. But even in the darkest plays we can always hear Levin's sense of humor, so that with him, like with many modern authors, the literary genres are often intertwined. Let us first say that the general tone of Levin's theater is very far from Sartre's. Levin is first of all the author of comedies, which means that his work essentially excels by humor, black humor and satire, burlesque and absurd. Like all authors of comedies, he insists mainly on the lowest dimensions of human life: sensual appetites, lust, desire for food and women, and all types of material pleasure. The characters in his plays are mostly simple people who belong to the lower and the middle classes; they are often mediocre or evil. Thus, one often evokes the names of Bertolt Brecht or Beckett to speak about his theater: Brecht for the political satire, Beckett for the absurd. In contrast, Sartre's theater and work in general seem to be very different from Levin's. Sartre is considered a philosopher and a 'serious' political writer, whose works are always situated in a high level of language. This is not the case for Levin's theater, whose political dimension mostly appears through grotesque satire. Thus, none of Sartre's major plays belong to the genre of comedy (the one exception could be *Nekrassov*); on the contrary, they are usually taken as highly philosophical or ideological works aiming to prove a specific thesis or idea. Their role is to illustrate an idea that Sartre had developed in one of his philosophical books. For example, *No Exit* shows, in a particular situation, the adequacy of the thesis concerning the relation to the others presented in *Being and Nothingness*; *The Flies* illustrate Sartre's thesis on freedom; *The Condemned of Altona* plays with these two theses alternately.

Thus, the first impression seems to say: there is no possible link between Sartre and Levin, the two authors definitively belong to two incompatible worlds. I would like to call into question this proposition on one specific point: the question of the relation to the Other.

*   *   *

My aim is not to invalidate the whole corpus of studies on Levin. Indeed, he is part of a modern tradition where one finds Brecht as well as Beckett. There is no point in negating this obvious proposition. I would rather like to show that, despite what may seem obvious, Levin's theater, especially of the 1970s, meets Sartre's work on a decisive point: the question of the relation to the Other, and the motive of the 'look'. It is not a question of influence. I do not intend to propose an academic study on influences or sources. Levin, while studying literature and philosophy at the Tel Aviv University in the 1960s, had probably heard of Sartre's work; but that is not the main point. More interesting seems to me to show the meeting between Levin's theater and Sartre's philosophy, not only on a single theme, or motif, but also to show a common sensibility, the same approach to human relations. It is striking that Levin's theater, like Sartre's, seems to present a 'no exit' situation. It evolves in circles between a few characters that are locked in relations made of jealousy, envy, and grief. Like Sartre's *No Exit*, Levin's *Ya'akobi and Leidental* offers the case of a trio which seems to be locked in a trap, although Levin's play is a comedy and Sartre's more of a drama. Yet the difference of genre is less important here than the common ground when we look at the conception underlying the two plays. Although Levin writes comedies, his view on human relations is particularly dark: people are tearing each other apart out of envy, competition, or simply pure sadism. I would like to illustrate the proximity between Sartre and Levin by taking examples from a few plays, focusing on Levin's masterpiece *Hefetz* (1972).

Indeed, *Hefetz* (the name of the main character, literally meaning a 'thing') is the play which promoted Levin as a 'serious' author. In the late 1960s, Levin began his theater career as a writer of political satires like *You, Me and the Next War*, or *The Queen of the Bathtub*. These plays mock the nationalism of the Israeli society after the victory of the Six-Day War, their military ethos which Levin depicts as pure stupidity. In the 1970s, he moved toward a more 'serious' theater, less directly political and more social and psychological. These plays are still comedies, but they deal with existential concerns, like solitude, the impossibility of communication, and especially the absurd cruelty of men in their relations with each other. *Hefetz* is his first step in this direction. The protagonist's very name is an indication that everybody considers him a pure object, mocking him. The play revolves around the relations inside his extended family with whom he has lived since his mother's death. The parents, Teigalach and Clamansea, are the pure product of Israeli petty bourgeois mentality: they are proud of themselves, always trying to show their social success and prosperity to everyone. This couple has a daughter, Fugra (literally 'figure'), who is the incarnation of the narcissistic young woman, totally absorbed in herself. Hefetz is secretly in love with her, a love that she perceives very well. She herself is engaged to Warshaviack, a handsome young man entirely subjected to his fiancée. Around these four main characters revolve few other figures, like for example Shukra (literally 'lie'), who, despite his name, is supposed to tell the truth of the whole story, a bit like the Greek chorus.

The story focuses mainly on Hefetz's relations with his family. These relations can be described as sadomasochistic in the sense that Hefetz is considered as nothing, as an object one laughs at, whereas Hefetz himself oscillates between self-pity and the attempt to resist the general disdain from which he suffers. Let us examine these relations in the first scene of the play, which shows Hefetz with Teigalach, the father. They are both in the kitchen:

> *Hefetz is eating a cake.*
> Hefetz: Ta-ta, ta-ta. *Break.* Ta-ta. Please excuse me for making such noises. It is pleasure. I take pleasure in this cake. Ta-ta. *Teigalach doesn't react.* What a pleasure I have. *Break.* This cake is giving me immense pleasure.
> Teigalach: No.
> Hefetz: How 'No'? *Break.* How 'No'?
> Teigalach: No.
> Hefetz: How 'No'?

Teigalach: You don't have any pleasure.
Hefetz: Why not?
Teigalach: Because you don't.
Hefetz: I have great pleasure.
Teigalach: You have pleasure in nothing at all.
Hefetz: Excuse me, really, I eat a cake with pleasure.
Teigalach: No.
Hefetz: How no? When you eat a cake, you don't feel any pleasure?
Teigalach: Me, yes, I do.
Hefetz: So you see, me too.
Teigalach: No.
Hefetz: Why do you talk to me like this?! I don't feel pleasure like everybody else?! No? No? *Break.* No? *Break.* No? *Break.* No?
Teigalach: So what do you want from me?!
Hefetz: That you tell me why you said so.
Teigalach: In order that you should not think that if you sometimes taste something sweet you feel happy like us.
Hefetz: I don't pretend to be happy like you. But acknowledge that as to the cake, I took some pleasure.
Teigalach: No, I won't acknowledge that. And don't try to make me say what I didn't say. You didn't take pleasure in this cake as you've never taken any pleasure in anything. Never. The conversation is over.
Hefetz: You behave as if you had the monopoly on pleasure.[1]

This scene, typical of Hanoch Levin, immediately introduces us into his world, the world of the conflict with the Other. This conflict arises from nothing, from the smallest detail in everyday life. It does not matter what gave rise to the conflict, since it is inescapable. Here, someone is eating a cake in front of someone else and tells him how much he enjoys it. The other denies him the right to enjoy the cake. Apparently, the same action—to eat a cake—does not produce the same effects on everyone, and those who have the right to deny forbid it to others. There are two types of men, two humanities: those who have all the rights, and those who have no rights at all. That is the immediate message of this scene.

---

[1] Levin (1999a, pp. 91–92). All quotations are from the Hebrew edition of Levin's plays: *Mahazot 1, Hefetz ve'aherim.* Tel Aviv: Hakibbutz Hame'uchad Editions, 1999. All translations by R.K.

One of the characters, Shukra, explains this elsewhere in a blunt and provocative way:

> But it is unbearable! This terrible hypocrisy will break my heart, in the end! You, bunch of cripples, you don't let the happy few enjoy their most elementary right: the right to see the unhappy in his misery. (Levin 1999a, p. 99)

This scene evokes many images in literature and philosophy. One can think of Beckett's two tramps in front of Pozzo in *Waiting for Godot*. Others will refer to Hegel's dialectic of lord and bondsman, who fight for mutual recognition. For me, this scene immediately recalls the encounter with the Other in Sartre's *Being and Nothingness*, and the torture of being-together in the play *No Exit*, even if here, we are in the presence of a one-to-one relationship, and not a trio. Indeed, the principle at work in Sartre's analysis of the encounter with the Other is the same that grounds Levin's depiction of the one-to-one relationship in this scene between Hefetz and Teigalach. Hefetz disturbs Teigalach not for a particular reason, but by his mere existence. The presence of this being in his house disturbs Teigalach, offends his wellbeing, as if he deprives him of the very air he breathes, and that without ever having done anything wrong to him. The Other is immediately perceived as an intruder; even worse than that, as an enemy who perpetually threatens one's space, one's private life, all the little pleasures of one's everyday life. He prevents one from enjoying life by his pure presence. When Sartre, in *Being and Nothingness*, presents the Other's appearance in the Self's world, how does he describe him? Let us turn to the famous example of the public garden. I am in a public garden. I think I am alone. Suddenly I see a man. How will I react? Sartre writes:

> The Other is first the permanent flight of things toward a goal which I apprehend as an object at a certain distance from me but which escapes me inasmuch as it unfolds about itself its own distances. [...] There is a total space which is grouped around the Other, and this space is made *with my space*; there is a regrouping in which I take part but which escapes me, a regrouping of all the objects which people my universe. [...] I apprehend

the relation of the green to the Other as an objective relation, but I cannot apprehend the green *as* it appears to the Other. Thus, suddenly an object has appeared which has stolen the world from me. Everything is in place; everything still exists for me; but everything is traversed by an invisible flight and fixed in the direction of a new object. (Sartre 1956, p. 343)

This description is puzzling: it begins with an objective analysis and finishes with a sudden affirmation according to which the Other "has stolen the world from me". It is as if I enjoyed first a privileged relationship with the world harmoniously arranged around my consciousness being at the center of the universe, and suddenly, the other man appears and steals the world from me. Indeed, I realize, as I see the other, that he is another consciousness—that is, someone who, like me, can organize the world around himself. I realize, in fact, that the world does not belong to me exclusively, that it also belongs to all the others I shall meet on my way. And being aware of this is unbearable since it is opposed to my narcissistic pleasure in the world as *my* world, *my* exclusive and inalienable property.

Let us come back to Levin's Hefetz and apply Sartre's analysis to our scene. What will we say? That Hefetz *steals* the cake from Teigalach! Indeed, when Hefetz enjoys a cake, Teigalach feels that he is dispossessed of his own pleasure, the pleasure to eat a piece of cake. What seems at first to be a funny situation in a sadomasochistic relationship between two persons, the perpetrator and the victim, becomes now, in the light of Sartre's analysis, the essence of all human relations, as it necessarily offends one's most elementary narcissism—a narcissism that consists in enjoying the world all alone in a happy solitude. In any case this is how Sartre describes the reaction of the person who walks in a public garden and suddenly realizes he is not alone. This reaction is depicted as almost physiological: this person immediately considers the presence of the Other as a threat to his pleasure, his feeling of the world. The Other is like a wolf which circles him ready to attack. We know that all the examples taken from *Being and Nothingness* confirm this idea. The Other's look is always a threat, but beyond this threat, it is evil in itself as a look. It is evil because it judges one, reduces one's freedom of a being-for-itself to nothing. This is the sense of the famous formula, "My original fall is the existence of the Other" (Sartre 1956, p. 352).

It is not necessary to analyze in detail Sartre's description of the look, which is quite known. What is striking is the closeness of Levin's perception of the look to Sartre's. From two examples, we will see that when he speaks of the look, he seems to quote from Sartre. The first is taken from the play *Young Varda'le* (1974). The scene shows Varda, a wealthy young woman desired by all the men in the play, with the cook and the gardener:

[the cook] to Varda: Let me just remind you that I admire you as I always did, whereas I only despise myself. (*She gets out. He addresses the gardener*) Your look accuses me, and you're right. And now, I am going to have a cup of tea and leave your look filled with accusation suspended in the air. (Levin 1999c, p. 246)

The Sartrean echo of these lines is obvious. First, let us observe that the tension between the two men is reinforced by their common desire for the young woman. They are rivals. But the most striking feature of this scene is the description of the look: it accuses, and 'it is right to accuse'. It is shame as 'confession', analyzed by Sartre, and what is left to the man accused by the look is only to try to escape those accusing eyes, like in the scene with the cook leaving the gardener alone. But this escape is vain: the cook will continue to carry in his thoughts the gardener's accusing look. In Sartre, the accusing look is answered by another accusing look: it becomes a war of looks. In Levin, the look provokes mostly a sadomasochistic relation, as we have seen in the case of Hefetz. The one becomes the slave of the other.

I take now a second extract, from the play *Schitz* (1975). Here are the words of Tsesha on her dying husband Schitz:

In the end, those eyes that are always looking at me, permanently requesting and accusing me, those eyes that encircle me for thirty years, like in a room filled with mirrors, as each shame, each failure is multiplied a hundred times. I order those eyes to close once and for all. Enough! (Levin 1999b, p. 331)

Here, again, the Sartrean character of the lines is absolutely obvious. The woman experiences her husband's look, here again an accusing look, as a real persecution. And like in the quotation above, the look provokes shame and makes the failure each time even more unbearable. The couple's relationship is seen through the prism of a searching look, the look of a perpetrator who does not let his victim go. Husband and wife are locked in the same place; hence, they cannot flee each other in a 'no exit' situation. In these scenes, Levin seems to adopt Sartre's formula: Hell is other people. Here, he can even write in a more minimalistic way: Hell is the Other. Indeed, for Levin, the single presence of one person is sufficient to plunge one into hell. A third person is not necessary. We are struck by this vision of the couple, filled with darkness and despair: the Other—here the husband or the wife—is always the one who, by his look, judges and accuses. All one can do is to wish his death!

To conclude, I will try to compare Sartre's vision of human relations with Levin's. The two authors come from very different backgrounds. Sartre's French intellectual and bourgeois family has nothing to do with the Polish-Jewish origins of Levin, who carried within him the world of the Eastern European Jewish *Shtetl*. But despite this cultural gap, their vision seems to meet on the question of human relations. Was it a secret influence of Sartre on Levin? Was it the experience of a young Israeli struck by the geo-political conflict of his country? The answer to this question remains obscure, and perhaps the question itself is vain. More essential seems to me the comparison of the works of the two authors. Whereas Sartre tried, all his life, to overcome the tragic war of the look, either in the elaboration of an ethics or in other realms, like in the late project of Flaubert's biography, Levin, on his side, remained on the level of the tragic war. This fact is surprising, as Levin could seek in his own Jewish tradition the means to take a step beyond this vision of human relations as an inescapable war. Indeed, in the Jewish tradition, the look is considered from a very different point of view, as Levinas showed in his philosophy.[2] Surprisingly enough, it is not the Jewish dramatist who sought to overcome the ontological tragic war between men, but the

---

[2] See, for example, in two of his major works: *Totality and Infinity* (1961) and *Otherwise than Being or Beyond Essence* (1974).

French philosopher and writer. First, he tried to do so with the ethics of the writer; then with the ethics of the revolutionary man; finally, with his Jewish secretary Benny Lévy, he discovered the Jewish dimension of ethics. Levin, on his side, will make of the tragic look the source of endless situations, funny or sad, in his plays. Perhaps this difference lies in the difference between the functions of philosopher and playwright: whereas the philosopher tries to surmount what seems to him a dead-end, the playwright is satisfied with the description of scenes likely to provoke tears or laughter, depending on the infinite variety of human relations.

References

Ben-Gal, Ely. 1992. *Mardi chez Sartre—un Hébreu à Paris*. Paris: Flammarion.
Levin, Hanoch. 1999a. Hefetz. In *Mahazot 1, Hefetz ve'aherim*, ed. Hanoch Levin, 87–171. Tel Aviv: Hakibbutz Hame'uchad Editions.
———. 1999b. Schitz. In *Mahazot 1, Hefetz ve'aherim*, ed. Hanoch Levin, 291–368. Tel Aviv: Hakibbutz Hame'uchad Editions.
———. 1999c. Young Varda'le. In *Mahazot 1, Hefetz ve'aherim*, ed. Hanoch Levin, 233–290. Tel Aviv: Hakibbutz Hame'uchad Editions.
Sartre, Jean-Paul. 1956. *Being and Nothingness*. Translated by Hazel E. Barnes. New York: Washington Square Press.

16

The Discovery of the Other in Post-War Japan: Two Sartreans on Kyoto School and Zainichi Koreans

Nariaki Kobayashi and Hiroaki Seki

This chapter aims to highlight Sartre's reception in Japan, notably regarding the following question: how did Sartre's philosophy, especially on the status of others, exert an influence on the shift of the intellectual scheme in post-war Japan? To tackle this question, one must notice first of all that a philosophy must be translated, then presented, and eventually practiced, in order to have an influence on a foreign country. Who, then, are the Sartreans that have played this mediator role between Sartre and his foreign public? What means were used? Which Japanese ideology did they fight against? How could the use of Sartrean philosophy help change the Japanese society after the war? From these perspectives, our chapter will focus on the academic reception of Sartre, but will also aim to go beyond academia and consider the impact of his philosophy within the whole society.

N. Kobayashi (✉)
Hitotsubashi University, Tokyo, Japan

H. Seki
University of Tokyo, Tokyo, Japan

© The Author(s) 2020
A. Betschart, J. Werner (eds.), *Sartre and the International Impact of Existentialism*,
https://doi.org/10.1007/978-3-030-38482-1_16

This choice of question requires putting aside other highly interesting aspects of the relationship between Sartre and Japan.[1] For example, we will not deal with the image of Japan in Sartre's works, nor with his personal relationship with Japan—application for a position as professor in Japan *circa* 1931—or Japanese people—for example, Shūzō Kuki (1888–1941), a young philosopher Sartre met in Paris around 1928 to whom he taught French philosophy.[2] Neither will we discuss Sartre and Beauvoir's 1966 trip to Japan that sparked strong enthusiasm in Japanese media.[3] Instead, we will deal with two Japanese Sartreans who, in the aftermath of the war, discovered Sartre, each in a different way in accordance with different interests, but who both did so with astonishment. We are talking of a philosopher, Yoshirō Takeuchi (竹内芳郎 1924–2016), and a French literature researcher, Michihiko Suzuki (鈴木道彦 born in 1929). In these two lives, we hope to catch a glimpse of the impact of Sartre's philosophy in post-WWII Japan, from a philosophical point of view as well as at a social level with particular respect to racial discrimination in Japan.[4] As an introduction, just a few words must be said to present Sartre's reception before and during the war.

Yasuhiko Masuda observes that "before and during the war, Sartre's reception was still in its infancy" and that "Sartre the philosopher did not catch the eye more than Sartre the writer".[5] This could be explained by the focus that academia had on German philosophy, that is, (neo)Kantian idealism, Husserlian phenomenology, and Heideggerian ontology. This was the case with the Kyoto School, the first school of modern Japanese

---

[1] For an overview of the relationship between Sartre and Japan see Sawada (2013, 2004) and Müller (2008). For an analysis of the reception in the field of publishing, see the Japanese article by Ishii (2006); the author comments: "all the insights we acquired from data on publications analysis lead to the following conclusion that 1966 is the acme year of Sartre's reception in Japan" (Ishii 2006, p. 103).

[2] The encounter with this Japanese philosopher who will later participate in the famous Kyoto School (京都学派) is not episodical if we consider that Sartre discovered German contemporary philosophy at an early stage thanks to this Japanese who studied with Heidegger. Cf. Light (1987).

[3] This visit has been commented many times: Tomiko Asabuki, Sartre and Beauvoir's guide and then friend, wrote the best testimony (Asabuki 1996). Regarding comments on the visit, see for example Suzuki (2011) and Suzuki and Sawada (2011).

[4] Nariaki Kobayashi mostly drafted the first part, while Hiroaki Seki did the latter.

[5] See Yasuhiko Masuda (2007). Surprisingly, *The Wall*, *The Room*, and an extract of *Nausea* were already translated before the war.

philosophy, which was often in dialogue with German phenomenologists with the aim to mediate between Western and Eastern philosophies.[6] Of course, some philosophers from this school—for example, Shuzō Kuki—did not ignore Sartre,[7] but their reception of Sartrean existentialism was, we should admit, not very intense. What mattered to them was to construct—in connection with German philosophy—a philosophy of a particular existence expressing the 'Japanese experience'. This was the ground paved by the Kyoto School and it was above all *against this backdrop* that Yoshirō Takeuchi started studying Sartre.

Yoshirō Takeuchi: Reception of Sartre as the Philosopher of the Post-War Period

We can understand how Takeuchi saw the particularity of Sartre's thought thanks to a mesmerizing quotation:

> For the Japanese intelligentsia to which we belong, there is only one unique and authentic place to directly receive Sartre's thought. This place is the Japanese reality, where we should use Sartrean thought as a weapon to fight against many foolish ideas. [...] Immersed in the Japanese spiritual climate, fitting exactly the world that Sartre described as "anti-value", we must radically get rid of obscure thoughts, obscure human relationships, and obscure daily behaviors. For this mission, no thought is stronger than Sartre's. (Takeuchi 1966, p. 314)

Takeuchi was born in 1924 to a well-off provincial family; at the age of 20, his mobilization during WWII was a capital event in his life. After the war, he discovered Sartre during his studies of French and German philosophies (Kant, Nietzsche, Bergson, Heidegger, etc.) and was fascinated by him. In 1956, he published his first work, *Introduction to Sartre's*

---

[6] For instance, Martin Heidegger mentions Shūzō Kuki in *Dialogue on Language Between a Japanese and an Inquirer* (Heidegger 1976).

[7] Another example is Kiyoshi Miki (1897–1945) who, also as a Kyoto School member, mentioned in his 1937 study on imagination the name of the author who published *L'imagination* during the previous year.

Philosophy, a first systematic perspective of the philosopher, from which the extract above is taken. In 1965, Takeuchi published *Sartre and Marxism*.[8] As he clearly stated, Sartrean philosophy is "a weapon" for him with which he wants to fight against the "Japanese reality". This practical approach to the philosopher, which is not detrimental to the scientific quality of Takeuchi's works, is indeed characteristic. In this way, the direct reference to Sartre gradually decreases in favor of Takeuchi's own interests regarding diverse topics of his time: student movement, Maoism, state violence and counter-violence, culture, and revolution during the late capitalist era, and last but not least, the *Tenno* system (Japanese emperor). Yet one fundamental attitude remains with Takeuchi: think *with* Sartre and *against* Japanese reality. What kind of reality is this?

Returning from a stay in Japan during 1936–1941, Karl Löwith exposed what we can still call 'the problem of Japan' today (see Washida 2014). In his "Postface to the Japanese Reader", Löwith criticizes the absence of a critical mind in Japanese philosophers and their failure to establish a clear distinction between the Self and the Other in the first place. According to Löwith, on the contrary, they enter a text of a European philosopher without noticing "*in primis* the incongruity of the philosopher's concepts in contrast with their own concepts". That is to say that they easily absorb a text from another culture as if there were no distance between the Self and the Other. In other words, Löwith accuses Japan of scorning the ipseity of the Self and the alterity of the Other. This double relationship to the Self and the Other seems to match well the Japanese reality that Takeuchi talks of.

This representation comes on top of the more general one of Japan itself. The doxa commonly represents Japan as a country without alterity, homogeneous, and which correspondingly does not admit individuality. This is not the place to analyze in detail this image, which would require comprehensive considerations of Japan's history and its representations. Rather, we want to limit ourselves here to some underpinning factors: the archipelago's remoteness, surrounded by the sea on all sides, enables the

---

[8] He also translated Sartre's philosophical writings such as *La transcendance de l'ego*, *Esquisse d'une théorie des émotions* and *La Critique de la raison dialectique*, and co-edited, with Michihiko Suzuki (to be presented in the next chapter) in 1966, the oeuvre entitled *The Totality of Sartre* which reproduced important articles written by various Japanese authors.

nation's relative homogeneity; following the country's modernization the *Tenno* system started to encompass the whole nation as its 'children'; the Japanese language is thought to have a uniqueness that inspires many beliefs about Japan's favorable status. This holistic image of Japan, though simplistic and often challenged, still weighs on intellectuals who, after the war, saw the deep roots of the disaster. For Takeuchi, who shares with them this question of a vague Japanese intersubjectivity, this representation is even more important as he looks at it from a philosophical point of view. Making use of Sartrean vocabulary, we say that the Japanese spiritual climate appears to him as "slimy", the ultimate area of the "anti-value". Subsequently, Takeuchi asks the essential question: how, in this Japanese reality that obscures all thoughts, human relationships, and daily behaviors, can we create the non-obscure thought?

With this perspective, Takeuchi insists on the radicalism of Sartrean thought from the beginning of his *Introduction*. Utterly convinced that "nowadays, real philosophical reflection cannot exist in academia", he recommends that the reader, who is supposed to "scorn and hate 'phenomenology' and 'philosophy of existence' as taught by university philosophers" "learn radicalism in philosophical reflection, and in this way, strive to fundamentally get rid of the obscure Japanese reality where collusion is dominant" (Takeuchi 1966, III–IV, V). What is the goal of this criticism of university philosophers? Thinking of the Kyoto School makes sense, since its studies of phenomenology and the philosophy of existence (Nietzsche and Heidegger, among others) were highly influential after the war. Therefore, we can make the following hypothesis: at the beginning of Takeuchi's Sartrean studies and fight against Japanese reality, there was also a struggle with the Kyoto School. Let us look into this.

At first sight, the Kyoto School's philosophical contribution is undisputed: it aimed to build an authentic Japanese philosophy that, influenced by Buddhism and Zen in particular, dialogued and/or competed with Western philosophy. In this sense, this school seemed not to be concerned about Löwith's criticism that targeted philosophers who absorbed Western philosophy without a critical mind. However, things got more complicated when, due to their intellectual fame, Kyoto School members got involved in building the imperialistic ideology during the Pacific war. Some participated in the roundtable called 'Overcoming

290 N. Kobayashi and H. Seki

Modernity' or 'The World-Historical Standpoint and Japan', which was retrospectively considered proof of the Kyoto School's political involvement (see for this subject *Rude Awakenings* 1995). Despite the philosophers' reluctance and intention to lead the military authority in a moderate direction, the nationalist arrogance that the titles of these roundtable seem to inspire was in fact proof for Löwith of a lack of critical mind. And this collaboration jeopardized the assessment of the Kyoto School's philosophy. Some pretended that their philosophical principle was intrinsically bound to a form of nationalism, imperialism, or even fascism (see for instance Van Bragt 1995). This question of the relationship between philosophy and politics provides topics for discussion still today. But especially after the war, when there were vivid memories of the purge of Kyoto School members from public administration, taking stock of their political responsibility was an urgent task. For Takeuchi, knowing that their philosophy was intrinsically bound to collaboration:

> In our country as well, in olden days, there were ultraconservative thoughts that, through excess of ontological hermeneutics, have absolutized the established order such as family, state, and nation as an ontological system. If it is obvious at an empirical stage that we live with the other and create the community with him, this does not mean, without misunderstanding phenomenological ontology, that the sense of the other's existence is "being-with". (Takeuchi 1966, p. 107)

Tetsuro Watsuji (1889–1960), an associate of the Kyoto School, has to be mentioned in this context.[9] Famous worldwide for his cultural studies on Japan, he tried notably in *Fūdo*, translated into English as *Climate and Culture*, to establish a typology of human beings according to the climatic conditions of the regions where they live, highlighting spatial rather than temporal determinations of *Dasein*, in opposition to Heidegger. This attempt reached its acme in his another book *Ethics* (1942), in which he tries to explain that humanity is ontologically made

---

[9] See the article "The Kyoto School" published in *Stanford Encyclopaedia of Philosophy*. Some refuse, however, to consider Watsuji in this School. In the *Encyclopaedia of Thinking and Philosophy* the article on The Kyoto School explains that Watsuji "is located at the periphery of this school" (Nakaoka 1998).

of intersubjective forms represented by family, nation, and state.[10] This book is controversial: under the aegis of the imperial regime, it can be considered an *ontological justification* of the Japanese Empire.[11] Tadashi Karube, an expert on Watsuji's political philosophy, confirms that "Watsuji's book that promoted the idea that the 'individual's return to the ultimate totality would be achieved by devotion to the State' was read as a justification of the mobilization for the war" (Karube 2010, p. 222).

Of course, Watsuji's thought cannot be likened to fanatical fascism. He often criticized war events and the government. Nevertheless, his philosophy comprised the idea that the community, which suspends the distinction between the Self and the Other, is superior to the individual. Is this philosophy intertwined with ultra-nationalism? Let us refer to the 'Heidegger affair' because it raises a similar question. European intellectual circles, especially in France, wonder whether Heidegger's collaboration with the Nazi regime was an accident.[12] For instance, Philippe Lacoue-Labarthe writes: "My starting hypothesis is that National Socialism is not an absurd or unconceivable phenomenon but is embedded in a rigorous fashion within the 'spiritual' German history. Only a historical and philosophical interpretation can provide access to the essence of National Socialism i.e. what makes it different from other similar phenomena in the first half of the century [...] and makes it stand out as an exception" (see Lacoue-Labarthe 2002, p. 159, *Epilogue: The Spirit of National Socialism and Its Fate*). The same is valid for the Kyoto School: Japanese ultra-nationalism is not an absurd or unconceivable phenomenon,

---

[10] See, for example, "the fusion of two [*the Nation* as the spiritual community and *the personality* as part of the nation] enables us to achieve, at the finitude of human being, the greater fusion of the two moments, the personal one and the collective one. The personality as individual comes back, through wiping any egotism away, to the totality of the nation with the holy" (Watsuji 1942, p. 452). "The individual's return to the ultimate totality can be achieved thanks to its devotion to the State. [...] Man can experience real human being which is removing egotism through courage and living in the totality" (Watsuji 1942, p. 505). "To have faithful subjects, we must build all the paths of human relationships from family to the State, through regional or cultural communities. [...] The Emperor wishes that all his subjects walk the human relationship path so they can answer to his holy heart and fully express their fidelity" (Watsuji 1942, pp. 506–507).

[11] Watsuji's thought goes beyond this political conception of course, which is imposed by time constraints. For a moderate conception, see Karube (2010).

[12] Number 14 of *Les Temps modernes* (January 1946) revealed the Heidegger affair for the first time in France. An anonymous op-ed says "it is possible to look at Heidegger's existentialism *for what* could promote accepting Nazism" (N.N. 1946). However, the author, who is said to be Sartre, did not go further.

but is embedded in the spiritual history of Japan including Japanese philosophers (see also Maruyama 1961). For Takeuchi, the question is whether an ontological conception such as "being-with" (*Mitsein*) justifies the Japanese reality and does not absolutize "the established order such as family, state and nation as an ontological system". In this point Sartre's philosophy became a "weapon" for him.[13]

In fact, Sartre's philosophy enables *encountering the Other*. Despite the importance given—qualitatively and quantitatively—to the description of concrete relations with Others, Sartre says in *Being and Nothingness* that "being-for-others is not an ontological structure of the for-itself" (Sartre 2010, p. 322). This means that the presence of the Other cannot be deduced from the ontological analysis of the for-itself, which is the first subject of his book. Yet this does not mean that the status of the Other is secondary to the status of the for-itself, but simply that the existence of the former cannot be reduced to the existence of the latter. The main fact is therefore that "we *encounter* the other; we do not constitute it" (Sartre 2010, p. 289). Correlatively, the first meaning of "being-for-others" is *conflictual encounter*.

This statement goes against the ontology of Heidegger and Watsuji. In the same way as with Heidegger, where *Mitsein* remains "a simple affirmation without foundation" (Sartre 2010, p. 286), with Watsuji, empirically obvious existences such as family, nation, and state enter into the ontological category by simple affirmation. These philosophers, even if they affirm the concrete existence of Others, finally eliminate it and do not enable encountering the Other's contingency. If Takeuchi appreciates Sartre's philosophy, it is because it succeeds in presenting this true nature of the Other:

> The Other's existence, how obvious it is, is an absolute and contingent event which has to be seen as such. No theory, no principle can reduce "the scandal of the plurality of consciences". (…) *The genuine meaning of the human relationship truly consists in "the encounter"*. (Takeuchi 1966, pp. 123–124)

---

[13] We observe that at the beginning Takeuchi was not highly critical of Watsuji. On the contrary, the young Takeuchi was close to Watsuji's thought. This aspect was highlighted by Nariaki Kobayashi, "'L'après-guerre' of Yoshirō Takeuchi" at the 39th symposium of the Japanese Sartrean studies association, on 15 July 2017. In that sense, Takeuchi's criticism of Watsuji and the Kyoto School is *auto-critique*.

It is the act of purifying reflection that, without bad faith, enables "encountering" the Other with authenticity and becoming aware of the meaning of the Other as ontology points out. The first step of existentialist ethics is therefore to acknowledge the Other's existence as a free being that is not mine (Takeuchi 1966, pp. 261–262).

Thus, according to Takeuchi, Sartre's philosophy can be used as a critical perspective of Japanese reality. This is the reasoning behind his statement that we quoted in the introduction: "For the Japanese intelligentsia to which we belong, there is only one unique and authentic place to directly receive Sartre's thought. This place is the Japanese reality, where we should use Sartrean thought as a weapon to fight against many foolish ideas". We can describe this attitude of Takeuchi as a 'post-war' thought because it was created from a deep reflection on philosophy's future after World War II. It enabled us, among other things, to discover the ontological meaning of the Other, which had previously eluded the other principal branches of Japanese philosophy.[14]

Michihiko Suzuki and the Zainichi, People Transformed into the Other

The philosophy of Others that we have in the precedent section naturally goes well beyond the academic framework and ventures into the society where we meet real Others. In the case of Japan, then, who is depicted as the Other? Without going into details of Japan's history, one can easily confirm that in Japan, throughout the decades of imperialism and war, the Others par excellence were considered the Koreans or, as we will call them hereafter, the *Zainichi*.[15]

---

[14] It is understood that the philosophy of alterity has not always been absent from Japanese philosophy. We can think of Shūzō Kuki, a Kyoto School member. He developed the unique philosophy of contingency in *Problem of the Contingency* (1935), in which he insisted on the contingent meaning of the Other's existence. This philosopher influenced Takeuchi's early works, as well as his comment on Nietzsche and his reception of Sartre, so it would be necessary to moderate comments on Takeuchi's relationship with the Kyoto School. This critical relationship is also a critical renewal. There is the need to prepare another article on the global influence of Kuki on the reception of Sartre in Japan.

[15] Zainichi (the term (在日) literally means "to stay in Japan") are the descendants of Koreans who came to Japan especially after Japan's 1910 colonization of Korea. Koreans were since then

If, as we have seen previously, the problem of the Other gained an actuality in post-war Japan, it could not be understood without this concrete relationship with the Zainichi. By focusing on the case of Michihiko Suzuki among the Sartreans, we intend to emphasize the role that Sartre's thought played in the encounter between Japanese and Zainichi.

Michihiko Suzuki was born in 1929 in Tokyo. His father was one of Japan's leading researchers of French literature, whose method can be described as positivism. Despite his ambiguous feelings for his father,[16] Michihiko himself became a researcher in the same field. Against the family, the society, and the nation he belonged to, he remained quite rebellious, so much so that it led him gradually to a subject and method quite different from those of his father. The distance particularly intensified when in 1954 he went to study in France where, several months later, he saw the outbreak of the Algerian War and its violent struggle against colonialism. Then he discovered the intellectuals—Franz Fanon, Francis Jeanson, and, of course, Jean-Paul Sartre—who were actively engaged in this fight. While promulgating their political engagement for the Japanese public, Suzuki in 1963 published his first book, *The Literature of Sartre*. Yet he was not content to introduce and translate rebellious European intellectuals; by mastering the issue of colonialism, he began to step into Japan's social problems, especially those surrounding the Zainichi.

Suzuki's commitment to the situation of the Zainichi is well known through his acts and articles on two Zainichi criminal cases, namely the Komatsugawa case in 1958 and the Kim Hiro case in 1968. We will focus here on the first case (to the second we will proceed shortly before the conclusion) with the help of a text Suzuki published first in 1966, "Jean Genet in Japan, or a people transformed into the Other". We consider it very important in the history of Sartrean studies because, on the one hand, it applies Sartrean thought to the concrete situation of Japan and,

---

considered as subjects of the Empire of Japan, which introduced many assimilation policies (the adoption of Japanese names, teaching of the Japanese language, etc.). However, many Koreans who came to Japan, often unwillingly, faced various forms of discrimination and in many cases, like that of the massacre during the Great Kantō earthquake in 1923, suffered from ferocious atrocities. They were considered as Others inside Japan, where ethnocentric ideology had a great influence.

[16] Regarding these ambiguous feelings, see Michihiko's 'existential' biography about his father Shintarō Suzuki (Suzuki 2014).

on the other hand, it is a reflection on colonialism which, starting from the analysis of a criminal case, questions the subjectivity of Japanese people in the face of the criminal's subjectivity.

First, let us summarize the Komatsugawa case.[17] On 1 September 1958, an 18-year-old man was arrested for raping and murdering two women. Born in Japan as a Korean descendant, the name of this young Zainichi was Shizuo Kaneko, while his Korean name was Ri Chin-u.[18] During the day, he was a factory worker and at night he studied at school. Before being arrested, he repeatedly called a newspaper company and a police station. Without revealing his name, he boasted about his crimes. In doing this, he seemed to be amusing himself. This caused a great scandal in Japanese society. When the trial started, which attracted strong attention from the public, several facts were controversial, including whether the rape even took place. In addition, the lawyer pleaded extenuating circumstances, such as a difficult family environment, poverty, and stigmatization because of his ethnic origin. He also asked the judges to consider that the suspect was not of sound mind during the crime. Yet, despite all these efforts, in February 1959, Ri Chin-u was sentenced to death. Successive appeals were rejected, and the execution—implemented quicker than normal—took place on 16 November 1962.[19]

How did Japanese society react to this case? On the one hand, the media immediately treated it as a sensational affair. In the newspapers, for example, the origin of the accused was superabundantly specified, as well as the composition of his family and his daily habits, as if his nationality was directly related to his criminality. To put it simply, this minor was treated as a "monster".[20]

---

[17] For details of the case, see the annex to *Crime, Death and Love* [*Tsumi to shi to ai to*], new edition by Park Soonam (Park 1984, pp. 249–270).

[18] For the Korean name, the pronunciations differ slightly in Japanese (Ri Chin-u) and proper Korean (Yi Chin'u). We adopt the Japanese pronunciation for Ri Chin-u and Kim Hiro (Kwon Hyi-ro), as was customary. For other Korean authors cited hereafter, we adopt the Korean pronunciation.

[19] Some have argued for the innocence of Ri Chin-u because of the dubious procedures used by the police and the courts. On this point, see the following books: Tsukiyama (1982), Ogasawara (1987), Nozaki (1994).

[20] See on this point the remark by Suh Kyung-Sik: "It is easy to imagine that the ethnic discrimination shared on average by the majority of Japanese at the time was inflicted not only on the police authorities, but also in the media world as well as in a good number of readers. In other words, the

On the other hand, artists and intellectuals did not fail to show a keen interest in this matter. Some published in September 1960 "a petition for the salvation of the young Ri", where they emphasized the responsibility of the Japanese people for the ethnic discrimination against the Zainichi and asked that attenuating circumstances be taken into consideration. But what really caught the artists' attention was the 'imaginary' character of this affair. Ri Chin-u was a literate man; he had stolen foreign literature books before the affair; he even wrote, between the two crimes, a short story entitled *A Bad Guy* [*Warui Yatsu*], where the young protagonist, after killing a man who persecuted him, explains and justifies the reason for his murder; finally, in prison he exchanged letters with a woman, Park Soonam, whom he intimately called his "sister". The correspondence, which continued until the day before his execution, was soon published under the title *Crime, Death and Love*, and played an important role in spreading Ri Chin-u's thinking to the wide public: it records his everyday mental states, the ambiguous and unspeakable affection for his correspondent, his reflections on his life, crimes, death, and the gradual awareness of his ethnicity. To all this should be added the fact that in court as well as in prison, Ri Chin-u remembered his crimes as something far removed from reality, as if they had been committed in a dream:

> The problem that has always remained in my mind was that I perceived what I did like in a dream of mine. When you do something and this thing, once has passed by, is perceived as something "like a dream", you would be embarrassed if someone asked you to have a real feeling about what happened. (Park 1984, p. 266)

Ri Chin-u, the imaginary man—this is the character that inspired various works of art following the affair.[21] Given all of the above, we now pay

---

way in which Japanese society looked at this affair was from the beginning strongly tainted by ethnic discrimination" (Suh 2010, p. 35).

[21] Of these works, two are particularly worth mentioning because they are works by two famous Sartreans. One is a film by Nagisa Ōshima, entitled *Death by Hanging* [Kōshikē] (1968). It is undoubtedly the best known among the works inspired by the case. The other is entitled *Cry* [Sakebigoe] (1963), a novel published by Kenzaburō Ōe, a future Nobel laureate. Regarding Sartre's influence on Nagisa Ōshima, see Müller (2009).

particular attention to Michihiko Suzuki's article "Jean Genet in Japan", where the author emphasized better than anyone else the ethnic responsibility of the Japanese people for the case.[22] Indeed, he considered this case as a "knife turned towards the Japanese society which deeply discriminated against him [Ri Chin-u]" (Suzuki 1969, p. 387).

It should first be noted that, although Suzuki was immediately aware of the case—he even signed the petition to spare the criminal's life—he did not grasp "the philosophical sense of the case" (Suzuki 1969, p. 370) until the publication of Ri's posthumous correspondence in 1963. In other words, his involvement was achieved only through the writing that the condemned criminal had left in prison and, in this sense, was totally different from his engagement in the Kim Hiro case, where, as will be discussed later, Suzuki faced the criminal in person. Anyway, having been "utterly defeated for days by this work" (Suzuki 1969, p. 372), he realized that this case was "one of the most upsetting philosophical affairs of post-War Japan". Since then, he devoted some years to understanding Ri Chin-u in his profound subjectivity with the help of the philosophical method Sartre had featured in *Saint Genet*, namely that of 'comprehension'. Suzuki proceeds to explicate the life of Ri Chin-u by dividing it into three moments: the inclination toward the imaginary world, the passage from the imaginary to the real, and finally, the deep reflection, conducted in prison, on the meaning of life.

Let us take a look at each of these moments in detail. In the first step, *the inclination toward the imaginary world*, Suzuki starts describing the general situation of the Zainichi. He notes that after colonization, massacre, and forced labor which were imposed on them during the colonization, the word "Korean" became in the Japanese language "the object that represents everything despicable, [...] even the symbol of Evil" (Suzuki 1969, p. 374). In other words, Japanese people discriminate Koreans as an unassimilable Other inside their territory. Since this discrimination is not a subjective but a structural one, Japanese people, regardless of their will, are inevitably involved in ethnic violence.

---

[22] This article, first published in 1966 under the title "The Choice of Evil" in the bulletin of his university seminar, was reprinted in February 1967 in the journal *New Japanese Literature* [Shin Nihon Bungaku] and later in his book *The Thoughts of Engagement* (Suzuki 1969, pp. 370–388). The quotations are from the last edition.

What made the situation of Ri Chin-u even more complicated was that he could only speak Japanese. This meant that, in addition to the fact that he had a Japanese name, he could only speak in a language which was not (ethnically) his own and which hence, in his eyes, embodied alienating values. In this sense, Ri Chin-u, writes Suzuki, is "altered not only in relation to others but also in the very depths of his subjective truth" (Suzuki 1969, p. 374). Faced with such an intolerable situation where he could not incarnate any positive value, he was tempted to take refuge in Evil, another name for the imaginary world.

In this world of imagination, he could enjoy freedom and almightiness, but such an attraction to the imaginary is not a mere escape but flows back to the former world with its *passage from the imaginary to the real*. By a strange "whirligig" (*tourniquet* in Sartrean terms) of Good and Evil, of Being and Non-Being, his choice of Self as Evil was gradually transformed into the behavior adopted in the real world. Then Suzuki writes: "Ri Chin-u rather thought of reversing real values by imagination. (…) The freedom of the imagination generated the crimes, it turned Ri Chin-u into a *real* strong man" (Suzuki 1969, pp. 376–378).

Thus, the crimes committed by Ri Chin-u were interpreted by Suzuki as the realization of his imagination where he had formerly enjoyed his almightiness. However, it is not Suzuki's intention to consider it a triumphant revenge by the discriminated against the discriminator. On the contrary, this realization is nothing more than a collapse of the sovereignty of the imaginary, even a sign of its failure, because the imaginary almightiness loses its power once it has entered the real world. The result, as we know, is that Ri was arrested and sentenced to death.

Then comes the ultimate moment when *he reflects in prison on the meaning of life*. This is the moment when, "dispossessed of his future, this man, condemned to death, yet builds himself as a solid existent" (Suzuki 1969, p. 380).

How did Ri Chin-u give meaning to his life? There is a tendency to believe that in prison he gradually became aware of his Korean ethnicity, which would in some sense give an account of the pain he had suffered. This is certainly the interpretation of Park Soonam, a correspondent and activist of ethnic nationalism, who had always had the intention to initiate Ri Chin-u into a new life where his ethnicity would play a more important role. Suzuki opposes to this concept his own idea that he had already coined elsewhere, namely that of "negative ethnic nationalism". While Park Soonam saw in the notions of homeland and ethnicity something positive, even goodness itself, Ri Chin-u, when he speaks about them in his replies to Park, cannot see them but through his own nature which, by being evil, contaminates them. Thus, even if Ri Chin-u could finally find solidarity with his people, it would only be at the end of his search for negativity in himself. In other words, he could reach the universal only by pursuing the logic of singularity and its responsibility. Only this could give a sufficient meaning to his life.

After summarizing Ri Chin-u's life, Suzuki compares it with that of Jean Genet. To what extent is this comparison relevant? Admittedly, the inclination to the imaginary world and evil, as described by Suzuki, reminds us of the case of Genet. Just as Genet is a monster in European society, Ri Chin-u is considered a monster by the Japanese society. However, adds Suzuki, we have to be aware of what separates them. Firstly, according to Sartre's explanation, Jean Genet "ceases to be *a* particular opponent of *a* historical society",[23] that is to say, his solitude becomes the example of everyone in any society as a whole. In the case of Ri Chin-u, however, Suzuki claims that the whole case cannot be understood without making the connection to the Japanese society that discriminated against him. Secondly, what is important to specify is that Genet is a *writer* and Ri Chin-u is a *murderer*. Jean Genet certainly writes about murders, but it is through his writing that he scandalizes his readers with his criminality. If then we consider the real murderer as 'Jean Genet in Japan', is there not a risk of falling into the aestheticization of crime?

We do not believe so, as even if Suzuki finds that "Ri Chin-u is literature itself, which is why it is the subject of the scandal" (Suzuki 1969, p. 387), we should immediately dismiss a misleading interpretation: it is not a question here of praising the triumph of the imaginary or of the crime. On the contrary, Suzuki categorically blames the facts of the crime and points out repeatedly Ri's failure and the limit of the imaginary.

---

[23] Sartre (2011, p. 659). Here the English translation (Sartre 2012, p. 596) makes an error when it writes: "In claiming absolute objectivity, Genet seems to be *a* particular opponent of *a* historical society" while the original is: "En revendiquant l'objectivité absolue, Genet cesse d'être *un* opposant particulier à *une* société historique".

Rather, he claims that "Ri is a starting point, and is *only* a starting point" (Suzuki 1969, p. 388). When Ri Chin-u himself admits and claims full responsibility for his own crimes, all we can do is to make him a point *from where* we ourselves begin to understand how and why 'we', the Japanese people, made a murderer like him, without depriving him of his subjectivity. That is why, as noted above, Suzuki saw this case as "one of the most upsetting philosophical affairs of post-War Japan", insofar as it forces us to radically reflect on our relationship with the Zainichi and, therefore, encourages us to engage actively in the problems related to the history of Japan and its discrimination. We can consider this type of reflection one of the most important considerations related to colonialism in Japan.

That said, we must ask whether the existence of Ri Chin-u has been sufficiently grasped in this reflection. Should we not rather consider that Suzuki, describing Ri Chin-u as the condemned in the imaginary world, has himself created his own imaginary character and this to the detriment of Ri Chin-u himself? In this sense, the presence of the Other totally remains problematic. The difficulty becomes clear when Suzuki, in his memoirs, characterizes his methods as sympathetic:

> For me, sympathy is first of all necessary to make me interested in a thing. It seemed to me that it would allow me at the same time to penetrate the existence of others. Even if an oppressive relationship separates us from each other, cannot we still cross that border? Or, to put it another way, is transborder not possible? Is it not a problem of imagination? These were my problems at that time. (Suzuki 2007, p. 69)

But both sympathy and imagination face serious difficulties: The Other, in exceeding our limit of sympathy, goes beyond what we imagine about him or her. Suzuki himself admits that communication based on sympathy can be an illusion, and we will see the conflict appear with the Kim Hiro affair, which also scandalized Japanese society.

Dating from 20 February 1968, the criminal case by Kim Hiro, who belonged, like Ri Chin-u, to the second generation of Zainichi, proceeded as follows. Kim Hiro, after killing two yakuza, locked himself in a hotel with 18 citizens as hostages. Through the media that interviewed him during the affair, Kim Hiro accused Japan of the discrimination he had suffered throughout his life—for this fact he would become later a 'national hero' in South Korea. As to the introduction to this case, in which Suzuki was involved from the beginning, we refer to the vivid article written by Suzuki himself and published at the request of Sartre and Beauvoir in the October 1968 issue of *Les Temps modernes* (Suzuki 1968; see also the interview Suzuki and Sawada 2011, p. 198).

This case was a real challenge for Suzuki. For him, whose engagement in the Ri Chin-u case was achieved only through writing, the Kim Hiro affair became the first opportunity to meet a real criminal Zainichi. The Other, once the fruit of his imagination, became suddenly the real existent.[24] But it goes without saying that these two Zainichi are different beings: unlike Ri Chin-u, who assumed full responsibility for his crimes, Kim Hiro shifted all the bad he had suffered onto Japan, thus refusing any responsibility he could have assumed for himself. It is apparent that for Suzuki the ideal posture was that of Ri Chin-u, while the figure of Kim Hiro, who might "spoil his own subjectivity", was almost unacceptable to him. In addition to the personality of Kim Hiro, which was far from being morally impeccable, this was the reason why his meeting with Kim Hiro in a prison room did not go well and finished in the termination of the talks. In this sense, the attitude of Suzuki and his sympathy-based method were put to the test by the real existence of the Other.

However, this does not mean that Suzuki's attitude should be evaluated as a self-oriented one. First of all, the sympathy-based method that Suzuki employs is not one ignoring otherness, but one that always tries to open itself up to the encounter with the Other.[25] In the Komatsugawa

---

[24] "My first impression is that the problem I had been thinking about for a long time in the Komatsugawa case really happened. However, in the Komatsugawa case, I put myself in a safe place when I was looking for Ri Chin-u's deep interiority, because he was already dead. But this Korean [Kim Hiro] is a living being and, according to the press, he openly declared that he would commit suicide soon. I feel troubled by the fact that things as I thought them were realized in this way" (Suzuki 2007, p. 152).

[25] In this sense, we couldn't agree with the criticism of Cho Kyung-hee, even if it should be taken into serious consideration: "We dare to say, without fear of misunderstanding, that the documents in which Ri Chin-u recorded his own universalistic thinking are suitable for Japanese writers and thinkers, including Suzuki, to draw their own sympathy and sentimentalism. (…) It is not only the problem of Suzuki. What matters here is the weakness of the intellectual base of thinking in Japan, which is incapable of assuming the legacy of the epoque of colonialism which deeply determined

case, Suzuki's intervention was limited to a one-way relationship because of the death of his interlocutor, but in the subsequent Kim Hiro case when he faced the real existence of the Other, despite his strained relationship with Kim and the solitude he suffered in Japanese society, Suzuki's anti-racist stance was not weakened; on the contrary, he continued being involved in the case for eight and a half years until the final verdict was brought in. This proves that his commitment to the Zainichi problem was total, to say the least. To end, we would like to share the lesson Suzuki drew from his long experience:

> Following this [difficult relationship with Kim Hiro], I learned that we cannot sufficiently assume our ethnic responsibility with the framework of aggressor/victim, oppressor/oppressed, discriminator/discriminated, but that we must, at the same time, make efforts to face the subjectivity of others. [...] All we can do is probably aiming, after accumulating such risky efforts, for the point where a reciprocal relationship becomes possible which goes beyond "ethnic responsibility". (Suzuki 2007)

Conclusion

At the end of this chapter, we cannot help but being surprised at the diversity of the activities of Takeuchi and Suzuki, the first two Sartreans in Japan. Although philosophy is Takeuchi's and literature Suzuki's principal domain, they have far exceeded the limits imposed by their disciplines. We can see here a fundamental characteristic they learned from Sartre—the passion for totalizing thought. Knowledge is not limited to a given field, but it must be integrated into society as a whole. It is certain that this was their firm conviction.

Sartre was their contemporary. They faced the same questions as the French philosopher did. This type of reception of European thought is noteworthy insofar as the researchers are actively involved in this reception. The reception of Sartre's thought exposed Takeuchi and Suzuki to the 'experience of the Other' in a double sense of the term. It was, on one

---

the way of being of Zainichi and tries instead of it to relativize it as a property of man in general in order to feel 'human' sympathy towards the Zainichi". See Cho (2017, pp. 247–248).

hand, the reception of *another* culture that is European, on the other hand, both experienced the problem of *the Other* in the intellectual environment of Japan.

Such a reception was, of course, the fruit of their long and critical reading of Sartre, for reception and criticism are finally one and the same. For our part, it goes without saying that we should also read their writings critically, considering them not as assimilable matter but as the Other. Such a reading, which is at the same time critical and sympathetic, is, as we believe has been demonstrated in this chapter, nothing but an 'encounter'.

References

Asabuki, Tomiko. 1996. *Vingt-huit jours au Japon avec Jean-Paul Sartre et Simone de Beauvoir (18 septembre—16 octobre 1966)*. Translated by Claude Peronny and Tanaka Chiharu; preface by Richard Chambon. Paris: Langues et Mondes-L'Asiathèque.

Cho, Kyung-hee. 2017. Composition of Appropriations of the 'Korean Condemned Criminal'—The Case of Komatsugawa and Japan/"Korean" [Chōsenjin shikeishū wo meguru sen-yū no kōzu—komatsugawa jiken to nihon/chōsen]. In *The Birth of "Post-war". Postwar Japan and the "Korean Border"* ["Sengo" no tanjō. Sengo nihon to chōsen no kyōkai], ed. Kwon Heok-tae and Cha Seung Ki, trans. from Korean into Japanese by Noriko Nakano and Toshio Nakano, 233–265. Tokyo: Shinsensha.

Heidegger, Martin. 1976. *Acheminement vers la parole* (Unterwegs zur Sprache). Translated by Jean Beaufret, Wolfgang Brokmeier, and François Fédier. Paris: Gallimard.

Heisig, James W., and John C. Maraldo, eds. 1995. *Rude Awakenings. Zen, the Kyoto School, & the Question of Nationalism*. Honolulu: University of Hawai'i Press.

Ishii, Motoko. 2006. A Reflection on Jean-Paul Sartre's Reception in Japan Based on Translation and Publication Analysis [Nihon ni okeru J.-P. Sarutoru no juyō ni tsuiteno ichi kōsatsu: Hon-yaku, Syuppanshi no shiten kara]. *Bulletin of Kyoto University Education Department* [Kyōto daigaku daigakuin kyōikugaku kenkyūka kiyō] 52: 93–107.

Karube, Tadashi. 2010. *The Kingdom of Light. Tetsuro Watsuji* [Hikari no ryōgoku. Watsuji Tetsuro]. Tokyo: Iwanami Shoten.

Lacoue-Labarthe, Philippe. 2002. *Heidegger. La Politique du poème.* Paris: Galilée.

Light, Stephen. 1987. *Shūzō Kuki and Jean-Paul Sartre: Influence and Counter-influence in the Early History of Existential Phenomenology.* Carbondale and Edwardsville: Southern Illinois University Press.

Maruyama, Masao. 1961. *The Thought of Japan* [Nihon no shisō]. Tokyo: Iwanami Shoten.

Masuda, Yasuhiko. 2007. How was Sartre Accepted in Japan? Study on a First Period [Sarutoru ha Nihon de donoyōni juyō saretaka: Sono reimeiki wo chūshin toshite]. *Jimbun* 6: 81–101.

Müller, Simone. 2008. Faszination eines universalistischen Denkers: Gedanken zu Jean-Paul Sartres Wertschätzung in Japan. In *Wege der Japanologie*, ed. Harald Meyer, 377–390. Münster: Lit Verlag.

———. 2009. Existentialist Impact on the Writing and Movies of Ōshima Nagisa. In *Sartre's Second Century*, ed. Benedict O'Donohoe and Roy Elveton, 191–201. Cambridge: Cambridge Scholar Press.

N.N. (Jean-Paul Sartre?). 1946. Deux documents sur Heidegger. *Les Temps Modernes* 4: 713.

Nakaoka, Narifumi. 1998. The Kyoto School. In *Encyclopaedia of Thinking and Philosophy* [Tetsugaku shisō jiten], 347. Tokyo: Iwanami Shoten.

Nozaki, Rokusuke. 1994. *Notebook for Ri Chin-u. A Zainichi Sentenced to Death* [Ri chin u nōto. Shikei ni sareta zainichi chōsenjin]. Tokyo: San-ichi Shobo.

Ogasawara, Kazuhiko. 1987. *Riddle of Ri Chin-u. Why Did He Admit Crimes?* [Ri chin u no nazo. Naze hankō wo mitometa noka]. Tokyo: San-ichi Shobo.

Park, Soonam. 1984 [1963]. *Crime, Death and Love* [Tsumi to shi to ai to]. New ed. Tokyo: San-ichi Shinsho.

Sartre, Jean-Paul. 2010. *L'Être et le Néant. Essai d'Ontologie Phénoménologique.* Paris: Gallimard.

———. 2011. *Saint Genet, Comédien et Martyr.* Paris: Gallimard.

———. 2012. *Saint Genet, Actor and Martyr.* Translated by Bernard Frechtman. Minneapolis: University of Minnesota Press.

Sawada, Nao. 2004. L'existentialisme au Japon: Réception, Impact et Influence. In *La Modernité Française dans l'Asie Littéraire (Chine, Corée, Japon)*, ed. Haruhisa Katō, 247–258. Paris: Presses universitaires de France.

———. 2013. Japon. In *Dictionnaire Sartre*, ed. François Noudelmann and Gilles Philippe, 259. Paris: Honoré Champion.

Suh, Kyung-Sik. 2010. The Shadow of a Monster—The Komatsugawa Affair and the Violence of Representations [Kaibutsu no kage—Komatsugawa jiken to hyōshō no bōryoku]. In *The Violence of Colonialism: From "The Prison of Words"* [Hyōron shū. Shokuminchishugi no bōryoku. "Kotobano ori" kara], 22–62. Tokyo: Koubunken.

Suzuki, Michihiko. 1968. L'affaire Kim Hiro. *Les Temps Modernes*, 722–737.

———. 1969. Jean Genet in Japan, or a People Transformed Into the Other [Nihon no june, mataha tashaka shita minzoku]. In *The Thoughts of Engagement* [Angājuman no Shisō], 370–388. Tokyo: Shobun-sha.

———. 2007. *The Time of the Transborder* [Ekkyō no Toki]. Tokyo: Shueisha.

Suzuki, Masamichi. 2011. How to Welcome an Intellectual Superstar: Sartre and the Japanese Press in 1966. In *Jean-Paul Sartre: Mind and Body, Word and Deed*, ed. Jean-Pierre Boulé and Benedict O'Donohoe, 167–181. Cambridge: Cambridge Scholars Publishing.

Suzuki, Michihiko. 2014. *Birth of the Man of French Letters. Journey to Mallarmé* [Furansu bungakusha no tanjō. Mararume heno tabi]. Tokyo: Chikuma Shobo.

Suzuki, Michihiko, and Nao Sawada. 2011. An Intellectual Star Remembered: Sartre's 1966 Visit to Japan. In *Jean-Paul Sartre: Mind and Body, Word and Deed*, ed. Jean-Pierre Boulé and Benedict O'Donohoe, 183–201. Cambridge: Cambridge Scholars Publishing.

Takeuchi, Yoshirō. 1966 [1st ed., 1956]. *Introduction to Sartre's Philosophy* [Sarutoru Tetsugaku Josetsu]. Tokyo: Morita Shoten.

Tsukiyama, Toshiaki. 1982. *Innocent! Ri Chin-u* [Muzai! Ri Chin-u]. Tokyo: San-ichi Shobo.

Van Bragt, Jan. 1995. Kyoto Philosophy—Intrinsically Nationalistic? In *Rude Awakenings. Zen, the Kyoto School, & the Question of Nationalism*, ed. James W. Heisig and John C. Maraldo, 233–254. Honolulu: University of Hawai'i Press.

Washida, Kiyokazu. 2014. *The Use of Philosophy* [Tetsugaku no tsukai kata]. Tokyo: Iwanami Shoten.

Watsuji, Tetsuro. 1942. *Rinrigaku*. Tokyo: Iwanami Shoten.

17

A Brief History of the Reception of Sartre in Argentina

Alan Patricio Savignano

Introduction

Jean-Paul Sartre's literature, philosophical system, and political opinions reached Argentina very early and were crucial for the intellectual history of the country. By the end of the 1930s, Sartre's short stories and his novel *Nausea* had arrived at the River Plate and the author was immediately lauded by some of the most important members of *Sur* (*South*), a very important Argentinian literary journal founded in 1931. That's when Victoria Ocampo's magazine decided to translate and publish Sartre in Spanish, lured by the excellence of his prose and his antifascist humanism during the post-war years. Around the same time, the publishing house Losada embarked on translating Sartre's books for similar reasons. Throughout the 1940s, in the philosophical academic field, a group of Argentinian professors associated with existentialism reviewed *Being and Nothingness* and judged its philosophical value.

A. P. Savignano (✉)
University of Buenos Aires, Buenos Aires, Argentina

© The Author(s) 2020
A. Betschart, J. Werner (eds.), *Sartre and the International Impact of Existentialism*,
https://doi.org/10.1007/978-3-030-38482-1_17

In the 1950s, Sartre's presence in the Argentinian intelligentsia became ubiquitous. The emerging Argentinian New Left took Sartre as an intellectual beacon. In fact, the denouncer mentality of the magazine *Contorno* (*Contour*) was mostly based on the Sartrean theory of *littérature engagée* (committed literature). The existentialist and humanistic reading of Marxism proposed by Sartre in the late 1950s and early 1960s offered this young generation an interesting alternative to the antiquated and determinist version of the communist orthodoxy, which was unable at that time to explain historical events like Stalinism, the Soviet intervention in Hungary and then in Czechoslovakia, the Cuban Revolution, and the independence struggles in Africa and Asia. On the other hand, in 1961 the preface of Fanon's *The Wretched of the Earth* written by Sartre touched the Argentinian New Left's nonconformist and revolutionary spirit, while also inspiring those who would later join rebel groups in favor of armed struggle.

Between the 1960s and the 1970s, Sartre's influence in Argentina gradually waned. Just like in France and other countries, new schools of thought, especially structuralism, gained momentum and displaced the philosopher of freedom from his hegemonic position in the cultural field. This happened as Sartre's health deteriorated; in 1973 he became completely blind. Meanwhile, Argentina and other Latin American countries entered a dark period of military dictatorships marked by state-sponsored terrorism: political persecution and cultural censorship put a drastic end to the intellectual production in Argentina. These events resulted in the eventual oblivion of Sartre's thought, the consequences of which are still persisting.

In this chapter I intend to briefly reconstruct the history of the reception of Sartre in Argentina as outlined above. I will describe the major milestones of the said process, prioritizing a more extensive than intensive approach. However, there are plenty of references to other more specific works for those who want to examine specific subjects in greater depth. Also, I offer some historical data in order to provide an overview of the historical contexts involved in the reception of Sartre's work. Finally, the attentive reader will notice that the historiographic method implemented here is profoundly indebted to the generational studies founded by Wilhelm Dilthey, José Ortega y Gasset, and Karl Mannheim.

Sur and *Losada*: First Spanish Translations of Sartre's Texts

The magazine *Sur* pioneered the translation of Sartre's writings in the Spanish-speaking world. Founded in 1931 by Victoria Ocampo, *Sur* was the most widespread literary and cultural publication in Argentina from its foundation until the 1960s.[1] Its main aim was to spread the latest and best works in international contemporary literature and to provide visibility to the new Argentinian writers. Among the most prominent members of *Sur* were: José Bianco, Adolfo Bioy Casares, Jorge Luis Borges, Carlos Alberto Erro, Eduardo González Lanuza, Eduardo Mallea, Silvina Ocampo, María Rosa Oliver, Ernesto Sábato, and Guillermo de Torre. The group's identity was characterized by the belief that they belonged to a small intellectual elite, tasked with guarding the cultural world and defending the liberal principles stemming from the national democratic tradition of Mayo and Caseros. During the twentieth century, *Sur* adamantly opposed the advance of totalitarianism in Europe and America. The magazine denounced—without drawing major distinctions— German Nazism, Italian Mussolinism, Spanish Francoism, Soviet Communism, and Argentinian Peronism.

Despite its defense of liberal ideals and the rejection of fascism in all its forms and manifestations, *Sur* proclaimed its apolitical stance countless times.[2] For Ocampo and her team, the art of writing should not involve itself in political quarrels. Thus the Argentinian cultural aristocracy followed Julien Benda's lessons in *The Treason of the Intellectuals* (1927). Moreover, the magazine's apoliticism contrasted paradoxically with its moral evaluation of literary works and their authors according to humanitarian values, as Judith Podlubne demonstrated (Podlubne 2009). For the members of *Sur*, works of fiction had true artistic value only if they reflected the universal spiritual ideals of an integral humanism like Jacques Maritain's style. Therefore, literary works were understood as an expression of the author's moral character, according to a personalist interpretation inspired by Emmanuel Mounier's ideas.

---

[1] On *Sur* and its history, see: King (1986), Villordo (1994), Pasternac (2002).
[2] On the paradoxical apoliticism of *Sur*, see: Donnantuoni Moratto (2015).

These notes regarding the idiosyncrasy of *Sur* are sufficient to explain the magazine's immediate—yet brief and restricted—interest in Sartre. A particular event drew Sartre to the attention of *Sur*'s talent scouts: his literary consecration in France due to the publication of *Nausea* in 1938 by the prestigious publisher Gallimard. This success could not go unnoticed by the Argentinian magazine, which was always eager to import into the country the great promises of world literature. In fact, as Anna Boschetti asserts, *Nausea* was a completely avant-garde novel: it proved the author's mastery of the most modern techniques of French (Louis-Ferdinand Céline, André Gide, André Malraux, Marcel Proust, Paul Valéry) and Anglo-Saxon literature (John Dos Passos, William Faulkner, Ernest Hemingway, James Joyce, Virginia Woolf) (cf. Boschetti 1985). Ocampo (King 1986, p. 84) and de Torre (1948, p. 22) used to say proudly that they recognized Sartre's talent the moment that they read his first *nouvelles*, even before he became a celebrity.

According to Carlos Correas (1994, pp. 105–106), the decision to publish Sartre in *Sur* was prompted mostly by Bianco, the secretary editor from 1938 to 1961.[3] The first text by Sartre published in *Sur* was the short story *The Room*, translated as *El Aposento*, which was split into two parts for the issues 54 (March 1939) and 55 (April 1939). Then the magazine published: *París bajo la ocupación* (*Paris Under the Occupation*) in issue 124 (February 1945); *Sobre un libro de Francis Ponge: 'A favor de las cosas'* (*About the Nature of Things*) in issue 127 (May 1945); *Retrato del antisemita* (*Anti-Semite and Jew*) in issue 138 (April 1946); and *El existencialismo es un humanismo* (*Existentialism Is a Humanism*), split into three issues, 147 (January 1947), 148 (February 1947), and 149 (March 1947). The famous lecture *Existentialism Is a Humanism* would also be published in book form by *Sur* in 1957. Finally, five years later, *Marxismo y existencialismo* (*Search for a Method*) was published in issue 279 (November–December 1962). This was the last text authored by Sartre that would come out in *Sur*.

The reason that Ocampo's magazine decided to publish Sartre's texts during the 1940s was the matching ideological stance—albeit superficial and equivocal—of the Argentinian periodical and the French author at

---

[3] It seems that Bianco was also the translator of the lecture *Existentialism Is a Humanism*, although he hid his authorship under the pseudonym of Victoria Prati de Fernández.

that time. Certainly, the Sartrean defense of individual freedom as the supreme value in his philosophical writings and his participation in the French Resistance were enough to earn the admiration of *Sur*. This positive relationship between the Argentinians and the Parisian came to an end with the latter's decision to support the French Communist Party in 1952. The Argentinian cultural elite could not forgive Sartre for supporting a political party in favor of a totalitarian regime during the Cold War.

However, it is worth mentioning that the estrangement between *Sur* and Sartre was also due to the existence of irreconcilable positions between them from the beginning of the relationship. First, the adamant antihumanism defended by Sartre in *Nausea* was clearly incompatible with the moral ideals of *Sur*. Second, because of her spiritualist aesthetic, Ocampo was very uncomfortable with the vile, low, carnal, and sexual themes of Sartre's existentialist literature. Last but not least, *Contorno* magazine, dominated by a group of the New Left in Argentina, played a crucial role by embracing Sartre's theory of committed literature in order to denounce the hypocrisies of the spotless, apolitical literature proposed by the literary generation behind *Sur*.

Losada, a publishing house in Buenos Aires, would take up the mantle of translating Sartre's *œuvre*. Losada was founded in 1938 by Gonzalo Losada Benítez. He was an immigrant from Madrid who had been managing the branch of Spanish publishing house Espada-Calpe in Buenos Aires since 1928. After Franco's victory in Spanish Civil War, he decided to split with the Iberian company and build his own publishing house in Argentina under his name. One of Losada's major aims was to publish books written by Argentinian and European writers who were censored in Spain by Franco's regime.[4] Among those forbidden by Spanish fascism was Sartre, whose books, it is worth recalling, were added to the *Index librorum prohibitorum* of the Vatican in 1948. Hence, Losada also pioneered the Spanish translation of Sartre's major literary, philosophical, and political works. For instance, among the large number of Sartre's books published by Losada, it is worth noting the canonical translation of *La nausea* (*Nausea*) by Aurora Bernárdez in 1946 and *El ser y la nada* (*Being and Nothingness*) by Juan Valmar in 1966.

---

[4] Regarding the censorship of Sartre's books in Spain during the Francoist dictatorship, see: Behiels (2006).

Existentialism in Argentina: Several Academic Studies About Sartre's Philosophical System

At the same time as Losada and *Sur* published the first Spanish transla-tions of Sartre's texts, a group of philosophers from Argentinian universi-ties carried out a rigorous study of the novel philosophical system in *Being and Nothingness* (1943). They were known as the 'existentialist gen-eration' or the 'generation of 1925' in the history of Argentinian philosophy,[5] whose most prominent members were Carlos Astrada, Alberto Erro, Vicente Fatone, Homero Guglielmini, Ángel Vasallo, Miguel Ángel Virasoro, and Rafael Virasoro. Their intellectual heyday was the period between 1925 and 1950 as a result of the imposition of existentialism in the Argentinian academic philosophy over rival schools of thought, such as positivism and Thomism. The First National Congress of Philosophy, held in Mendoza in 1949, with its plenary section devoted exclusively to existentialism, is regarded as the consecrating moment of Argentina's existentialist current.

The origins of this group date back to the Argentinian university reform of 1918 and to what historian Francisco Romero called the "pro-cess of normalization of Argentinian philosophy" during the 1910s and the 1920s (Romero 1961). Thus, philosophical practice turned into an institutional profession, especially as a result of the reorganization of the university degree in philosophy according to modern reformist values. This period was also marked by an update of philosophical knowledge. In the first decades of the twentieth century, renowned European thinkers such as Ortega y Gasset, Bendetto Croce, Eugenio D'Ors, and Maritain visited Argentina. They introduced into the country the new currents of spiritualism, existentialism, axiology, phenomenology, and historicism. Furthermore, several professors and students went on study trips to Europe, where they acquired first-hand knowledge about the philosophi-cal doctrines in vogue on the Old Continent. Astrada was the best exam-ple of this trend. He made his first trip to Germany in 1927 to complete

---

[5] On the Argentinian existentialist generation, see García Losada (1999), Pró (1973), Correas (1994).

his education at the universities of Cologne, Bonn, and Freiburg with Max Scheler, Edmund Husserl, Martin Heidegger, and Oscar Becker.

Among the members of the Argentinian existentialist generation, Astrada, Fatone, and the Virasoro brothers carried out a critical and scholarly review of Sartre's philosophy. For this group of scholars, Sartre's thinking was very appealing, given that it was a vast and coherent system of ideas in open discussion with the great contemporary exponents of German thought (Hegel, Husserl, and Heidegger). Astrada et al. carried out a meticulous reading of Sartre's two main philosophical works available at that time: the essay *Being and Nothingness* and the transcription of the lecture *Existentialism Is a Humanism*. Broadly speaking, the Argentinian existentialists admired Sartre's efforts in thinking freedom as the human being's own way of being. However, they denounced the subjectivism and relativism that they believed were implied by the main principles of the *Essay on Phenomenological Ontology*.

Miguel Ángel Virasoro (1900–1966) was perhaps the largest contributor to the reception of Sartre's philosophical thought.[6] He published in 1948 the first Spanish translation of *El ser y la nada*, which incidentally was the first translation of *Being and Nothingness* from French into any other language. In a prologue written by him by way of an introduction to the essay, Virasoro did not hide his enthusiasm about Sartre, whom he considered "an exceptional thinker"[7] [un pensador de excepción] and a "new supreme master of existentialism" [nuevo maestro máximo del existencialismo] (Virasoro 1948, p. IV). For his part, his brother Rafael Virasoro (1906–1984), lauded Sartre's existentialism for "having exhausted the idea of human freedom" [haber llevado a sus últimas consecuencias la idea de la libertad humana] and having built "a passionate defense of freedom" [una apasionada defensa de la libertad] (Virasoro 1957, p. 59). Despite these compliments, both brothers rejected fundamental theses of Sartre's thought. Miguel Ángel, for example, completely rejected the being-in-itself and being-for-itself dualism. He found it unacceptable to think that there is, on the one hand, a being of consciousness and, on the

---

[6] A more detailed exegetical analysis of Miguel Ángel Virasoro's and Fatone's texts on Sartrean philosophy can be found in my paper Savignano (2016).

[7] All translations from Spanish into English by A.P.S.

other hand, a being of things: the being is actually something unitary (Virasoro 1947, p. 375). In a text written in 1950, he warned of the depiction of the being-in-itself as identical and solid. These features, he judged, result from a Parmenidean prejudice, alien to an authentic phenomenological description, (Virasoro 1947, p. 380).

Both Virasoros also found Sartre's definition of freedom exclusively as self-determination inadmissible. According to Rafael, this leads to a subjectivist relativism, since a freedom which chooses itself as freedom does not have any objective values to differentiate between good and bad deeds (Virasoro 1957, p. 59). Sartrean freedom would paradoxically be able to justify totalitarian doctrines and attitudes as a consequence (Virasoro 1957, p. 61). On the other hand, Miguel Ángel stated that self-determination and autonomy are not enough to describe the essence of freedom as Sartre believed, because a philosophy of existence must also recognize that freedom is a positive and mundane power, which may result in a successful or failed action according to the effective realization of a project (Virasoro 1950, pp. 97–98).

In *La revolución existencialista* (1952, *The Existentialist Revolution*), Astrada also criticized Sartre's notion of freedom and harshly labeling it "artificial" (Astrada 1952, p. 97). The reasons for this reproach were several. First, according to the Argentinian professor, Sartrean freedom is not based on existentialist ontology but rather on modern metaphysics. The descriptions of the in-itself and the for-itself follow the Cartesian model of *res extensa* and *res cogitans* (Astrada 1952, p. 98), states Astrada. Second, this scheme leads to an insurmountable ambiguity in the Sartrean definition of *Dasein*, since it results in a being which is simultaneously a thing and a conscience. Therefore, man is described as a *compositum*, that is, a patchwork of diverse realities without a true link between them (Astrada 1952, p. 102). Third, agreeing with the Virasoro brothers' criticism, Astrada states that Sartre's freedom of choice is "purely negative", since it is defined as "an indetermination of the will" [una indeterminación de la voluntad] (Astrada 1952, pp. 99–100). This steers the French existentialist away from a correct conception of freedom, which would consist precisely of the determination of the will in a more Kantian way, and not, as Sartre claims, a choice without reason or motive—that is, a completely absurd choice. Finally, Astrada declares in his essay that "Sartre's humanism leads to a subjectivism that prevents man from accessing his being" [el humanismo de Sartre se resuelve en un subjetivismo que impide al hombre accede a su ser] (Astrada 1952, p. 156), closely mirroring Heidegger's criticisms against Sartre in *Letter on Humanism* (1947).

The most extensive and complete Argentinian exegesis of Sartre's philosophy is without doubt Fatone's book *El existencialismo y la libertad creadora: una crítica al existencialismo de Jean-Paul Sartre* (1948; *Existentialism and the Creative Freedom: A Critique of Jean-Paul Sartre's Existentialism*). In this book, the author analyzes not just philosophical texts but also literary writings in order to provide a broad outlook on Sartrean existentialism. In the first place, he explores the philosophical influences in Sartre's work: Kierkegaard, Stirner, Heidegger, and Pascal. Then, he exposes the central theses of Sartre's ontology and ethics during the 1940s. In the final chapters, Fatone presents his interpretation of certain affinities between existentialist philosophers and mystics (one of Fatone's favorite subjects, having devoted his life to the historical and philosophical study of religions).

Fatone's main criticism of Sartre's thought is that the anthropology stated in *Being and Nothingness* inevitably falls into moral pessimism, despite the Parisian philosopher's attempts to argue otherwise in *Existentialism Is a Humanism*. Fatone argues that a notion of freedom, as creator of projects and values, is nothing but a source of misery (Fatone 1948, p. 81). Such seems to be the moral lesson taken from the life of the protagonists of Sartrean literature (e.g., Roquentin in *Nausea*, Mathieu in *The Age of Reason*, *The Reprieve*, and *Troubled Sleep*, Hugo in *Dirty Hands*, Garcin in *No Exit*). The paradox of Sartre's existentialism is that human freedom is useless, since its ultimate goal (i.e., to be God in terms of in-itself-for-itself) is by definition impossible. On the other hand, Sartre is criticized by the Argentinian professor for thinking that personal identity is a mere theatrical performance, a farce (Fatone 1948, pp. 82–83). According to Fatone's understanding of the well-known chapter on bad faith, the human person, his character, his habits, and his actions are nothing more than the performance of a role. This means that we are never completely the character that we perform because of the law of consciousness: being what it is not and not being what it is. For Fatone, there are no people in Sartre's world, only characters (Fatone 1948, pp. 82–83).

In conclusion, during the 1950s there was in Argentina a large production of essays introducing, interpreting, and criticizing Sartre's philosophy. This allows us to state that Sartrism was well received in Argentinian academia by several members of the Argentinian existentialist generation.[8,9] However, this process did not go beyond this period and Argentinian universities quickly lost interest in Sartre's contributions to the study of being and consciousness. This is further supported by Sartre's 'marginal presence' in the *curricula* in philosophy at the Faculty of Philosophy and Literature of the University of Buenos Aires between 1949 and 1955.[10]

The New Argentinian Left and *Contorno* Magazine: Intellectuals' Social Engagement

The disappearance of academic studies on Sartrean theoretical philosophy coincided with the arrival of a second reception, this one undertaken from the fringes of academia by a group of young people charmed by the rebellious spirit of *Les Temps modernes* and the Sartrean proposal of an existentialist and Marxist humanism. They were, in the terms of Oscar Terán, the "New Argentinian Left" of the 1960s, whose origins actually dated back to the 1950s (Terán 1991). Deterred by the traditional political parties (e.g., liberals, Peronists, communists, socialists), this new generation was inspired by foreign thinkers such us Hegel (as taught by

---

[8] Apart from the existentialists, some Catholic neo-Thomist philosophers from Argentina also analyzed Sartre's existentialism. For instance, Ismael Quiles wrote *Sartre: el existencialismo del absurdo* (1949), where he reproduces the classic criticisms against Sartre from French Catholic philosophers such as Roger Troisfontaines and Régis Jolivet. Likewise, Octavio Derisi published in the issue 5 of *Revista de Filosofía* a paper titled "El materialismo subyacente en la concepción antropológica de Jean-Paul Sartre".

[9] Recent studies show that the Egological Theory of Law developed by Argentinian philosopher of law and jurist Carlos Cossio was significantly influenced by Sartre's ideas (cf. Méndez 2018).

[10] These statements are based on some inputs from Luciano Barreras' PhD thesis titled *Existencialismo y estructuralismo en la cultura universitaria argentina* (currently unpublished).

Kojève), Marx (especially the *Manuscripts of 1844*), and Gramsci. However, the spotlight of the Argentinian intellectual scene unquestionably belonged to Sartre, who embodied the model of the committed intellectual in Argentina. It was precisely in this period that the Argentinian cultural field went through a gradual politicization.

Within the New Left, the group around *Contorno* played a central role in the appropriation of Sartre's concept of committed literature. *Contorno* was a journal of literary, cultural, and political criticism published in Buenos Aires from 1953 to 1959. The main contributors were Ramón Alcalde, Carlos Correas, Adelaida Gigli, Noé Jitrik, Rodolfo Kusch, Oscar Masotta, Adolfo Prieto, León Rozitschner, José Sebreli, Francisco Solero, David Viñas, and Ismael Viñas. They formed a group of young people, many of them students from the Faculty of Philosophy and Literature at the University of Buenos Aires. As stated by Nora Avaro and Analía Capdevila, their cultural position in the magazine's early years was mainly parauniversity (*Denuncialistas* 2004, p. 12), since their activities during Perón's government were carried out outside or on the fringes of the university (e.g., in the faculty's Student Center, known as the CEFyL).[11]

The magazine's political-cultural identity was defined as taking equal distance from the liberal sector (*Sur*) and the orthodox left (the Communist Party and the Socialist Party of Argentina). This was reflected in its distinctive valuation of the Peronist phenomenon, well evidenced in the articles of the double issue 7/8 of July 1956. Despite not having any sympathy for Perón as a leader and having criticized the management of universities during his rule, the *contornistas* understood the populist movement in a Beauvoirian-Sartrean way as the rebellion of the humiliated in Argentinian history. Therefore, as explained by William Katra, *Contorno* saw in Peronism not a contingent, external, and pernicious event, but a prelude to an authentic and forthcoming socialist revolution in Argentina and Latin America (Katra 1988, p. 77).

In its early days, the magazine, led by the Viñas brothers, was mainly "*un ajuste de cuentas* (a grievance)", an intellectual grievance against previous generations of writers, as Beatriz Sarlo points out (Sarlo 1983).

---

[11] Many of them contributed to *Centro* magazine, a CEFyL publication, considered by Omar Acha a prelude to *Contorno* (cf. Acha 2008, p. 158).

The denouncer mentality of the young critics was shaped by the Sartrean conception of committed literature, well known in Argentina because of the book *¿Qué es la literature?* (1950; *What Is Literature?*), the Spanish translation of Sartre's *Situations II: littérature et engagement* (1948) done by Aurora Bernárdez for Losada. Indeed, many of the articles by the *contornistas* supported the belief that literature cannot be separated from the existential situation of the writers and that writers are responsible for the social and ethical messages spread through their works.[12] In view of these principles, the *contornistas* denounced the ludic literature of the contributors of the *Martín Fierro* magazine, the falsely apolitical literature of those at *Sur*, Ezequiel Martínez Estrada's and Murena's deterministic and metaphysical essays, the naive and stereotyped realism of the literature of the Boedo group, and so on.[13] Due to this ruthless trial against their 'elders', the young generation were dubbed "patricidal" by Emir Rodríguez Monegal in 1956 (Rodríguez 1956).

Among the members of *Contorno* the trio formed by Correas, Masotta, and Sebreli held a special place in the history of Sartrism in Argentina. They were the only self-proclaimed 'Sartrean' members of the magazine and regarded the thinker from Saint-Germain-des-Prés as a faraway master. Many of their writings are full of Sartrean theses, which were applied to figure out major problems of Argentinian reality. The article "Celeste y Colorado (Sky Blue and Red)" by Sebreli, published in issues 217–218 (November–December 1952) of *Sur*, is, for example, the first essay aiming to think "the Argentine problem from the perspective of freedom [el problema argentino desde la perspectiva de la libertad]" (Sebreli 1984). In order to achieve this goal, Sebreli linked the Sartrean philosophical dichotomy between realists and idealists to the political rivalry between "colorados" (Federalists, nationalists, Peronists) and "celestes" (Unitarians, liberals, anti-Peronists) in Argentinian history. The author's proposed solution was the abandonment of abstract principles in public debates and a responsible acceptance of the intrinsic impurity of political action. Thus he repeated *mutatis mutandis* Hugo's lesson at the end of *Dirty Hands*.

---

[12] For a more detailed analysis of the role of Sartre's *¿Qué es la literatura?* in *Contorno*, see my article Savignano (2014).

[13] In addition to the aforementioned reference texts about *Contorno*, see also Croce (1996).

The Argentinian existentialist trio read a large part of the Sartrean *corpus* and had a deep admiration especially for *Saint Genet, Actor and Martyr* (1952). They all considered it one of the masterpieces of the twentieth century. From the existential psychoanalysis of the thief and writer Genet, they inferred that writing is an ontological adventure undertaken by some in order to either free themselves from social alienation or accept it as an *a priori* essence by means of bad faith. *Saint Genet* certainly provided them with the tools necessary to understand fully the life and work of Argentinian wordsmiths. Correas's, Masotta's, and Sebreli's studies on Argentinian writer Roberto Arlt are the most representative attempts to apply the heuristic theses of *Saint Genet* to the Argentinian literary world. In chronological order, Sebreli published "Inocencia y culpabilidad de Roberto Arlt" (Roberto Arlt's Innocence and Guilt) in issue 223 (July–August of 1953) of *Sur* (Sebreli 1953); Masotta wrote *Sexo y traición en Roberto Arlt* (*Sex and Betrayal in Roberto Arlt*) between 1957 and 1959, but he published it only in 1965; finally, Correas published his essay *Arlt, literario* (*Arlt, Literary*) in 1996, although it was written between 1977 and 1984. These works contributed to build an image of Arlt as a precursor of existentialist literature (see Capdevila 2005).

Lastly, Masotta, too, made a valuable contribution to Sartrean phenomenological studies. In issue 13 (1959) of *Centro* (*Centre*) magazine, he published his translation of "La trascendencia del ego" (*The Transcendence of the Ego*), followed by a critical and introductory article titled "La fenomenología de Sartre y un trabajo de Daniel Lagache" (Sartre's Phenomenology and a Daniel Lagache's work). This translation would later be republished in 1968 in book format by another publishing house, Caldén, which added the introduction, notes, and appendices of the 1965 French edition curated by Sylvie Le Bon. In 1959, Masotta's decision to translate and comment on Sartre's early essay was intended to defend Sartre from the philosophical attacks of Merleau-Ponty in *Adventures of the Dialectic* (1955), while also taking his 'master' political stance during the Cold War when the two French phenomenologists broke up their alliance. Masotta's comment also meant to show that Sartre's early ideas were not as incompatible as they seemed with the Merleau-Pontinean phenomenology of the body, Marxism, and even psychoanalysis. These statements prompted an intervention by Eliseo Verón, another of the most outstanding figures of the New Argentinian Left and a key member of *Centro* at the time. In the following issue of the magazine, Verón published "Notas sobre la conciencia y el yo en la fenomenología de Sartre" (Notes on Consciousness and the 'I' in Sartre's Phenomenology), where he condemned Masotta's conciliatory approach and criticized his lack of rigor in his analysis of phenomenological concepts.[14]

The Fall of Sartre and the Rise of Structuralism in Argentina

By the early 1960s, Sartre's project of revitalizing Marx's theory through existentialism was very well received by the New Argentinian Left. The thesis of *Search of Method* (1956) and the first volume of *Critique of Dialectical Reason* (1960) were discussed in Argentinian magazines such as *Cuestiones de filosofía* (1962; *Philosophical Questions*) and *Pasado y presente* (1963–1965; *Past and Present*). The latter, despite its Gramscian orientation, appreciated Sartre's dialectic conception of the *praxis*, as evidenced by the article "Sobre la realidad objetiva de la contradicción" (On the Objective Reality of the Contradiction) written by the Italian philosopher Enzo Paci for the first issue. In that text, Paci built a defense of Sartre's dialectical vision of history from the criticisms of the Levi-Straussian ethnology, which was gaining international recognition at that time.[15]

Nevertheless, during the 1960s, the Argentinian intellectual scene would echo the cultural events in France, with the gradual replacement of existentialism by structuralism as the dominant school of thought. "Existentialism, as a philosophy of subjectivity and of the subject, came under attack and the subject and conscience gave way to rules, codes, and structure", Dosse pointed out in his *History of Structuralism* (Dosse 1997, p. 5). In France, the conflict was sparked when Claude Lévi-Strauss

---

[14] On the debate between Masotta and Verón, see Scholten (2001, pp. 140–152).
[15] Regarding the reception of structuralism in Argentina, see Barreras (2015, 2016).

stated in *The Savage Mind* (1962) that dialectical reason is a myth and then Foucault, in *The Order of Things* (1966), proclaimed the death of man. Sartre counterattacked by saying that the new schools of thought were nothing more than "the last barrier that the bourgeoisie can still raise against Marx" [*le dernier barrage que la bourgeoisie puisse encore dresser contre Marx*] (Sartre 1966, p. 87). Even so, his hegemony over the French cultural field came to an end. In the 1970s his deteriorating health prevented him from keeping up with his writing and considerably reduced his interventions in social and cultural debates.

In Argentina, as the social sciences developed, Sartre's ideas came to be replaced. This was part of a new process of modernization of universities and higher educational institutions. It entailed the creation of new university degree courses, such as sociology and psychology, and the foundation of new private institutions in the artistic and scientific vanguard, such as the Instituto di Tella. The most outstanding protagonists in this process were Masotta and Verón.[16] These 'modernizing heroes' of Argentinian culture, as Barreras calls them, played a central role in the new cultural scene of the 1960s and represented the model of the theoretical-critical intellectual open to international cultural innovations, especially doctrines related to structuralism (Saussure's linguistics, Lévi-Strauss's ethnology, Althusser's Marxism, Lacan's psychoanalysis, etc.).[17] Both proclaimed that social scientists should remain distant from social and political conflicts for the sake of an objective vision, in conformity with Lévi-Strauss's and Foucault's methodology. This methodological ideal suggested the separation between knowledge and political action, while also attacking the Sartrean model of the committed intellectual. The battle between existentialism and structuralism was fought mainly in the dispute over who was the legitimate heir of Marxist doctrine. In fact, in 1965, Masotta—who had abandoned his early Sartrism and had turned to the study of semiology, contemporary art (comics, pop art, and

---

[16] Verón attended Lévi-Strauss's classes when he went to Paris in 1961 in order to study anthropology.

[17] On the dissemination of structuralism in Argentina, *Los libros* magazine, directed by Héctor Schmucler in its early years, played an influential role. In fact, Schmucler had studied with Roland Barthes in France.

happenings) and Lacanian psychoanalysis—proclaimed in his presentation of *Sexo y traición en Roberto Arlt* that Marx's theory "is not a philosophy of the consciousness at all, and that, for the same reason, and in a radical way, it excludes phenomenology [no es, en absoluto, una filosofía de la conciencia; y que, por lo mismo, y de manera radical, excluye la fenomenología]", adding: "the philosophy of Marxism must be rediscovered in modern theories (or 'sciences') of the languages of structures and the unconscious" [La filosofía del marxismo debe ser reencontrada en las modernas teorías (o 'ciencias') de los lenguajes de las estructuras y el inconsciente]" (*Arlt, yo mismo* in Masotta 2010, p. 228). On the other hand, Verón in "Ciencia social y praxis social" (Social Science and Social Praxis), an article published in issue 4 (1963) of *Discusión* (Discussion) magazine, argued that Marxism is incompatible with phenomenology and considered that the pretension of totality of the dialectical reason is "an illusion of omnipotence over the real" [una ilusión de omnipotencia sobre lo real] (Verón 1972, p. 229), as Levi-Strauss had already proved. Thus, the new theories of human sciences in France and Argentina judged Sartre's philosophical thought obsolete, for it falsely exaggerated the role of conscious and voluntary actions of the subjects in history.

During the waning years of Sartrism and the rise of structuralism, the intellectual beacon that Sartre had been for Argentina and other Latin American countries had a last chance to shine. The Third World and anti-colonialist humanism of his prologue to Fanon's *The Wretched of the Earth* in 1961 had a strong impact on the mentality of the New Left and groups that favored the armed struggle that would emerge between the 1960s and the 1970s. (e.g., las Fuerzas Armadas Revolucionarias, Montoneros, el Ejército Revolucionario del Pueblo). The prologue synthesized fundamental ideas that were circulating in the new generations: anti-imperialism, dependency theory, voluntarism, and, for some, the apology for revolutionary violence. In fact, Fanon's and Sartre's ideas about the manufacturing of sub-men by colonialism are an essential part of *La hora de los hornos* (1968; *The Hour of the Furnaces*), an Argentinian testimonial documentary directed by Octavio Getino and Fernando 'Pino' Solanas showing the tragic consequences of material and ideological domination of neo-colonialism in Argentina and Latin America, similar to European or American colonialist domination in underdeveloped countries of

Africa and Asia. On the other hand, the experience of the *Cátedras Nacionales*[18] in sociology at the University of Buenos Aires between 1968 and 1972 was also partially inspired by Sartre's Third World position, especially among intellectuals sympathetic to Sartre's ideas, such as Horacio González (González et al. 2006) and José Pablo Feinmann.

Finally, on 24 March 1976, the coup d'état by the Armed Forces against President Isabel Martínez de Perón inaugurated the civic-military dictatorship known as the National Reorganization Process. The severe repressive censorship of Argentina's scientific, cultural, and artistic output, along with the persecution, kidnapping, and extermination of left-wing intellectuals, ended with the circulation of Sartre's ideas and those of other thinkers labeled as 'subversives' by the military junta. The reception of Sartrism in Argentina was abruptly halted and it will take several years for universities to resume the teaching and research of the philosopher of freedom.

References

Acha, Omar. 2008. *La nueva generación intelectual*. Buenos Aires: Herramienta.

Astrada, Carlos. 1952. *La revolución existencialista: hacia un humanismo de la libertad*. La Plata: Nuevo Destino.

Avaro, Nora, and Capdevila Analía, eds. 2004. *Denuncialistas: literatura y polémica en los '50 (Una antología crítica)*. Buenos Aires: Santiago Arcos.

Barreras, Luciano. 2015. Estructuralismo en la Argentina: filosofía, ciencia (social) y política. *Avatares Filosóficos* 2: 3–13. Accessed August 3, 2020. http://revistas.filo.uba.ar/index.php/avatares/article/view/305.

———. 2016. *Existencialismo y estructuralismo en la cultura universitaria argentina. Entre la 'modernización' y la radicalización*. Unpublished PhD thesis, FFyL-UBA. Accessed August 3, 2020. http://repositorio.filo.uba.ar/bitstream/handle/filodigital/4382/uba_ffyl_t_2016_se_barreras.pdf?sequence=1&isAllowed=y.

Behiels, Lieve. 2006. La recepción de Sartre en España: el caso de *La nausée*. *Espéculo* XI: 32. Accessed August 3, 2020. http://webs.ucm.es/info/especulo/numero32/sartrees.html.

---

[18] The so-called *Cátedras Nacionales* were university chairs devoted to developing a new sociology to study Argentine and Latin American social problems.

Boschetti, Anna. 1985. *Sartre et "Les Temps Modernes": Une entreprise intellectuelle*. Paris: Les Éditions de Minuit.

Capdevila, Analía. 2005. Arlt, existencialista. Acerca del buen uso del Saint Genet. *La Biblioteca* 2–3: 404–417.

Correas, Carlos. 1994. Historia del existencialismo en Argentina. *Cuadernos de filosofía* 40: 103–114.

Croce, Marcela. 1996. *Contorno: izquierda y proyecto cultural*. Buenos Aires: Colihue.

Derisi, Octavio N. 1952. El materialismo subyacente en la concepción antropológica de Jean-Paul Sartre. *Revista de Filosofía* 5: 48–54.

Donnantuoni Moratto, Mauro. 2015. Políticas de la revista Sur: formas retóricas de una identidad "liberal". In *Polémicas intelectuales, debates políticos. Las revistas culturales en el siglo XX*, ed. Leticia Prislei, 119–148. Buenos Aires: FFyl-UBA.

Dosse, François. 1997. *History of Structuralism, Vol. I: The Rising Sign, 1945–1966*. Translated by D. Glassman. Minneapolis: University of Minnesota.

Fatone, Vicente. 1948. *El existencialismo y la libertad creadora: una crítica al existencialismo de Jean-Paul Sartre*. Buenos Aires: Argos.

García Losada, Matilde I. 1999. *La filosofía existencial: sus introductores*. Buenos Aires: Editorial Plus Ultra.

González, Horacio, et al. 2006. *Jean-Paul Sartre, actualidad de un pensamiento*. Buenos Aires: Colihue.

Katra, William H. 1988. *Contorno: Literary Engagement in Post-Peronist Argentina*. Cranbury: Associated University Presses.

King, John. 1986. *Sur: A Study of the Argentine Literary Journal and Its Role in the Development of a Culture, 1931–1970*. Cambridge: Cambridge University Press.

Masotta, Oscar. 2010. *Conciencia y estructura*. Buenos Aires: Eterna cadencia.

Méndez, Eduardo. 2018. *Fenomenología existencial en el derecho: la teoría egológica como nueva cultura jurídica*. Remedios de Escalada: Universidad Nacional Lanús.

Pasternac, Nora. 2002. *Sur, una revista en la tormenta: los años de formación, 1931–1944*. Buenos Aires: Paradiso.

Podlubne, Judith. 2009. Compromiso espiritual e independencia creadora. Una moral humanista para la literatura en la revista Sur (1935–1945). *Iberoamérica* 35 (IX): 19–38. https://doi.org/10.18441/ibam.9.2009.35.19–38.

Pró, Diego F. 1973. *Historia del pensamiento filosófico argentino*. Mendoza: Instituto de Filosofía de la Universidad Nacional de Cuyo.

Quiles, Ismael. 1949. *Sartre: el existencialismo del absurdo.* Buenos Aires: Espasa-Calpe Argentina.

Rodríguez Monegal, Emir. 1956. *El juicio de los parricidas: la nueva generación argentina y sus maestros.* Buenos Aires: Deucalión.

Romero, Francisco. 1961. Sobre la filosofía en Iberoamérica. In *Filosofía de la persona y otros ensayos*, ed. Francisco Romero, 147–156. Buenos Aires: Losada.

Sarlo, Beatriz. 1983. Los dos ojos de Contorno. *Revista Iberoamericana* XLIX (125): 797–807. https://doi.org/10.5195/reviberoamer.1983.3839.

Sartre, Jean-Paul. 1966. Sartre répond. *L'Arc* 30: 87–96.

Savignano, Alan P. 2014. El rol de *¿Qué es la literatura?* de J.-P. Sartre en la formación generacional del grupo *Contorno*. *Cuadernos de materiales*, 26. Accessed August 3, 2020. https://cuadernodemateriales.wordpress.com/2015/02/01/cdm-26-el-rol-de-que-es-la-literatura-de-j-p-sartre-en-la-formacion-generacional-del-grupo-contorno-a-patricio-savignano/.

———. 2016. La recepción del pensamiento de Jean-Paul Sartre en Argentina: la generación existencialista del 25 y la nueva izquierda de *Contorno*. *Revista Ideas* 4: 34–61. Accessed August 3, 2020. http://revistaideas.com.ar/wp-content/uploads/2016/12/Ideas.Revista-de-filosof%C3%ADa-moderna-y-contemporanea-N%C2%BA4.pdf.

Scholten, Hernán. 2001. *Oscar Masotta y la fenomenología: un problema de la historia del psicoanálisis.* Buenos Aires: Atuel.

Sebreli, Juan J. 1953. Inocencia y culpabilidad de Roberto Arlt. *Sur* 223: 109–119.

———. 1984. Celeste y colorado. In *El riesgo del pensar: ensayos 1950–1984*, ed. Juan J. Sebreli, 25–36. Buenos Aires: Sudamericana.

Terán, Oscar. 1991. *Nuestros años sesenta: la formación de la nueva izquierda intelectual en Argentina 1956–1966.* Buenos Aires: Puntosur.

de Torre, Guillermo. 1948. *Valoraciones literarias del existencialismo.* Buenos Aires: Ollantay.

Verón, Eliseo. 1972. *Conducta, estructura y comunicación: escritos teóricos: 1959–1973.* Buenos Aires: Tiempo Contemporáneo.

Villordo, Óscar H. 1994. *El grupo Sur: una biografía colectiva.* Buenos Aires: Planeta.

Virasoro, Miguel Ángel. 1947. La filosofía de J. P. Sartre. El ser en sí y el para sí. *Realidad* I (3): 368–381.

———. 1948. Prólogo. In *El ser y la nada*, ed. Jean-Paul Sartre, vol. I. Buenos Aires: Ibero-Americana.

———. 1950. La idea del hombre en el Congreso de Filosofía de Lima. *Cuadernos de Filosofía* III (7): 84–103.

Virasoro, Rafael. 1957. *Existencialismo y moral: Heidegger y Sartre.* Santa Fe: Castellví.

18

Existentialism Against Colonialism: Sartre, Fanon, and the Place of Lived Experience

Robert Bernasconi

The global impact of Frantz Fanon's *The Wretched of the Earth* extends far beyond academia and it has served as a Bible to numerous anti-colonial movements. One thinks especially of its importance to the Black Panther Party in the United States and the Black Consciousness movement in South Africa. Indeed, there is still today no shortage of passionate readers of *The Wretched of the Earth* in South Africa up to and including proponents of the Rhodes Must Fall Movement (See, for example, Sayles 2010; Ramuga 1986; and More 2017). The question therefore in the context of the present volume on the reception of existentialism is only the extent to which it can be seen as an existentialist text. I have argued elsewhere that *The Wretched of the Earth* must be read in conjunction with Jean-Paul Sartre's *Critique of Dialectical Reason* (Bernasconi 2010). Fanon himself left this in no doubt. When he arranged for a third-party to approach Sartre to ask him to write an Introduction to *The Wretched of the Earth*, he asked that Sartre be told: "each time I sit down at my desk, I think of

R. Bernasconi (✉)
Department of Philosophy, Pennsylvania State University,
University Park, PA, USA

© The Author(s) 2020
A. Betschart, J. Werner (eds.), *Sartre and the International Impact of Existentialism*,
https://doi.org/10.1007/978-3-030-38482-1_18

him" (quoted by Cohen-Solal 1987, p. 431). Nevertheless, the tendency in recent literature has been to try to separate the late Fanon from Sartre which, by implication, might separate him from existentialism.[1]

That Frantz Fanon's first book, *Black Skin, White Masks*, is a major existentialist text is not in doubt. Recently the focus of major commentators has been more on his understanding of psychopathology than on his understanding of Sartre, but this is mainly because the recent publication of his dissertation has shown the extent of his reading in that area and in so doing has opened up new and highly productive lines of research (Fanon 2018). Current research on Fanon's relation to Sartre is less robust. Just as some scholars of Simone de Beauvoir have thought that to enhance her reputation it was necessary to create a gulf between her and Sartre, promoters of Black existentialism have been anxious to distance him from Sartre as if the connection diminished his work. Such efforts strike me as misguided not only because neither Beauvoir, nor Fanon, sought to minimize their debt to Sartre, but also because their own contributions are sufficiently incisive not to need such help. But this tendency has had an unfortunate effect on studies of the relation of Fanon to Sartre. The focus of almost all of them has been his critical remarks on the latter's account of the negritude movement in *Black Orpheus* in the fifth chapter of *Black Skin, White Masks*, entitled "The Lived Experience of the Black" (Fanon 2008, pp. 111–117). Before turning to *The Wretched of the Earth* I will briefly examine the questions that discussion raises for reception history (on this debate, see Bernasconi 2007).

The context of Sartre's *Black Orpheus* should not be forgotten. This was not a gratuitous intervention into a discussion where he had no place. Sartre had been invited to write a Preface to an anthology of poetry by Black Francophone writers who identified with the Negritude movement (Julien 1948). Instead of a brief introduction he wrote a major interpretive essay in which many of his more problematic claims derive directly from the material he was discussing, such as a tendency toward a kind of racial essentialism, as when he talks of "the black soul" (Sartre 2001a, p. 115).

---

[1] Monolingual readers of Fanon in the English-speaking world are deprived of the resources to see the proximity of Sartre and Fanon because none of Fanon's English translators seem to have been familiar with Sartre's vocabulary and so they have systematically, albeit unwittingly, erased these connections. On the translations, see Etherington (2016).

In the course of bringing together the different strands of that movement, he reduced them to two dominant tendencies. In so doing he privileged the dialectical account offered by Aimé Césaire over the backward-looking perspective of Léopold Sédar Senghor. To that extent his perspective was not so different from Fanon's own. That is what allowed Fanon to say in the following chapter that "we can understand why Sartre sees in the black poets' Marxist stand the logical end to negritude" (Fanon 2008, p. 174; Bernasconi 2002). Furthermore, Fanon praised *Anti-Semite and Jew*: "Certain pages of *Anti-Semite and Jew* are some of the finest we have ever read" (Fanon 2008, p. 158). His striking, albeit deeply problematic, claim there was that the anti-Semite makes the Jew.[2] Fanon took this up and applied it to anti-Black racism: "it is the racist who creates the inferiorized" (Fanon 2008, p. 73). He did so without in any way minimizing the differences in lived experience that separate Blacks from Jews (Fanon 2008, p. 150). But just as Jews questioned Sartre's account of what is to be a Jew, so Fanon questioned his account of what it is to be Black: "Jean-Paul Sartre forgets that the black man suffers in his body differently from the white man."[3] As Fanon explained in a footnote, Sartre's account of relations to the other in *Being and Nothingness* was "correct" as far as it went, but could not be applied to a Black consciousness for whom the other is "the master, whether real or imaginary" (Fanon 2008, p. 117n24). This is what Sartre at this point of his life did not appreciate and where he overstepped.

According to Fanon, the early Sartre not only lacked the lived experience of being Black, he also had not paid sufficient attention to the power differential between Blacks and Whites and the way it gave rise to certain oppressive mechanisms. As soon as one understands this difference that derives from what is sometimes called an author's subject position, the importance of Fanon's voice becomes clear. The difference lies in the lived experience from which he can speak and what that lived experience allows him to say. All of this is familiar and yet easily forgotten. The famous

---

[2] Sartre (1948, p. 69). For the history of the criticisms this claim elicited see Judaken (2006).

[3] Fanon (2008, p. 117). Fanon repeatedly uses the term *man* to refer to both men and women in a way that, quite properly, is not acceptable today. He also uses it in its narrower sense. Often it is undecidable which sense he is using it in. I am retaining the word both in quoting and paraphrasing him as this is not the place to try to decide in each case which sense is to be understood.

opening lines of *Black Orpheus* make a related point: "When you removed the gag that was keeping these black mouths shut, what were you hoping for? That they would sing your praises?" (Sartre 2001a, p. 115). And yet within a few pages, as Fanon points out, Sartre forgets his limitations.

"The Lived Experience of the Black" has given rise to a whole sub-field within critical philosophy of race.[4] Multiple scholars have written autobiographical studies of their experiences of racism and in so doing brought the experience of being racialized as Black or Native American or Latin American, alive for many White readers. Through this single chapter existentialism has left its mark on how race is thought within academia in the United States. But the chapter is often read in isolation. It is not only cut off from Sartre, who in *Being and Nothingness* had provided the account of freedom as well as a basis for thinking of race as an aspect of the body's facticity (Sartre 2018, p. 440. See Bernasconi 2008). It is also, and more importantly, cut off from the historical context of the anti-colonial wars that Fanon references in praising the Vietnamese, who, in their colonial struggle, "accept death for the sake of the present and the future" (Fanon 2008, p. 202). And above all it is cut off from the rest of the book. Indeed, it is not even in this chapter that Fanon marks his most significant advance on Sartre. In the sixth chapter, "The Negro and Psychopathology," where Fanon demonstrates that racism cannot be adequately approached in terms of the individual situations that dominated the discussed in the previous chapters. Fanon's point is that one has to go beyond the looks and actions of individual racists to investigate the societal mechanisms, such as "cultural imposition," through which Black people were inferiorized (Fanon 2008, p. 167). In 1952 Fanon had a richer understanding of the operation of structural racism than Sartre did, but the book was not only a diagnosis. It was a call for action in which the oppressed, by risking their lives, could find the means to overcome the inferiority complex that society had produced. In *The Wretched of the Earth* actions of this kind would be described as disintoxicating violence (*la violence désintoxique*): it could address a person's inferiority complex at the individual level

---

[4] "The Lived Experience of the Black" was first published as a stand-alone essay in 1951 before its republication with minor changes the following year.

(Fanon 2004, p. 51). But to transform the society these actions needed to lead to a restructuring of the world (Fanon 2008, p. 63).

In *Anti-Semite and Jew* Sartre had already recognized that, although he had begun with the individual anti-Semite, only a transformation of society could bring about the eradication of anti-Semitism: "it could not exist in a classless society" (Sartre 1948, p. 149). But it seems that at this point he lacked the resources to take the diagnosis further. He had been inducted into racial politics already by his visits to the United States in 1947 and 1948 (Cohen-Solal 1987, p. 241; see also Bernasconi 1995). This enabled him to see subsequently that beyond the immediate confines of the Cold War seen as a joust between two superpowers lay the transformative process by which across the 1950s the colonized world was liberating itself. The dominant context in which Sartre wrote *Critique of Dialectical Reason* and Fanon wrote *The Wretched of the Earth* was the global fight against colonialism as a racist material system, and its most immediate impact for both of them was, of course, the Algerian War of Independence.[5] Sartre took a major step in his theorization of this struggle when in 1956 he gave a talk under the title "Colonialism is a System" (Sartre 2001b). In the following year, in response to Albert Memmi's *The Colonizer and the Colonized*, which itself was an existentialist account that borrowed heavily from Sartre, he claimed that Memmi saw only a situation, whereas racism is built into the system.[6]

Sartre's adoption of the term *system* might seem to challenge a standard conception of existentialism, but he was not attempting to readjudicate Kierkegaard's protest on behalf of the individual against the Hegelian system. For both Sartre and Fanon what was at issue was a racist material system, not, as with Hegel, a system of ideas. Sartre in *Search for a Method*, in preparation for publishing *Critique of Dialectical Reason*, offered a detailed discussion of the role of existentialism in his work at that time. Using the explanation Sartre offered in *Search for a Method* of how his writing continued to be in line with existentialism, one need only

---

[5] On the role of *Les Temps modernes* during the Algerian War of Independence, see Burnier (1967, pp. 99–107, 114–115, and 121–132).

[6] Sartre, "Introduction," in Memmi (1965, p. xxiii). Sartre's Introduction was originally published as a review of the first edition for *Les Temps modernes*, July–August 1957, nos. 137–138: 289–293. See Azzedine Haddour (2011, pp. 88–89).

demonstrate the clear parallels between *The Wretched of the Earth* and *Critique of Dialectical Reason* to have integrated Fanon's late work into an account of the reception of existentialism.

Existentialism aims at the concrete. Indeed, according to Sartre, it is "the only concrete approach to reality" (Sartre 1963, p. 21). He also writes of the *Critique of Dialectical Reason* that the concrete was "the hidden conclusion of the entire investigation" (Sartre 1976, p. 521). By contrast, to begin with individual experience and stay with it is ultimately to remain in the abstract. Both Sartre and Fanon acknowledge that to focus exclusively on individual acts of racism, as still so often happens, is to abstract from the real problem, which is colonialism as a racist material system. The racialized individual is racialized less by the gaze than by cultural imposition. This insight takes one beyond *Anti-Semite and Jew*, and the account of cultural imposition in *Black Skin, White Masks* only goes part of the way.

Fanon takes a further step on the way to the concrete in 1956 in "Racism and Culture" when he describes racism as "one element of a vaster whole: that of the systematized oppression of a people" (Fanon 1966, p. 63). Subsequently, at the very beginning of *The Wretched of the Earth*, he marks in two sentences the integration of the individualist dimension of his account with the broader systemic perspective that makes sense of it: "It is the colonist who *fabricated* and *continues to fabricate* the colonized subject. The colonist derives his truth, i.e., his wealth, from the colonial system" (Fanon 2004, p. 2, translation modified). In these two sentences, first, Fanon adapts Sartre's famous formulation that the anti-Semite makes the Jew to the colonial context and then, secondly, he locates that experience within the colonial system that sustains it.

Sartre in *Critique of Dialectical Reason* makes a similar point when he revisits the account of the gaze, albeit this time it is the gaze of the worker toward the employer, who in turn realizes himself concretely as an object of hatred in the form of "a common individual."[7] He had already, earlier in the book, modified the account of how one is made this or that by lodging it into an account of the passive syntheses of materiality (Sartre

---

[7] Sartre (1976, p. 757). Sartre had already reversed the gaze at the beginning of *Black Orpheus* (Sartre 2001a, p. 115).

1976, pp. 231–232). Whereas in *Being and Nothingness* and *Anti-Semite and Jew* it is the direct gaze that determines relations with another, in *Critique of Dialectical Reason* our relations to others are mediated by materiality and also our relations to others across other others. The dominant understanding of racism that locates it primarily in the idea or sentiments of the individual is thereby overturned: "racism is a passive constitution in things before being an ideology" (Sartre 1976, p. 39). This does not mean that theories play no part in racism, but rather that racism is lived before it is thought: "racism is the colonial interest lived as a link of all the colonialists of the colony through the serial flight of alterity."[8] More precisely, it is "a praxis illuminated by a theory ('biological', 'social', or empirical racism, it does not matter which) aiming to keep the masses in a state of molecular aggregation, and to use every possible means to increase the 'sub-humanity' of the natives" (Sartre 1976, p. 721).

The distortion of racism in ordinary understanding, whereby it is reduced to a thought or sentiment, is no accident. It is racism as a material system that itself produces the tendency to individualize the experience of racism as a means to conceal and distort the all-pervasive character of systemic racism. To paraphrase Sartre's early essay on intentionality, racism is outside in the world, among things, among others (Sartre 2013, p. 6). It is not lodged in the deep recesses of hearts and minds, but within the system, as the account of colonialism in *Critique of Dialectical Reason* demonstrates (see especially Sartre 1976, pp. 716–734. See also Arthur 2010, pp. 77–94.). It is in the same spirit that Fanon in *The Wretched of the Earth* equates existential problems with objective problems (Fanon 2004, p. 153). Existentialism is not reducible to the subjective as some of its critics want to maintain.

Sartre's *Critique of Dialectical Reason* and Fanon's *The Wretched of the Earth* are preoccupied with the same two questions. First, how does the existentialist render the material system visible? Secondly, once that had been done, where does that leave the accounts of lived experience on

---

[8] Sartre (1976, p. 300n). By "serial alterity" Sartre understands the way all colonialists act in each of them, so that when a colonialist beats a native each does so through the beatings given to other natives by other colonialists: they each act in this way "because this is *what one does*" (Sartre 1976, p. 731n).

which existentialists have frequently relied? The first of these questions is explicitly formulated in *Search for a Method* when Sartre asks how it is possible to "conceive of the appearance of systematic processes such as capitalism or colonialism" (Sartre 1963, p. 100). His immediate response was not only that contemporary Marxism was incapable of doing so, but that the capacity to do so had already been blocked by Engels. What the Marxism of Sartre's day allegedly lacked was "the existential project," that is to say, "the project which throws him toward the social possible in terms of a defined situation" (Sartre 1963, p. 181). So while it might seem at first sight that existentialism, as normally conceived, lacks a conception of the system and might even be thought to be inimical to it, in fact it is on Sartre's account indispensable for its role in producing the path to a dialectical conception of the system.

To be sure, the existential account itself needs the help of a revivified Marxism. From the very first pages of *Search for a Method* Sartre indicates that existentialism needs Marxism to free it from the inherited abstract forms of thought that limit our conceptions of class (and race) and thereby promote a form of theoretical isolationism (Sartre 1963, pp. 5–6). A one-sided focus on the abstract individual removed from the concrete conditions in which he or she finds him- or herself is characteristic of contemporary society and deprives that society of the resources it needs in order to identity and stay focused on the problems created by systemic racism. Without these resources all the problems that have come to be endemic to the institutions themselves are restricted to the local with the result that the big picture is missed. One can, for example, try to sustain an account of slavery in terms of abuses and can interpret colonialism in terms of bad administrators. In this way one reduces slavery and colonialism to individuals abusing for their own selfish ends a framework that is presented as in and of itself neutral.[9] One can offer a similar approach in the context of police violence against racial minorities which is so often reduced to serial cases of rogue cops who are said to be merely bad apples. Hence the importance of Sartre's conclusion at the end of *Critique of Dialectical Reason* that dialectics can establish the conditions for such

---

[9] The argument can be traced back to G. W. G. Hegel's *Lectures on the Philosophy of World History* (Hegel 2011, p. 501). See also James (1981, p. 76).

things as classes, whereas analytical reason, through its atomization of society and denial of material reciprocity, is "an oppressive praxis for dissolving them" (Sartre 1976, p. 804). Those are the options facing the theorist.

Sartre presents dialectics "as the practical consciousness of an oppressed class struggling against its oppressor" (Sartre 1976, p. 803). That is to say, it is not something rarefied, possessed only by a few who have studied closely the writings of Hegel and Marx.[10] It belongs to the oppressed and they share in it insofar as they engage in praxis (Sartre 1963, p. 172). What is understood by praxis here? Sartre in the *Critique of Dialectical Reason* defines it as "an organizing project which transcends material conditions an end and inscribes itself, through labour, in inorganic matter as a rearrangement of the practical field and a reunification of means in the light of the end" (Sartre 1976, p. 734). However, beyond this generalized sense of the term, praxis in Sartre has a definite sense: "Concrete thought must be born from *praxis* and must turn back upon it in order to clarify it" (Sartre 1963, p. 22).

It is even more clear that in *The Wretched of the Earth* it is not lived experience as such that reveals the operation of the colonial system, but revolutionary praxis understood dialectically. The masses themselves have a "a voracious taste for the concrete" that they receive from the praxis that throws them into a desperate struggle (Fanon 2004, p. 52. Translation modified). It is through praxis, the deployment of violence, and "the project of liberation," that "the colonized subject discovers reality and transforms it" (Fanon 2004, p. 21). "Praxis enlightens the agent" because it shows the agent the means and the end (Fanon 2004, p. 44). That is to say, there is an understanding that belongs to concrete praxis. Whereas praxis helps to reveal the situation, the project locates it within a larger totalizing frame, and when the praxis takes the form of revolutionary praxis aimed at undermining the material system, then it is the system itself that comes to light. The relation of praxis to dialectical reason is crucial here where new meanings arise from this action. Fanon writes: "The nationalist militant who fled the town, revolted by the demagogic and reformist maneuvers of the leaders, and disillusioned by 'politics,'

---

[10] Fanon insists on the same point (Fanon 2004, p. 141).

discovers in concrete praxis a new politics which is no way resembles the old."[11] The same kind of considerations had already led Sartre to the conclusion that the dialectic cannot experience itself "except in and through the *praxis of struggle*" (Sartre 1976, p. 804).

But if it is through praxis, rather than in lived experience, that systemic racism is revealed, where does that leave Fanon's appeal to the lived experience of the Black in *Black Skin, White Masks*? It is an important question given the prominence of lived experience in contemporary work in critical philosophy of race that takes its inspiration from him. The organization of the book suggests that the evidence of lived experience on its own was already in question there. The fifth chapter ends in tears: "Not responsible for my acts, at the crossroads between Nothingness and Infinity, I began to weep" (Fanon 2008, p. 114). By contrast, the book ends on a very different note with Fanon asking the reader to feel the open dimension of every consciousness to which is added a final prayer, "O my body, always make me a man who questions!" (Fanon 2008, p. 206) It seems that one cannot rely on the evidence of lived experience. It does not know itself. Hence, in the evolution of Fanon's thought, lived experience, as described in chapter five of *Black Skin, White Masks*, gives way later in the book to action, and that, in turn, points to what in *The Wretched of the Earth* is described as the experience of revolutionary praxis.

In *Search for a Method* Sartre provides the theoretical basis for such a trajectory when he gives a revised account of what he calls "the method of the existentialist approach," but what is most remarkable is how he provides here for the first time an account of the place of lived experience (Sartre 1963, p. 148). He describes this method as "a regressive-progressive and analytic-synthetic method." By "progressive" he understands movement toward the objective result and by "regressive" a going back toward the original conditions (Sartre 1963, p. 154). He explains that this is nothing other than the "dialectical movement which explains the act by its terminal signification in terms of its starting conditions" (Sartre 1963,

---

[11] Fanon (2004, p. 95). Translation modified. Richard Philcox seems to have an allergy to translating the French word *concret* as "concrete." Of at least six occurrences in *The Wretched of the Earth*, he takes this route only once.

p. 153). In other words, the existential method and the dialectical method fold into one another. It remains only to understand how that happens.

To appreciate Sartre's attempt to place existential phenomenology at the service of a dialectical Marxism, it is helpful to look at a footnote in *Search for a Method* which he devotes to Henri Lefebvre (Sartre 1963, p. 51n). In his 1952 essay "Perspectives on Rural Sociology" Lefebvre presented an account of how sociology and history can be integrated into a materialist dialectic. He identifies three phases of the inquiry: descriptive, analytico-regressive, and historical-genetic (Lefebvre 2003, p. 117). In recounting them, Sartre changes Lefebvre's meaning by recharacterizing the first phase in terms of "phenomenological description" (Sartre 1963, p. 2n). He seems to understand by that a description of the situation does not yet attain to the level of the system as such.

Sartre's existential-dialectical method can be illustrated by a brief reference to Sartre's account of colonization as developing history in the *Critique* where he distinguishes three levels of intelligibility that correspond to Lefebvre's account. Sartre writes: "The play of flat appearances which can be studied by economic Reason has no intelligibility except in relation to the anti-dialectical system of super-exploitation. And this in turn is not intelligible unless one begins by seeing it as a product of human labour which created it and continues to control it" (Sartre 1976, p. 729). The description of appearances has no meaning unless related to an account of power that is accessible only to the analytico-regressive movement, but this meaning gives rise to understanding only when seen through an historical dialectics. Analytical reason is both indispensable but in and of itself inadequate to the task of investigating "oppression as a historical *praxis* realizing itself, determining itself and controlling itself in the milieu of passive alterity" (Sartre 1976, p. 729). If phenomenological description is to be placed in the service of politics, it must be seen dialectically, which means referring it back to the meanings sedimented in past praxis.

In *Search for a Method* Sartre writes of "the profundity of the lived" (*la profondeur du vécu*) (Sartre 1963, p. 145). This gives to lived experience a significance that one is surprised to discover that it lacked in his earlier thought. It was not from the early Sartre but, most likely, from Merleau-Ponty's *Phenomenology of Perception* that Fanon took the idea of lived experience. Lived experience can be described phenomenologically, but its depth and intelligibility is given only when it is located within an analysis of power relations. This, using the terms Fanon deploys in *The Wretched of the Earth*, would mean evoking the reciprocal exclusion of colonizer and colonized governed "by a purely Aristotelian logic" (Fanon 2004, p. 4). This corresponds to the way in *Search for a Method* the lived is said to be revealed through the regressive moment of the investigation where one begins from the absolute concrete and descends to its most abstract conditioning in the sense of the material conditions as they are given as lived by abstract subjects (Sartre 1963, p. 145). But, as Sartre warns, this offers at most only an outline of the dialectical movement, which only fully emerges when the progressive moment of the investigation is fueled when the impasse is broken by the new meanings arising from historical praxis.

Long before Sartre formalized the approach in this way, Fanon had enacted it. In the sixth chapter of *Black Skin, White Masks* he introduces an objection made against Sartre's *Black Orpheus* by Gabriel d'Arbousier. D'Arbousier argued that by describing the negritude poets as a movement Sartre had ignored the historical and social realities of the different countries from which they came and that had the effect of separating them.[12] Fanon defends Sartre and at the same time acknowledges that the objection, if valid, would apply to him too. Fanon begins *Black Skin, White Masks* by recalling his own subject position: "As those of an Antillean, our observations and conclusions are valid only for the French Antilles" (Fanon 2008, p. xviii). However, in response to d'Arbousier he acknowledges that in pursuing his account he had had no choice but to lift the restriction: "At the start we wanted to confine ourselves to the Antilles. But the dialectics, at all cost, got the upper hand and we have been forced to *see* that the Antillean is above all a black man" (Fanon 2008, p. 150). Fanon conceded that the negro race is dispersed and no longer unified, that insofar as one operates simply by way of descriptions located at the phenomenal level one simply opens the door to an infinite number of perspectives, but he insists that at the concrete level the

---

[12] D'Arbousier (1949, pp. 38–39). For some of the context, albeit perhaps oversimplifying the issues, see Birchall (2004, pp. 81–82).

problem is resolved: "The universal situation of the black man is ambiguous, but this is resolved in his concrete existence" (Fanon 2008, p. 150. Translation modified). He presents as evidence the fact that "wherever he goes the negro remains a negro" (Fanon 2008, p. 150. Translation modified). Dialectics is vindicated but only to the extent that it attains the concrete by passing through the account of lived experience.

The importance Sartre in his late work gives to lived experience is indicated in *Search for a Method* in the last part of the text and further demonstrated throughout the multi-volume study of Flaubert where it is constantly in play. It is explained further when in an interview from 1969 entitled "Itinerary of a Thought" Sartre marked the place he now gave to lived experience. He acknowledged that it was absent from his early thought and that its introduction marked the major change of his late work from his thinking in *Being and Nothingness*. "My early work was a rationalist philosophy of consciousness" that "in the end becomes an irrationalism, because it cannot account rationally for those processes which are 'below' consciousness and which are also rational, but lived as irrational" (Sartre 2006, pp. 21–22). This is at first sight surprising. One might imagine that the turn of history was the major shift as he indicated at another point (Cohen-Solal 1987, p. 412. See Sartre 1976, p. 716). Or one might highlight his turn to dialectical reason as the major innovation of his late thought because it allowed him, for example, to think colonialism as a system. But for Sartre the notion of lived experience changes everything because it was for him a dialectical concept when seen through the lens of the regressive-progressive method. He indicates this explicitly: "What I call *le vécu*—lived experience—is precisely the ensemble of the dialectical process of psychic life, in so far as this process is obscure to itself because it is a constant totalization, thus necessarily a totalization which cannot be conscious of what it is" (Sartre 2006, p. 20).

Sartre explains in *Search for a Method* that lived experience does not know itself: "It is the terrain in which the individual is perpetually overflowed by himself and his riches and consciousness plays the trick of determining itself by forgetfulness" (Sartre 2006, p. 22). Lived experience is "so opaque and blind before itself that it is also an absence from itself" (Sartre 2006, p. 22). Fanon knew all that implicitly and this is reflected by the way that the lived experience of the Black described in the fifth chapter in terms of inferiority can be given a different meaning when in the following chapter it is presented in the context of an account of the cultural imposition that produces that experience together with an account of the action or praxis that promises to free Blacks from the sense of inferiority opposed on them. On this basis one can say that the existential method Fanon deploys in *Black Skin, White Masks* and refines in *The Wretched of the Earth* finds its formal exposition in *Search for a Method*.

It was the need to address the colonial system as such and their shared commitment to the Algerian War of Independence in particular that led Sartre and Fanon to retool existentialism. The later Sartre and Fanon not only do not leave existentialism behind, they also show why an existentialism that remains locked into the paradigm of the gaze at the risk of bypassing material structures loses sight of the historical context. The global reception of *The Wretched of the Earth* suggests that, even though theoreticians may dismiss his conception of an existentialist dialectics, he found a language that resonates with the oppressed and their understanding of colonialism as a racist material system that comes to them through lived experience informed by praxis.

References

Arthur, Paige. 2010. *Unfinished Projects. Decolonization and the Philosophy of Jean-Paul Sartre*. London: Verso.

Bernasconi, Robert. 1995. Sartre's Gaze Returned: The Transformation of the Phenomenology of Racism. *Graduate Faculty Philosophy Journal* 18 (2): 201–202.

———. 2002. The Assumption of Negritude: Aimé Césaire, Frantz Fanon, and the Vicious Circle of Racial Politics. *Parallax* 23: 68–83.

———. 2007. On Needing Not to Know and Forgetting What One Never Knew: The Epistemology of Ignorance in Fanon's Critique of Sartre. In *Race and the Epistemologies of Ignorance*, ed. Nancy Tuana and Shannon Sullivan, 231–239. Albany: SUNY Press.

———. 2008. Can Race Be Thought in Terms of Facticity? A Reconsideration of Sartre's and Fanon's Existential Theories of Race. In *Rethinking Facticity*, ed. François Raffoul and Eric Nelson, 195–213. Albany: SUNY Press.

———. 2010. Fanon's *The Wretched of the Earth* as the Fulfilment of Sartre's Critique of Dialectical Reason. *Sartre Studies International* 16 (2): 36–46.

Birchall, Ian H. 2004. *Sartre Against Stalinism*. New York: Berghahn.

Burnier, Michel-Antoine. 1967. *Choice of Action. The French Existentialists in Politics*. Translated by Bernard Murchland. New York: Random House.

Cohen-Solal, Annie. 1987. *Sartre. A Life*. Translated by Anna Cancogni. London: Heinemann.

D'Arbousier, Gabriel. 1949. Une dangereuse mystification: La théorie de la négritude. La nouvelle critique. *Revue du marxisme militant* I (5): 34–47.

Etherington, Ben. 2016. An Answer to the Question: What is Decolonization? Frantz Fanon's *The Wretched of the Earth* and Jean-Paul Sartre's *Critique of Dialectical Reason*. *Modern Intellectual History* 12 (1): 151–187.

Fanon, Frantz. 1966. *Toward the African Revolution*. Translated by Haakon Chevalier. New York: Monthly Review Press.

———. 2004. *The Wretched of the Earth*. Translated by Richard Philcox. New York: Grove Press.

———. 2008. *Black Skin and White Masks*. Translated by Richard Philcox. New York: Grove Press.

———. 2018. Mental Alterations, Character Modifications, Psychic Disorders and Intellectual Deficit in Spinocerebellar Heredodegeneration. In *Alienation and Freedom*, ed. Jean Khalfa and Robert J.C. Young, 203–275. London: Bloomsbury.

Haddour, Azzedine. 2011. Being Colonized. In *Reading Sartre*, ed. Jonathan Webber, 73–89. London: Routledge.

Hegel, G.W.G. 2011. *Lectures on the Philosophy of World History*. Translated by Robert F. Brown and Peter C. Hodgson. Oxford: Oxford University Press.

James, C.L.R. 1981. *Spheres of Existence*. Westport, CT: Lawrence Hill.

Judaken, Jonathan. 2006. *Jean-Paul Sartre and the Jewish Question*. Lincoln: University of Nebraska Press.

Julien, Ch.-André. 1948. Avant-Propos. In *Anthologie de la nouvelle poésie nègre et malgache de langue française*, vii–viii. Paris: Presses universitaires de France.

Lefebvre, Henri. 2003. Perspectives on Rural Sociology. In *Henri Lefebvre: Key Writings*, ed. Stuart Elden, Elizabeth Lebas, and Elonore Kofman, 111–120. New York: Continuum.

Memmi, Albert. 1965. *The Colonizer and the Colonized*. New York: Orion Press.

More, Mabogo Percy. 2017. Locating Frantz Fanon in Post-Apartheid South Africa. *Journal of Asian and African Studies* 52 (2): 127–141.

Ramuga, Thomas K. 1986. Frantz Fanon and Back Consciousness in Azania (South Africa). *Phylon* 47 (3): 182–191.

Sartre, Jean-Paul. 1948. *Anti-Semite and Jew*. Translated by George J. Becker. New York: Schocken.

———. 1963. *Search for a Method*. Translated by Hazel Barnes. New York: Alfred A. Knopf.

———. 1976. *Critique of Dialectical Reason. Volume I. Theory of Practical Ensembles*, trans. Alan Sheridan-Smith. London: NLB.

———. 2001a. Black Orpheus, trans. John MacCombie. In *Race*, ed. Robert Bernasconi, 115–142. Oxford: Blackwell.

———. 2001b. Colonialism is a System. In *Colonialism and Neocolonialism*, ed. Jean-Paul Sartre, 30–47. London: Routledge.

———. 2006. Itinerary of a Thought. In *Conversations with Jean-Paul Sartre*, 3–66. London: Seagull Books.

———. 2013. A Fundamental Idea of Husserl's Phenomenology: Intentionality. In *We Have Only This Life to Live*, ed. Ronald Aronson and Adrian Van den Hoven, 3–6. New York: NYRB Books.

———. 2018. *Being and Nothingness*. Translated by Sarah Richmond. London: Routledge.

Sayles, James Yaki. 2010. *Meditations on Frantz Fanon's Wretched of the Earth. New Afrikan Revolutionary Writings*. Montreal: Kersplebeded.

Part IV

Science and Arts

19

Existential Psychoanalysis in America

Cameron Bassiri and Matthew Senie

It is the task of the present chapter to demonstrate the manner in which Sartre's existential psychoanalysis was received by American psychology in the 1950s and 1960s. We will argue that Sartre's own form of analysis, developed most explicitly toward the end of *Being and Nothingness*, together with his critique of Freudian psychoanalysis, the most sustained form of which is found in the chapter of *Being and Nothingness* entitled "Bad Faith," served as an alternative to the predominance of orthodox psychoanalysis and behaviorism in the United States. As we will show, Sartre represents a movement away from the conception of the human being determined by biological givens and unconscious forces, or as an entity governed by patterns established through operant conditioning.

C. Bassiri (✉)
Department of Philosophy and Religion, American University, Washington, DC, USA
e-mail: bassiri@american.edu

M. Senie
American University, Washington, DC, USA
e-mail: ms3937a@american.edu

© The Author(s) 2020   **345**
A. Betschart, J. Werner (eds.), *Sartre and the International Impact of Existentialism*,
https://doi.org/10.1007/978-3-030-38482-1_19

Both of these schools and approaches, it is worth noting, fall under what Ludwig Binswanger termed *homo natura* (Binswanger 1963, p. 150). However, in critiquing the biological reductionism and determinism of the tradition of psychology, Sartre moves toward a non-essentialist humanism which interprets neurosis through a confrontation with one or more of the following themes—namely, freedom, death, isolation, and meaninglessness—and interprets the behavior of the subject as rooted in a fundamental life-choice. This existentialist critique and orientation influenced the development of American psychology during these decades and continues to do so up to the present day. In thus influencing and re-orienting American psychology, we would also like to signal its philo-sophical import, demonstrated in the shift of focus from the Kantian categories of causality, actuality, and necessity, to those of community, possibility, and contingency. And finally, we would like to show the man-ner in which Sartre's critique of Freud and behaviorism is similar to that which Kierkegaard leveled at Hegel, only, instead of not wanting to kneel before the system, Sartre did not want to drown in the depths of the unconscious (Kierkegaard 1941, pp. 97–98). Thus, while providing an account of the history of Sartre's reception, we also hope to provide a conceptual account of his influence on the history of American psychology.

In order to account for this development and influence, we will divide the text into two Parts. Within Part One, we will begin by explaining the background against which American psychology was developing, and to which Sartre's work served as both a response and an alternative. We will emphasize the essentialist character of both orthodox psychoanalysis and behaviorism, and show the way in which these forms of essentialism required corresponding methods which neglected fundamental aspects of the life of the patient, most notably his immediate lived-experience. Within this Part, we will also begin to explain the relation between patient and therapist, and in so doing help set the stage for the discussion of the development of this relation in Part Two. Then, within the second part of this work, we will devote particular attention to the reception of Sartre's thought through the writings of prominent American psycholo-gists from this period. In addition to providing such an account, we will also demonstrate the inconsistency between certain of their views of Sartre's philosophy and psychological principles and their own orientations. This discussion will then allow us to move to an analysis of the manner in which Sartre influenced the clinical encounter between patient and therapist, and show the importance of his ontology for existential-humanistic psychology, represented most clearly in the work of James Bugental (Bugental 1978, pp. 36–38; Bugental 1987, pp. 49–66). Finally, we will conclude with some of the more current attempts to integrate Sartre into existential psychology by briefly discussing the work of Irvin Yalom and Betty Cannon, and will conclude with a few directions for future research.

Before beginning the text proper, however, there are a few issues with the field of existential psychology itself that we would like to note. First, existential psychoanalysis or psychology, as stated by several of its greatest representatives, among them Rollo May and Abraham Maslow, is not itself an independent school of psychology, comparable to the school of Freud. It is, as May himself claims, "an *attitude*" (May 1969a, b, p. 15). As such, it is not clearly demarcated from other schools, as psychoanalysis is from behaviorism, but permeates all schools of psychology to a greater or lesser extent, and raises questions fundamental to all psychology and clinical practice as such (May and Yalom 2000, p. 274). Moreover, it is accused of being unnecessarily obscure, so much so in fact that Abraham Maslow claims, in large part in reference to Heidegger and Jaspers, that "There is much in the existentialist writings that I find extremely difficult, or even impossible, to understand and that I have not made much effort to struggle with" (Maslow 1969, p. 49). Nevertheless, he managed to make use of its core principles and thought it essential to the present state and future of psychology. He writes, when discussing its impact:

> Perhaps this is why I have found it to be not so much a totally new revelation as a stressing, confirming, sharpening, and rediscovering of trends already existing in American psychology (the various self psychologies, growth psychologies, self-actualization psychologies, organism psychologies, certain neo-Freudian psychologies, the Jungian psychology, not to mention some of the psychoanalytic ego psychologists, the Gestalt therapists, and I don't know how many more. (Maslow 1969, pp. 49–50)

Thus we are faced with the paradoxical, if not contradictory, question: how can a school of psychology, which is in truth no school at all, affect the already existing framework of psychology and provide an alternative approach, method, and understanding?

The second issue, which further complicates matters, is the critique of Sartre found in several prominent American existential psychotherapists, perhaps above all by Rollo May and Gordon Allport. We will quote their work extensively below, but make brief mention of their views for the moment to highlight the tension in the reception of Sartre in America. Moreover, in addition to this critique is the American preference for other European existentialist thinkers, in particular Martin Heidegger and Søren Kierkegaard, as found again in May, Carl Rogers, and so on. How, then, we may ask, can Sartre have had a significant impact on American psychology if he was received in this way, and what are we to make of this reception itself? Is this not in fact a rejection, rather than a reception, of Sartre?

Part I: Psychology Without a Subject

It is important to note from the beginning that the reception of existentialist philosophy by American psychology was ambiguous. By such ambiguity, and with reference to our opening remarks, we mean that existentialism did not come on the American intellectual scene and establish an entirely new and unheard of theory or practice of psychology. Rather, and this we argue is part of the virtue of its approach, it deepened the existing theories and methods by injecting its unique philosophical concepts and new life into them. This, however, is not to say that existential psychoanalysis did not become a field in its own right; again, what we hope to emphasize is that it also built on, developed, and in various respects transformed the extant and dominant psychoanalytic and behavioral frameworks already in place. We would like to focus on the peculiar relation that these two schools of psychology have to the unique presence of existentialist psychology in America. Before doing so, however, it is necessary to acknowledge that these schools of thought are enormously broad and complex, with many adherents and dissenters. Thus, while we will generalize some of their principles for our purposes here, we recognize in advance the provisional character of our account. As a result, we will devote particular attention to how these schools of thought conceived of the *individual subject* in the context of the therapeutic relationship between patient and therapist.

The main element of existential philosophy that allows it to offer an alternative to Freudian psychoanalysis and behaviorism is its unique conception of the subject as a situated freedom responsible for itself, its values, and its relations to others, in a word, its *non-essentialism*. And in truth it is just this Sartrean concept of a *subject without an essence* that made possible a corresponding form of therapy which both complemented and challenged orthodox Freudian psychoanalysis and behaviorism so effectively. Both of the latter schools, though each in its own way, are defined by what we will term an "essentialization" of the individual. In fact, this view is shared by Rollo May. He writes: "In endeavoring to separate reality into its discrete parts and to formulate abstract laws for these parts, Western science has by and large been *essentialist* in character" (May 1969b, p. 12). In the case of Freud, the essentialization, or the fixing of the nature, "form," or essence of the subject, was rooted in his natural-scientific and psychodynamic view of the individual as biologically determined by conflicting unconscious forces. While for Skinner, his essentialization comes in the form of his rejection of "autonomous man," or any notion of subjectivity at all, and his replacement of it with an organism whose life *is* its behavior as it has been developed through operant conditioning and which can be understood purely through "a science of behavior."[1] Both schools, then, given their theoretical frameworks and their conceptions of human existence, *are psychologies without a subject*.

As is well known, Freudian psychoanalytic theory conceives of the true individual as a reserve of hidden impulses and drives. Furthermore,

---

[1] Skinner (2002, p. 14) and Skinner (1953, p. 11). It is also worth noting that Skinner was aware of this charge. In *Walden Two*, clearly referring to Sartre and existentialism, he has his character Castle say: "When you deny your own freedom for the sake of playing with a science of behavior, you're acting in plain bad faith. That's the only way I can explain it" (Skinner 2005, p. 242). Moreover, for certain of his evaluations of phenomenology and existentialism, see Skinner (1976, pp. 243, 248–249).

mental life is deterministic and mechanistic. In the "Editor's Introduction" to *The Psychopathology of Everyday Life*, James Strachey writes: "Moreover, there was another fundamental belief of Freud's which could be convincingly supported by the examination of parapraxes—his belief in the universal application of determinism to mental events. This is the truth which he insists upon in the final chapter of the book: it should be possible in theory to discover the psychical determinants of every smallest detail of the processes of the mind" (Freud 1965, p. 8). The history of the individual, it follows, is determinative of its present, and when a patient enters therapy, it is precisely this history and this causal series that is of central importance. Thus, within the "psychoanalytic situation," through an exclusive orientation to the past and personal history of the patient, the various psychosexual stages of development, and working through transference, resistance, and so on. psychoanalysis provides insight into the origin of the neurosis of the patient with the ultimate aim of "the translation of what is unconscious into what is conscious. Yes, that is it. By carrying what is unconscious on into what is conscious, we lift the repressions, we remove the preconditions for the formation of symptoms, we transform the pathogenic conflict into a normal one for which it must be possible somehow to find a solution" (Freud 1966, p. 541). This conception of the subject as determined by its unconscious and amenable to "analytic therapy" through the therapeutic apparatus involving free association, resistance, relieving repression, transference, and so on reduces the subject to an identifiable and yet modifiable essence (Arlow 2000; Freud 1966, p. 557, for the complete discussion pp. 557–576).

Although an independent school of psychology, behaviorism falls into the same essentializing trap. Rather than plumbing the depths of the unconscious, it is fundamentally concerned with properly understanding and modifying the behavior of the patient. As Wilson has described it in general terms:

> Applied behavior analysis, derived directly from Skinner's radical behaviorism, restricts itself to the study of overt behavior and environmental conditions that presumably regulate behavior. Covert, unobservable elements, such as needs, drives, motives, traits, and conflicts, are disregarded. Skinner's analyses of behavior, for example, are couched in terms of

conditioning processes, such as reinforcement, discrimination, and gener-
alization. (Wilson 2000, p. 212)

There is no hidden or inner life of the individual, no hermeneutic of
associations or dreams designed to reach a cure. There is simply behavior,
nothing more and nothing less. The therapist, it follows, attempts to
understand the situation within which various behavior patterns were
established, that is, the reinforcement achieved through reward and pun-
ishment, and then has the task of constructing a scenario to reinforce new
behavior meant to replace the old. In this sense, it *essentializes* the patient
by *reducing* it to behavior. Moreover, the clinical approach essentializes
the patient by scientifically understanding it as an organism with behavior patterns which have been formed and can change without consciousness, choice, and, perhaps above all, freedom. Thus, in neither orthodox
psychoanalysis nor behaviorism does the analyst empathically engage
with the patient as a subject, but rather as a purely natural-scientific
object with various symptoms, neuroses, or undesirable behavior patterns
in need of modification. The therapist, therefore, observes the patient
from the outside, evaluating the data "objectively." Nevertheless, while
there will invariably be nuances to each patient-therapist relationship, the
formula for the interaction between the two remains constant, and the
essence of the patient—unconscious forces or behavior—is preserved for
the therapeutic work to be successful.

It is here that we can begin to see the importance of existential psychology and where it diverges most sharply from the traditional theories. It is
defined by a rejection of essentialism, and, though not always acknowledged, this can be traced largely to Sartre and his early ontology of the
subject. Sartre, late in *Being and Nothingness*, develops his own concept of
existential psychoanalysis, which views the patient as a free, responsible
subject whose various neuroses or behaviors are rooted in a fundamental
life-choice. As such, Sartre's emphasis in the clinical encounter was on the
individual as a freedom, his lived-experiences, and understanding the
fundamental life-choice at the root of the neurotic behavior. In contrast
to psychoanalysis and behaviorism, existential psychoanalysis attempts to
make contact with the present lived-reality of the living subject on the
basis of its past, rather than looking into the past or operant conditioning

alone. As Sartre writes of his own form of analysis in *Search for a Method*: "Psychoanalysis alone allows us to discover the whole man in the adult; that is, not only his present determinations but also the weight of his history" (Sartre 1968, p. 60). And the way into this patient's unique present with its historical depth is through a particular kind of relationship between the analyst and the patient—a relationship that relies on a non-essentialist conception of the individual and the corresponding empathic concern of the therapist.

In any psychoanalytic encounter, when the analyst looks at the patient, a moment of objectification occurs. However, we argue that according to existential analysis, in this moment of objectification, of the understanding of the patient as *living through*, not *having*, various neuroses, the subjectivity of the subject is maintained. The question, however, is how to establish the interaction between two subjectivities without falling into an essentialism and turning the empathic relation between the patient and therapist into Hell. To look at the patient is to develop a certain view of him, that is, as this specific individual who has made various choices, is suffering from ailments. Now, based on what we have seen thus far, it appears that a tension exists in our interpretation. We identified the act of objectification as part of the problem that arose in psychoanalysis and behaviorism. However, we have just claimed that objectification occurs in the therapeutic process. There is a difference, however, in that the kind of objectification that results from the Freudian and behaviorist frameworks is different from the kind found in the existential approach. This is because the former schools assume that the objectified view of the patient provides an exhaustive account of the essence of the patient. The existential approach by contrast recognizes the dangers of objectification and works to prevent it from becoming essentialization through the empathetic connection between patient and analyst, wherein each subject sees the other as a subjectivity, rather than as a mere object whose essence is being uncovered. Freudianism looks at the patient and sees a collection of drives which need to be scientifically excavated and polished, as though fossilized. The assumption is that to uncover this supposed essence of the individual is to cure the afflicting neurosis. But to brush off a fossil is not to resurrect the dinosaur. Similarly, behaviorism looks at the patient and sees behavior, which can be mechanistically reinforced or altered.

Existential psychoanalysis recognizes the moment of objectification for what it is, that is, a part of the process, and nothing more than a reference to what is behind it: the free and responsible subject who experiences neurosis as anxiety, fear, uncertainty, and so on.

Part II: Sartre's Reception and the Therapeutic Encounter

In what follows, we will pick up the guiding thread from Part One and devote particular attention to the relation between the therapist and the patient. We will also further expand on the theme of ambiguity, and develop it in another direction. However, before doing so, we would like to make a few comments about the presence of existentialism and existential psychology in America during the late 1950s, 1960s, and on into the 1970s. First, as seems to be universally known, existentialist psychology came on to the scene with the publication of the anthology *Existence*, edited by Rollo May, Ernest Engel, and Henri F. Ellenberger in 1958. This text involved two introductory essays by May explaining exactly what is meant by existential psychology, that is, its "origins," "significance," and "contributions" (May 1958a, p. 37, b, p. 3). These first two essays by May can be read as manifestos of existentialist psychology, materializing this specter, as it were, and heralding its future and that of American psychology. In the wake of this publication, several other journals, articles, and so on were founded and published. In a section entitled "Since *Existence*" in Herbert Spiegelberg's *Phenomenology and Psychology in Psychiatry*, he notes the *Journal of Existential Psychiatry* in 1960, which ultimately became the *Journal of Existentialism* in 1964, the *Review of Existential Psychology and Psychiatry* in 1961, *Existential Inquiries* in 1959, the *American Association for Existential Psychology and Psychiatry* in 1959, and so on (Spiegelberg 1972, pp. 164–165). And in the final entry of *Existential Psychology*, "Existential and Phenomenological Psychology: A Selective Bibliography," Joseph Lyons writes:

When an earlier edition of this bibliography was prepared, less than eight years ago, it was possible to include in 185 items a nearly exhaustive listing of 'writings in English in which phenomenological or existentialist conceptions are applied explicitly to issues in the field of psychology.' An attempt to do the same today would result, quite probably, in close to 1000 entries. Existentialism and phenomenology are no longer doctrines or even movements, but, like modern psychoanalysis, influences that pervade every aspect of the current intellectual and artistic scene. (Lyons 1969, p. 99)

These brief remarks represent in broad strokes the impact of existential thought on American psychology and psychiatry. However, after reading through the material, and poring through many of the subsequent lectures and texts, any observant reader will note the lack of references to Sartre and the critical reception of him. Rollo May, for example, in the first essay of *Existence*, "The Origins and Significance of the Existential Movement in Psychology," writes: "Sartre represents a nihilistic, subjectivist extreme in existentialism which invites misunderstanding, and his position is by no means the most useful introduction to the movement" (May 1958b, p. 11). Moreover, in the opening essay entitled "The Emergence of Existentialist Psychology" of the collection *Existential Psychology*, he writes: "I agree with Sartre when he emphasizes, 'We *are* our choices,' but I would add, 'within the limits of our given world'" (May 1969b, p. 13). And again, Gordon Allport, in summarizing this collection and existentialist thought itself, writes: "Trends in American existentialism will be (and are) far more optimistic. Sartre says there is 'no exit.' One is reminded of Epictetus the Stoic, who long ago wrote, 'So your nose runs? What, then, you fool, be glad you have a sleeve to wipe it on.' Can anyone picture Carl Rogers offering such counsel?"[2] Moreover, of a piece with this critique is the American preference for other European existentialist thinkers, in particular Martin Heidegger and Søren Kierkegaard.

---

[2] Allport (1969, p. 96). The clear answer to this question is "No," and one does not need to look far to see that it is Rogers's reading of Sartre that in part confirms this response. In his account of "The Sixth Stage," he writes: "*Self as an object tends to disappear.* The self, at this moment, *is* this feeling. This is a being in the moment, with little self-conscious awareness, but with primarily a reflexive awareness, as Sartre terms it. The self *is*, subjectively, in the existential moment. It is not something one perceives." Could one ever imagine Rogers not giving this advice? (Rogers 1989, p. 147).

However, we would argue that this reception is misguided, both on its own terms and with regard to Sartre's work itself. We will therefore continue to expound this understanding of Sartre, while also citing some passages from Sartre which are perfectly consistent with, and in fact supplement, the critiques from May and Allport. First, May remarks that existential psychology is "the endeavor to understand man as *experiencing*, as the one to *whom* the experiences happen" (May 1969b, p. 9). Sartre writes: "The *principle* of this psychoanalysis is that man is a totality and not a collection. Consequently he expresses himself as a whole in even his most insignificant and his most superficial behavior. In other words, there is not a taste, a mannerism, or a human act, that is not *revealing*" (Sartre 1984, p. 726). And finally: "Thus existential psychoanalysis will have to be completely flexible and adapt itself to the slightest observable changes in the subject. Our concern here is to understand what is *individual* and often even instantaneous. The method which has served for one subject will not necessarily be suitable to use for another subject or for the same subject at a later period" (Sartre 1984, p. 732). Moreover, the comment by Allport coheres with a fairly common interpretation—what we consider a misinterpretation—of Sartre's view of the Other, which finds emphatic expression in the work of Mary Warnock, who states that "other people are essentially, in themselves, and by their very existence, a danger to us" (Warnock 1970, p. 116). Clearly, all of these remarks problematize the concept or the view of the reception of Sartre and his influence on American psychology. In fact, we are arguing that while American psychology was critical of Sartre—and receptive of him to an extent, as we have seen—it is in truth the case that American psychology was more Sartrean than it would have liked to admit. And, of course, even if it wasn't, it should have been. Furthermore, when May states that "consciousness itself implies always the possibility of turning against one's self, denying one's self," he is clearly making use of Sartrean concepts, most of all bad faith, in an attempt to show the manner in which clients are able to deny their own self-consciousness, awareness, freedom and responsibility, and so on (May 1969a, p. 82). In addition, Rogers, after referring to himself as an existentially oriented psychologist in line with Maslow and May, and with clear reference to Skinner, writes that "*human* behavior is, in some significant ways, something more than the behavior of our laboratory animals" (Rogers 1969, p. 86). He further claims that the most important thing he can do as a therapist is "be real," view therapy as "a meeting of two *persons*," and that 'The way to do is to *be*" (Rogers 1969, p. 87). All of these quotations presuppose a uniquely Sartrean concept of authenticity—one not relying solely on the phenomenon of death—in order to help the patient realize his potential. Sartre writes: "Precisely because the goal of the inquiry must be to discover a *choice* and not a *state*, the investigator must recall on every occasion that his object is not a datum buried in the darkness of the unconscious but a free, conscious determination—which is not even resident in consciousness, but which is one with this consciousness itself" (Sartre 1984, p. 732). Finally, however much, in other words, Rogers may have been influenced by Kierkegaard, unless he wants to impose the necessity of religious fulfillment in this context, he is still making use of a Sartrean concept, and ultimately requires it for the complete development of his own form of therapy.

Moreover, these authors emphasize consciousness. In the same stroke, however, they refer to the significance of Heidegger's concepts of *Dasein* and being-in-the-world. As should be clear from *Being and Time*—the text they are working with most closely—Heidegger's analyses are not primarily concerned with consciousness. In addition, these theorists credit Heideggerian ontology with having overcome the subject-object distinction, expelling various dualisms and erroneous concepts from philosophy and psychology. However, it still seems to us that such an overcoming—assuming it is achieved—is not necessary therapeutically useful or an accurate depiction of the life of the patient. If one is attempting, as von Gebsattel did, for example, to live in "the world of the compulsive," and if the compulsive himself perceives objects in various ways, most notably as threatening, unless as a potential goal for therapeutic practice, it is not clear how such overcoming is significant or even appropriate in this context (Gebsattel 1958, p. 170). This issue surrounding the elimination of the subject-object distinction is also stressed by Viktor Frankl. He writes: "Those authors who pretend to have overcome the dichotomy between object and subject are not aware that, as a truly phenomenological analysis would reveal, there is no such thing as cognition outside of the polar field of tension established between object and subject" (Frankl

1969, pp. 50–51). Thus, *contra* May, rather than "representing an extreme form of subjectivism and nihilism in existentialism," Sartre recognizes and appreciates the subject, or, as we could say, each subject, in its subjectivity (May 1958b, p. 11). On the basis of such a recognition, Sartre makes possible a new orientation in accordance with which each subject, as his or her own world, is treated uniquely by the therapist in such a way that a collaboration leads to understanding, insight, behavior modification, and, ultimately, more consciousness of the subject's freedom and responsibility.

And here, we would like to state more clearly the change in patient-therapist relations that one finds in American psychology as a result of Sartre's work. A further comment, in truth a critique, from Viktor Frankl is particularly relevant at this point. In *The Will to Meaning*, to further clarify his own view, he writes: "Meanings are discovered but not invented. This is opposed to the contention of Jean-Paul Sartre that ideals and values are designed and invented by man. Or, as Jean-Paul Sartre has it, man invents himself" (Frankl 1969, p. 60). First, we would just like to disagree with this statement, and show such a view implies a metaphysics that limits the possibilities of the therapeutic encounter. Within the therapeutic context, and emphasized by Bugental for example, *presence* is a fundamental concept (Bugental 1978, p. 36). To define presence, he writes: "*Presence* is the quality of being in a situation in which one intends to be as aware and as participate as one is able to be at that time and in those circumstances. Presence is carried into effect through mobilization of one's inner (toward subjective experiencing) and outer (toward the situation and any other person/s in it) sensitivities" (Bugental 1978, p. 36). Thus, Sartre has made possible a therapeutic "We," and in such a way that each member maintains its irreducibility in its forming a pair. Moreover, through the concept of presence, Sartre has established the possibility carried out by Bugental of having both therapist and patient act together to "invent" a meaning in the life of the subject that does not demand an essentialism of the patient or the world, which is the danger and one of the limitations of Frankl's approach (Frankl 1969, p. 60). If a meaning is to be "found," it must already "be there," implying a metaphysical order with inherent, hidden meaning or meanings which simply need to be uncovered (Frankl 1969, p. 61). In other words, Sartre's ontology and correlative concepts make possible a truly free and open therapeutic process wherein patient and therapist create meaning together without various methodological principles or metaphysical commitments blocking the way. If the therapist can make the subject aware of his bad faith and "denial of consciousness"—as stated by May—by being present, caring, empathetic, and engaged, rather than being absent, indifferent, cold, and passive, then the ontology of the for-itself can come to light and the patient can become aware of his freedom and the corresponding responsibility in a positive way (May 1969a, p. 82).

Finally, to conclude, we think it prudent to mention certain recent developments. First, just as the reception of existential analysis is divided into two periods—the phenomenological and the existential—so we think existential psychology itself can be divided into two periods as well—the implicitly and the explicitly Sartrean. What we have discussed over the course of this presentation in part speaks to the implicit Sartreanism of the first phase of existential psychology. Irvin Yalom, mentioned earlier, systematized all of these ideas in his comprehensive *Existential Psychotherapy*. He emphasizes the fact that the European authors included in the anthology *Existence* are still not appreciated to the extent to which they should be in the United States, and provides a definition of existential therapy that he develops over the course of his text (Yalom 1980, p. 17). He writes: "Existential Psychotherapy is a dynamic approach to therapy which focuses on concerns that are rooted in the individual's existence" (Yalom 1980, p. 5). He develops theoretical accounts of the four themes of this area of psychology—death, freedom, isolation, and meaninglessness—and provides detailed case histories.

Moreover, ten years later, Betty Cannon integrates Sartrean principles into her metatheory and practice in *Sartre and Psychoanalysis: An Existentialist Challenge to Clinical Metatheory*. One thing that makes this text so unique and so important to the future of the field is that Cannon not only makes use of the early principles in her clinical work and explains precisely why she found Sartre more insightful and useful in certain respects than other schools of psychology, but in so doing she also integrates concepts from the *Critique* into her theory and practice. And here we think we can see the challenge to current Sartrean practice and an indication of at least one of the directions it should develop in, that is, the incorporation of concepts from the *Critique*, such as "the third" and "fraternity-terror," to further understand the basic life-choice of the patient and how the therapist can help *create* or "invent," not "discover," new meanings to help the patient live a meaningful life with full consciousness of his or her freedom and responsibility (Frankl 1969, p. 60). Thus Cannon writes:

> The difference between Sartre's earlier and later work is that the fundamental project in his later work has acquired a sociomaterial dimension which is foreign to *Being and Nothingness*. Although human freedom still lies at the heart of the Sartrean dialectic, it is a freedom which discovers itself in an inescapable social world within which the power of humanized matter, of groups, and of series, is recognized in a new way. Existentialist therapy must no longer simply discover the individual depths to a client's project; it must also elucidate the sociomaterial depths of that same project. (Cannon 1991, p. 220)

Furthermore, a final line of research would involve incorporating Sartre's concepts from the *Critique* into the practice of group psychology. Now, a beginning in this direction has been made by Yalom in his comprehensive text *The Theory and Practice of Group Psychotherapy* which, in its most recent, fifth edition, was edited with Molyn Leszcz. How, we might ask, on the basis of the principles discussed over the course of this chapter and the concepts just listed from the *Critique*, could Sartre's later thought be integrated into the various views of the "cohesiveness" of the group? (Yalom and Leszcz 2005, pp. 55–56). This cohesiveness of groups has a peculiar transcendental status within the realm of group psychology in so far as it serves as a condition for possibility for subsequent group work. Yalom writes: "I must point out that group cohesiveness is not only a potent therapeutic force in its own right. It is a precondition for other therapeutic factors to function optimally." And given this importance, the question is how Sartre's concepts can be used to help strengthen the ties between group members. Moreover, how would his concept of "the third," for example, contribute to an understanding of both groups with leaders and leaderless groups? And, more generally, how can his understanding of the genesis and maintenance of groups help group therapists maintain the interest and focus of the group, work with disruptive members, and provide an existentially oriented group wherein each member recognizes and is recognized by the other members as they empathically work through the specific tasks of the group?

Finally, we would like to end this presentation on a light note. After all that we have discussed, it should be readily apparent that Sartre had a tremendously important impact on American psychology—at times even in an unrecognized manner—and that he made possible a number of developments within the field. Rollo May states that "every psychotherapist is existential to the text that he is a good therapist" (May 1969b, p. 15). We would like to add that every great psychotherapist is Sartrean.

References

Allport, Gordon W. 1969. Comment on Earlier Chapters. In *Existential Psychology*, ed. Rollo May, 93–98. New York: McGraw-Hill.

Arlow, Jacob A. 2000. Psychoanalysis. In *Current Psychotherapies*, ed. Raymond J. Corsini and Danny Wedding, 16–53. Itasca: F.E. Peacock.

Binswanger, Ludwig. 1963. Freud's Conception of Man in the Light of Anthropology. In *Being-in-the-World: Selected Papers of Ludwig Binswanger*, 149–181. New York: Basic Books.

Bugental, James F.T. 1978. *Psychotherapy and Process: The Fundamentals of an Existential-Humanistic Approach*. New York: McGraw-Hill.

———. 1987. *The Art of the Psychotherapist*. New York: W.W. Norton and Company.

Cannon, Betty. 1991. *Sartre and Psychoanalysis: An Existentialist Challenge to Clinical Metatheory*. Lawrence: University Press of Kansas.

Frankl, Viktor E. 1969. *The Will to Meaning: Foundations and Applications of Logotherapy*. New York: Plume.

Freud, Sigmund. 1965. *The Psychopathology of Everyday Life*. New York: W.W. Norton and Company.

———. 1966. *Introductory Lectures on Psycho-Analysis*. New York: W.W. Norton and Company.

von Gebsattel, V.E. 1958. The World of the Compulsive. In *Existence*, ed. Rollo May, Ernest Angel, and Henri F. Ellenberger, 170–187. New York: Rowman & Littlefield.

Kierkegaard, Søren. 1941. *Concluding Unscientific Postscript*. Princeton: Princeton University Press.

Lyons, Joseph. 1969. Existential and Phenomenological Psychology: A Selective Bibliography. In *Existential Psychology*, ed. Rollo May, 99–117. New York: McGraw-Hill.

Maslow, Abraham. 1969. Existential Psychology—What's in it for us? In *Existential Psychology*, ed. Rollo May, 49–57. New York: McGraw-Hill.

May, Rollo. 1958a. Contributions to Existential Psychotherapy. In *Existence*, ed. Rollo May, Ernest Angel, and Henri F. Ellenberger, 37–91. New York: Rowman & Littlefield.

———. 1958b. The Origins and Significance of the Existential Movement in Psychology. In *Existence*, ed. Rollo May, Ernest Angel, and Henri F. Ellenberger, 3–36. New York: Rowman & Littlefield.

———. 1969a. Existential Bases of Psychotherapy. In *Existential Psychology*, ed. Rollo May, 72–83. New York: McGraw-Hill.

———. 1969b. The Emergence of Existential Psychology. In *Existential Psychology*, ed. Rollo May, 1–48. New York: McGraw-Hill.

May, Rollo, and Irvin Yalom. 2000. Existential Psychotherapy. In *Current Psychotherapies*, ed. Raymond J. Corsini and Danny Wedding, 273–302. Itasca: F.E. Peacock Publishers.

Rogers, Carl. 1969. Two Divergent Trends. In *Existential Psychology*, ed. Rollo May, 84–92. New York: McGraw-Hill.

———. 1989. A Process Conception of Psychotherapy. In *On Becoming a Person*, 125–159. New York: Houghton Mifflin Company.

Sartre, Jean-Paul. 1968. *Search for a Method*. New York: Vintage Books.

———. 1984. *Being and Nothingness*. New York: Washington Square Books.

Skinner, B.F. 1953. *Science and Human Behavior*. New York: The Free Press.

———. 1976. *About Behaviorism*. New York: Vintage Books.

———. 2002. *Beyond Freedom and Dignity*. Indianapolis: Hackett Publishing Company.

———. 2005. *Walden Two*. Indianapolis: Hackett Publishing Company Inc.

Spiegelberg, Herbert. 1972. *Phenomenology in Psychology and Psychiatry*. Evanston: Northwestern University Press.

Warnock, Mary. 1970. *Existentialism*. Oxford: Oxford University Press.

Wilson, G. Terence. 2000. Behavior Therapy. In *Current Psychotherapies*, ed. Raymond J. Corsini and Danny Wedding, 205–240. Itasca: F.E. Peacock.

Yalom, Irvin. 1980. *Existential Psychotherapy*. New York: Basic Books.

Yalom, Irvin, and Molyn Leszcz. 2005. *The Theory and Practice of Group Psychotherapy*. New York: Basic Books.

20

Existentialism and Cinema: The Dialectic of Bad Faith and Authenticity in Federico Fellini's *8½*

Maria Russo

Film and Existential Philosophy

There are two possible ways of studying the influence of existentialism. The first approach is related to a documented reception of this philosophy by an author—for example, when it is possible to trace a critical debate. The second way is related to the implicit connections between existentialist themes and issues, even outside the borders of philosophy. In fact, existentialism was not just a philosophy but also a European cultural movement and trend. Even intellectuals who had never considered philosophy in their work were influenced by existentialism and its atmosphere especially in literature and cinema.

First of all, an important question must be asked: can films do philosophy in some way? It is necessary to distinguish between films that are only the result of a mass production and films that are aware of their metaphorical potentiality. The latter often include philosophical premises, even if they are not presented in the form of a theory or argumentation,

M. Russo (✉)
Lecturer in Moral Philosophy, San Raffaele University, Milan, Italy

© The Author(s) 2020
A. Betschart, J. Werner (eds.), *Sartre and the International Impact of Existentialism*,
https://doi.org/10.1007/978-3-030-38482-1_20

but through main characters' actions and choices. Is this still philosophy? One may recognize that not all philosophers have written their ideas in the form of a rigid argumentation or a series of syllogisms. At the dawn of ancient Greek philosophy, Plato used to resort to myths; St. Augustine employed the form of confession; and, in another modality, Michel de Montaigne utilized it in his *Essays*. French moralists often used moral tales; Nietzsche expressed himself using aphorisms. And, of course, existentialists have mixed up phenomenological descriptions with several narrative parts. In fact, Sartre and Beauvoir were philosophers and writers in a wider sense. Hence, the history of philosophy is full of episodes in which philosophical content was communicated in a narrative way.

This is one of the reasons why several authors, such as Stanley Cavell or Stephen Mulhall, think that films can contribute to the philosophical discussion. For Mulhall, movies are even able to philosophize better than the traditional text-based medium because they communicate not only on a rational level, but also on an emotional one. It is not clear whether films can do every kind of philosophy, but we believe that films can do existentialist philosophy. In fact, the Seventh Art could list many authors who have reflected on themes such as human existence, freedom of choice, and forms of alienation in their era. There were those who developed tragic and anguished aspects of existentialism, such as Ingmar Bergman, offering voice and image to Heideggerian themes; and there were those who meditated on specifically Sartrean themes, such as the concrete possibility to act freely in a world full of limits and constraints or the opposition between bad faith and authenticity.

One should not forget that Sartre even tried to write several screenplays (such as *Typhus* or *Freud* for John Huston) and he entitled his most important periodical *Les Temps modernes* in honor of Charlie Chaplin. He loved the Marx Brothers, Buster Keaton, Orson Welles, and even Donald Duck (as remembered by Simone de Beauvoir). He analyzed the structure of image in his *Imagination: A Psychological Critique* (1936) and in *The Imaginary* (1940), and he made a very passionate apology for cinema in which he expressed his esteem toward the Seventh Art and its ethical, philosophical, and narrative potential (Sartre 1990).

Existentialism and Italian Cinema

While there are several obvious connections between existentialism and cinema in France, in Italy this link is more implicit and has to be analyzed in its peculiarity. Certain authors developed a sort of existentialist cinema starting from neorealism, an artistic movement based on the choice to use non-professionals as actors and to reproduce reality without trimmings, especially in its roughest aspects. The two most eccentric authors of this prolific trend were Michelangelo Antonioni (with his so-called *internal existentialism*) and Federico Fellini (with his *magic realism*). For the former an existentialist influence is evident in his masterpiece *Red Desert* (1964) and in the so-called trilogy of alienation (*The Adventure, The Night*, and *The Eclipse*, between 1960 and 1962). In different ways, Antonioni and Fellini both depicted the individual discomfort in perceiving one's existence as devoid of any aim or meaning. This interior affliction also includes the relationship with others and the assumption of a role inside society. Though we do not know whether Antonioni and Fellini read Sartre's and Camus's essays and narratives, existentialism was quite present in the Italian film industry. Antonioni developed the idea of the unavoidable depression tied to an awareness of the human condition, whereas Fellini tried to offer a therapy for this spiritual disease. Both directors also carried out an autopsy on the bourgeois mentality. This aspect was also well developed by Pier Paolo Pasolini, one of the most influential intellectuals of the past century in Italy. Over the years, many other Italian movie directors developed existentialist themes in their films, such as Bernardo Bertolucci, Marco Bellocchio, Nanni Moretti, Giuseppe Tornatore, Emanuele Crialese, and, most recently, Paolo Sorrentino and Luca Guadagnino.

It is not possible here to analyze all the implicit references to existentialism within Italian cinema, so let us take Federico Fellini's Oscar-winning movie *8½* as an example. In this film, there are several analogies with Sartrean early philosophy but also an original contribution to the theme. The film is about a movie director who struggles with his inability to complete the script of his forthcoming film. According to our thesis,

8½ is not only an intellectual movie, but an existentialist argumentation in the form of a narration.

Also William Pamerleau, who wrote a book titled *Existentialist Cinema*, thinks that Fellini developed existentialist themes: "With respect to existentialism, let us say that certain films and certain philosophers try to describe the same thing: the human condition" (Pamerleau 2009, p. 41).

The aim of this chapter is not to offer a complete parallel between the two authors, but to focus on *8½* as an example of an existentialist movie developing a Sartrean argument that goes even beyond Sartre himself.

8½: An Existentialist Interpretation

Fellini was an omnivorous reader, but he did not like to show off his culture. For this reason, it is quite difficult to trace his readings. However, after the success of the *Existentialism Is a Humanism* conference, Sartre and his cultural and philosophical trend became well known throughout Europe. In effect, Sartre and Fellini thought alike on the same themes by different means: a phenomenological description of the human condition beyond the surface of reality, the complexity of identity and choices, the lack of a strong will that is recognizable both in Guido Anselmi (the protagonist of *8½*) and in Sartre's characters such as Mathieu (*The Age of Reason, The Reprieve, Troubled Sleep*) or Antoine Roquentin (*Nausea*).

At this point, it is appropriate to describe briefly the plot of the movie. Guido Anselmi is a famous movie director (exactly like Federico Fellini at that time: he had just been applauded for *La Dolce Vita*). He is about to prepare his forthcoming movie but he is suffering from a sort of artistic block. He is not able to write a complete script, choose the actors, and understand what he wants to say. He is working under pressure because the budget is very tight. Even if the producer and an unpleasant well-known movie critic are very skeptical about his current work, he prefers to distract himself with his mistress who reminds him of his childlike wet dream (a prostitute named Saraghina he met on a beach). In the middle of the movie, Guido's wife appears on the set, and they start to argue about his continuous cheating and lies. Even the beautiful Claudia, the actress who should play a girl who can save him in this movie, is not able to inspire Guido. The movie seems to end with the failure of an entire existence, but just when Guido is about to leave the set, an illusionist suggests to him how to start the movie. The set becomes a sort of circus, with all characters holding their hands in a circle.

Beyond all this stratified puzzlement, it is possible to recognize two levels of narration. Firstly, the storyline Guido is trying to complete is nothing but a representation of himself in the kingdom of bad faith. He intends to depict the many women in his life, but he is not capable of penetrating and illustrating their existential truth in a cinematic form. The same occurs in dealing with his self-portrait, as he is unable to represent his contradictory personality. He fails to outline a strong critique against Catholic education and he tries to hide his inadequacy and insecurity behind his artistic portrait.

But there is also another level of narration, which is the tale in which Federico Fellini reveals himself as a man and as a director through the multitude of Guido's masks. In this *hiddenness*, that is also a voluntary *disclosure*, lies the dimension of authenticity. Fellini and Guido will coincide in the final scene. As Pamerleau points out, "Fellini's highly personal, semi-autobiographical films provide specific examples of the search for authenticity on the part of the film's characters and the filmmaker himself" (Pamerleau 2009, p. 165).

The Nightmare of Alienation and the Look

The movie opens with a sort of a nightmare. Guido is stuck in very chaotic traffic, a situation not so improbable for somebody who drives in Rome. This nightmare takes place in a claustrophobic atmosphere and Guido has to make an incredible effort to get out of his car. Already here we can find at least two Sartrean themes that will be present in the whole movie: (1) the remarkable bond between the individual's modality of being and their representation of the world and (2) the infernal relationship between the for-itself and the others. In *Being and Nothingness*, the for-itself, in its incessant sequence of choices, makes not only oneself, but also its representation of the world as a correlative of these choices. In this interpretation, the world appears as a magical and irrational world or as a technical one. In Guido's case it is a suffocating world, in which every-body makes demands. This is really evident in the way Fellini-Guido transfigures reality, not only dreaming when asleep but also daydreaming. The most famous scene in the movie is the sequence of the harem. In this quite chauvinistic fantasy, all the women in Guido's life live together without conflict, with the purpose only of loving him. But the harem is only a failed attempt to escape from reality. Guido cannot avoid the expectations of his women just as he cannot escape from the producer's demands. Sartre had masterfully described this relationship between the for-itself and the world in his *Sketch for a Theory of Emotions*:

> The horrible can appear only in the kind of world whose existants are magi-cal by nature [...]. This is rather well shown in the universe of the dream where doors, locks, walls, and arms are not recourses against the menaces of the thief or the wild animal because they are perceived in a unitary act of horror. [...] We see the murderers cross these walls and doors. In vain do we press the trigger of our revolver: the shot does not go off. In short, to perceive any object whatsoever as horrible is to perceive it on the basis of a world which reveals itself as already being horrible. (Sartre 1962, p. 89)

At the end of the initial sequence, the producer captures Guido with a rope tied to his foot while he is trying to fly above the beach. Guido feels distraught, and immediately the world around him becomes overwhelm-ing. While everybody lives in the technical world, made of promises, deadlines, and rules, Guido prefers the magical world, in which he meta-phorically elaborates his ghosts and hidden desires. This preference will return at the end of the movie.

Starting from this initial sequence, it is also possible to introduce the second theme: the infernal relationships with others. Guido is never authentic with anybody, because he needs to represent himself as an art-ist, as a Latin lover, as an intellectual not entrapped in the bourgeois logic and set of rules. This lack of authenticity leads to the infernal dynamics described in the third part of *Being and Nothingness*. Guido is unable to establish equal relationships, especially with women. In the background, there is certainly Fellini's social critique of the Italian male of his time, often growing up with the myth of the macho man (in *Amarcord* this will be connected to the representation of Mussolini and fascism), and with a clear distinction between a mother or wife based on the model of the Virgin Mary and a female as a sexual object, based on the model of a prostitute. In fact, there is a scene in the film where Guido has just had sex with his mistress and begins to daydream. In this fantasy, he meets his mother by his father's gravestone, and her face suddenly becomes his wife's. His mother and wife represent moral judgment, whereas his desires are situated in a parallel life. He suffers from other people's look. Primarily, he is afraid of disappointing his parents. There is a dream sequence in which his producer complains about Guido's behavior with his deceased father. Another example is his childlike encounter with Saraghina. His school priests discovered and scolded him for his curiosity. The Catholic look is totally identified with the education itself, at the point that one of the priests has the face of Guido's mother.

Another alienating look is represented by the movie critic he invites onto his set to examine the script. He continues to criticize and disapprove Guido. For example, he says:

So, what does it mean? (…) No connection with a real critical conscience. No, if you really want to make a polemical piece about the Italian catholic consciousness, you would need a much higher degree of culture as well as inexorable logic and clarity. Forgive me, but … your naiveté is a serious failing.

One of the mistakes the movie critic insists on underlining is Guido's tendency to reduce every character to a specific function or a precise symbol: a typical inclination of bad faith.

Existence and Things: How Sad Having to Play a Role

Guido is fake in everything he does, in his relationships as well as his work. As we have mentioned, one of the most evident examples of bad faith is the attempt to reduce others to mere characters. Claudia should represent innocence and rebirth. Nevertheless, this is a mere didactic symbol. Also during casting, Guido is unable to choose the right actresses to interpret his wife, his mistress, and other people because he treats them as essences, objects, and fixed identities. Luisa, Guido's actual wife, later says: "How sad having to play the bourgeois wife who doesn't understand." Guido himself will become victim of this narrative entrapped in bad faith. When his wife reproaches him for his cheating, he shouts: "I don't know what you think my life is like, reducing it all to the pettiness of somebody stealing from the cookie jar." There is a very similar description in Sartre's *Saint Genet* (even if Fellini did not read it). Talking about Genet's childhood, Sartre mentions an episode that would have been fundamental in the construction of his personality:

> The child was playing in the kitchen. Suddenly he became aware of his solitude and was seized with anxiety, as usual. (…) There is no one in the room. An abandoned consciousness is reflecting utensils. A drawer is opening; a little hand moves forward. Caught in the act. Someone has entered and is watching him. (…) In a moment the whole village will know … The child alone is in ignorance. (…) A voice declares publicly: "You're a thief." The child is ten years old. (Sartre 2012, p. 17)

This was also something that happened to Guido. When he was a child, he was caught in the act of dancing with the prostitute Saraghina. He was seen and deemed as a pervert. In a similar way to Genet, Guido shapes his life through the repetition of this forbidden relationship. He directs movies and actors, but he is the first one who plays a role. Sartre was really critical toward the reduction of an individual to a character long before he started to write psycho-biographies and the *Critique of Dialectical Reason*. Already in the *War Diaries* composed over a two-year period between 1939 and 1940, he disapproved of this reduction of human existence. In regard to his companion-in-arms Pieter, Sartre wrote that for him:

> There exist only types. These types, moreover, are formed by the intersection of their inherited nature and their professional activity. He'll never say "Paul's scared", but "Paul's the scared type". Not just out of a basic vulgarity that makes him choose instinctively the most vulgar turns of phrase, but out of a need to refer to clear cut categories. This is why, to him, I'm "the

bohemian", "Montparnasse", etc. And he'll explain my every reaction by my bohemian character and intellectual calling. (Sartre 1999, p. 13)

Pieter, like everyone who lives in bad faith, thinks that there is a limited number of human characters. For Sartre, this is a sort of "psychology of the customer": the individual is reduced to a set of uniform needs. Nevertheless, human existence cannot be reduced to a state, a thing, or a character. This is one of the most important claims of Sartrean existentialism, the reason why Sartre separated the for-itself from the in-itself, the being of the stone from the existence of a free subject.

Fellini interprets his character in a similar way. Guido fails on a dual level: not finding a fixed and acceptable identity for himself and reducing other people to a role. He adapts himself to a set of conventions, like the famous waiter in the Parisian café described in *Being and Nothingness.*

> He applies himself to chaining his movements as if they were mechanisms, the one regulating the other; his gestures and even his voice seem to be mechanisms; he gives himself the quickness and pitiless rapidity of things. He is playing, he is amusing himself. But what is he playing? We need not watch long before we can explain it: he is playing at being a waiter in a café. (Sartre 1978, p. 59)

One could say that Guido is actually playing the part of a movie director and we could also question whether Fellini is also playing the part of a movie director and if Sartre was also trying to play the part of a writer. From an existentialist point of view, what is the difference between playing a role and living outside bad faith dynamics? It has been argued that Fellini is authentic while he is telling us the story of Guido entrapped in bad faith. Are people all equally condemned to bad faith and failure? Benny Lévy, in Sartre's last interview published as *Hope Now*, asks something similar: "A café waiter, a public leader, a revolutionary militant Marxist, and Jean-Paul Sartre all seemed to have this much in common: even though they all assigned themselves goals, all, such as they were, failed" (Sartre and Lévy 1996, pp. 53–54). Sartre replied: "I think the way in which I wanted immortality, the way I conceived it, was not very different from that of the café waiter or Hitler, but the way in which I worked at my writings was different. It was clean, it was ethical" (Sartre and Lévy 1996, p. 58).

What is Sartre's interpretation of being ethical? If we consider the final promise in *Being and Nothingness*, the attempt to build the existentialist moral philosophy drafted in *Notebooks for an Ethics*, his most famous conference *Existentialism Is a Humanism*, and even his last interview, being ethical corresponds to be truly free. What Sartre means here is to focus constantly on a project and try to achieve it without using violence toward others. Even if Guido explicitly declares that he would like to be honest without wounding anybody, this social and political aspect is not sketched at all in Fellini's movie. However, there is an analogous reflection on authenticity as a moral and truthful conduct. The difference between Guido and Fellini is that while Guido is trying to hide himself in his movie with masks and excuses based on bad faith, Fellini is authentically showing his inadequacy and fragility through his alter ego.

Bad Faith and Authenticity: How to Live Without Fleeing from Responsibility

In *Notebooks for an Ethics*, Sartre wrote a sort of praise of human finitude. If the individual consciousness could be immortal it could achieve all possibilities, without choosing anything. It would not be recognized as unique, because what makes individuals unique is the totality of their limited choices. This set of preferences and values defines the identity *in fieri* of every human being.

> There is freedom if there is a choice among possibles. And an irremediable choice. If a being were endowed with a temporal infinity, he could realize every possible, he would therefore be nothing more than the development in an infinite and necessary series of every possible, therefore he would disappear as an individuality (the realization of these possibles to the exclusion of all the rest) and as freedom (the dangerous and irremediable choice of some possibles). (Sartre 1992, p. 326)

Guido is unable to make his movie not because he has nothing to say, but because he wants to say everything. He wants to talk about human relationships, make a critique against Catholic consciousness, and indicate a salvation for humanity—all of this in a science fiction movie with an enormous spaceship during a thermonuclear world war. "In my movie I have all sorts of things happening. I'm putting everything in. Even a tap-dancing sailor," he says to Rossella, his best female friend. He does not want to exclude anything. In a word, he is not able to choose. "I'm the one without the courage to bury anything at all." In Fellini's movie, this confession opens the possibility to exit the vicious circle of bad faith. Guido recognizes he is living among excuses and superficial justifications without taking any responsibility. Rossella says: "You are free, but you must learn to choose." "We are condemned to be free," stated Sartre in *Being and Nothingness*, but it is not necessarily a tragic condition. One may choose in order to concretely realize one's ends. What separates Guido from achieving his artistic effort and authentic relationships is his inability to choose possibilities that will be irremediable, without the cinematic possibility to repeat the scene. As Pamerleau points out, "Authenticity (...) consists in having a true and lucid consciousness of the situation, in assuming the responsibilities and risks that it involves, in accepting it in pride or humiliation, sometimes in horror and hate." (Pamerleau 2009, p. 167).

Fellini imagines an exit from the hell of bad faith. This possibility was not analyzed in *Being and Nothingness* and was only sketched in the unfinished *Notebooks for an Ethics* (which, of course, could not have been read by Fellini). For Sartre, this possibility took the shape of a radical conversion. For Fellini, this conversion is basically the confession of our fragility beyond any self-representation.

Paradise Is Other People

At the end of the movie, the illusionist Maurice suggests to Guido the way to become authentic. All characters get off the spaceship (instead of getting on it to leave the planet) and they join hands in a circle in which nobody is excluded. The nostalgic atmosphere, the meditation on death present in the entire film, and the grotesque emphasized by Maurice and by the spaceship's skeleton remind us all of the fragility of human finitude. Nevertheless, our limits, difficulties, efforts, and hard choices are the elements that constitute our uniqueness and specific individuality, as Sartre pointed out in his early philosophy. At the end Guido says to his wife:

> It's so natural accepting you, loving you. And is so simple. (...) But this confusion is ... me. Not as I'd like to be, but as I am. I'm not afraid anymore of telling the truth, of the things I don't know, what I am looking for and haven't found.

When Guido accepts himself as an existence *in fieri*, he is also able to establish equal relationships. The existence *in fieri* is represented by the movement of the circle of which Guido is also part. In the conclusion of this movie, unlike Sartre's writings, excluding the unfinished *Notebooks*, it is possible to move beyond the infernal dynamic of "Hell is other people".

In a very famous Italian movie dictionary, Morandini writes: "Sartre says: '*L'enfer, c'est les autres*' [in *No Exit*, M.R.]. Fellini overturns this claim: life and movies are the others, both those who are alive and those who are dead, both real and creative creatures. It is necessary to accept all of them with love, gratitude and solidarity" (Morandini et al. 2002, p. 972).

For Fellini bad faith leads to failure; nevertheless, if one is able to recognize this failure, admitting one's fragility, it is possible to live, without masks, in an authentic relationship with oneself and others. Authenticity is not just the opposite of bad faith, or a definitive radical conversion: it is instead the weak attempt to accept human freedom and its challenges. Guido confesses:

> This is the only way I can feel alive and I can look into your faithful eyes without shame. Life is a celebration. Let's live it together! This is all I can say to you Luisa, or the others. Accept me for what I am, if you want me. It's the only way we might be able to find each other.

And the Other can finally answer: "I can try if you help me." If Garcin, Inès, and Estelle of *No Exit* are trapped for eternity and they cannot exit from hell, here somebody tries to open a window. Curiously, Fellini develops the dialectic between bad faith and authenticity in the same direction as in the *Notebooks*. Sartre believed intermittently in the possibility of overcoming the vicious circle of bad faith, basically in *Notebooks* and in his last interview when he talked about fraternity in a way different from the *Critique*. However, in the major part of his works, he describes the dynamics of violence and oppression. Differently, Fellini considers life and freedom as opportunity, even if they are often wasted and fail. In this sense, it is possible to start the movie, love others, and learn to make your own choices.

References

Morandini, Laura, Luisa Morandini, and Morando Morandini. 2002. *Il Morandini. Dizionario dei film 2003*. Bologna: Zanichelli.

Pamerleau, William C. 2009. *Existentialist Cinema*. Basingstoke: Palgrave Macmillan.

Sartre, Jean-Paul. 1962. *Sketch for a Theory of the Emotions*. London: Methuen & Co.

———. 1978. *Being and Nothingness: An Essay on Phenomenological Ontology*. New York: Pocket Books.

———. 1990. Apologie pour le cinéma. In *Ecrits de jeunesse*, ed. Michel Contat and Michel Rybalka, 388–404. Paris: Gallimard.

———. 1992. *Notebooks for an Ethics*. Chicago: The University of Chicago Press.

———. 1999. *War Diaries. Notebooks from a Phoney War 1939–1940*. London: Verso.

———. 2012. *Saint Genet. Actor and Martyr*. Minneapolis: University of Minnesota Press.

Sartre, Jean-Paul, and Benny Lévy. 1996. *Hope Now. The 1980 Interviews*. Chicago: The University of Chicago Press.

Index[1]

---

[1] Note: Page numbers followed by 'n' refer to notes.

© The Author(s) 2020
A. Betschart, J. Werner (eds.), *Sartre and the International Impact of Existentialism*,
https://doi.org/10.1007/978-3-030-38482-1

377

Printed by Printforce, the Netherlands